AF251132

Burhan Dogançay: Works on Paper 1950–2000

BURHAN DOGANÇAY

Works on Paper 1950–2000

Essay by RICHARD VINE

Introduction by THOMAS M. MESSER

HUDSON HILLS PRESS / *New York & Manchester*

First Edition
© 2003 Burhan Dogançay

Published in the United States by Hudson Hills Press LLC, 74-2 Union Street, Manchester, Vermont 05254.
Distributed in the United States, its territories and possessions, and Canada by National Book Network, Inc.
Distributed in the United Kingdom, Eire, and Europe by Windsor Books International.

Founding Publisher: Paul Anbinder
Executive Directors: Randall Perkins and Leslie van Breen

Editor: Richard Carter
Designer: Howard I. Gralla
Composition: Angela Taormina
Proofreader: Margot Page
Indexer: Karla Knight
Color separations by Pre Tech Color, Wilder, Vermont
Printed and bound by CS Graphics Pte., Ltd., Singapore

Library of Congress Cataloguing-in-Publication Data

Vine, Richard.
Burhan Dogançay : works on paper, 1950–2000 / Richard Vine ;
introduction by Thomas M. Messer. — 1st ed.
    p. cm.
Includes bibliographical references and index.
ISBN 1-55595-226-7 (hardcover)
1. Dogançay, Burhan, 1929– Catalogues.   I. Dogançay, Burhan, 1929–
II. Title.
NC139.D64A4 2003
760'.092 — dc21

                                    2003001110

Contents

Acknowledgements

I would like to express my sincere appreciation to Paul Anbinder of Hudson Hills Press for the great enthusiasm with which he took on the publication of this book, the third book by Hudson Hills Press on my art. I am also grateful to Randall Perkins and Leslie van Breen for taking over this project from Paul Anbinder and for having given their utmost in seeing this project through.

I express particular thanks to Thomas M. Messer for his encouragement and unwavering faith in my art during the past forty years. Like so many times in the past, he has provided once again a wonderful introduction, for which I am deeply grateful.

I would also like to thank Richard Vine for his comprehensive and insightful text.

The following photographers have recorded my work over the course of my career, and I thank them: Özgür Bakır, Razi Canikligil, Cevat Dosembet, George Emrl, Önder Ergün, David Heald, Hülya Kolabaş, Ömer Tüzel, Norman Wightman.

Last, but not least, my deep gratitude goes to my wife, Angela, without whose diligence and long hours of hard work this project would not have been possible.

B. D.

Introduction

BURHAN DOGANÇAY's art is above all an authentic optical testimony derived from an irrepressible visual curiosity and pursued on a global scale. Only thereafter does it become technique, i.e., a means through which insights are translated upon a flat surface, to result, finally, in a personal style.

This book, which is the third major published survey dedicated to Dogançay, is wholly devoted to his works on paper. Within this general category, it is neatly divided into: I: Drawings and Sketches (pencil, India ink, crayon); II: Watercolors and Gouaches; III: Fumages; IV: Collages; and V: Mixed Media — subdivisions that partly overlap and, in their totality, encompass the years from the early 1950s into the new millennium, to represent the intense striving of half a century.

Viewing the work sequentially, one may point to the mid-1960s as the crucial moment in the artist's liberation from an essentially impressionist and post-impressionist heritage in favor of up-to-date sensibilities that went hand in hand with the appropriation of contemporary techniques. Such a development followed in the wake of the Turkish-born artist's departure from Europe and the initial stage of integration within the New York art world — an integration that remained qualified, thereby retaining a healthy measure of independence and confidence in the validity of a personal mode of expression.

What then defines Dogançay's mature work? In terms of subject matter, it is about faces and the expressions marked on them; about hearts, love and sex; about objects, letters and inscriptions; as well as about assorted shapes and colors, their harmonies and dissonances and their definition on flat paper and cardboard surfaces. In their final rendition, such a form language harmonizes within a field suggestive of collage, regardless of the particular technical procedure that may have been applied. The resulting composition then reflects changing moods and periods, zeitgeist, ethnic characteristics, and much that remains undefined. The viewer is left with a measure of freedom in the ultimate formulation of specific meanings.

The process chosen by Burhan Dogançay in his search for contents is laborious. Traceable to a passion for travel, it amounts to a gathering process of imagery selectively drawn from sources throughout the world and thus to a documentation of life at large. Dogançay's photographic archive is very extensive. It was assembled over a period of forty years of travel and diligent observation in 112 countries. Such a visual reservoir then assumes the function of a supply mechanism for his art and as such reflects historical, social, political, and societal phenomena that remain implicit and without propagandistic intent.

A few specific references support such assertions through random examples of Doğançay's work: *Oligarchy,* (1992), with its insinuating inscription denoting an unspecified political comment addressed to an identifiable recipient. *Red Lips* (1997) provokes responses to some undefined sexual perversion, while *Dualistic Heart* (1997) makes us think of searing inner conflict rendered in an abstract expressionist idiom that intensifies tensions conveyed through explicit features. *Billboard* (1964), with its scribbled names in seeming chaos, provides stark and unmodified color contrast next to tasteful tonal adjustments, as if to suggest coexistence of spontaneous expression with finely calibrated aesthetic control. Works like these are indicative of the artist's capacity to formulate separateness and contrast within a harmonious framework of a pervasive unity.

Among the artist's most impressive late works is a series executed in mixed media and entitled "Post no Bills." The source for its contents will, no doubt, be found on the walls that Burhan Doğançay has so assiduously investigated in many parts of the world — walls that in Victor Hugo's words "whisper, cry, and sing." In their paper incarnation, the artist's achievement is effectively summed up through a by-now familiar vocabulary of hands and hearts, lettered inscriptions, and color contrasts. Perhaps more strongly than in any previous series, "Post no Bills" is no less compelling for having been left, pending as it were, as a sequence of implications rather than as a conclusive statement — "mirrors of human consciousness," in the artist's own words.

February, 2002

Thomas M. Messer
Director Emeritus,
The Solomon R. Guggenheim Foundation

Burhan Dogançay: The Fine Art of Detection

by Richard Vine

For Burhan Dogançay, as for many artists, works on paper are the leading edge of experimentation, the first — and often most dynamic — drafts of a new composition, and sometimes of an entirely new vision. Thus the sketches and drawings, watercolors and gouaches, fumage pieces, collages, and mixed-medium renderings that he has produced in profusion over the last five decades not only provide the basis for his more deliberate paintings and sculptures but also serve, along with photography, as Dogançay's primary means of apprehending the world. That this artist's mind works in solitude, intuitively, concretely — through his eyes and his hand — is consonant with his formal procedures, the course of his life, and his themes. For his career is, in all these senses, singular.

Modern art, the art for which Dogançay abandoned a diplomatic career and has lived in a long and (especially in the early years) difficult exile from his homeland of Turkey, is largely a story of groups and movements — fauvism, cubism, futurism, dada, surrealism, abstract expressionism, arte povera, minimalism, pop art, conceptualism, etc. — or of aesthetic fashion: performance art and installation, trans-avant-garde figuration, the politicized work of the 1980s, and the electronic art of today. But collectivism of this sort Dogançay has always refused. Indeed, his project — one is tempted to say his "mission" — has been to work unencumbered (and so also unaided) by artworld trends, cliques, and paradigms. In his determination to *see* for himself, and to record visual phenomena as they impinge directly on an isolate, independent consciousness, he has embodied a philosophical program that arose four centuries ago in France (Dogançay's first foreign abode, from 1950 to 1955) with the cogito of Descartes, then evolved via the flaneur aesthetic of Baudelaire into the radically free *soi* of Sartrean existentialism. In America (Dogançay's second home since 1962), popular imagination has transformed the solitary observer into the lone cowboy and the tough, tellingly named "private eye." In both traditions, whether highbrow or low, the task of the individual mind is to sort through conflicting evidence, take account of the tricks to which our senses are heir, and decide what is true. The artist is, in effect, a witness and a detective.

Dogançay's investigations began with naturalistic exercises in form and line — the disciplined drawing that was formerly the foundation skill for all serious artists. The son of an army cartographer who was himself a part-time artist, the young Dogançay (born 1929) was, from infancy, taken on surveying expeditions into the Turkish hinterlands, where his father set him to drawing as a distraction. Yet, since the elder Dogançay's precisely calibrated charts were anything but fanciful self-indulgences, something of the cartographer's allegiance to reality must have infiltrated the boy's thought process at a very early age. His talent was groomed both through coaching by his father and through drawing lessons with the well-known painter Arif Kaptan. By Dogançay's high school years in Ankara, when making art and playing soccer were his ruling passions, he was able to render subjects with such speed and accuracy that his teacher, Nusret Bey, accused him of presenting his father's drawings as his own — an error corrected only after Dogançay senior spoke up on the boy's behalf.

We can see this facility clearly in such early images as *Nude* (1951), a crayon study of a young woman sitting bent-legged on the floor with her back to the viewer. The simple furnishings of the room — a wooden chair, a door, a stretched canvas leaning against a wall — speak of the student-bohemian simplicity of Dogançay's life at the time. Completion of a law degree in Ankara had been followed by stints as a professional soccer player, a reluctant conscript soldier, and a racetrack gambler. Now the young man, having been sent for graduate studies to the University of Paris by his father, to whom he vowed not to pursue soccer or art, was living in the Cité Universitaire — drawing and painting assiduously, playing soccer, and about to attend art courses at La Grande Chaumière. In the stolen moment depicted here, we seem to glimpse, along with the aspiring artist who was forced to study economics, a secret and forbidden life — voluptuously satisfying, we suspect, if only its sensually fleshed representative would turn toward us to be fully seen and embraced. Great poignancy lies in the short but seemingly inviolable distance that separates the artist from the object of his desire. Dogançay's drawings of this era are a veritable catalogue of people, things, and places subject to his delectation, but studied at a curious remove.

How different is the diagonally composed *Reading Female* (1962) of eleven years later: a plump torso with ample breasts pressed near to the picture plane, the woman's face and identity blocked out by a book. No distance intervenes now, no tentativeness slows the thick India ink strokes. A world of experience has been assimilated, recorded in hundreds of sketches — e.g., *Sidewalk at Night in Calcutta* (1959) — by the thirty-three-year-old diplomat who, his doctorate finished, has assumed a series of governmental posts that have taken him literally around the world.

In images from the early 1950s, the artist seemed to be asking, "Why can't this be mine?" Here, a decade later, he has asserted an answer: "It can." By this time, Dogançay had mounted three successful shows with his father at the Art Lovers Club in Ankara, and five of his paintings had been selected for the capital city's Twenty-second State Exhibition in 1961. He was working in New York, the world nexus of contemporary art, as director of the Turkish Information Office. But his diplomatic appointments, though successively more prestigious, had left him harried and discontent. Within two years, he made the wrenching decision to forego reassignment to Paris, resign his diplomatic commissions, and dedicate himself to his art.

If the black-and-white sketches demonstrate most clearly Dogançay's talent for close observation and compositional rigor, disclosing his visual understanding of how the world is structurally knit together, his colorful watercolors and gouaches capture the fleeting, incidental effects of light and shade — and thus mark his attunement to the subtleties of passing time. Evolving from relatively traditional shore scenes and cityscapes such as *Honfleur* (1950) and *Monmartre* (1954), figure studies like *Hasan* (1952), and classic tabletop *vanitas* works like *Still Life (Apples and Ballantine),* (1963), his formal inquiries soon extended to deliberately flattened forms and fields of solid color, images tending implicitly toward abstraction.

This radical stylization ran parallel with Dogançay's realist tendencies even from his student days in Paris. As early as 1953, the blank-faced *Nude on Red*, depicting a minimally modeled but still-recognizable female body on a red divan, could be offset by the geometrically designed *Destiny*, in which body parts have become triangles and circles of flat color. In short, as the artist matured, his work — or at least half of it — modernized. He increasingly employed a Matisse-like collapse of space and arbitrariness of hue — tendencies that Matisse himself, ironically, derived in part from Eastern decorative motifs. From this point on in Dogançay's work, academic "correctness" and fidelity to everyday appearance — evident, for instance, in the beautifully scenic *Antalya* (1960) — were frequently employed in counterpoint to proto-abstract qualities, seen in images like *Population Explosion* (1960) with its volumeless jumble of fleshy humanoid forms displayed against a solid wash of mottled blue. Numerous 1963–64 scenes from Mexico, Arizona, and New York feature an immense sky of uninflected scarlet (a shade reminiscent of Hawthorne, as well as of *The Red Studio*), which engulfs landscape, figures, and architecture. Even such deceptively conventional views as *Sailing Boats* (1963) and *Park Avenue at 54th Street* (1964) are composed of energetic blots and smears of color that nearly escape their referential function altogether.

From the mid-1960s onward, the temporal became less of a preoccupation for Dogançay; he began to dwell on enduring patterns — creating a material dialogue between time and eternity. Perhaps the precipitating incident was a 1963 epiphany before a patch of wall on East Ninety-sixth Street in Manhattan, where the artist perceived in the bits of torn poster, faded orange paint, mud streaks, and rough masonry a chance "composition" as compelling as any abstract painting imaginable. Thereafter, he experimented, more and more obsessively, with renderings that brought found traces from the urban milieu — its signs and graffiti, its walls and doors — close up and flat against the picture plane. His techniques range from the Cy Twombly–like scribbles of *Richard First* (1964) to the torn-paper illusionism of the aptly titled *Residue of Human Beings* (1969) to the distinct, though fragmentary, lettering of *Simply No* (1971).

This period was not an easy one. Though Dogançay had shown twice at Ward Eggleston Galleries, he had no sales and no collectors. Thomas Messer, then director of the Guggenheim Museum, was an early supporter who oversaw the acquisition of the gouache-and-collage

Billboard (1964) — Doğançay's first museum placement — in 1965; but when the artist came to him in total despondency the following year, Messer could offer Doğançay only a galvanizing admonition to believe in his own talent and stick to his work. It was enough. Doğançay cast aside the temptation to quit and rededicated himself to his artistic labors. Three years later, a recommendation from the Metropolitan Museum's legendary modern art curator, Henry Geldzahler, gained Doğançay admittance to the renowned Tamarind Lithography Workshop in Los Angeles. There, during a two-month residency, the artist produced a set of sixteen lithographs (in editions of twenty each) — images composed of bright, flat, often letter-based forms — that sold readily to collectors and museums, thereby establishing Doğançay's name in the United States and abroad.

By the late 1970s, a new stylistic element appeared in Doğançay's gouaches and watercolors: lively, multicolored "curling-paper" forms set on a monochrome background, often accompanied by their own swooping, calligraphic "shadows." In *Untitled* (1977), for instance, a stately tangle of bright "scraps," looking as though it has broken through the background barrier into the viewer's presence, occupies the middle of the visual field in complicated equilibrium with its depicted shadow. *Spiderweb* (1982) presents thin strips of color entwined in the sort of pliant tension associated with its title, or with the creature that creates such attenuated constructs. At once self-sufficient and vulnerable, these central forms read as Doğançay's metaphor for the complex self, the node of Cartesian consciousness, isolated within the flux of what T. S. Eliot described in *The Waste Land* as "Your shadow at morning striding behind you / Or your shadow at evening rising to meet you."

THESE compositions mark a return, in Doğançay's semiabstract work, to his longstanding fascination with figure and ground, volume and depth. Facing the question of how three dimensions can be simulated graphically without resort to elaborate, Renaissance-style linear perspective, the artist had been exploring two unusual methods: smoke drawing and projectivist collage.

The first of these procedures, *fumage*, is a difficult technique used by only a few patient practitioners such as France's Noël Dolla, who "paints" abstract traces of soot on monochrome canvases, and Germany's Czechoslovakian-born Georg Dokoupil, who uses candle smoke to draw delicate, soft-focus figurative scenes. Doğançay, however, working independently and without direct reference to these younger artists, employs smoke for more oblique, depth-enhancing purposes. Standing above a bathtub filled with water, he holds the drawing or collage in one hand over a burning candle, which he then moves about with the other hand to attain his atmospheric effects. (Occasionally, the work takes flame and must be quickly dropped, utterly ruined, into the waiting tub.) This existential gesture of risking all for the sake of a potential improvement is

essential to Dogançay's art and life. The resulting marks — translated as shape, shadow, or veil —
serve three principal functions: depiction, modeling, and concealment.

In *Smoking Orange* and *Friendly Ghost* (both 1974), the sober clouds of carbon residue
dominate the smaller, sharply delineated color elements, while in *Smoke All Over* (1972) and
Mela Man (1973) — rather more typical examples — the elongated stains mix equally with other
forms, and so yield a chromatically and psychologically darker and more intricate composition.
Recession of space, and thus protrusion of objects, is conveyed in works like *Turning the Corner*
(1973) and *Letter Fragmentation* (1973), where smoke is used as a chiaroscuro medium to define
the volume of the depicted folds and crinkles of the surface, giving the trompe l'oeil image its
punch. Finally, smoke softens, darkens, and partially hides the two hearts, paired insignia of love,
in *Burning Hearts* (1984) — suggesting a balance, and an inherent conflict, between public dec-
larations and secret emotional truths.

In this sense, *Burning Hearts*, deploying one of Dogançay's lifelong motifs, is emblematic
of his entire *fumage* enterprise. Smoke is the displaced evidence of fire, not the flame itself — as
graffiti (particularly the amorous and political types found in most of these images) are often the
by-products and signifiers of passions enacted elsewhere. The minds of others, like their lives,
ultimately remain a black box. We make our inferences, imperfectly, on the basis of outward
manifestions, some intentional (premeditated language acts — verbal, visual, bodily, sartorial,
etc.), some inadvertent. Such is the "art" of living as social creatures. In this murky environment, love, even for those who think they know each other well, is at root an act of faith.

Interestingly, it was while deeply immersed in the *fumage* series that Dogançay met and,
in 1978, married Angela Hausmann — following an initial encounter in the most "social" of all
possible settings, the Hungarian Ball in New York. German by birth, trilingual, an international
banker, Angela soon brought to his professional life an orderliness and savvy that contributed
substantially to his burgeoning success. In 1982, Dogançay — who by then had exhibited at galleries in Sweden, Switzerland, and Germany, as well as in Turkey and the United States — was
given a large one-man show at the Centre Georges Pompidou in Paris. *Les Murs Murmurent, Ils
Crient, Ils Chantent* (The Walls Whisper, They Cry Out, They Sing), drawn from the countless
photographs of walls that the artist had shot in diverse international cities (as part of the "Walls
of the World" project that continues to this day), subsequently traveled to twenty international
venues over the course of three years.

The theme of that breakthrough show also pervades the large body of collages that Dogançay
has produced since the mid-1960s. These works represent for Dogançay an exceptional fusion of
meaning and method. Collage is, of course, one of the signature techniques of the twentieth cen-

tury. In the hands of avant-garde masters like Ernst, Schwitters, Heartfield, and Cornell, it has proved an exceptional vehicle for communicating, on an intimate scale, shared experiences of fragmentation and bafflement, of wrenching physical and spiritual displacement. For Dogançay — raised in part in the fields and villages of a seemingly timeless Anatolia, only to be thrust into the hyper-sophisticated milieu of postwar Paris and the multi-ethnic turbulence of New York — the procedure is a natural methodological choice.

In early pieces like *Wipe Out Slums* (1964) and *Black 7* (1970), bits of paper from widely varied sources, many bearing partial images or words, are brought together with acrylic and other applied pigments in arrangements that evoke the visual chaos of urban "message" walls. The broken, jumbled statements thus recorded, which the artist finds to be remarkably similar across the globe, bespeak, he believes, the common fears and desires of humanity. Each work reflects a shared need to express one's situation and one's self, even when such efforts are mingled with and overlaid by those of others. More purely formal concerns infuse the many later collages, such as *Yellow Curls* (1986), that offer a surface thickly studded with cones of furled paper. So complete is the shift of emphasis here that the scrolled portions of *Newsprint* (1986) actually hide the news of the day, and the historic tale in *The Story of World War II* (1987) is wrapped up tight and unseen.

Such pieces relate directly to the curled-metal sculptures that the artist had begun making in Switzerland in 1983, a year after his father-in-law, the German engineer Gerhard Hausmann, introduced him to the exceptionally malleable and durable properties of aluminum. Earlier, in preparation for some of his paintings, prints, and drawings, Dogançay had made three-dimensional paper maquettes that allowed him to study, in various light, the elaborate shadows that his abstract forms cast against the flat surfaces to which they were attached. These models he had routinely discarded until Thomas Messer one day urged the artist to retain them for exhibition — or as mock-ups for full-scale sculptures yet to be realized.

The issues explored in these sculptural pieces, as in the cone collages with their nearly indistinguishable mix of real and "fictive" (i.e., depicted) forms, are also brought to high resolution in the tapestries that Dogançay designed for the venerable Atelier Raymond Picaud in Aubusson, France, beginning in 1983. As in his graphic works of this time, Dogançay's woven ribbonlike images strike an eerie balance between "object" and "shadow," the two constituents of the quasi-calligraphic central motif. This "subject," resembling a pictograph or a character from Arabic script, is, in effect, a visual device that has become almost a verbal symbol as well.

Dogançay's play on the nature and meaning of language thus recalls one of the key intellectual issues of the twentieth century: the conflict between referential and self-reflexive modes of discourse. Does a symbol in a given language derive its meaning from that to which it refers ("car" = a type of vehicle) or simply from its relationship to other symbols within the sign system? By what rules, if at all, can the two modes be combined? Such questions — which have occupied thinkers such as Wittgenstein, Saussure, and Derrida — are not ones that we can expect any visual artist to resolve definitively. Yet Dogançay's works, in their frequent fusion of documentation and metaphor, elegantly enrich the debate.

If we regard the shadow-casting form in an untitled 1998 crayon study as a "character" in a dual sense of the word, it becomes an icon of cognitive transformation. The image is, depending on how one chooses to look at it, either the composite of a crinkled paper strip and its shadow, or else a single wordlike entity — or both. Thus the thing beheld becomes an emblem for the very process of perceiving it. The "shadow" especially serves Dogançay's point, suggesting that the mind, in every situation, projects its own future and trails its own past. Such works are a rebuttal — clear, simple, and cunning as a parable — to those who would argue that the cogito is a myth. Postmodernists have asserted that the Cartesian model is fundamentally flawed, because it posits an impossibly pure, empty, and unmediated consciousness. Dogançay's shadow works counter, in effect, that the solitary consciousness can learn to take into account its own conditioning factors — psychological, social, perceptual — and thus learn to see clearly and think truly.

Dogançay's reportorial penchant was put before the curatorial staff of the State Russian Museum in St. Petersburg when its members examined slides of his documentary door images and his abstract "House Painter" series featuring vivid "test" swatches of acrylic on canvas. Their response, in keeping with the era's heady spirit of *glasnost* and *perestroika*, was to offer him the first solo exhibition ever to be granted to a foreign artist at their museum. The massively attended *Walls and Doors 1990-91* exhibition of paintings opened at the museum in 1992 and traveled to the Artists' Union in Moscow.

TODAY, as is most evident in his mixed-media works, Dogançay retains formal command of abstractionist techniques (e.g., *Two White Tracks*, 1990, with its black rectangle superimposed over yellow-bordered white curves on a pale blue field) but endows most of his images with direct references to building or subway walls and the palimpsests of poster scraps and anonymous markings found there. Some images — such as those prompted by the black paper covering the windows of a disused Alexander's department store in New York (e.g., *Gray Symphony*, 1998) or by the black plastic hung across potentially distracting billboards before drivers commence the Grand Prix in Monte Carlo (e.g., *Rainbow*, 1990, from the "Formula One" series) — deal explicitly with degrees of disclosure, suggesting an undeniable beauty in the hidden and obscure. Others, like the celebrity-imaged *Diana & Che* (1998), manifest the high legibility and strong, though fractured, narrative content favored by practiced *décollage* artists like Jacques de la Villéglé and Mimmo Rotella.

Perhaps Dogançay's most transparent, meaning-laden works are those associated with his truth-telling alter ego, Grego. In *Grego's Wall* (1992), the all-caps message "AIDS WON'T WAIT," tattered and half lost, fights for the viewer's attention amid a lifelike clutter of competing political statements and blinding distractions in the form of high-color rectangles. *Grego's Eyes* (1992) confronts us with a wall that, thanks to a pair of collaged and painted eyes, stares back — a *tabula* returning the viewer's gaze — as though to assert that all perception is also projecton as well. Looking at the image is like encountering one's conscience.

In treating the man-made world as a sign, Dogançay gives his work a sly, half-disguised ethical dimension. Our moral choices are indeed written in, and on, our urban structures. Walls can shelter or can act as a barrier, be a site for the expression of shared passions — erotic, political, commercial — or a place where such communiqués are torn, obliterated, and weathered away. Doors, another prime Dogançay motif, are instruments of both access and exclusion. In Dogançay's oeuvre, they are always closed and often locked. Such lessons must have been indelibly etched on the mind of the boy who left home and country, the man who gave up security for a personal quest, a life of exasperating but revealing detours (the theme of many works such as *What Will I Wear?*, 1995). What is it he hoped, and still hopes, to learn in those hundreds of cities traversed on foot? What is this artist's invisible grail?

In classics of the detective genre, the private eye notes everything, gathering key material evidence. Yet, to break the case, he must also look *through* as astutely as he looks *at*. So, too, in Dogançay's art. A second plane of his "double" works (for example the cone series) attests that the artist knows what it is to work, materially and philosophically, on two levels at once. He even hinted once at a binary creed distilled from his wide travels and ceaseless aesthetic labors: "Only love can solve our problems — love and also beautiful compositions."[1]

Many honors and awards have been bestowed on Dogançay: the Enka Art and Science Award (1984); participation in the first Istanbul biennial (1987) and the ninth Bienal Internacional de Arte in Valparaiso, Chile (1989); medals from the governments of Russia and Turkey (including the latter's National Medal of the Arts for Lifetime Achievement and Cultural Contribution, 1995); nearly a score of exhibition catalogues and monographs; and a full-scale retrospective at the Dolmabahçe Cultural Center, Istanbul (2001). He is thus a bridge figure who has repeatedly brought critical attention, and modern artistic practice, to his native Turkey — just as he simultaneously spurred awareness of his Islamic homeland among Western artworld observers.

Dogançay's wide-ranging works variously combine naturalism and good drawing, traditional qualities instilled by his father and early teachers, with a drive toward radical innovation derived from the Euro-American idea of "progress." He is a man living simultaneously in two worlds, and so a representative figure of our times. His work is pervaded by numerous contemporary dichotomies — East/West, old/new, bourgeois/bohemian, native/expatriate, collective/

individual, illustration/sign, volume/flatness, image/text, fictive/real — whose oscillations give off intense artistic sparks.

In his spacious SoHo loft, Dogançay continues to work these days in many mediums, moving easily from photography to collage to drawing and watercolor to painting — a man at one with his métier. From an artist of such technical facility, buoyed by fifty years of experience, many fresh insights are yet likely to flow. As Dogançay again walks the streets with sketch pad at the ready, what message will he discover, tomorrow, in the writing on the walls? What new form or theme will come to life under his remarkable hand? What future doors will open?

1. Quoted in Eleanor Flomenhaft, "Dogançay: A Heroic Quest," from *Burhan Dogançay: A Retrospective* (Istanbul: Duran Editions, 2001), 73. Biographical information in my article is drawn primarily from this multi-author catalogue and from personal interviews with the artist in the early weeks of 2002.

I

Drawings & Sketches

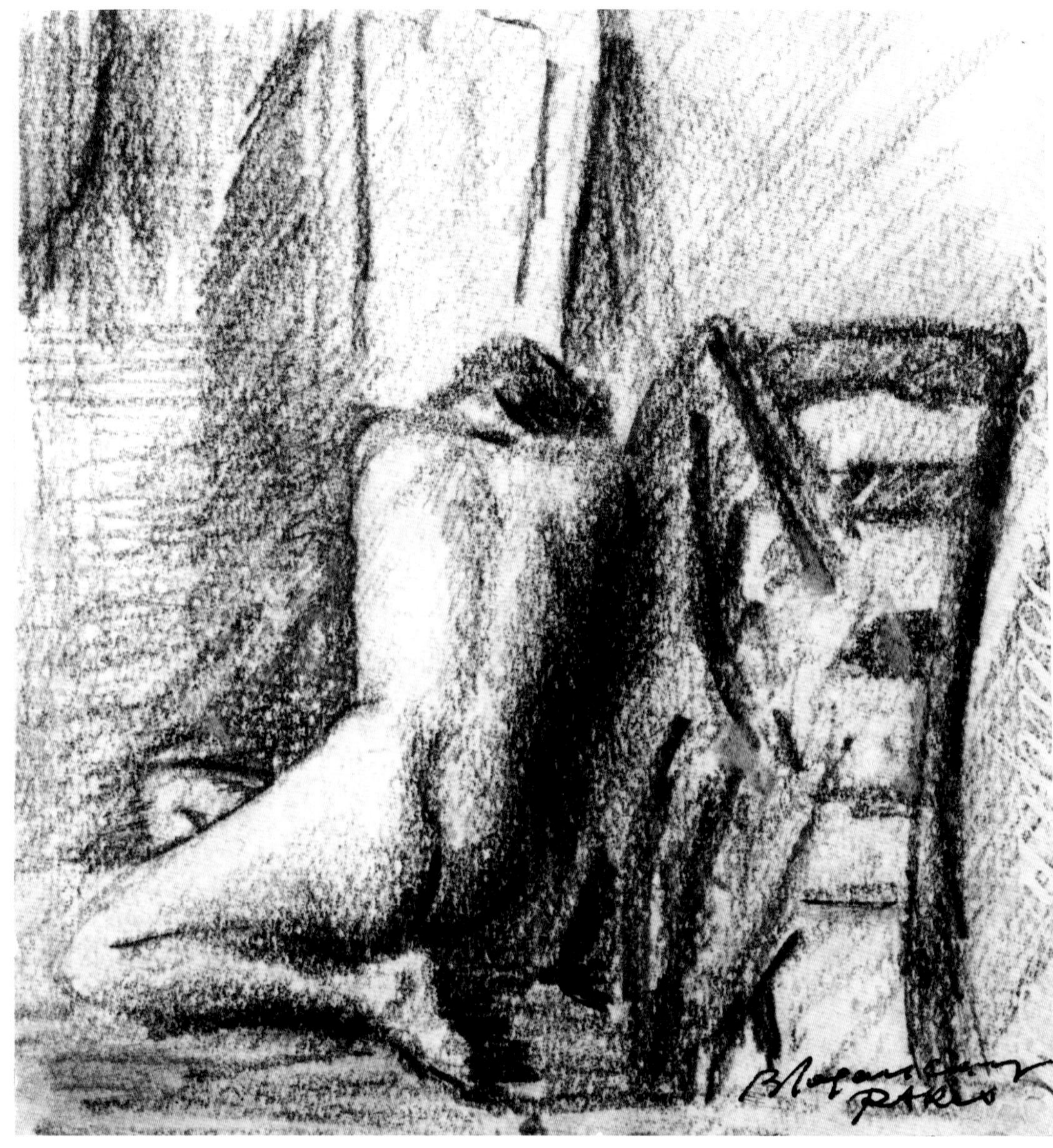

Nude, 1951. Crayon on paper, 6 × 6 in. (15.2 × 15.2 cm). Collection of the artist

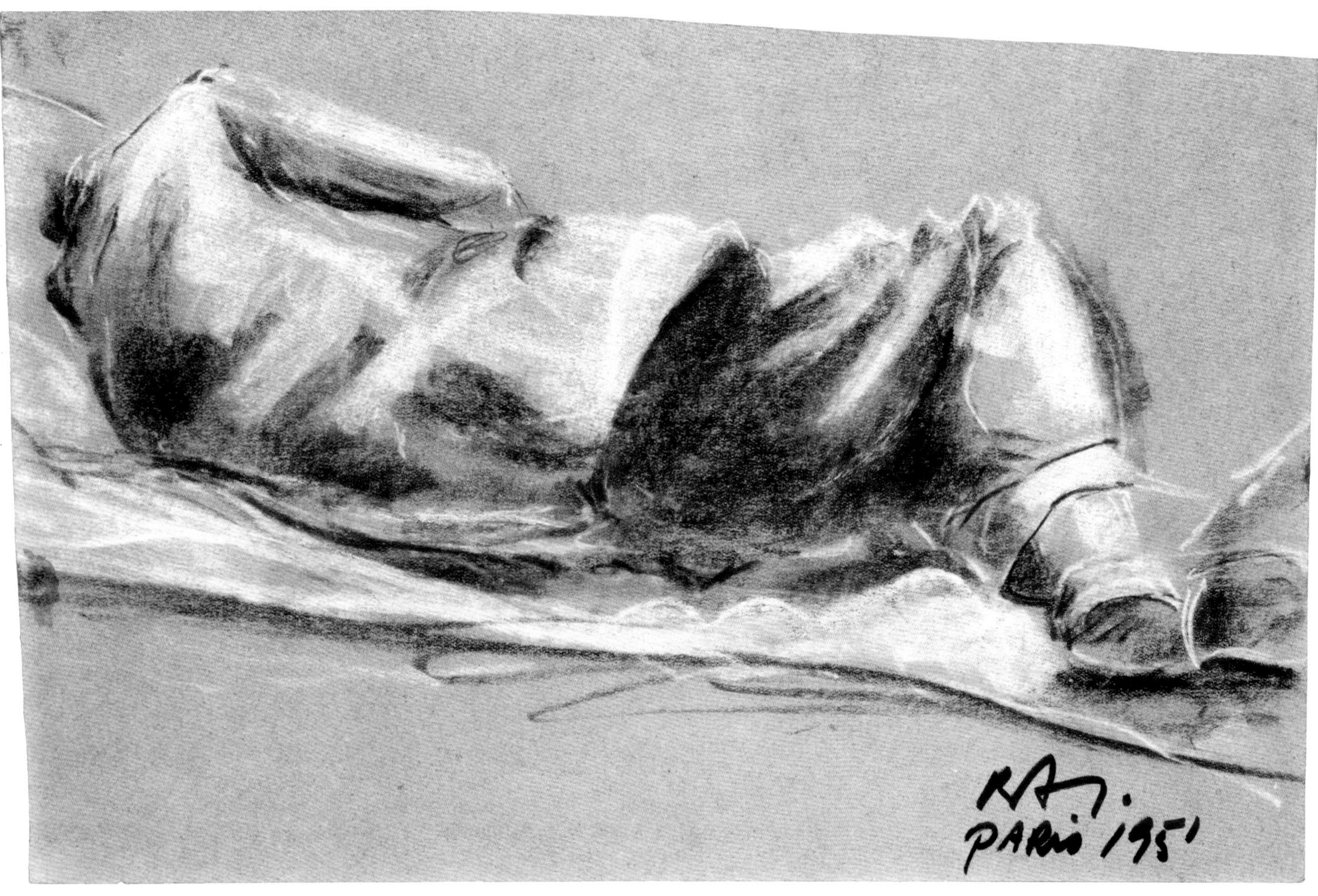

Vagrant, 1951. Charcoal on paper, 7 × 10¾ in. (17.8 × 27.3 cm). Collection of the artist

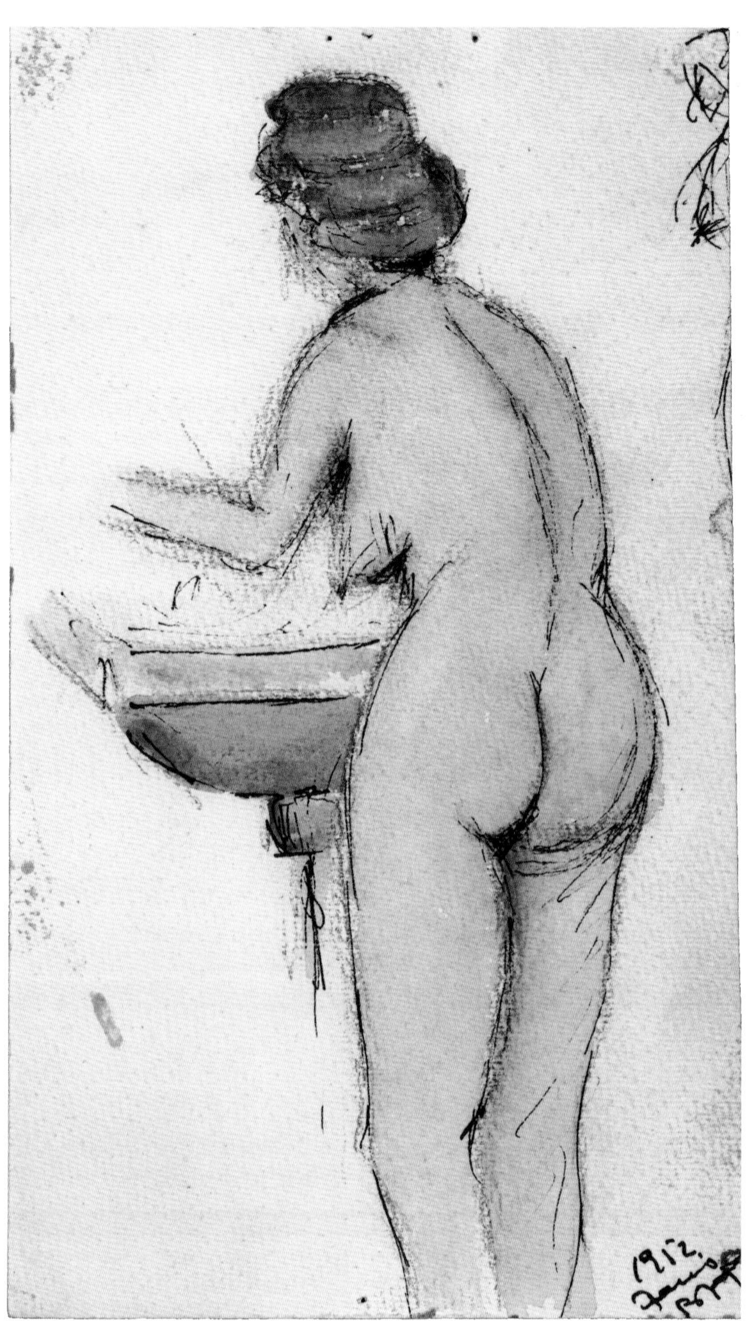

Nude at Sink, 1952. India ink and watercolor on paper, 8½ × 5 in.
(21.6 × 12.7 cm). Collection of the artist

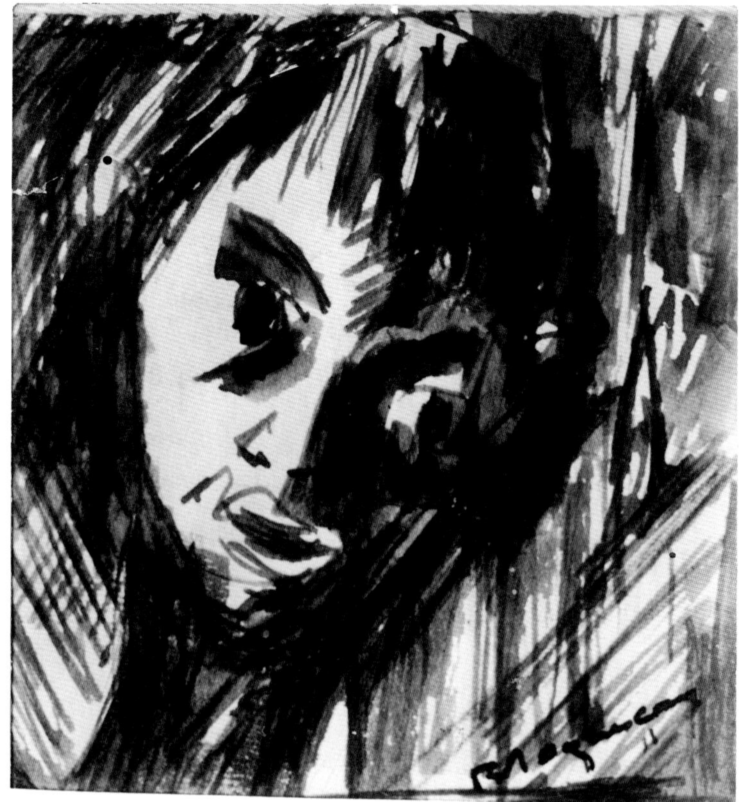

Despair, 1955. India ink on paper, 4 × 4 in. (10 × 10 cm).
Private collection, France

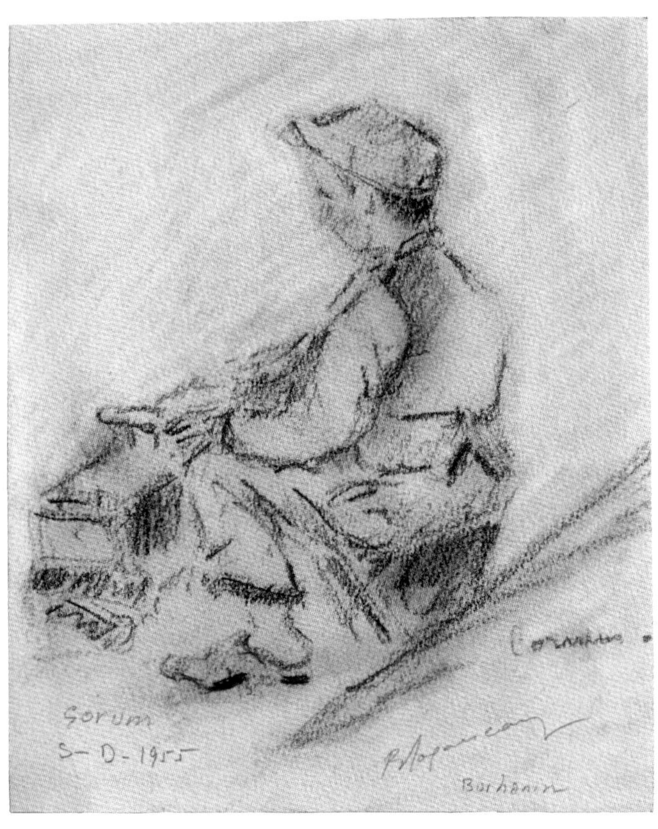

Shoeshine Boy, 1955. Pencil on paper, 7⅛ × 6 in. (18 × 15 cm).
Collection of the artist

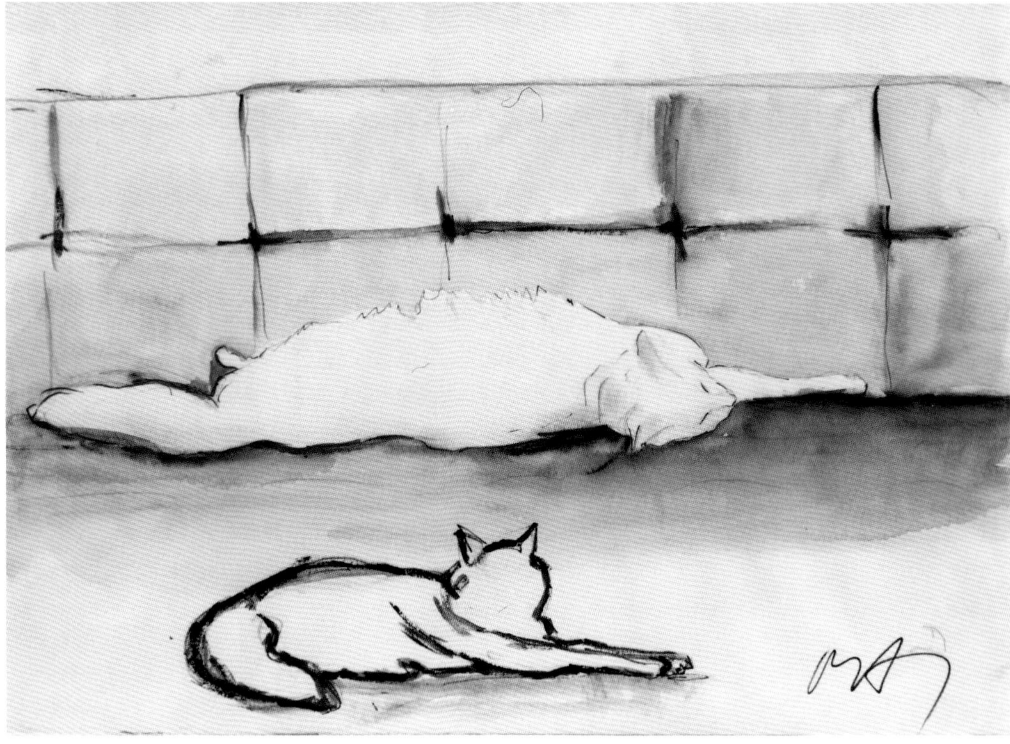

Pamuk, 1959. India ink and watercolor on paper, 12 × 17 in. (30 × 43.2 cm). Collection of the artist

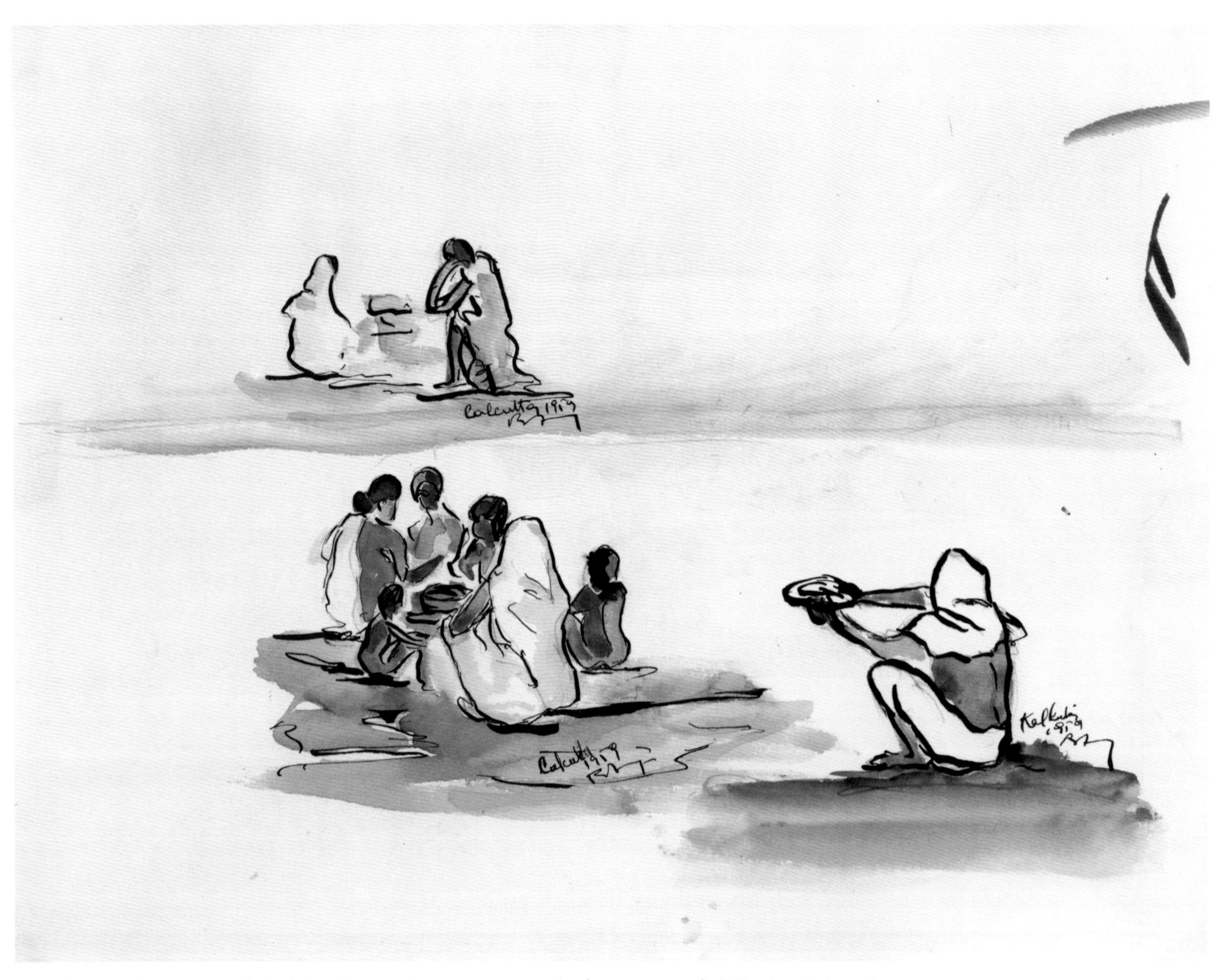

Sketch Done in Calcutta, 1959. India ink and watercolor on paper, 9 × 12 in. (22.9 × 30.5 cm). Collection of the artist

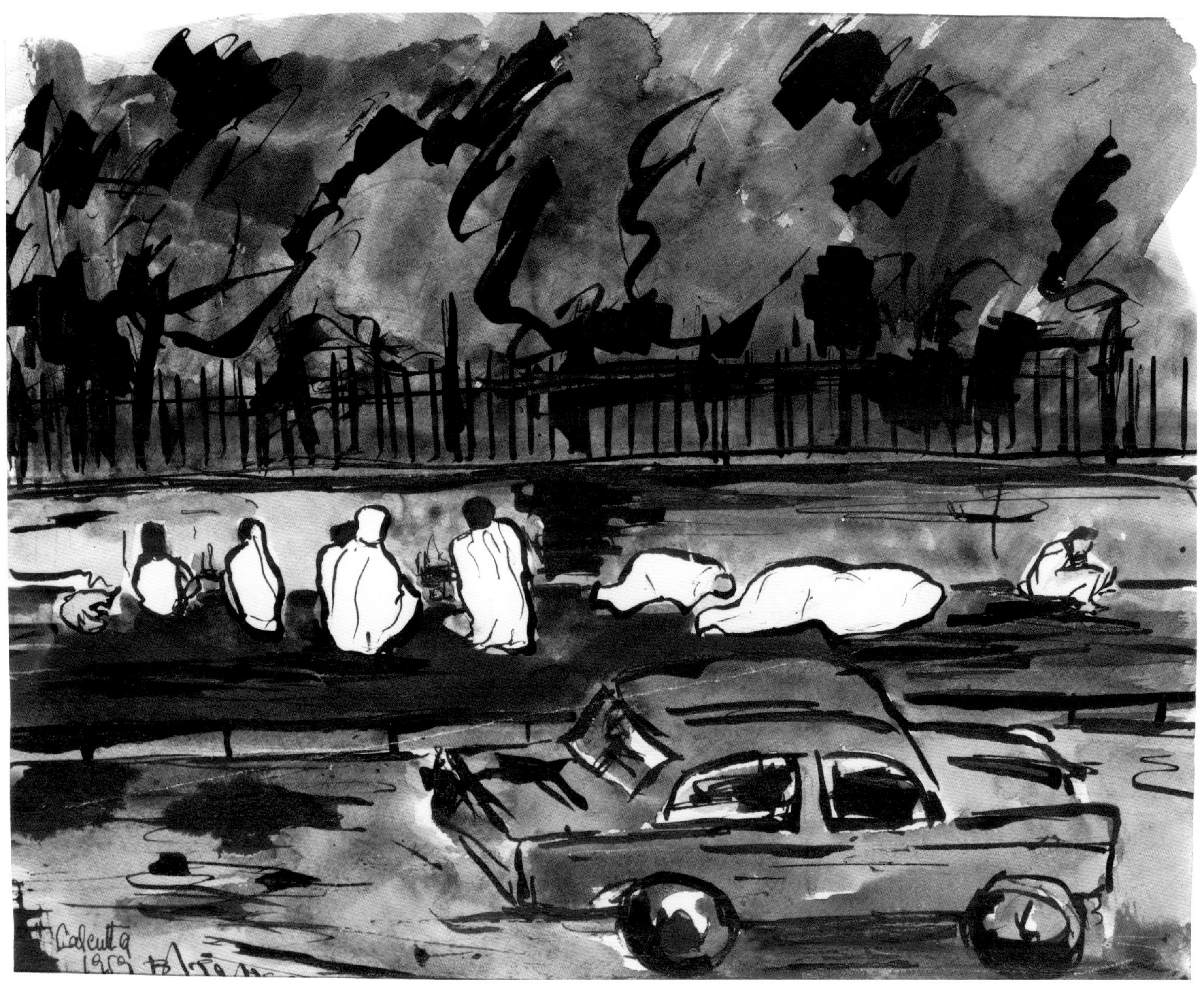

Sidewalk at Night in Calcutta, 1959. India ink and watercolor on paper, 8½ × 11 in. (21.6 × 27.9 cm). Collection of the artist

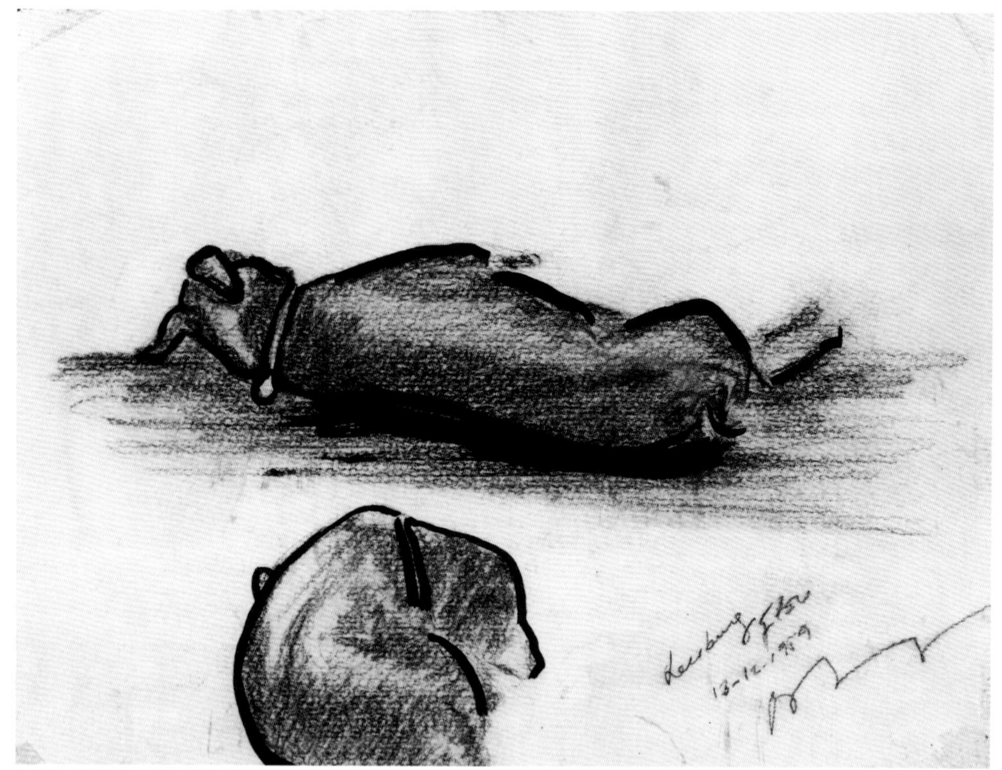

Dog, 1959. India ink and crayon on paper, 9 × 11 in. (22.8 × 27.9 cm). Collection of the artist

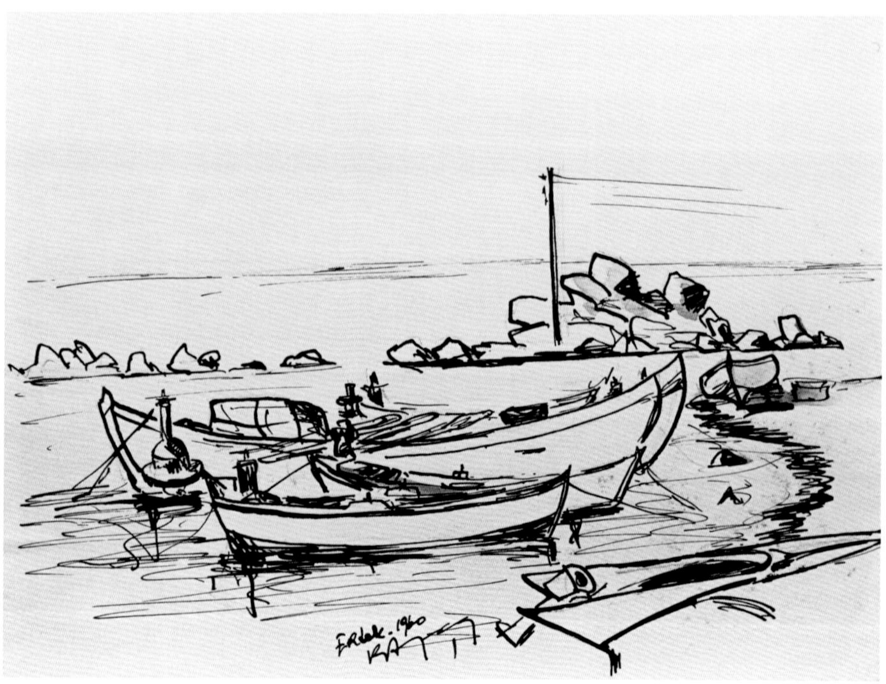

Erdek, 1960. India ink on paper, 6¾ × 9⅛ in. (17 × 23 cm). Collection of the artist

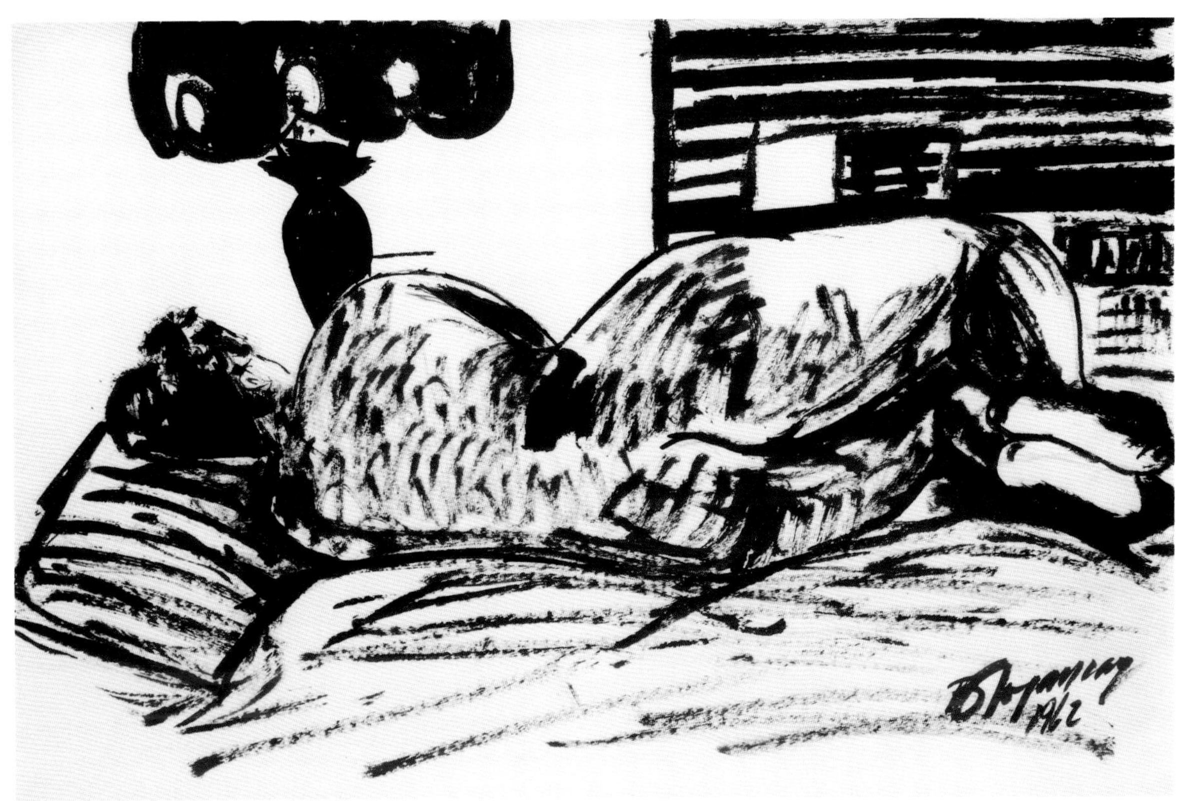

Resting Woman, 1962. India ink on paper, 22 × 30 in. (55⅞ × 76¼ cm). Private collection

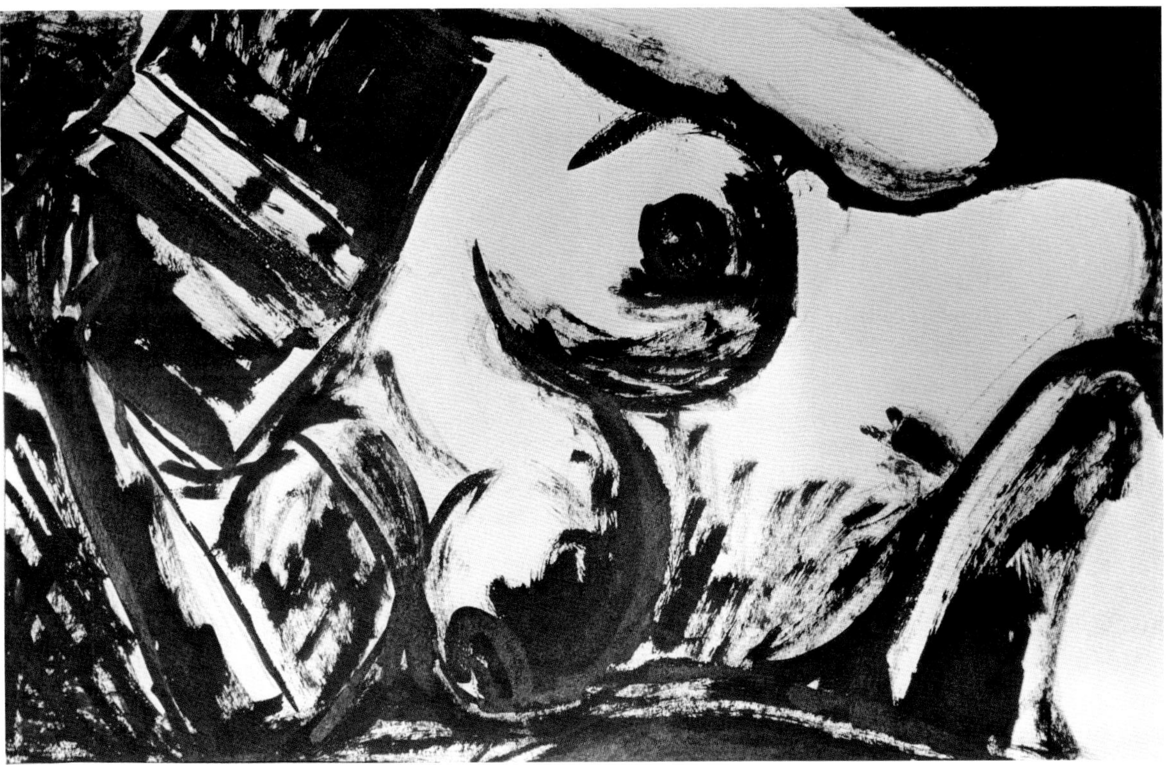

Reading Female, 1962. India ink on paper, 22 × 30 in. (55⅞ × 76¼ cm). Private collection

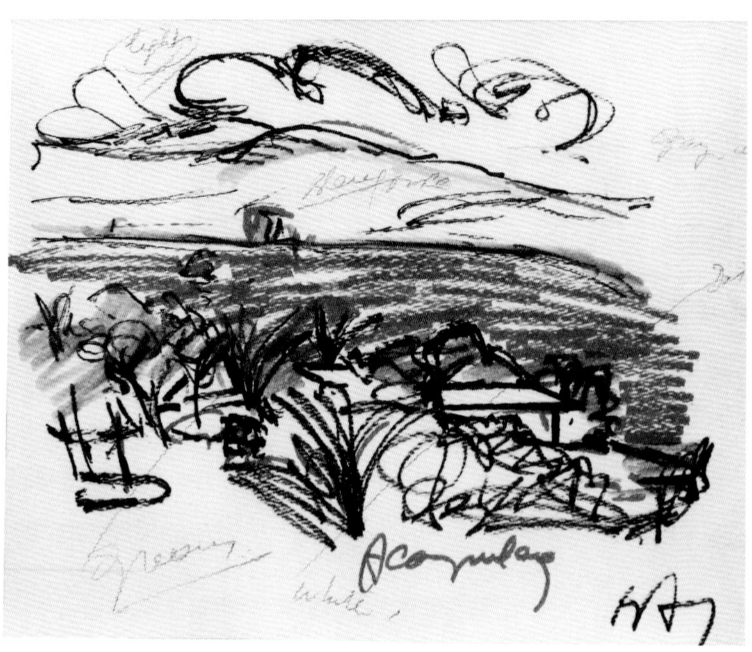

Acapulco, 1963. Crayon on paper, 8½ × 10½ in. (21.6 × 26.7 cm).
Collection of the artist

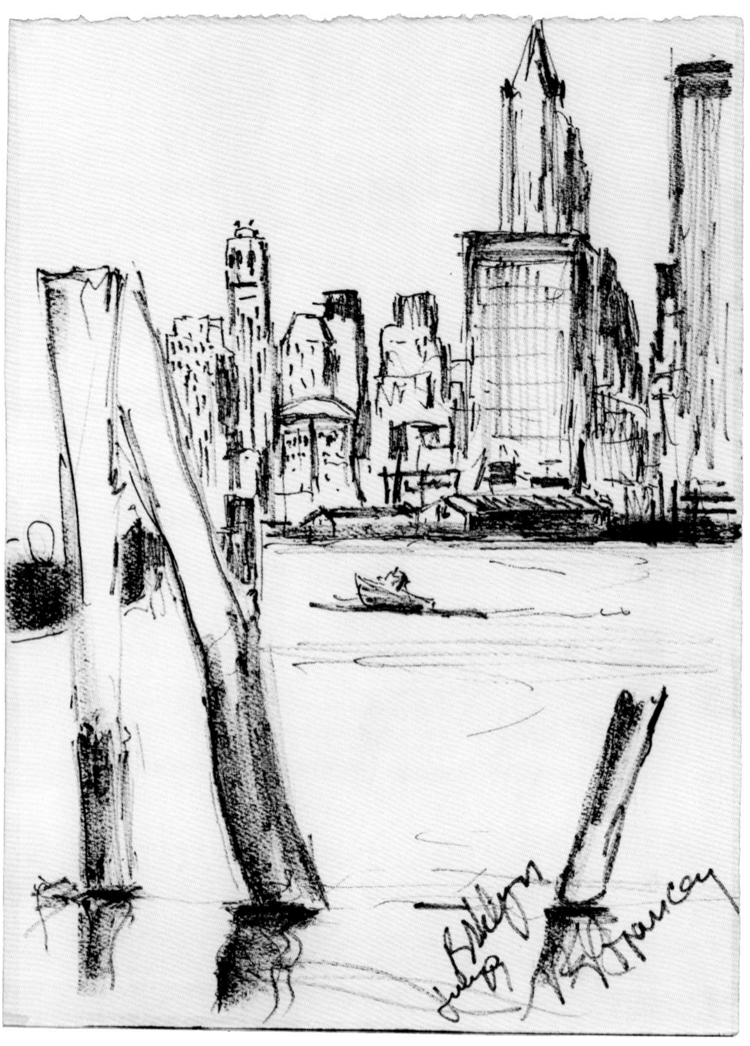

View of Manhattan from Brooklyn, 1963. India ink and crayon,
13 × 9¾ in. (33 × 24.8 cm). Collection of the artist

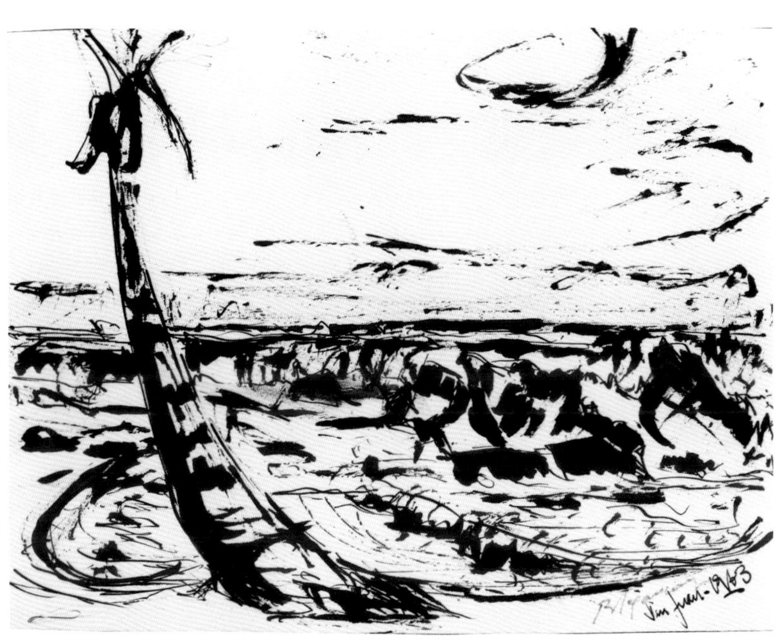

Storm at Sea, 1963. India ink on paper, 9 × 11 in. (22.8 × 27.9 cm).
Collection of the artist

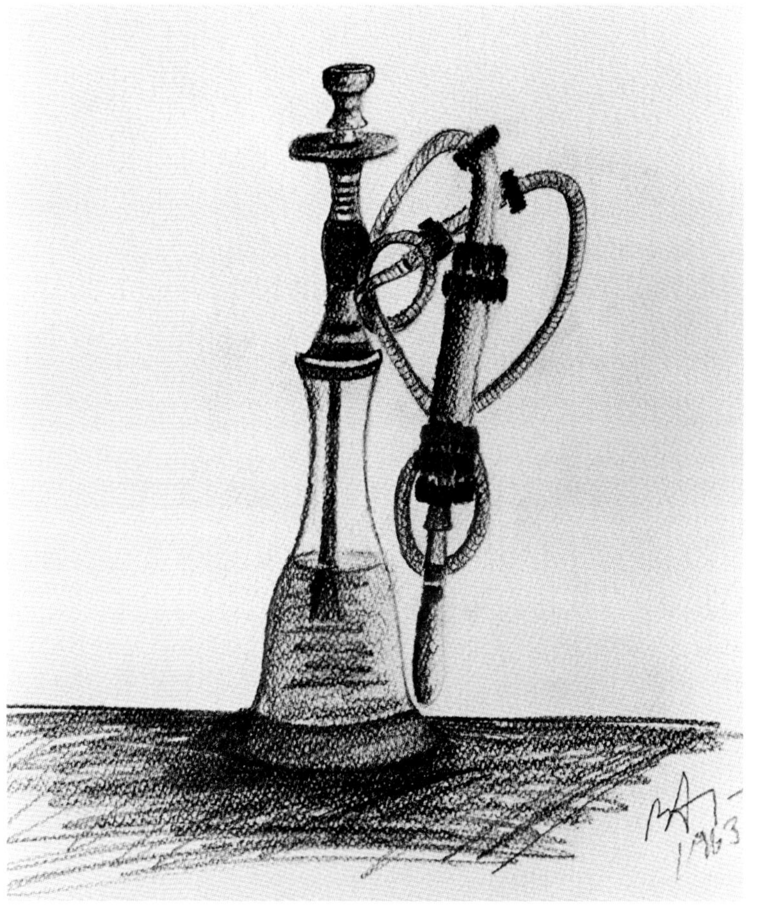

Waterpipe, 1963. Pencil on paper, 10¼ × 8¾ in. (26 × 22 cm).
Collection of the artist

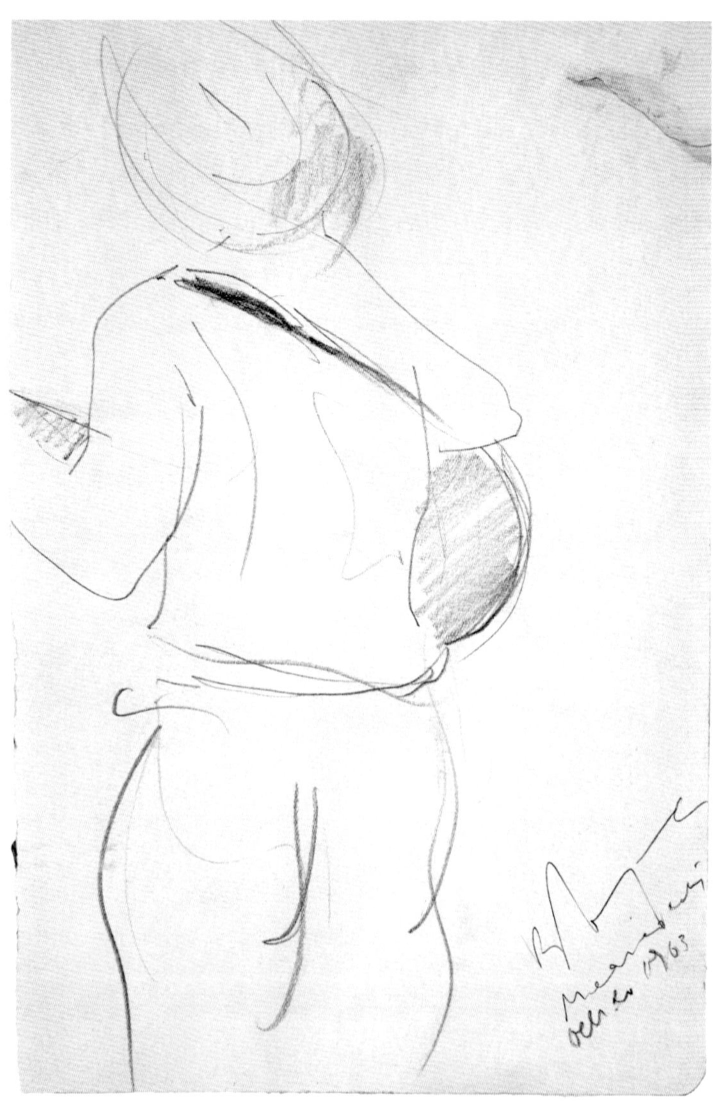

Mexican Guitar Player, 1963. Pencil on paper, 9⅜ × 6 in.
(24 × 15 cm). Collection of the artist

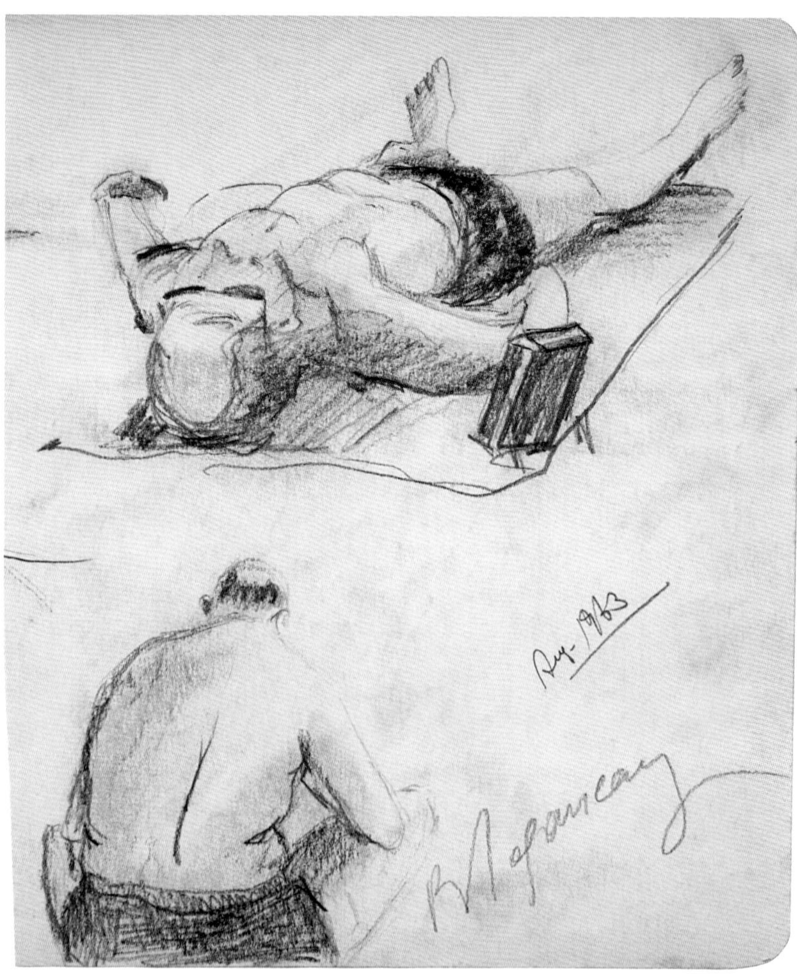

Men Sunbathing on the Roof, 1963. Pencil on paper, 9 × 7½ in.
(22.9 × 19 cm). Collection of the artist

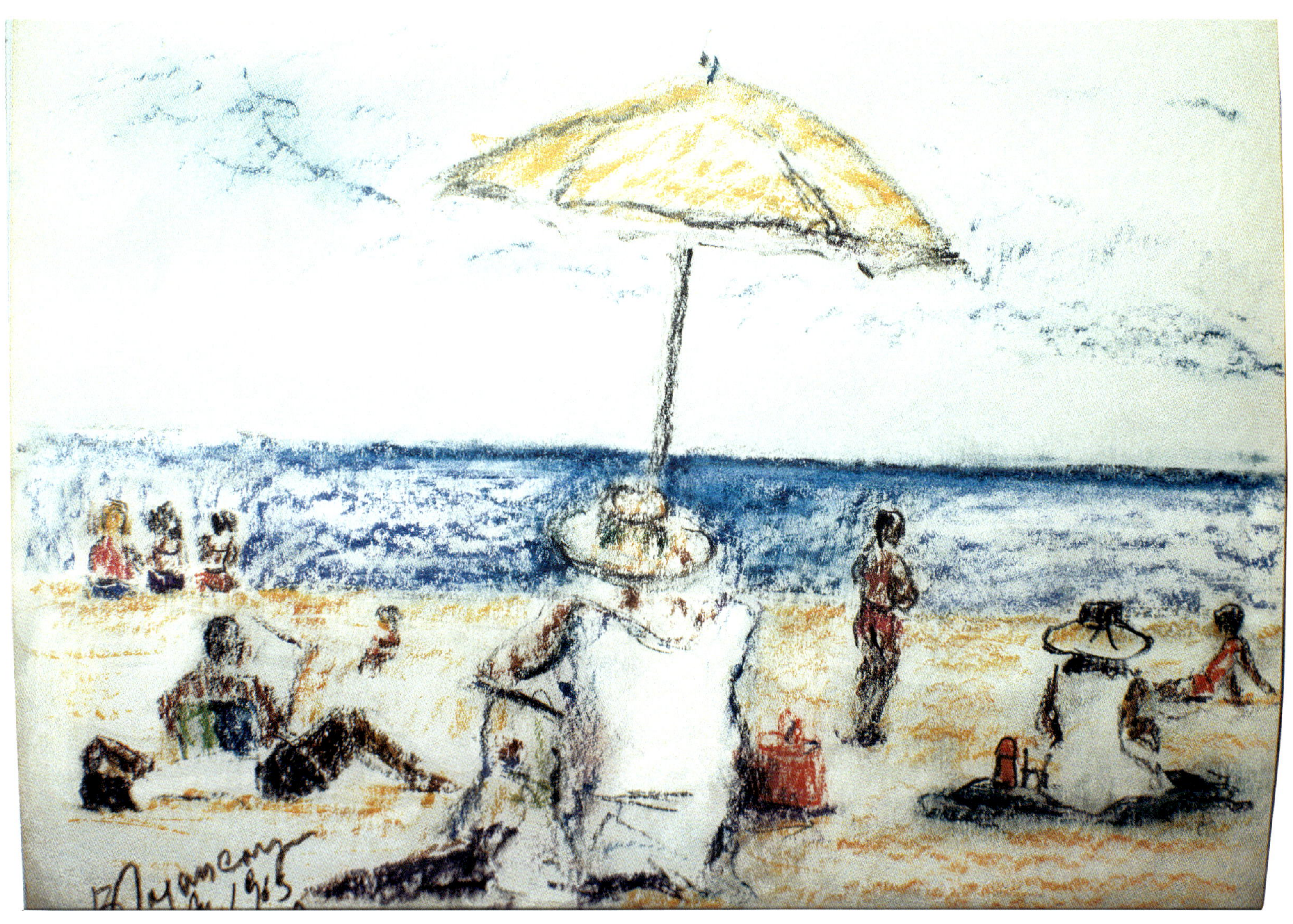

Beach with Yellow Umbrella, 1963. Crayon on paper, 8¾ × 11⅞ in. (22.1 × 30 cm). Collection of the artist

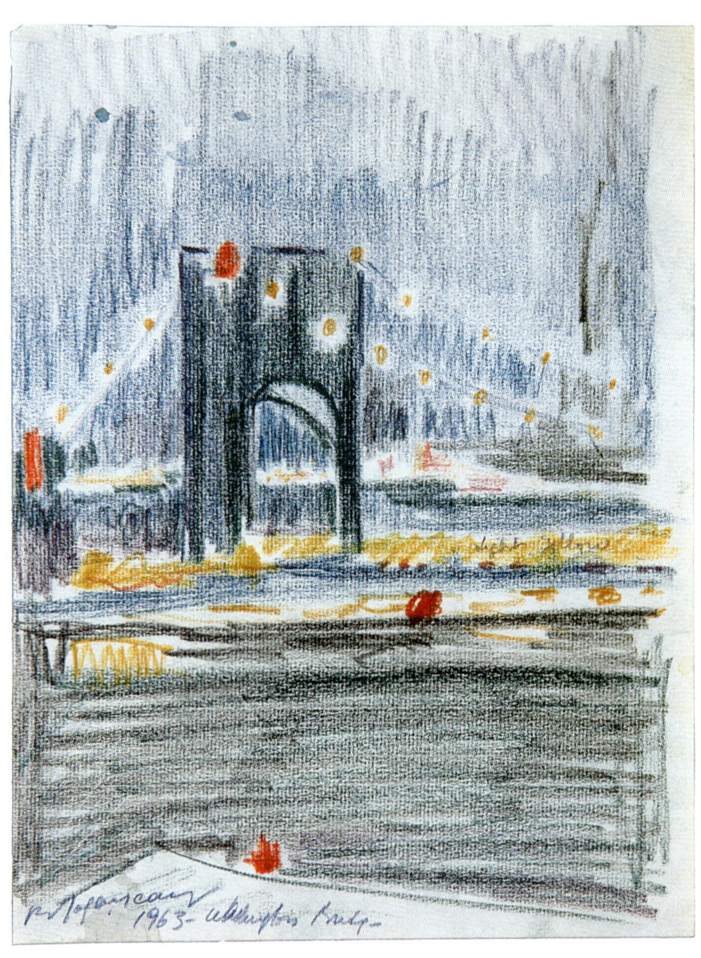

George Washington Bridge, 1963. Crayon on paper, 11 × 8¾ in. (28 × 22.1 cm). Collection of the artist

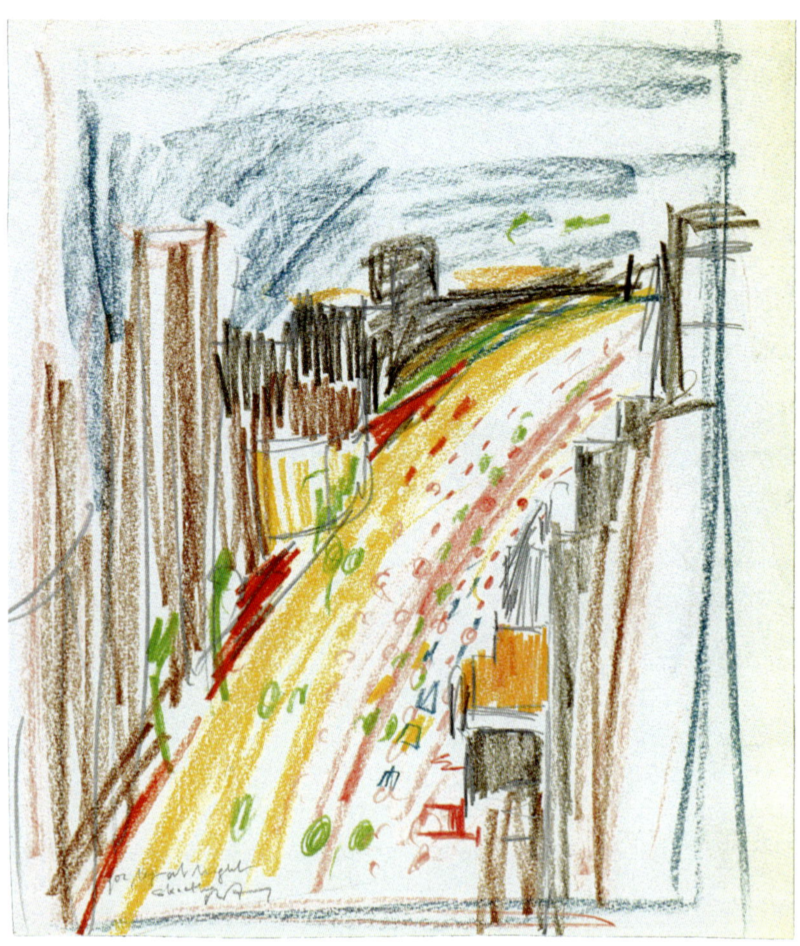

New York, Sketch, 1963. Crayon on paper, 11½ × 10 in. (29.2 × 25.4 cm). Collection of the artist

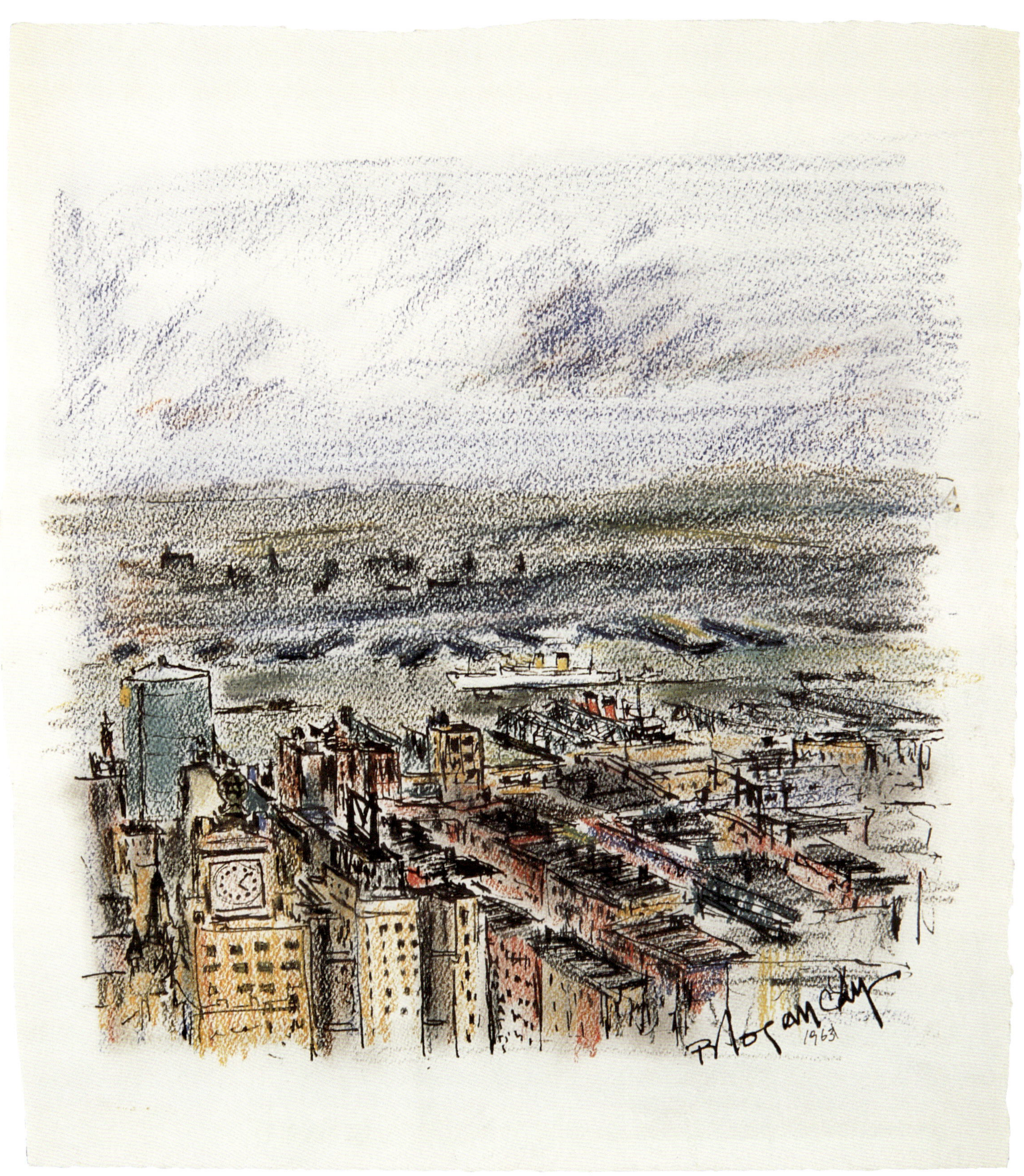

View from 500 5th Ave., 1963. Crayon and India ink on paper, 11½ × 10 in. (29.2 × 24 cm). Collection of the artist

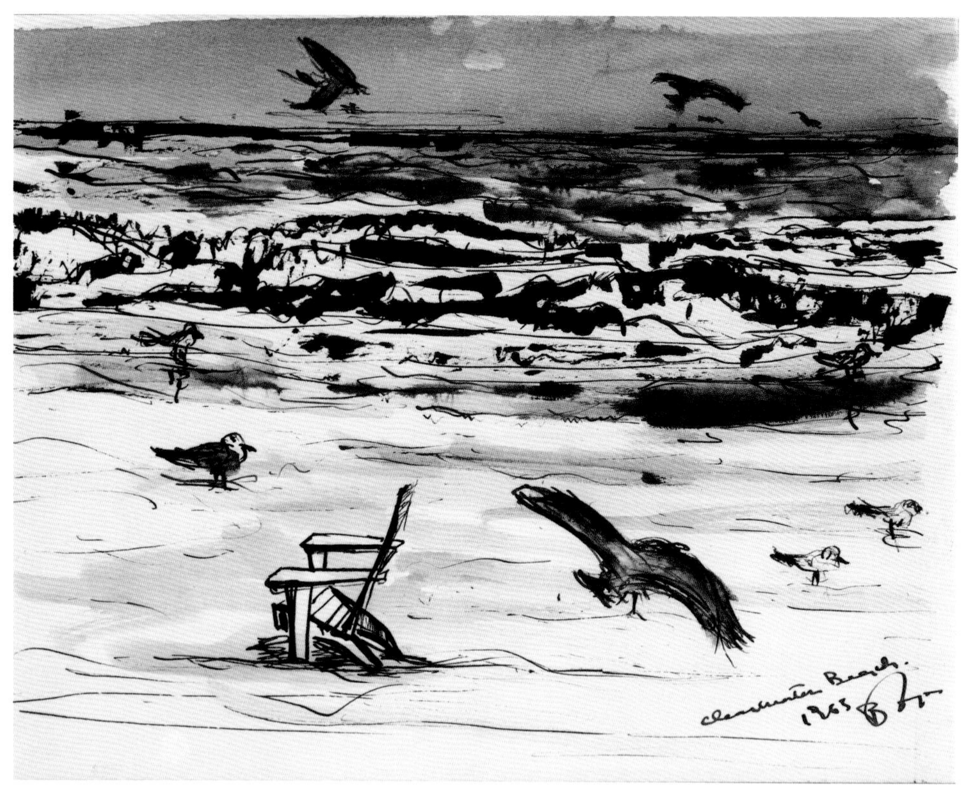

Beach in Clearwater, 1963. India ink on paper, 9 × 11 in. (22.8 × 27.9 cm). Private collection

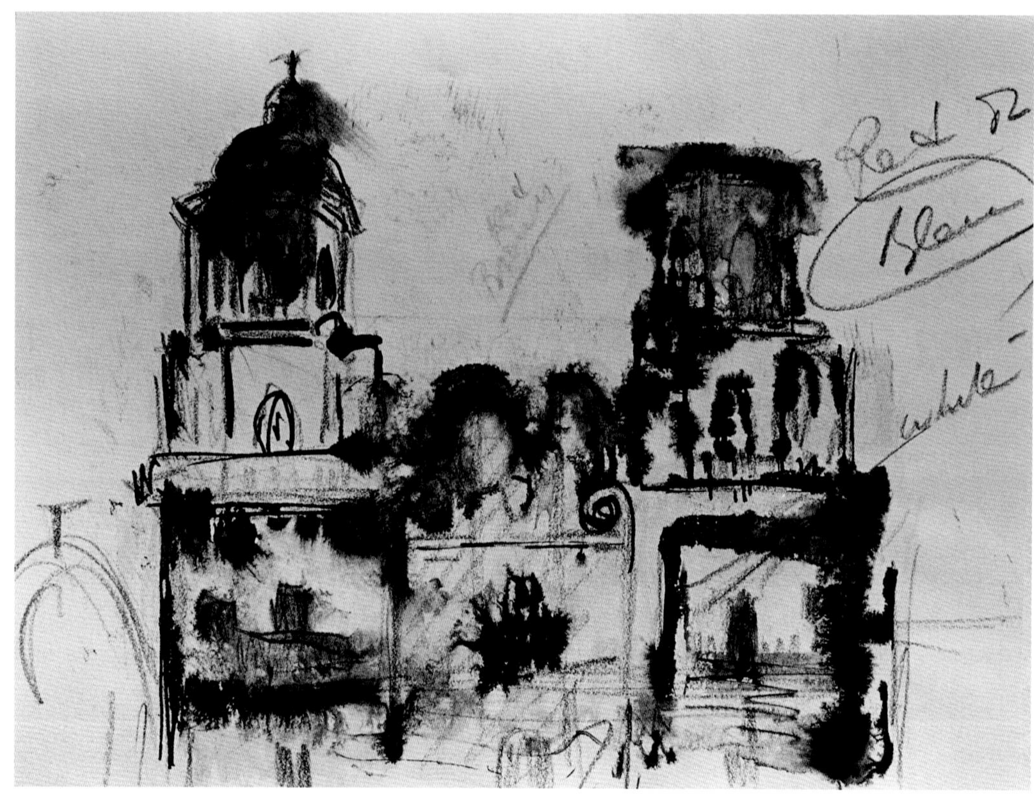

An Old Church in Arizona, 1963. India ink on paper, 9 × 12 in. (22.9 × 30.5 cm). Collection of the artist

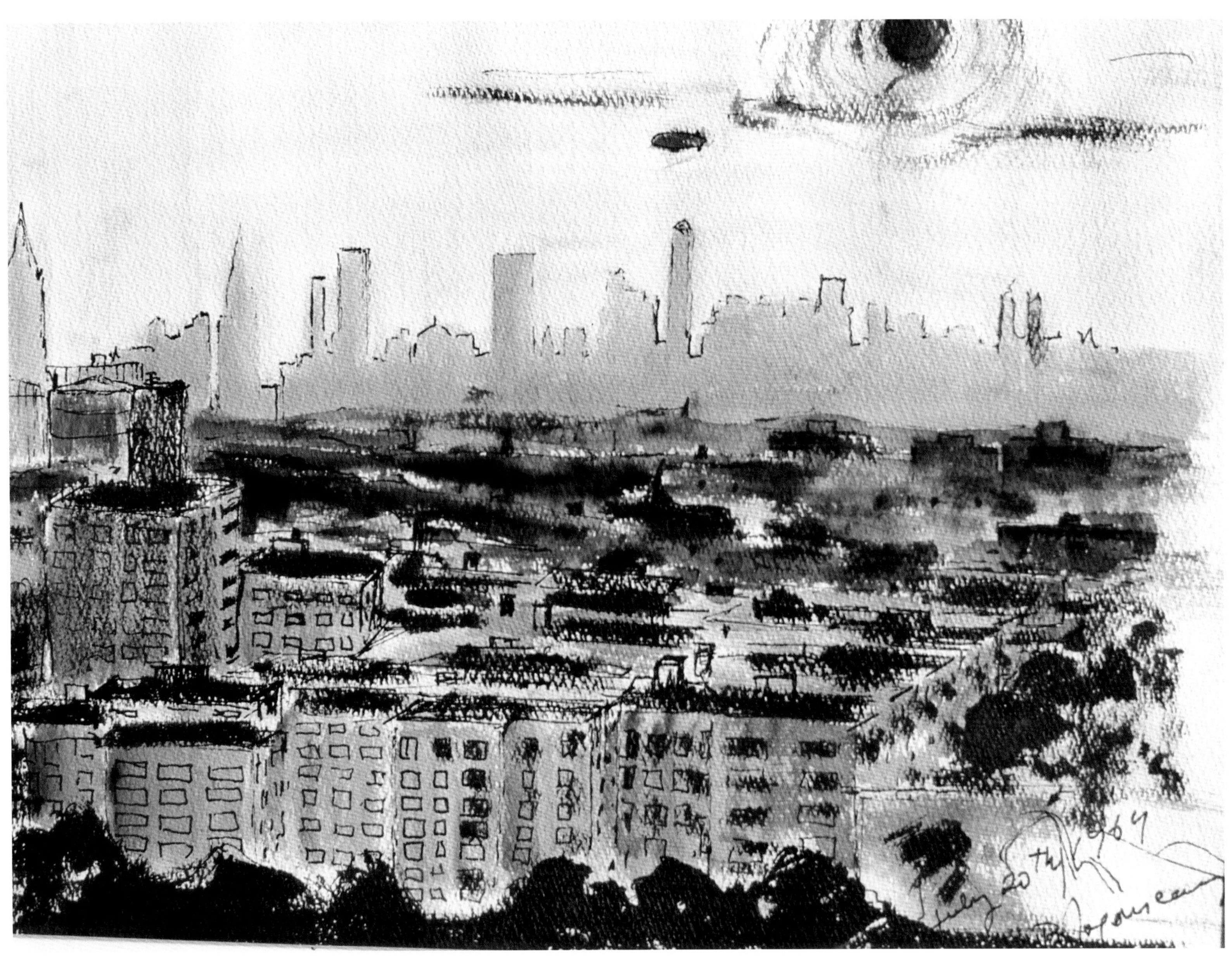

Manhattan Skyline from Queens, 1964. India ink and gouache on paper, 11 × 15½ in. (27.9 × 39.4 cm). Collection of the artist

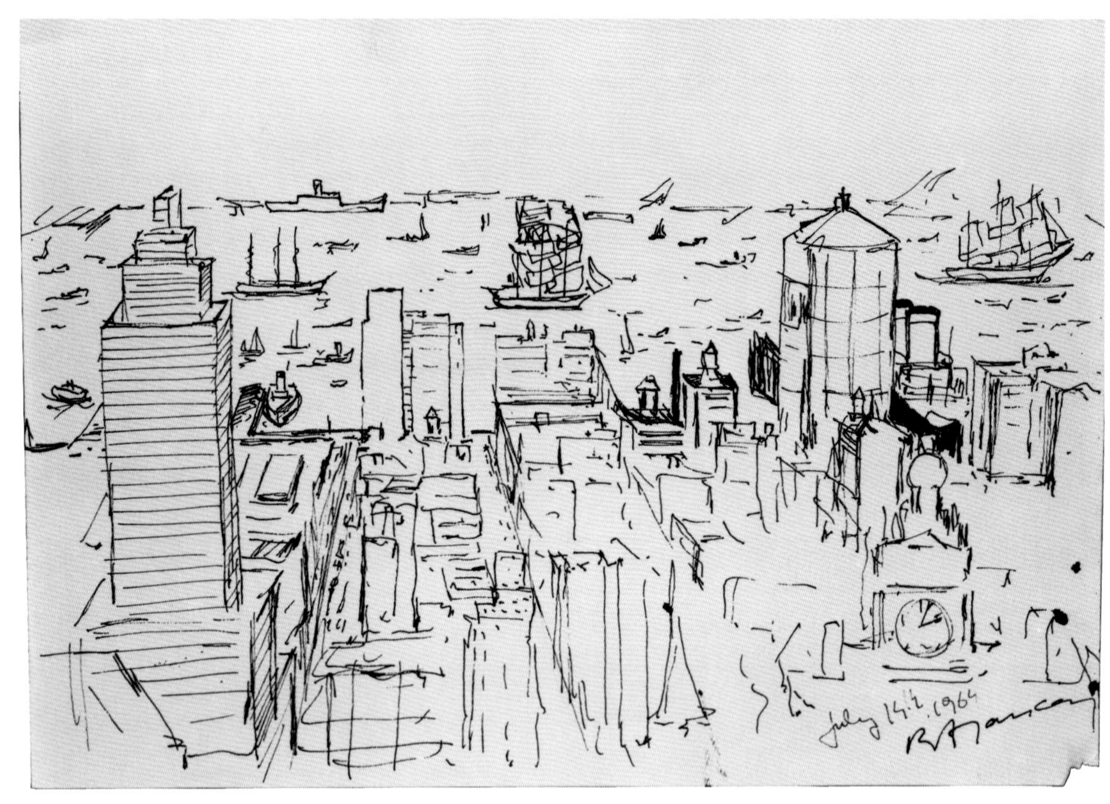

Tall Ships on the Hudson, 1964. India ink on paper, 15 × 22 in. (38.1 × 55.9 cm). Private collection

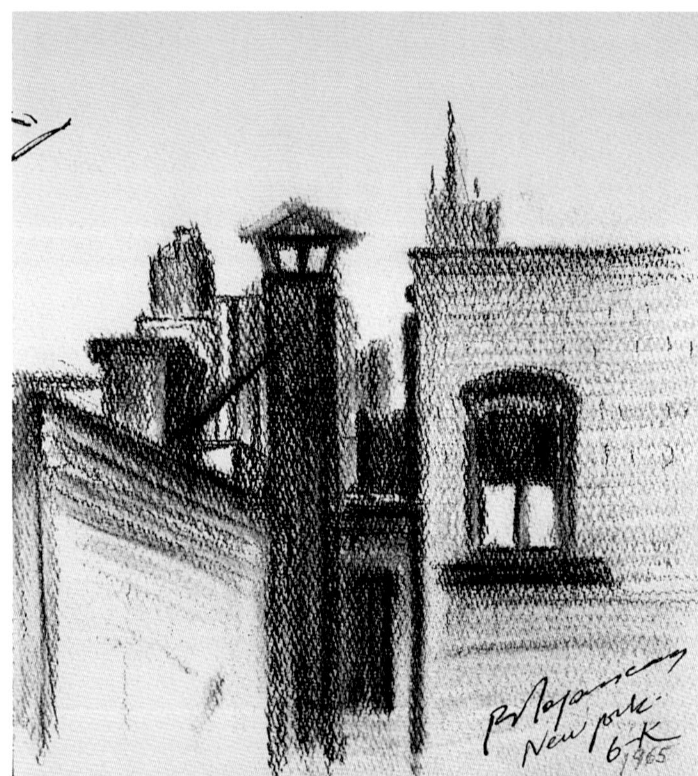

Manhattan Rear View, 1965. Pencil on paper, 9⅜ × 8¾ in.
(24 × 22 cm). Collection of the artist

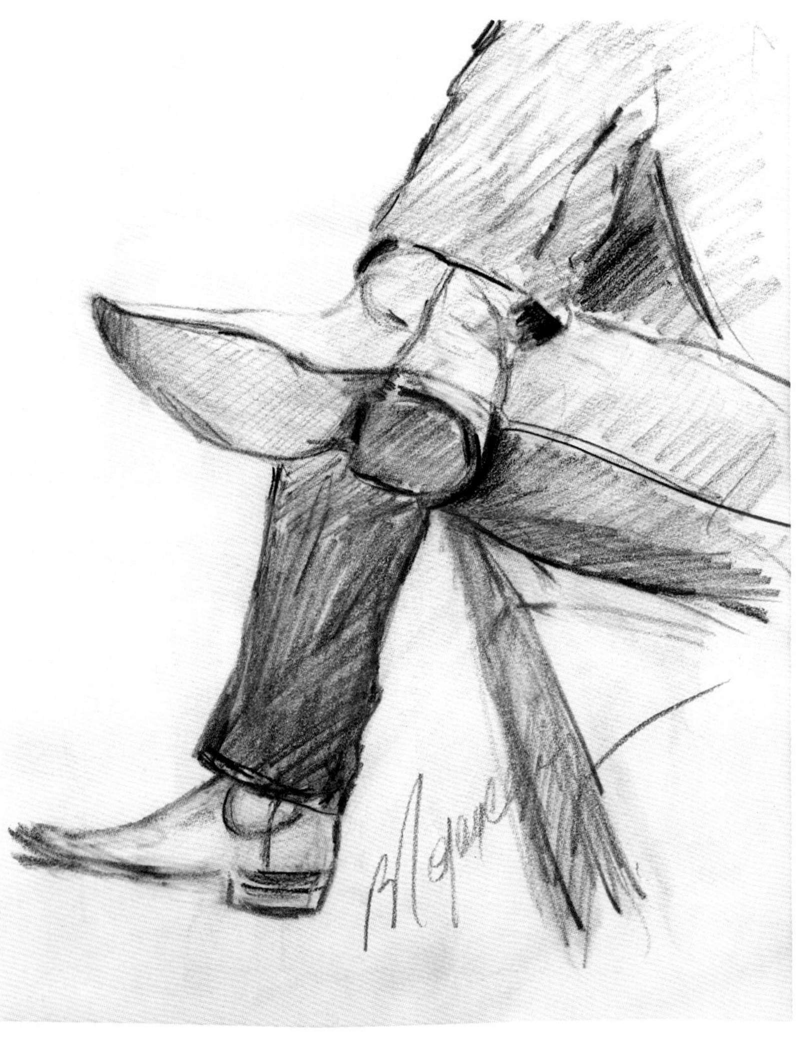

Cowboy Boots, 1965. Crayon on paper, 10½ × 8½ in. (26.7 × 21.6 cm).
Collection of the artist

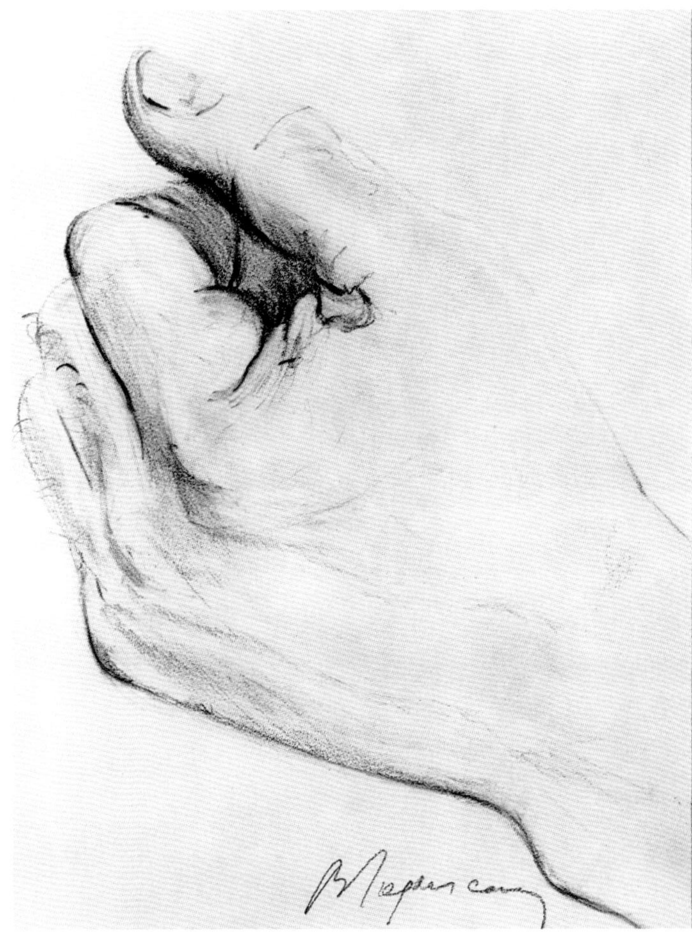

Hand, 1965. Crayon on paper, 8 × 6 in. (20.3 × 15.2 cm).
Collection of the artist

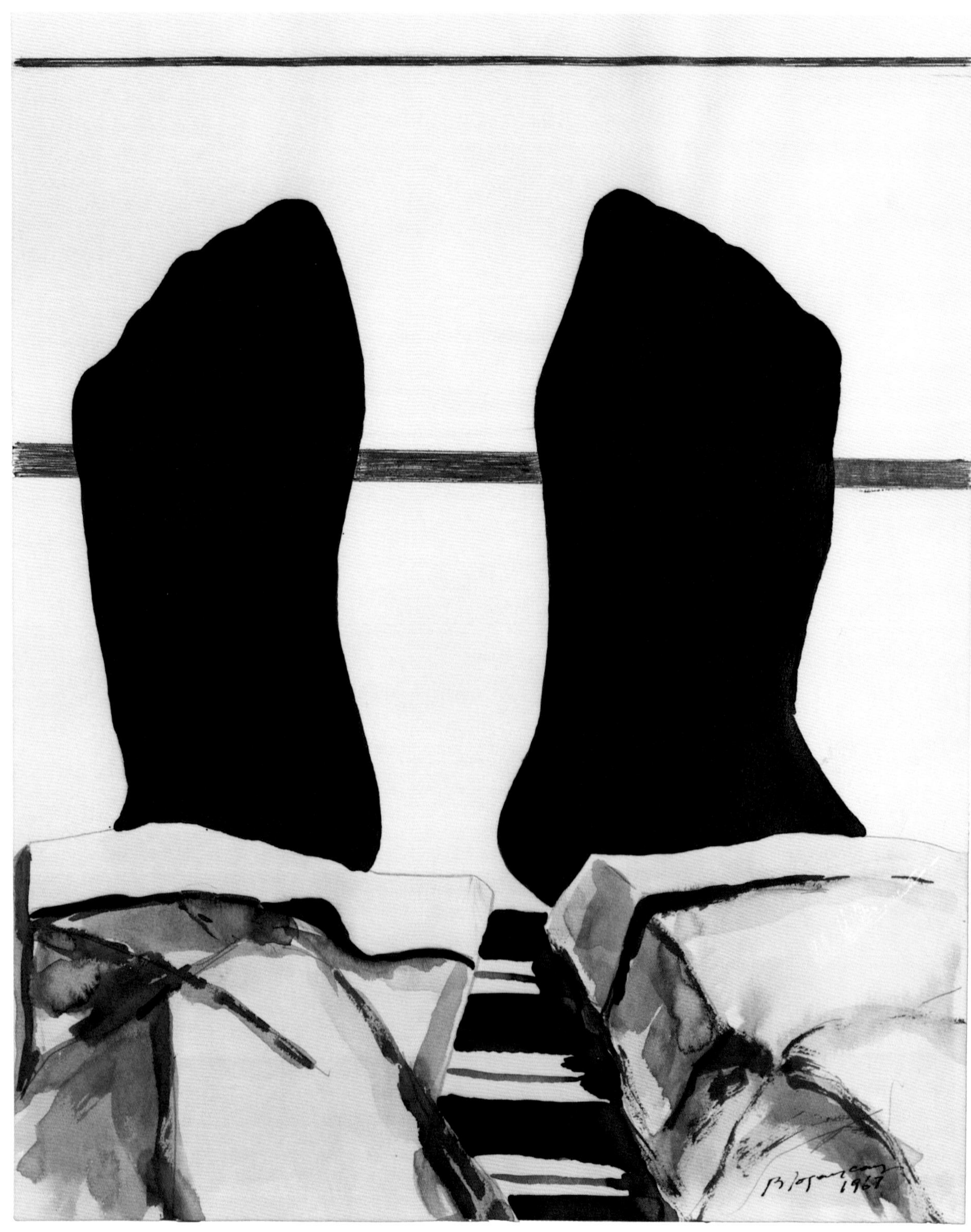

Feet, 1967. India ink on paper, 13½ × 11 in. (34.3 × 27.9 cm). Collection of the artist

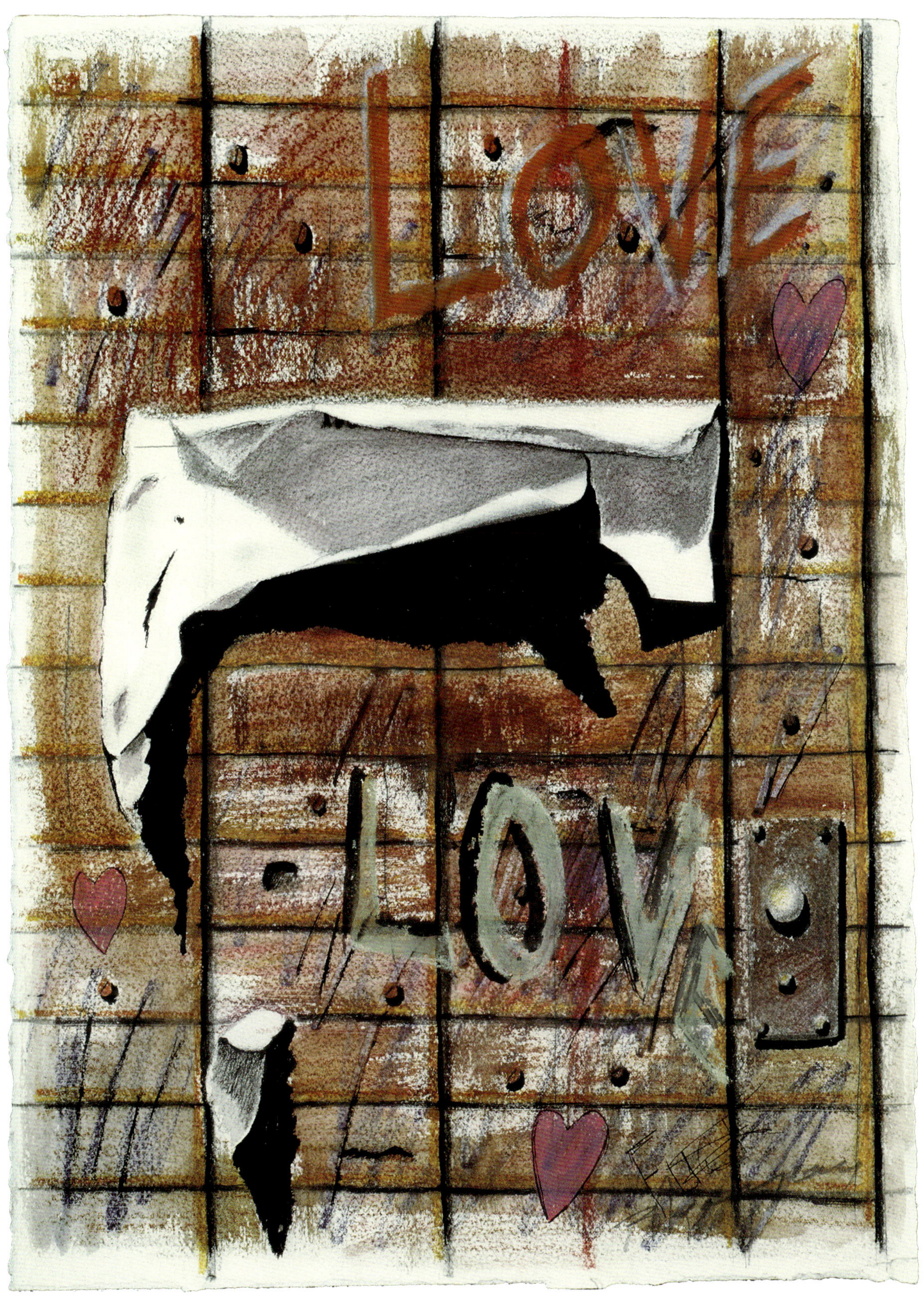

Love, 1969. India ink, crayon, and gouache on paper, 14½ × 10½ in. (36.8 × 26.7 cm). Private collection, Istanbul

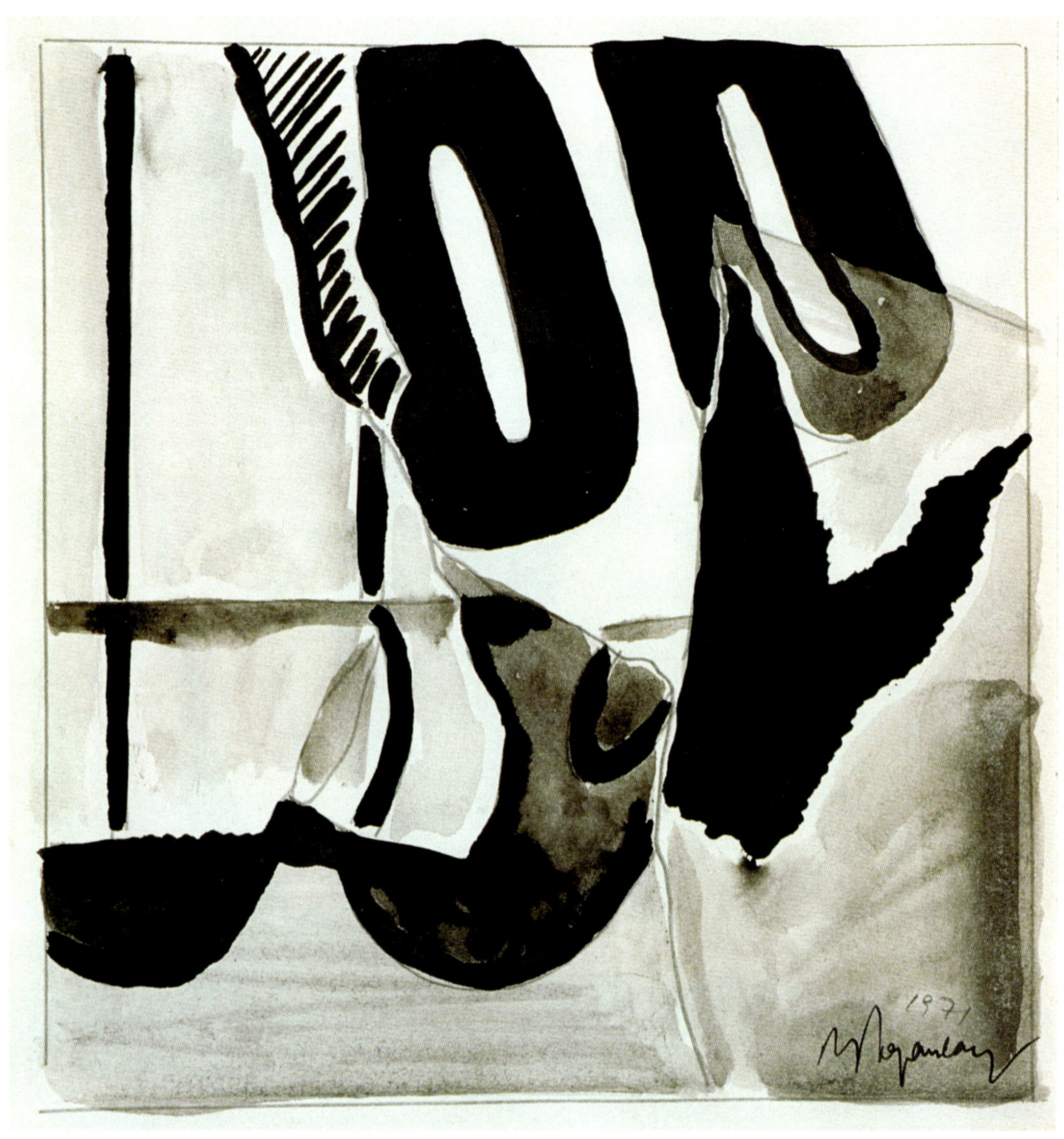

From Book E: Double oos; Study, 1971. India ink and crayon on paper, 6½ × 6½ in. (16.5 × 16.5 cm). Collection of the artist

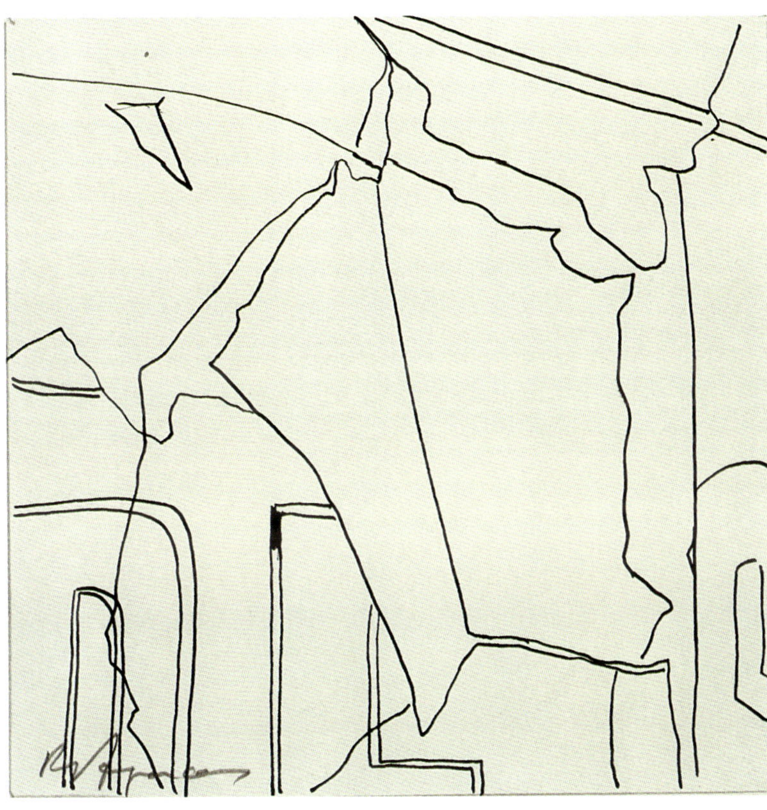

From Book E; Study, 1971. India ink on paper, 7 × 7 in. (17.8 × 17.8 cm).
Collection of the artist

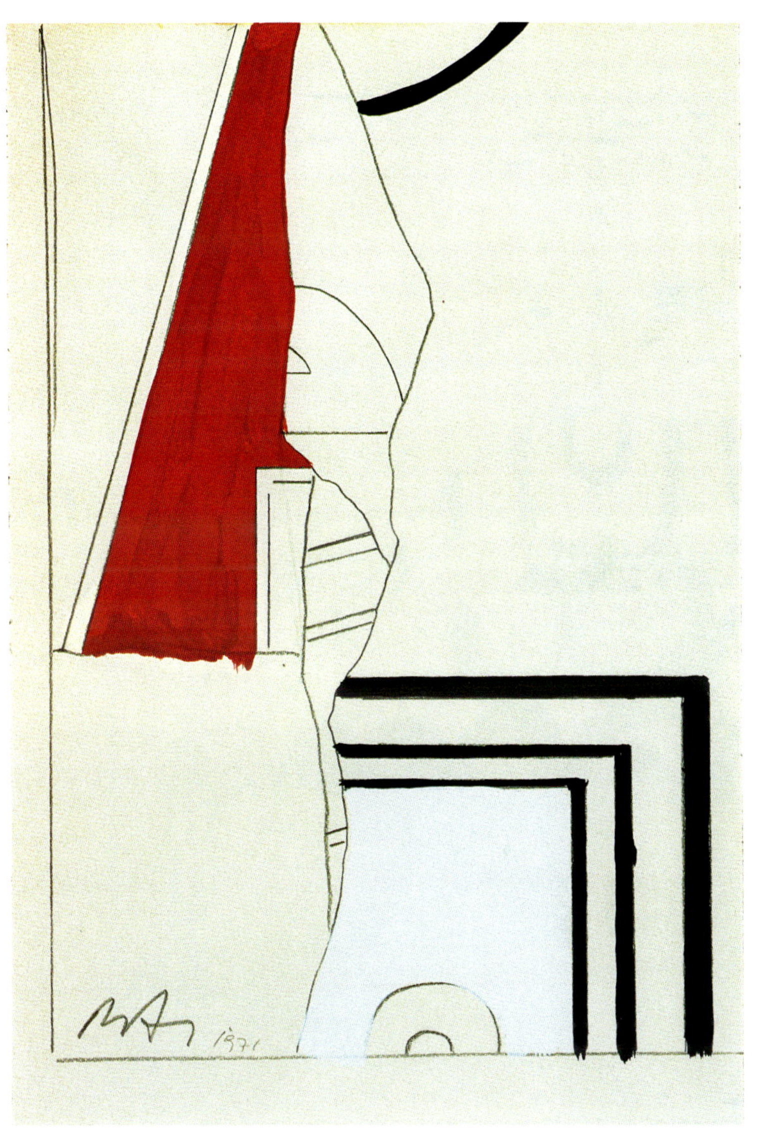

From Book E; Study, 1971. Crayon and gouache on paper,
9½ × 8 in. (24.1 × 20.3 cm). Collection of the artist

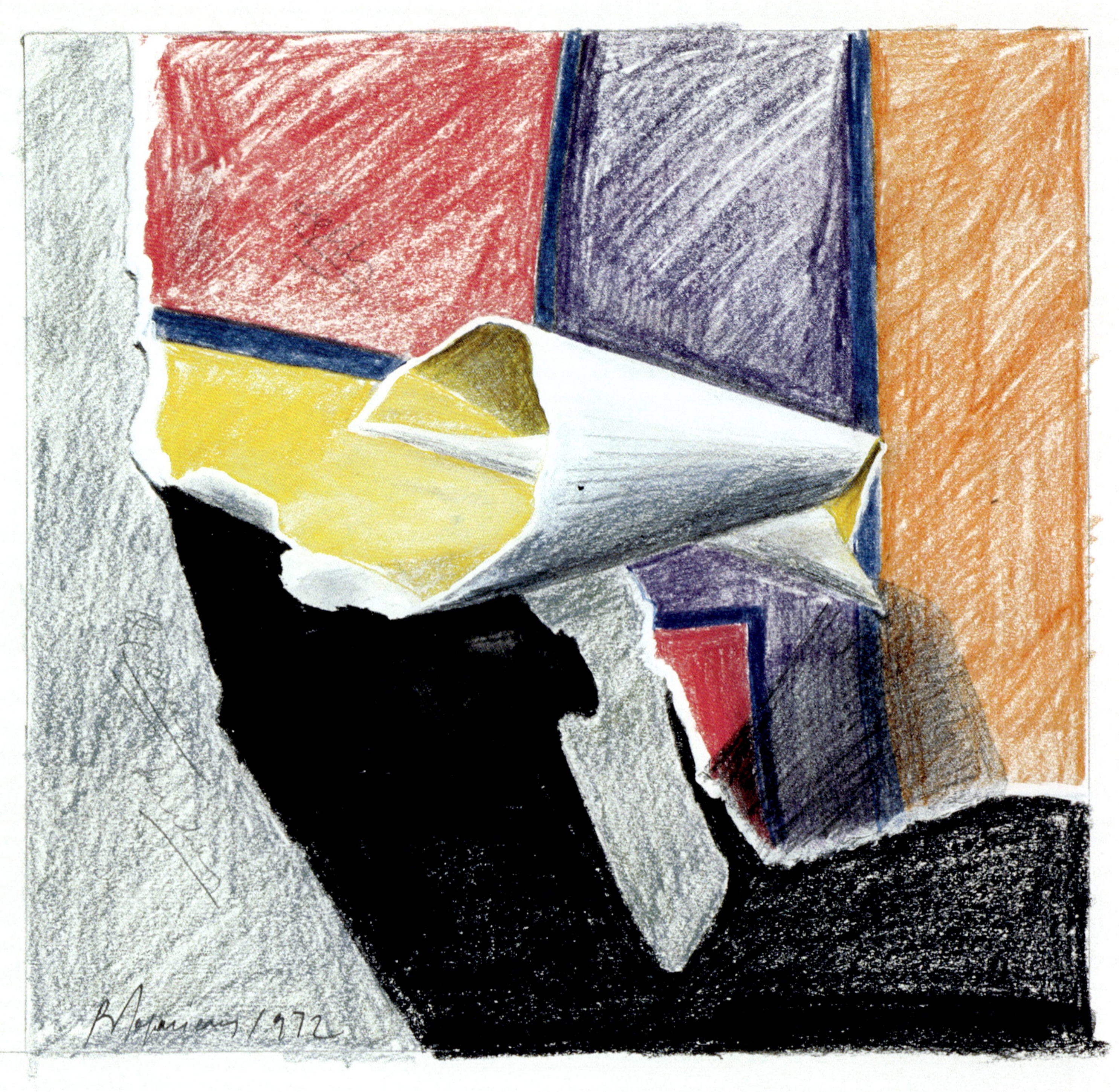

Torn Poster; Study, 1972. Crayon on paper, 9¼ × 10 in. (23.5 × 25.4 cm). Collection of the artist

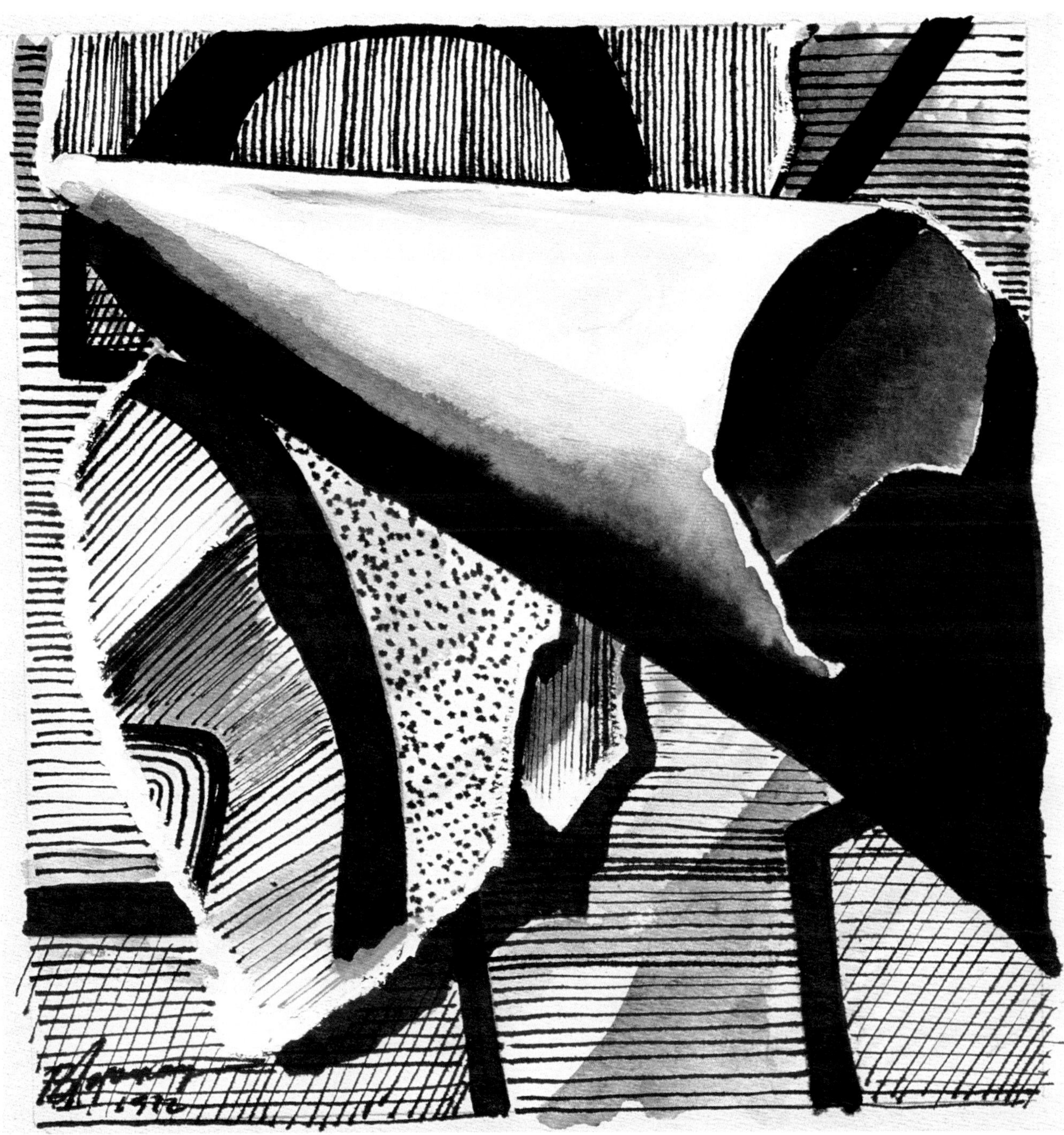

From Book C: Untitled, 1972. India ink, acrylic, and gouache, 7×7 in. (17.8 × 17.8 cm). Collection of the artist

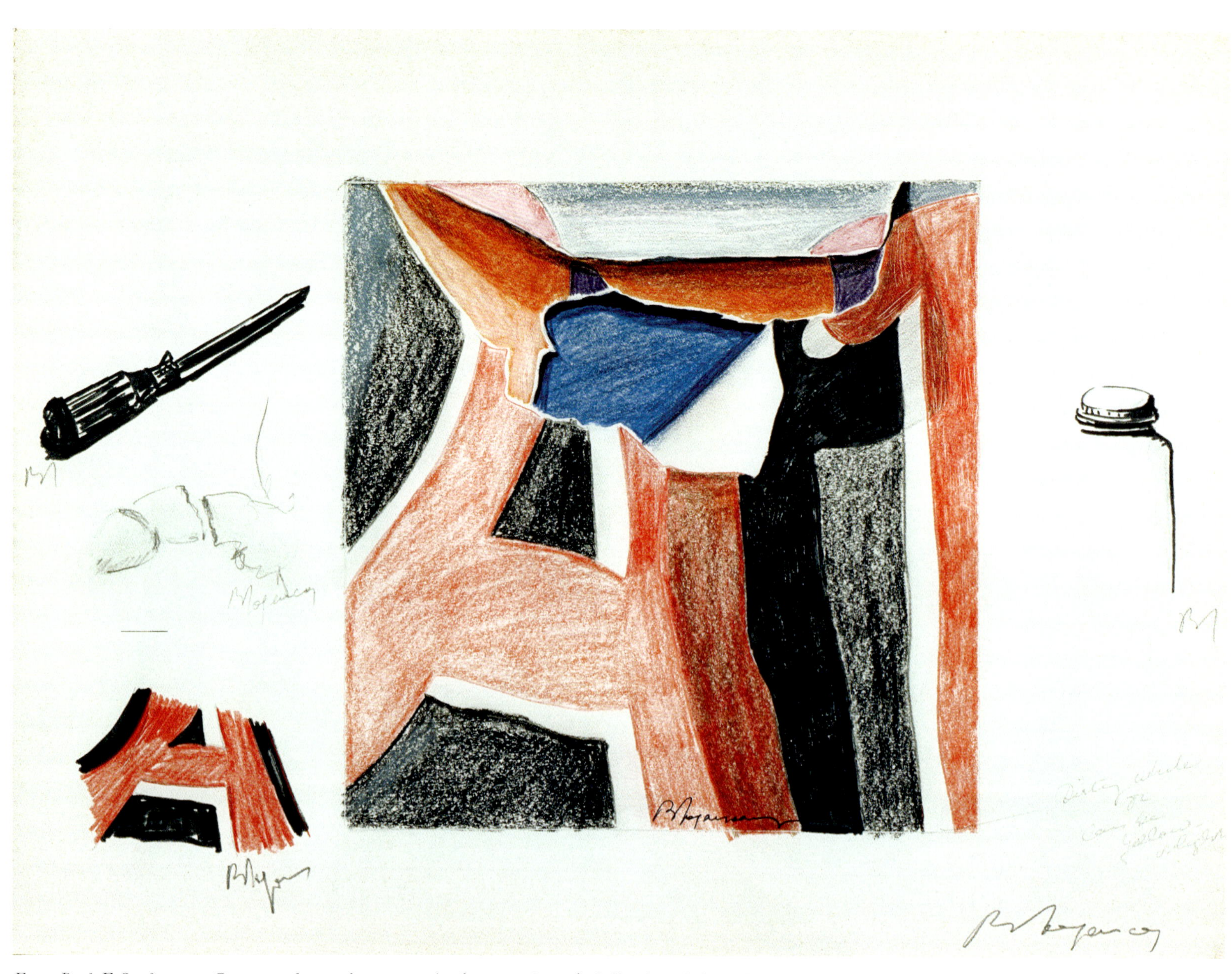

From Book F; Study, 1972. Crayon and gouache, 10 × 15 in. (25.4 × 38.1 cm). Collection of the artist

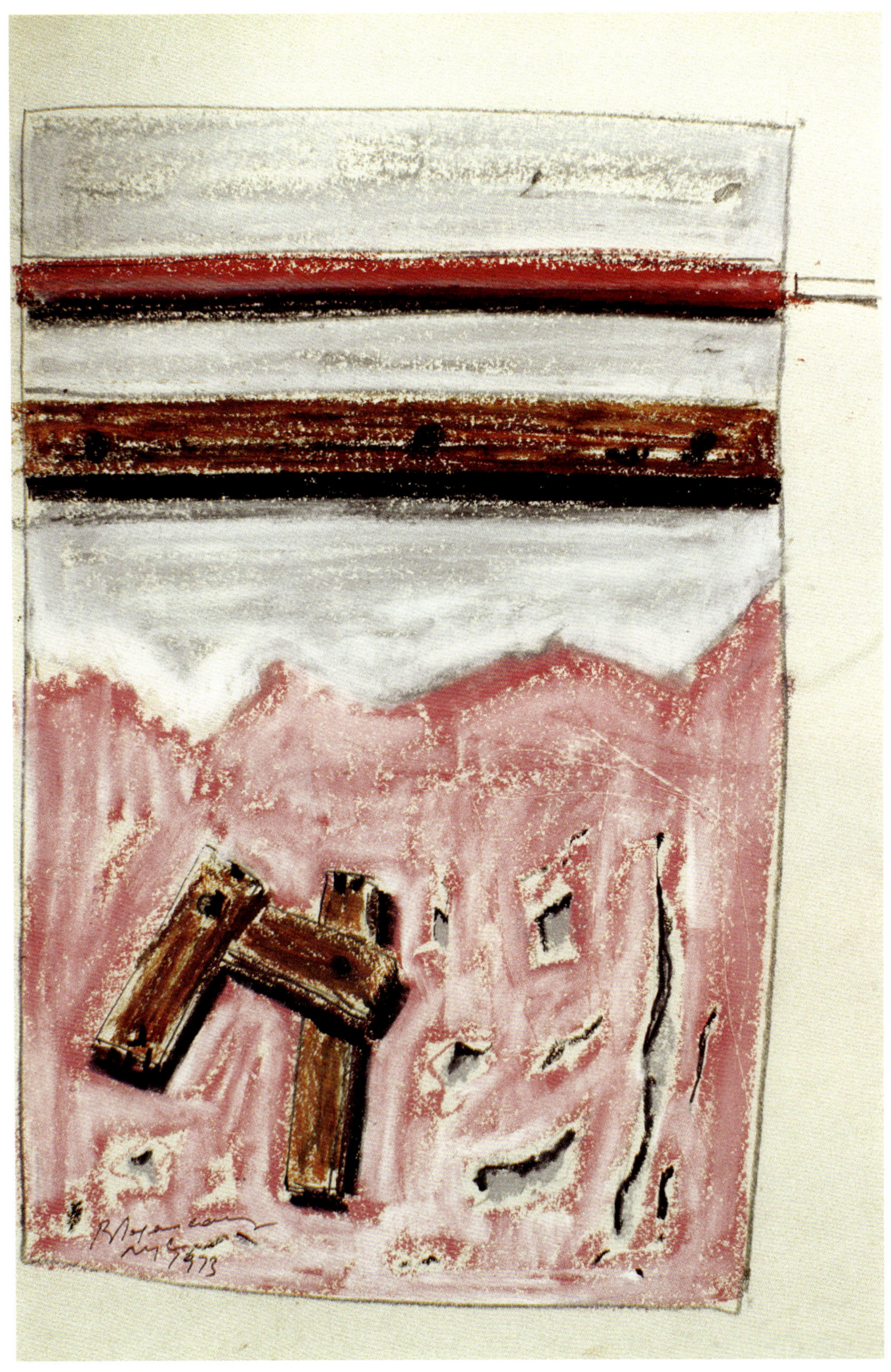

Study for Large Canvas, 1973. Crayon on paper, 9½ × 7 in. (24.1 × 17.8 cm). Collection of the artist

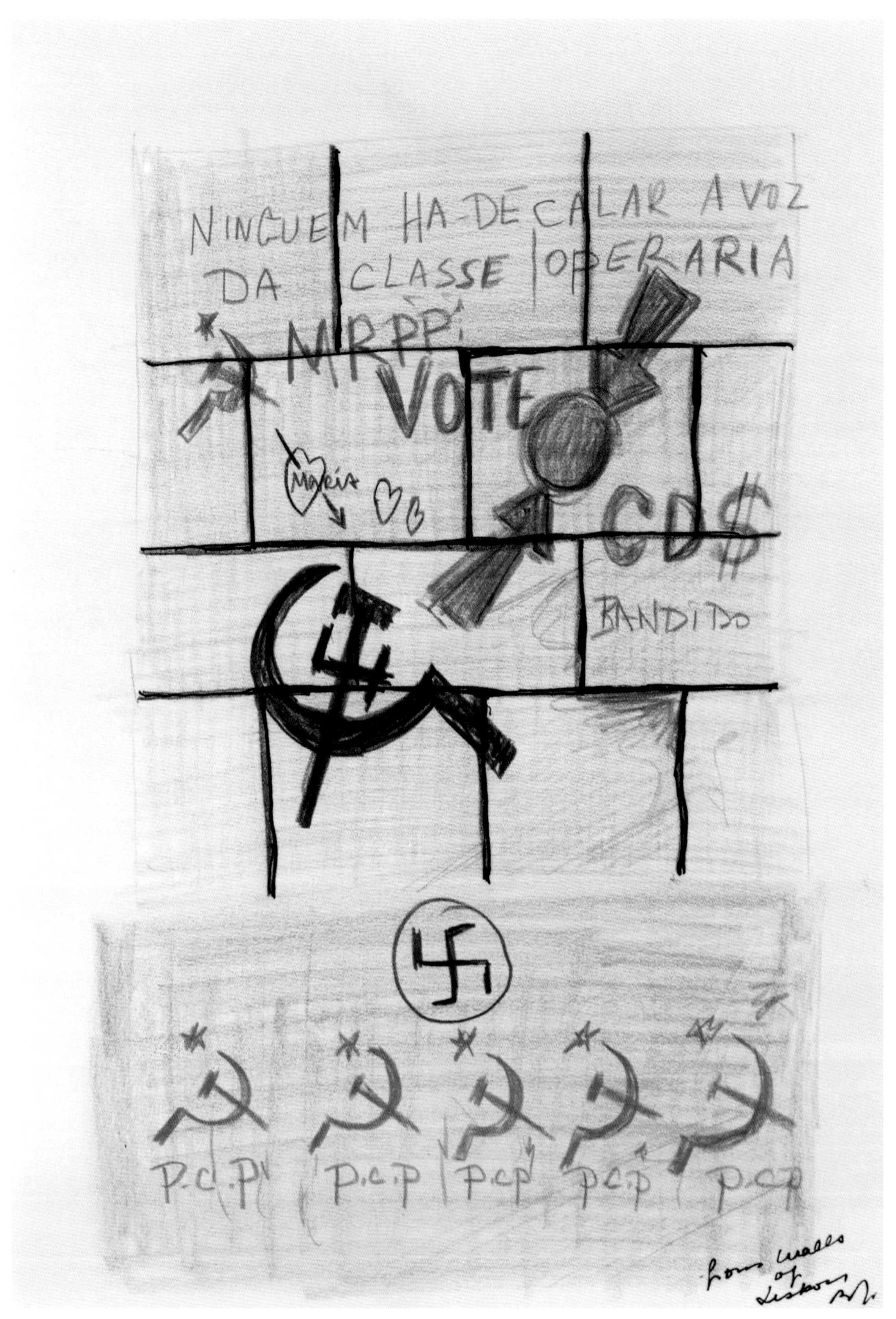

Study: From Walls of Lisbon, 1977. Pencil on paper, 9½ × 7 in. (24.1 × 17.8 cm). Collection of the artist

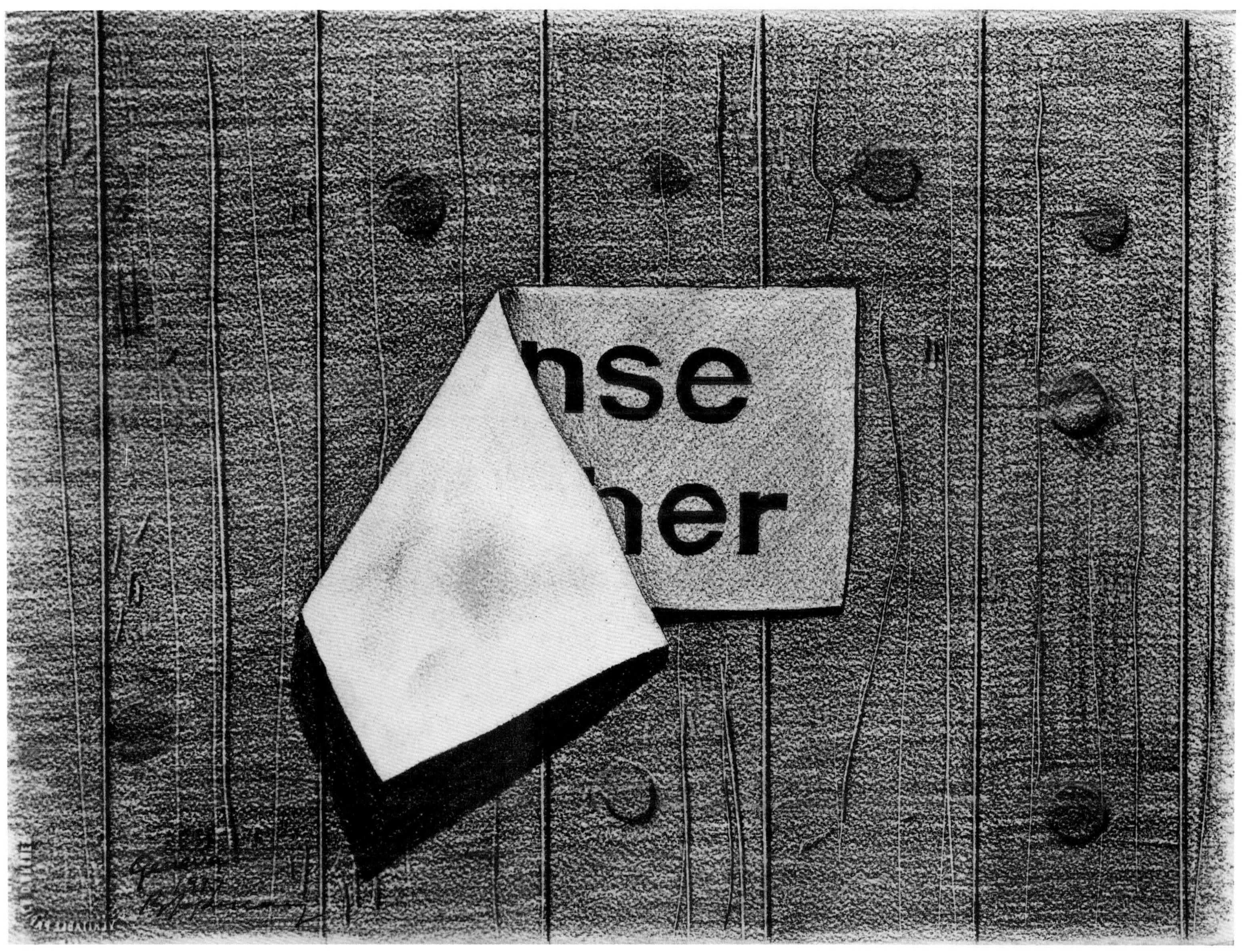

Défense d'Afficher, 1977. Crayon on paper, 10 × 12 in. (25.4 × 30.5 cm). Collection of the artist

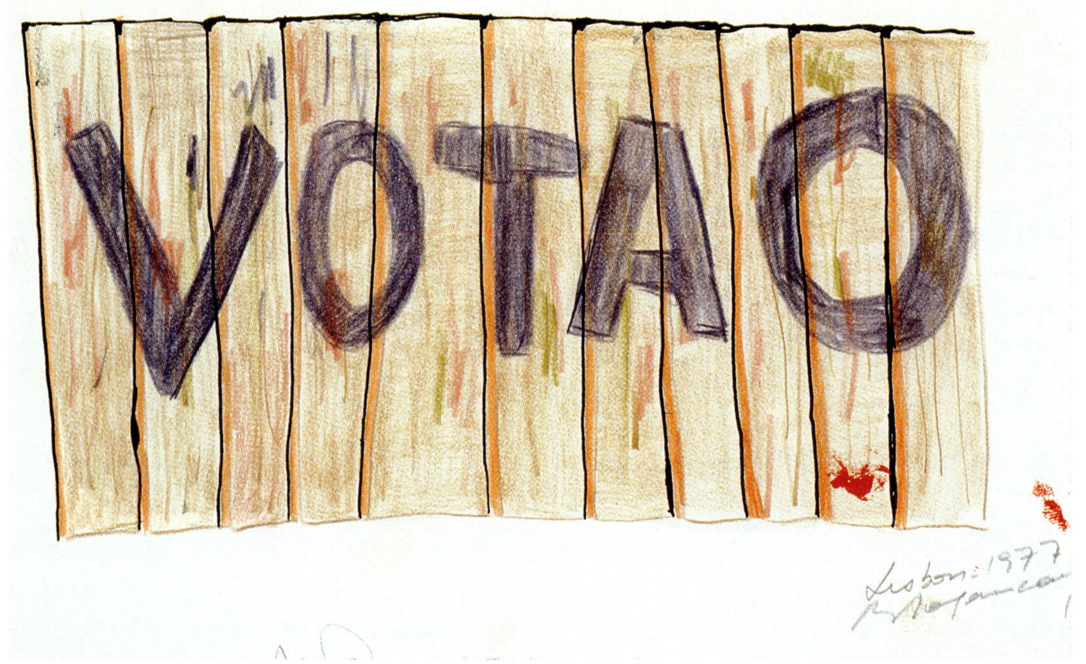

Study for Walls from Portugal, 1977. India ink and crayon on paper, 4½ × 8 in. (11.4 × 20.3 cm).
Collection of the artist

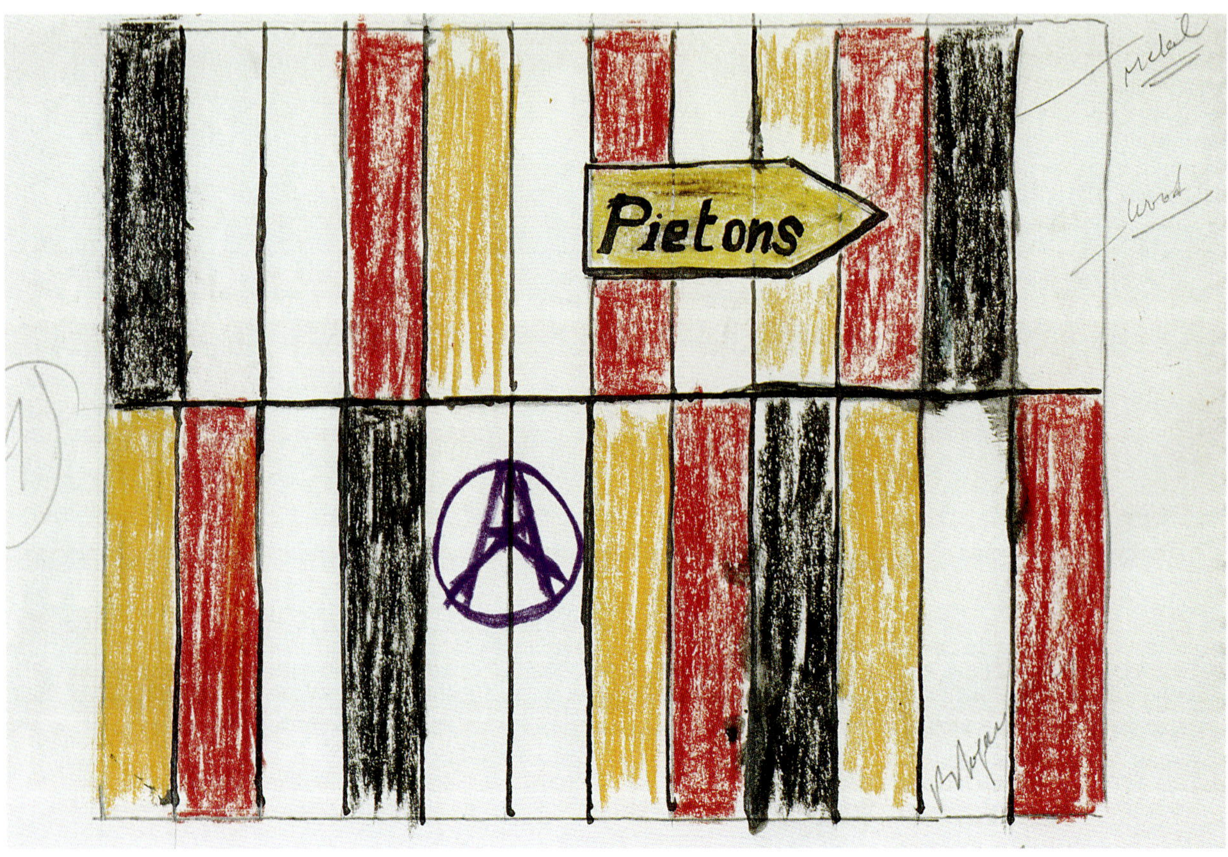

From Book 11: From Walls of Paris, 1979. India ink and crayon on paper, 5½ × 9 in. (14 × 22.9 cm). Collection of the artist

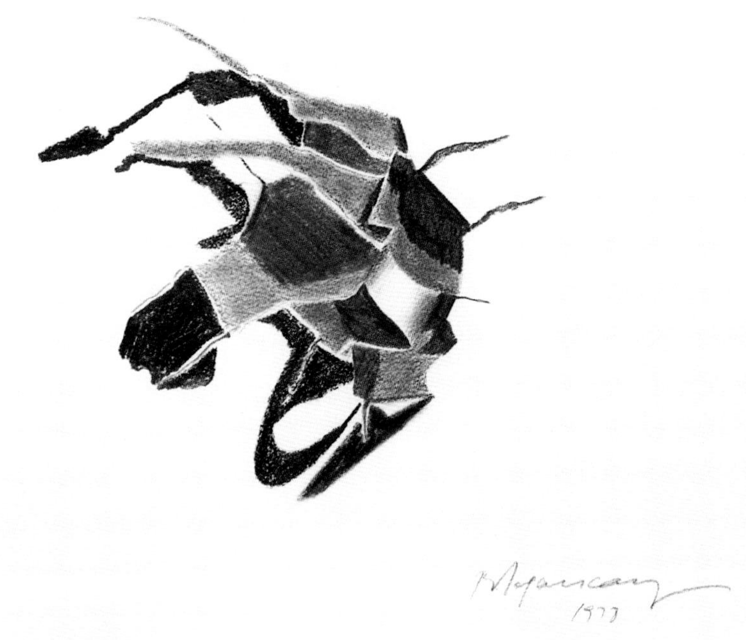

Study for Large Canvas, 1978. Crayon and pencil on paper, 11 × 15 in. (27.9 × 38.1 cm).
Private collection, Dusseldorf

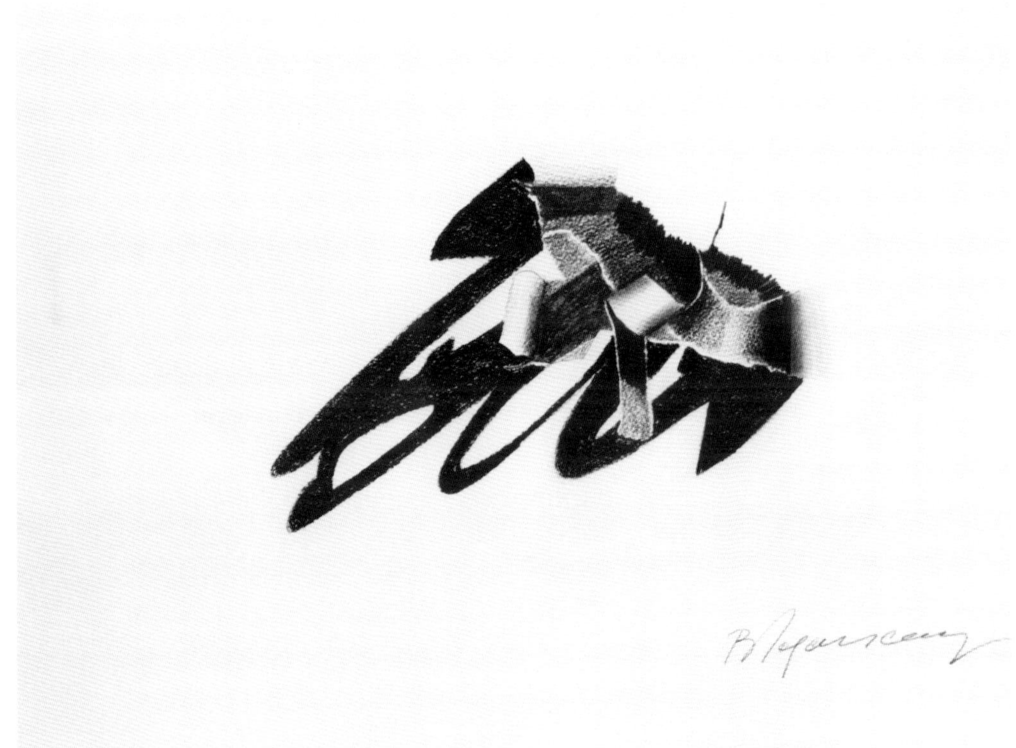

Study for Large Canvas, 1978. Crayon and pencil on paper, 11 × 15 in. (27.9 × 38.1 cm).
Collection of the artist

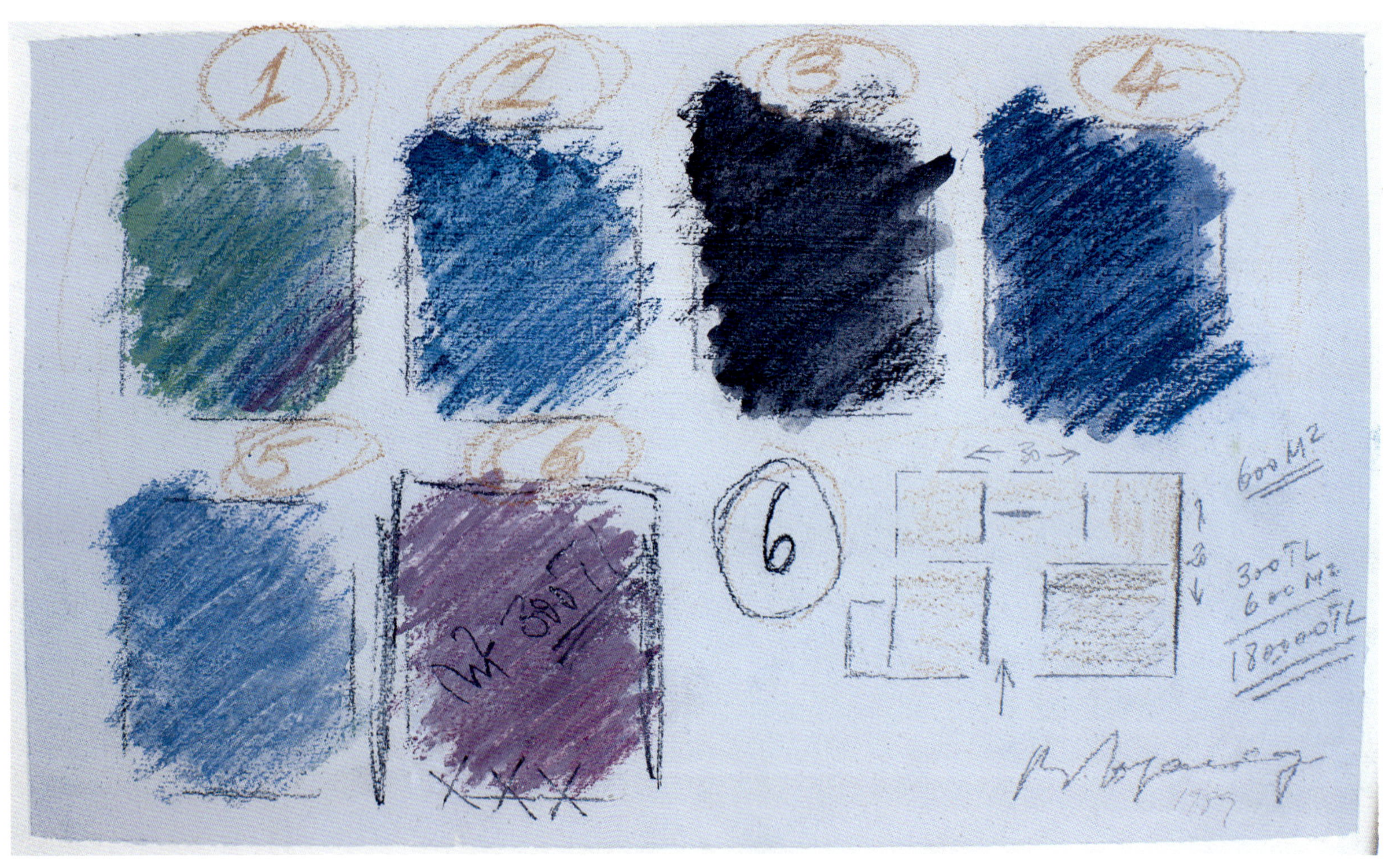

Study for Housepainter Series, 1989. Pencil and acrylic on paper, 8 × 14 in. (20.3 × 35.6 cm). Collection of the artist

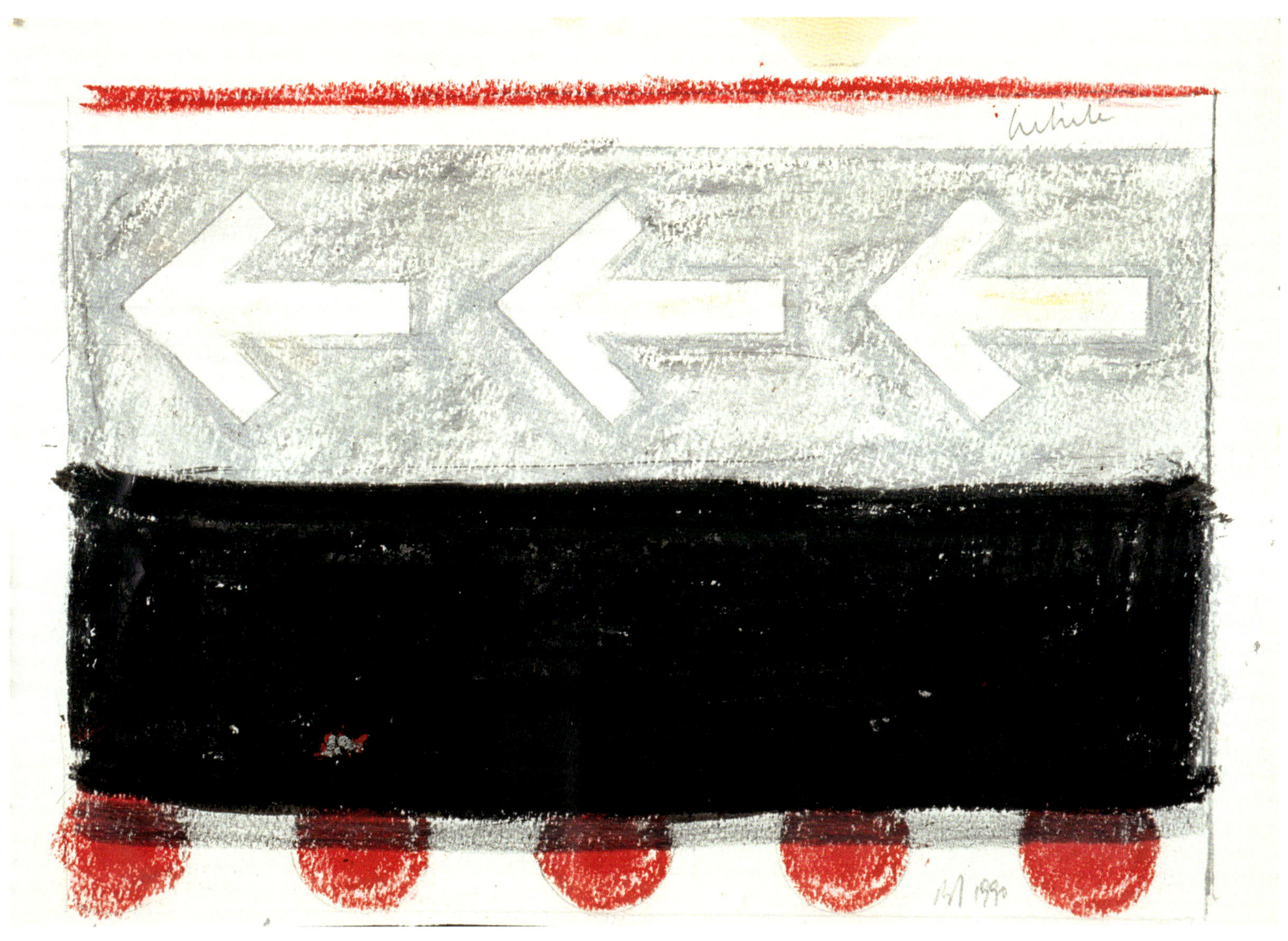

Study for Formula I Series, 1990. Crayon and gouache on paper, 6½ × 9 in. (16.5 × 22.9 cm). Collection of the artist

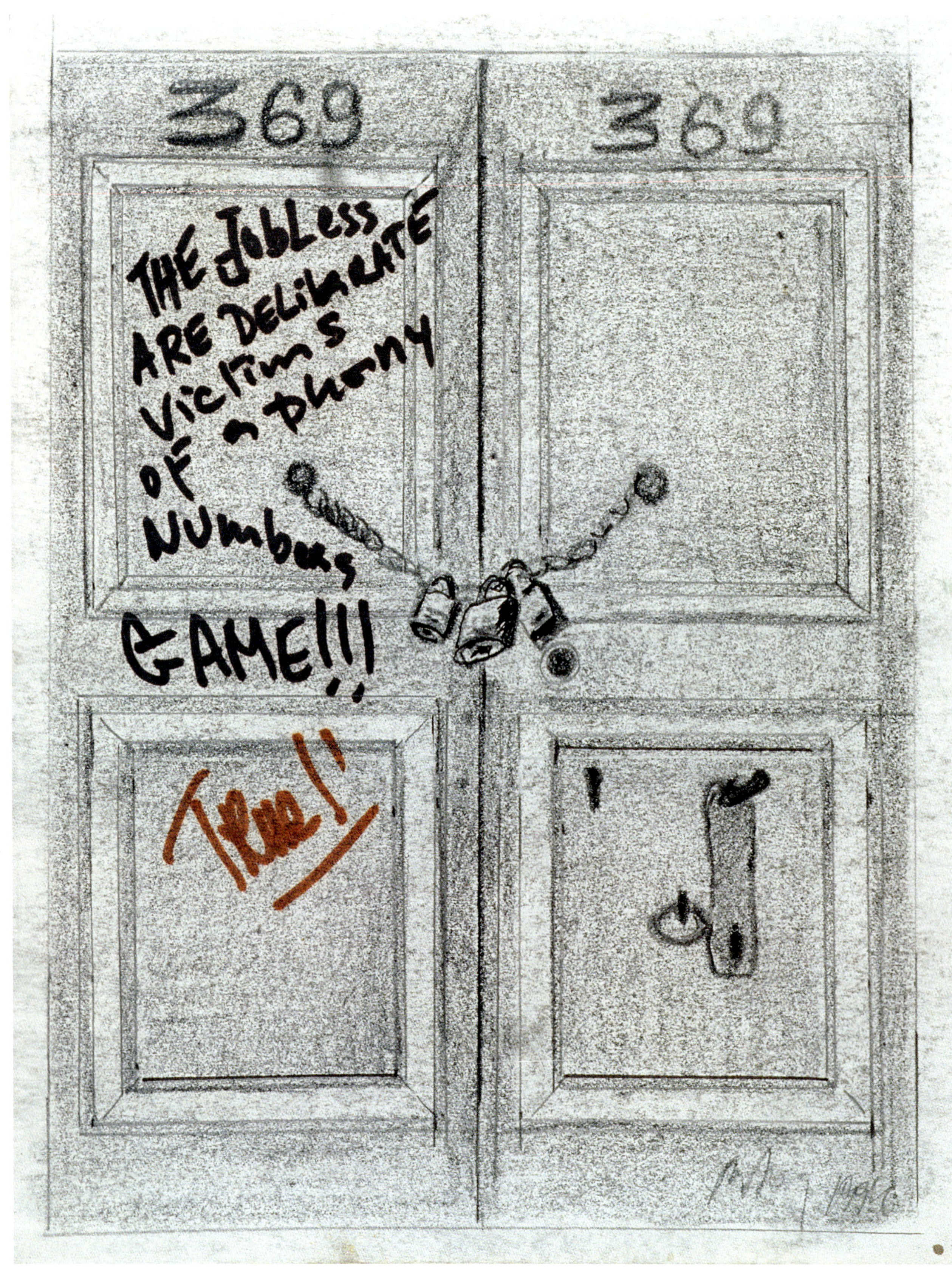

Study for Doors Series, 1994. India ink and pencil on paper, 9 × 6½ in. (22.9 × 16.5 cm). Collection of the artist

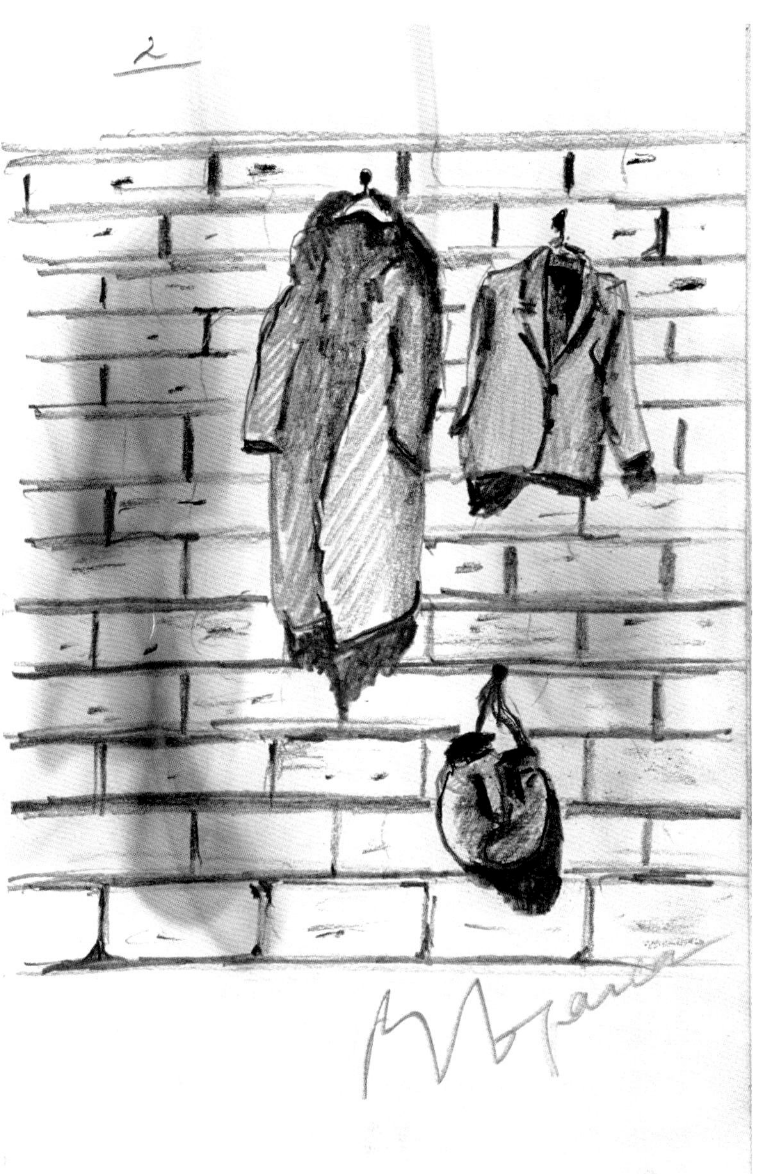

Coats on a Wall 2, 1994. Pencil on paper, 7 × 5 in. (17.8 × 12.7 cm).
Collection of the artist

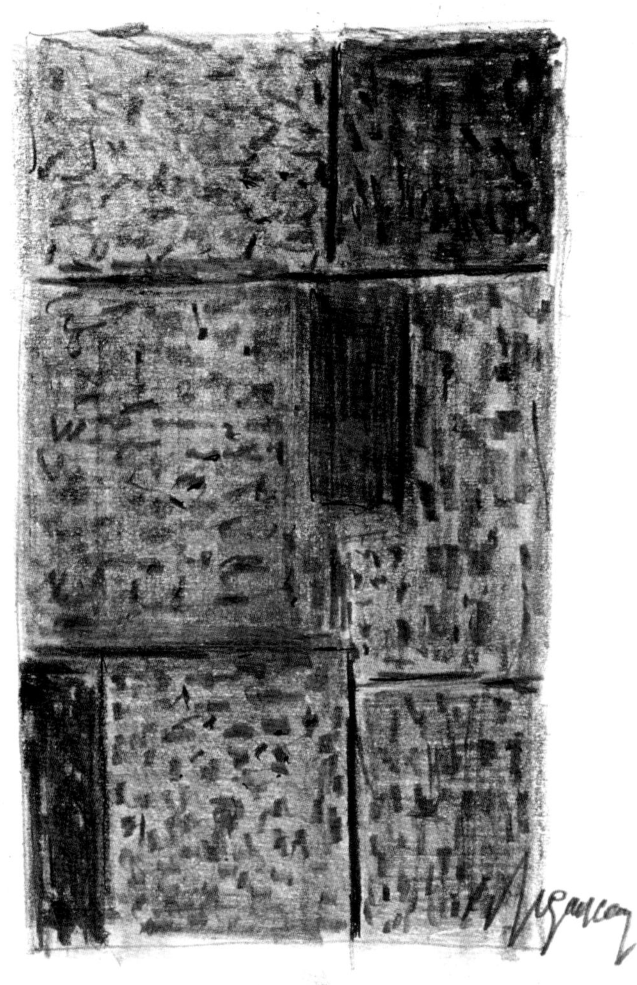

Study for Alexander's Wall Series, 1994. Pencil on paper, 7 × 5 in.
(17.8 × 12.7 cm). Collection of the artist

II

Watercolors & Gouaches

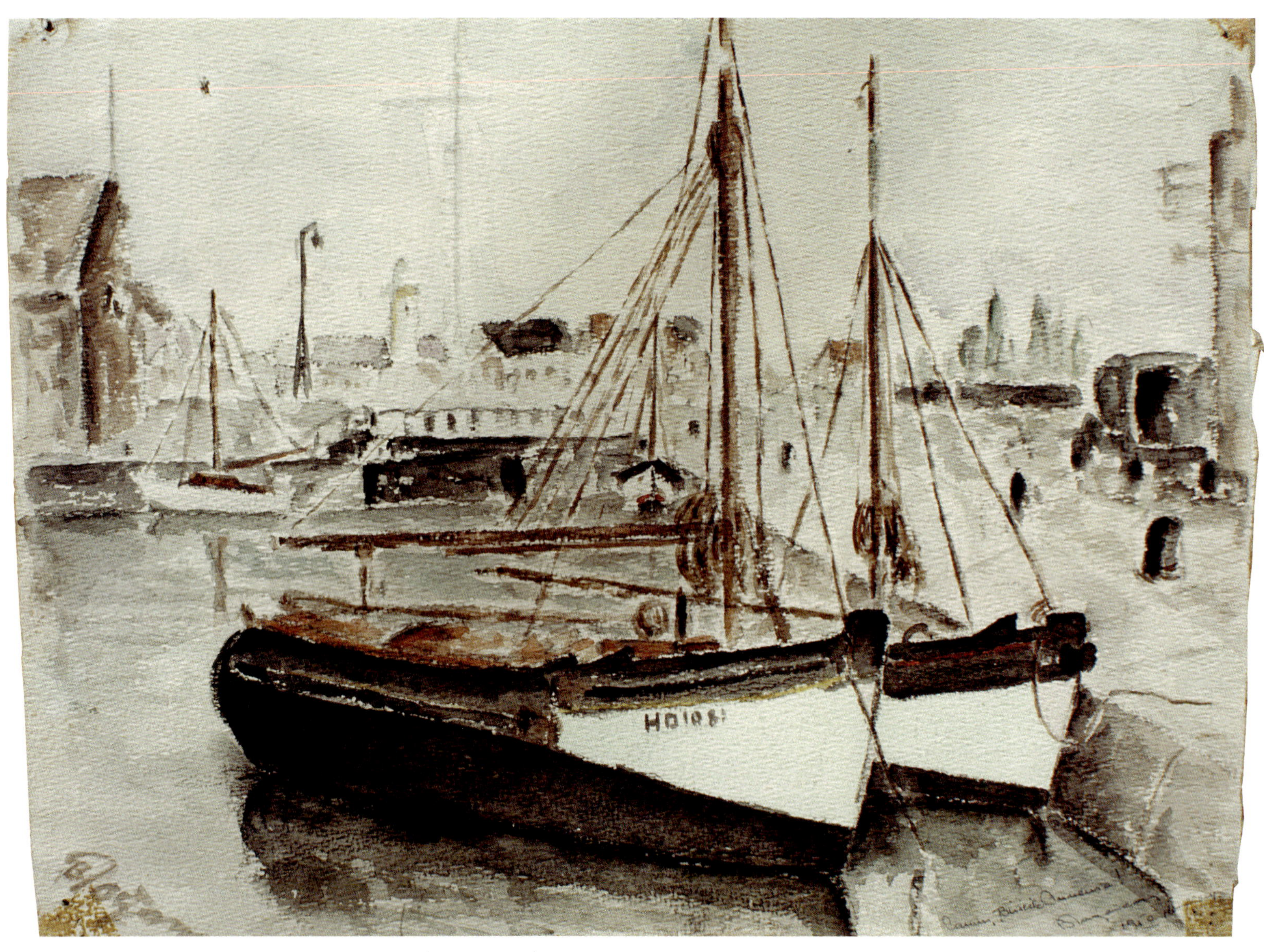

Honfleur, 1950. Watercolor on paper, 10 × 13 in. (25.4 × 33 cm). Collection of the artist

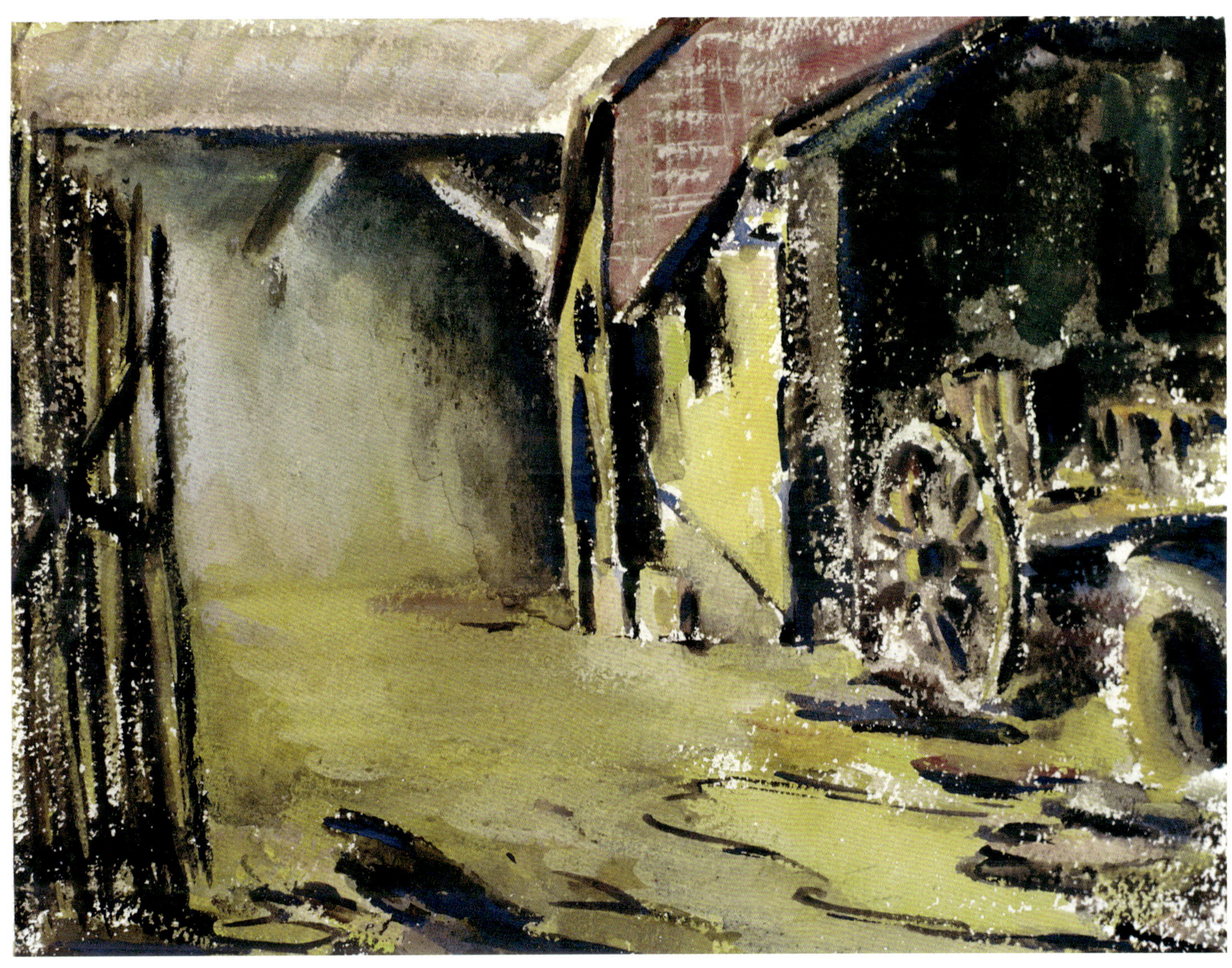

A Farm House in France, 1952. Watercolor on paper, 7 × 10 in. (17.8 × 25.4 cm). Private collection, Ankara

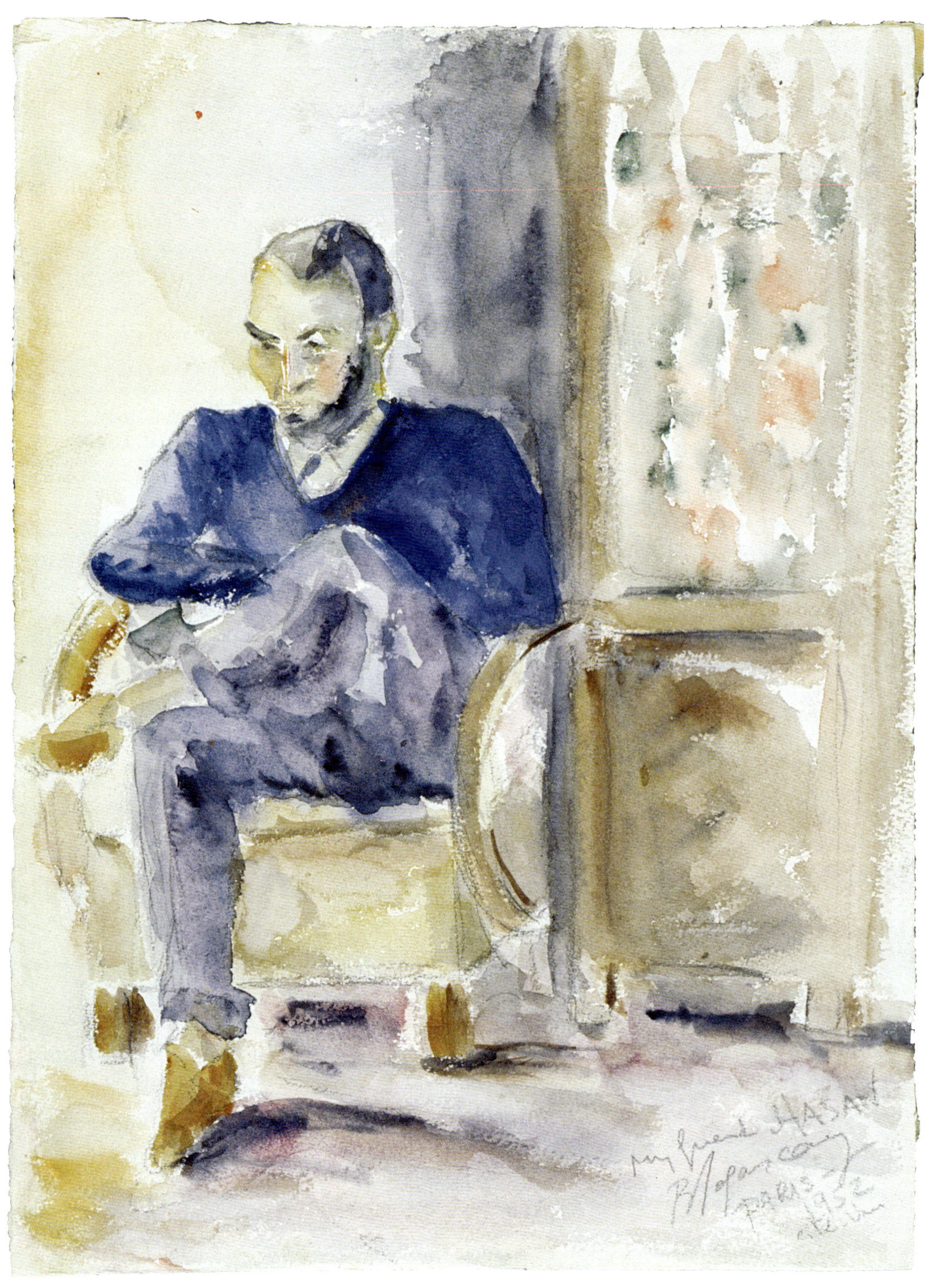

Hasan, 1952. Watercolor on paper, 14½ × 11 in. (36.8 × 27.9 cm). Collection of the artist

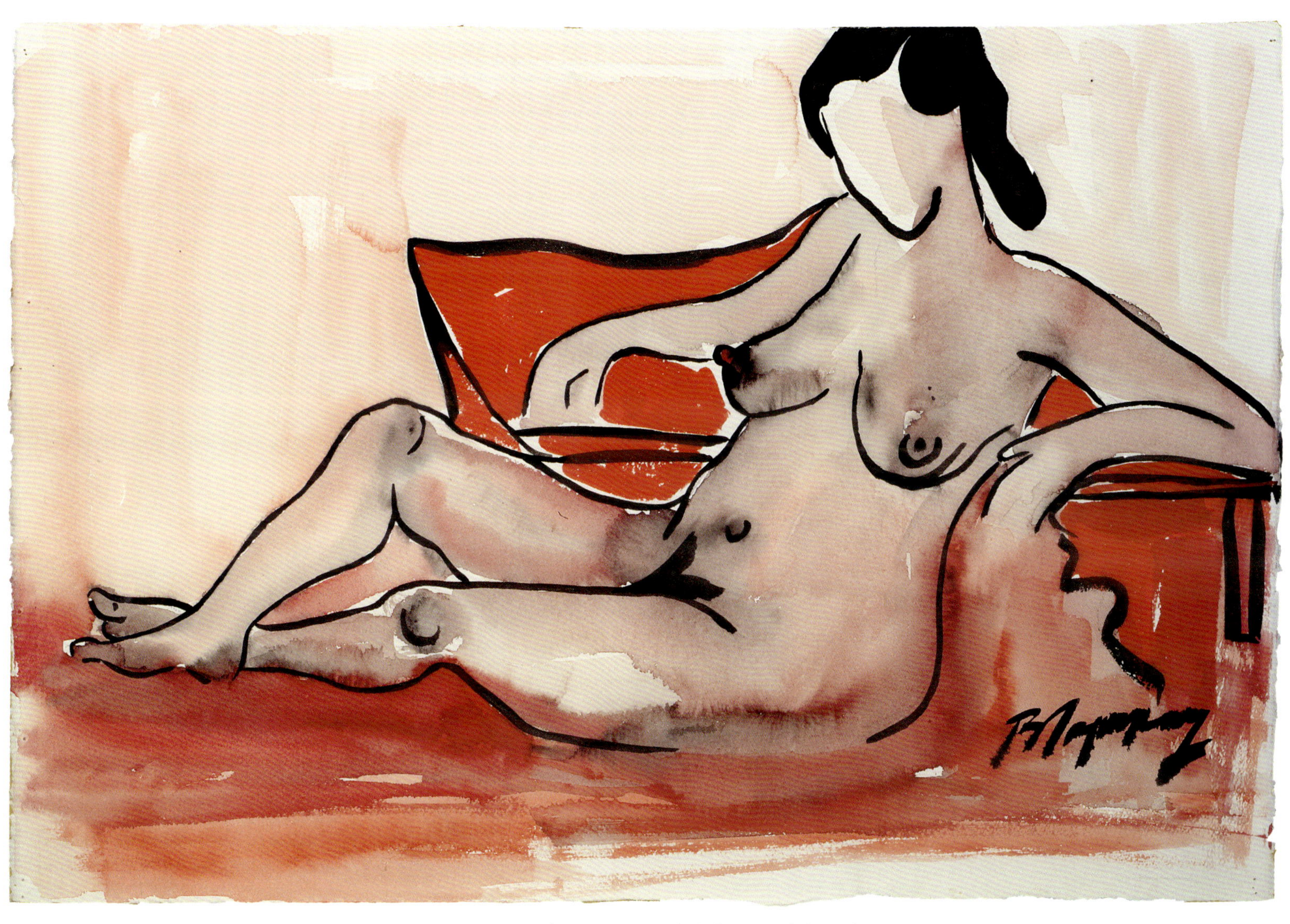

Nude on Red, 1953. Gouache and India ink on paper, 13½ × 22 in. (34.3 × 55.9 cm). Collection of the artist

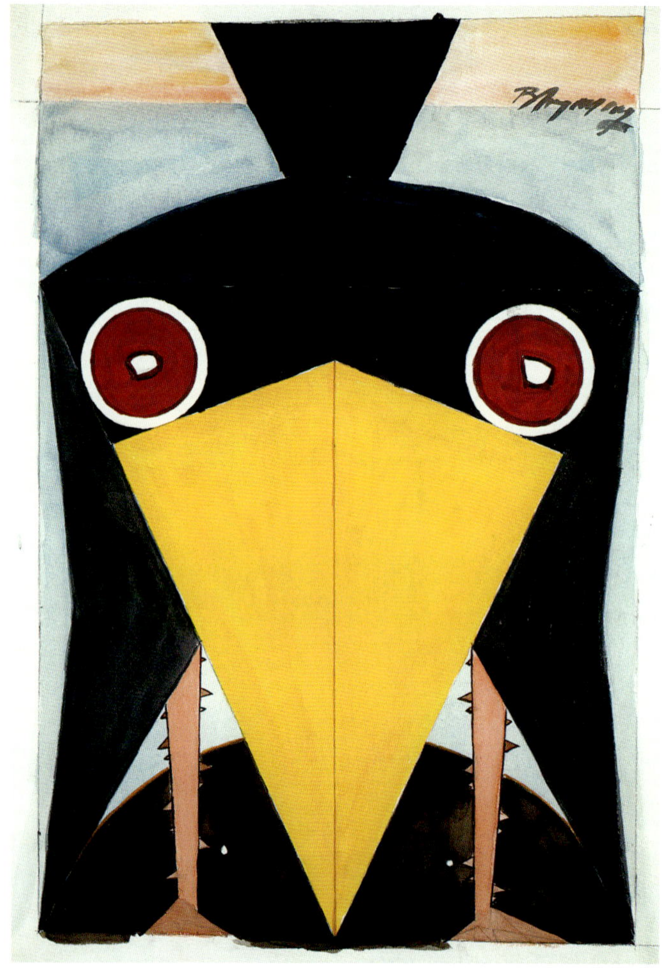

Destiny, 1953. Watercolor on paper, 5 × 4 in. (12.7 × 10.2 cm).
Collection of the artist

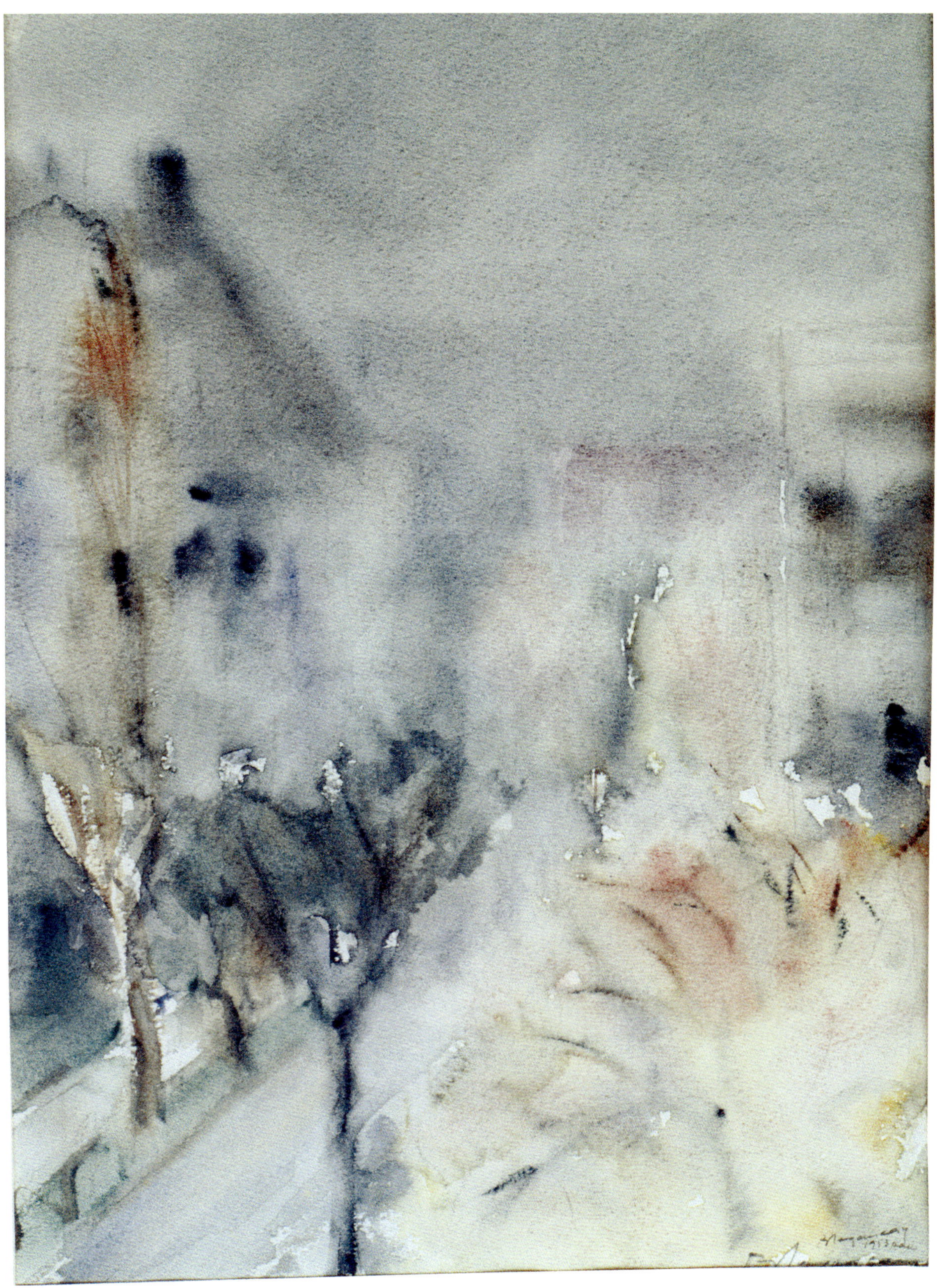

Foggy Day at the Cité Universitaire, 1953. Watercolor on paper, 14½ × 11 in. (36.8 × 27.9 cm). Private collection, Istanbul

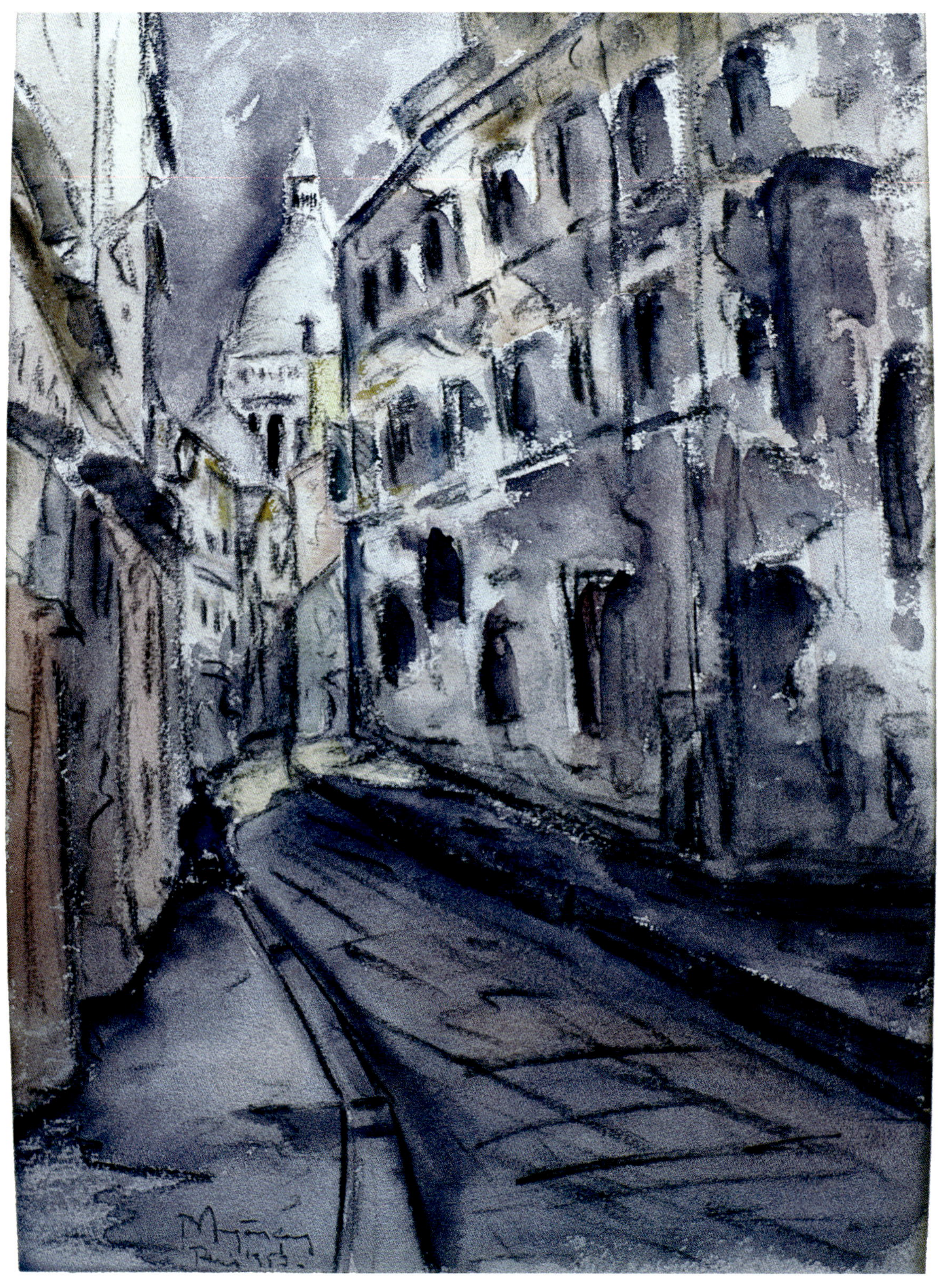

Montmartre, 1953. Watercolor and India ink on paper, 8⅝ × 6½ in. (21.8 × 16.5 cm). Private collection,
Strasbourg

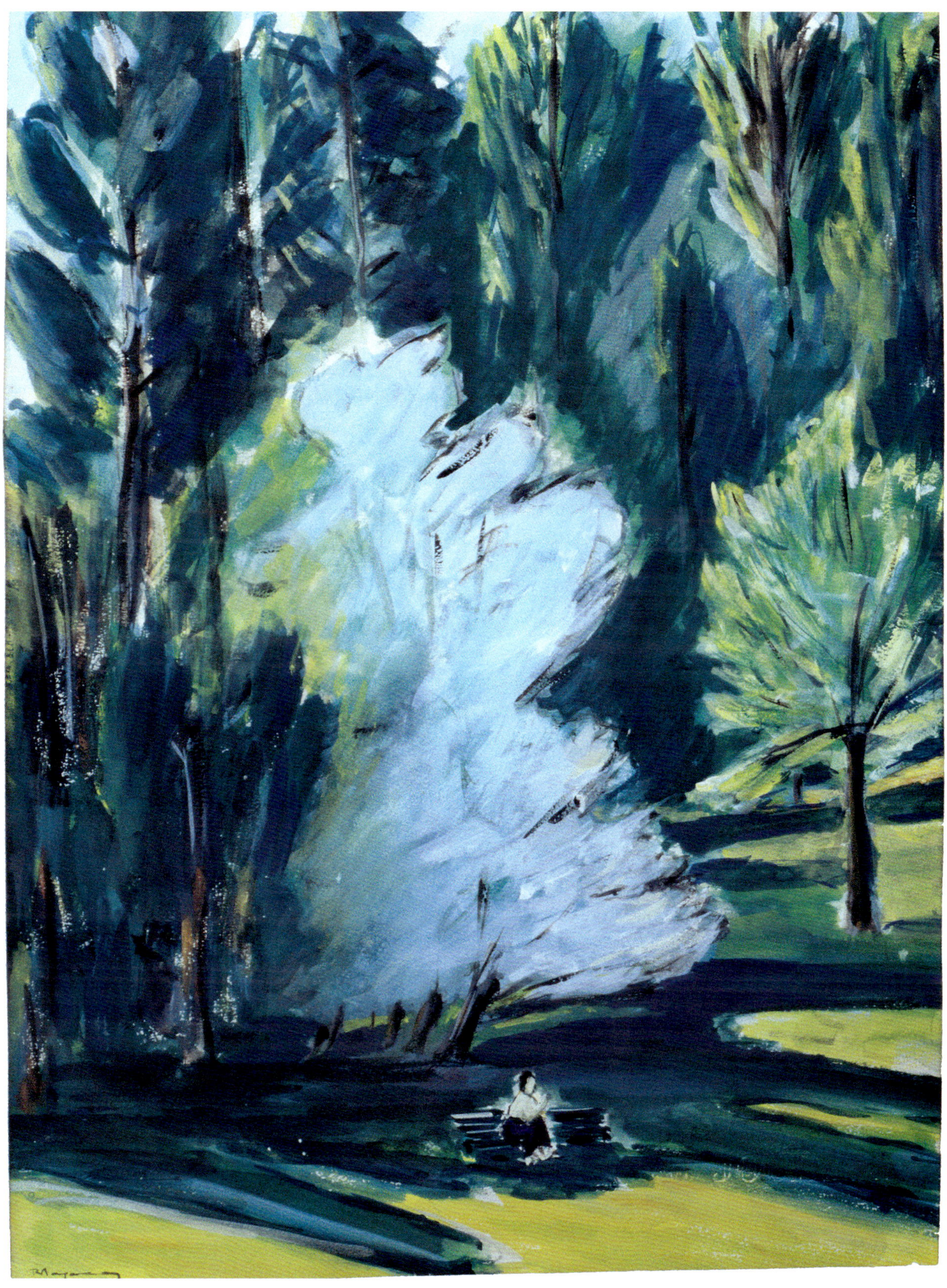

Spring in Paris II, 1954. Gouache on paper, 12 × 9 in. (30.5 × 22.9 cm). Private collection, Istanbul

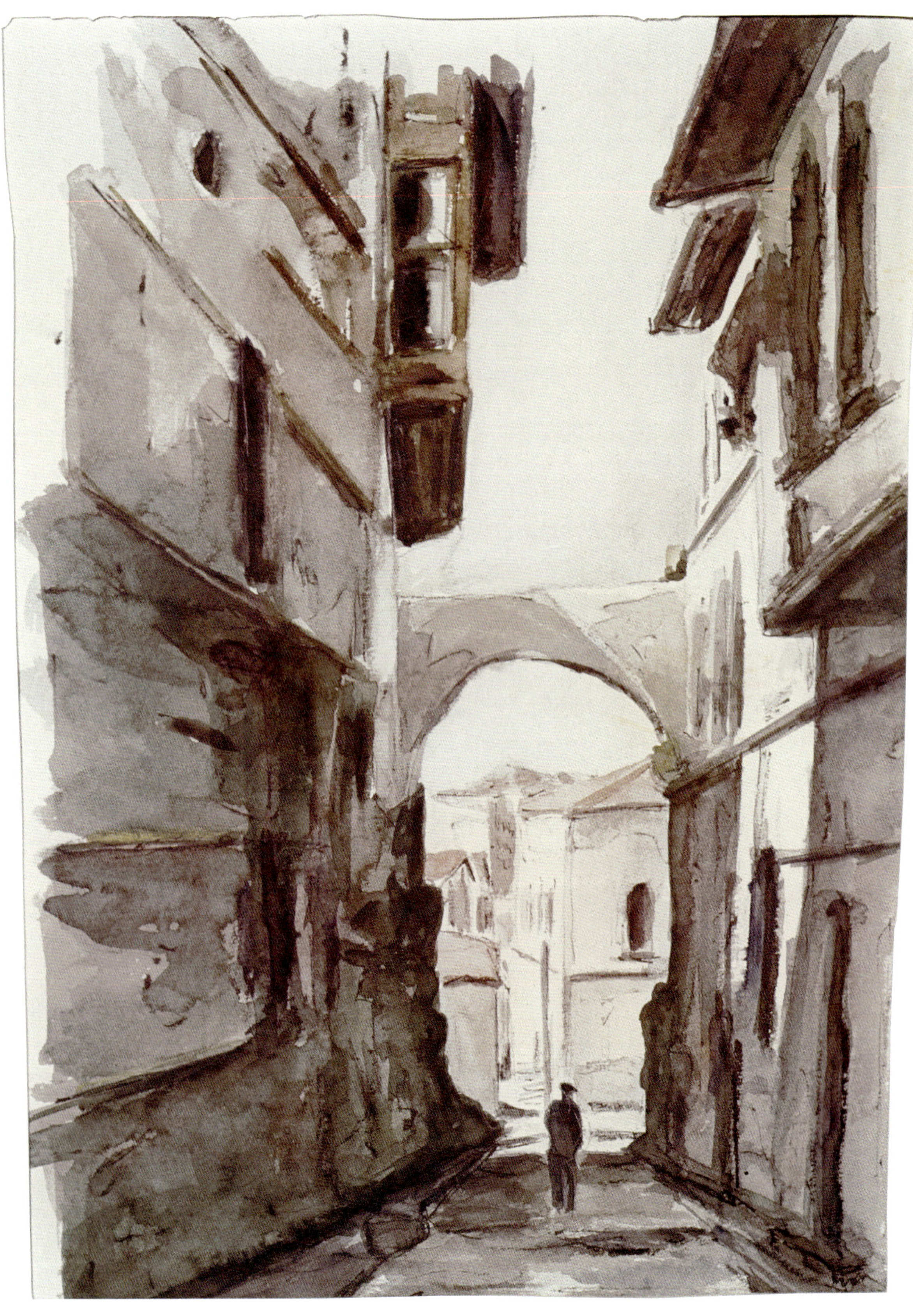

Old Ankara, 1958. Watercolor on paper, 11 × 9 in. (27.9 × 22.9 cm). Private collection, Istanbul

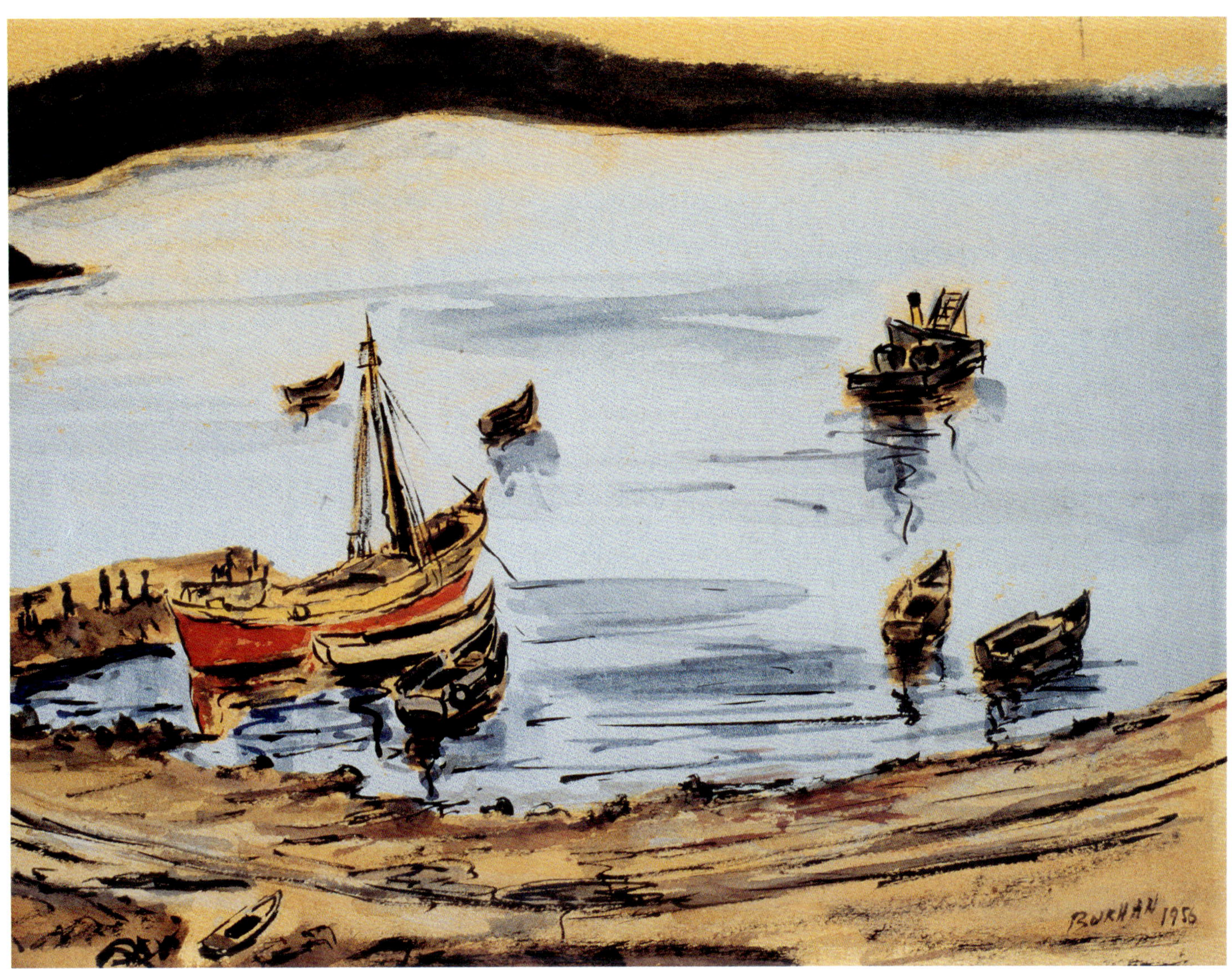

Silifke'den, 1956. Watercolor and India ink on paper, 9⅛ × 11⅞ in. (23 × 30 cm). Collection of the artist

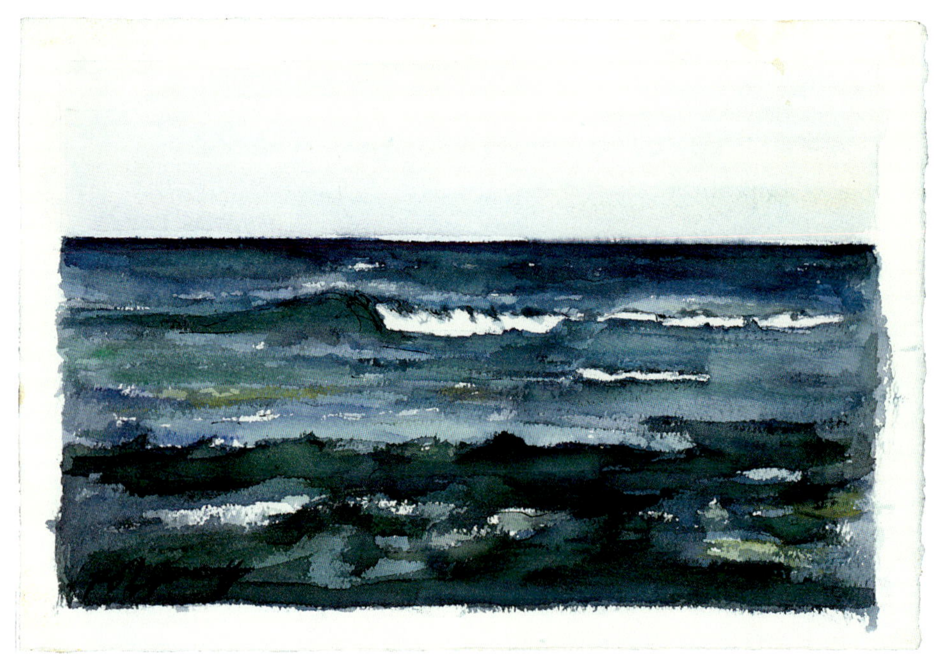

After the Storm, 1959. Watercolor on paper, 6 × 10 in. (15.2 × 25.4 cm). Collection of the artist

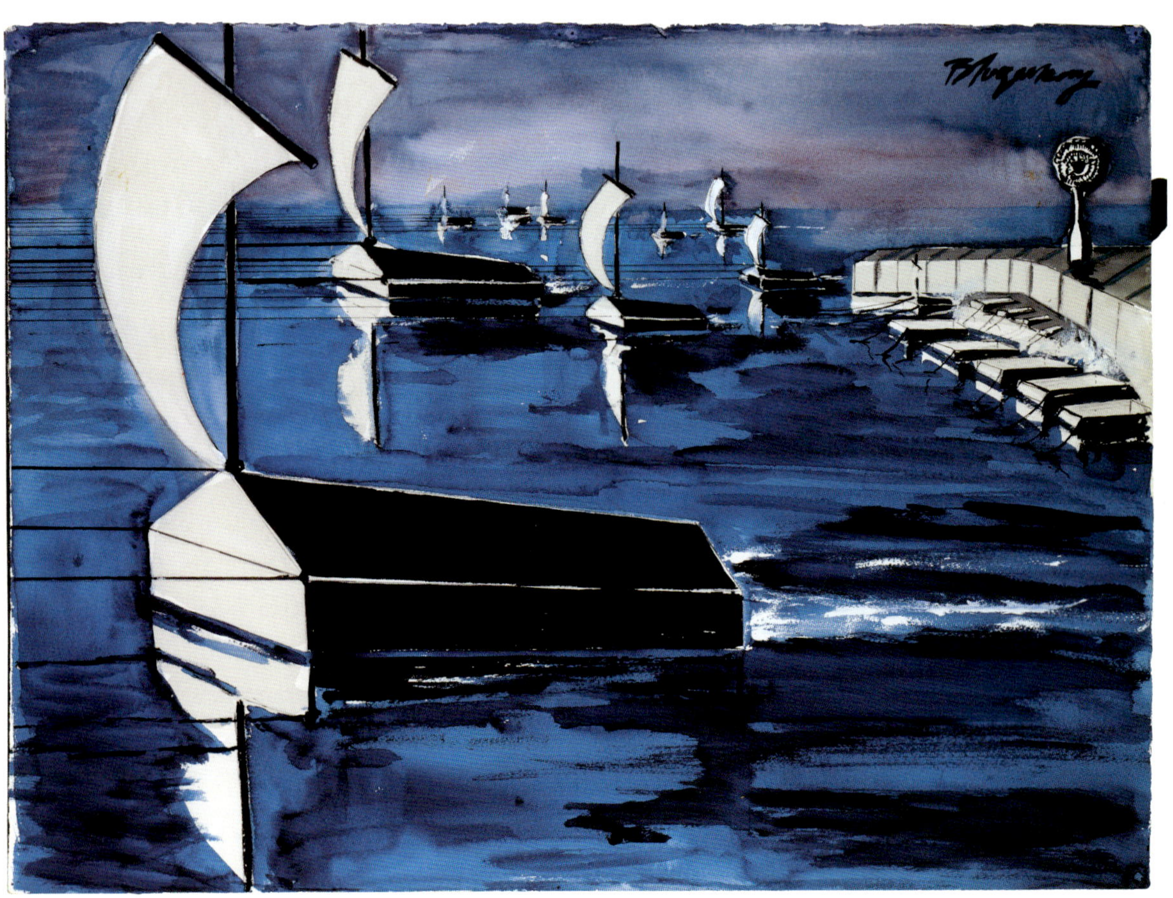

Silent Ships, 1960. Watercolor on paper, 22 × 30 in. (55.9 × 76.2 cm). Collection of the artist

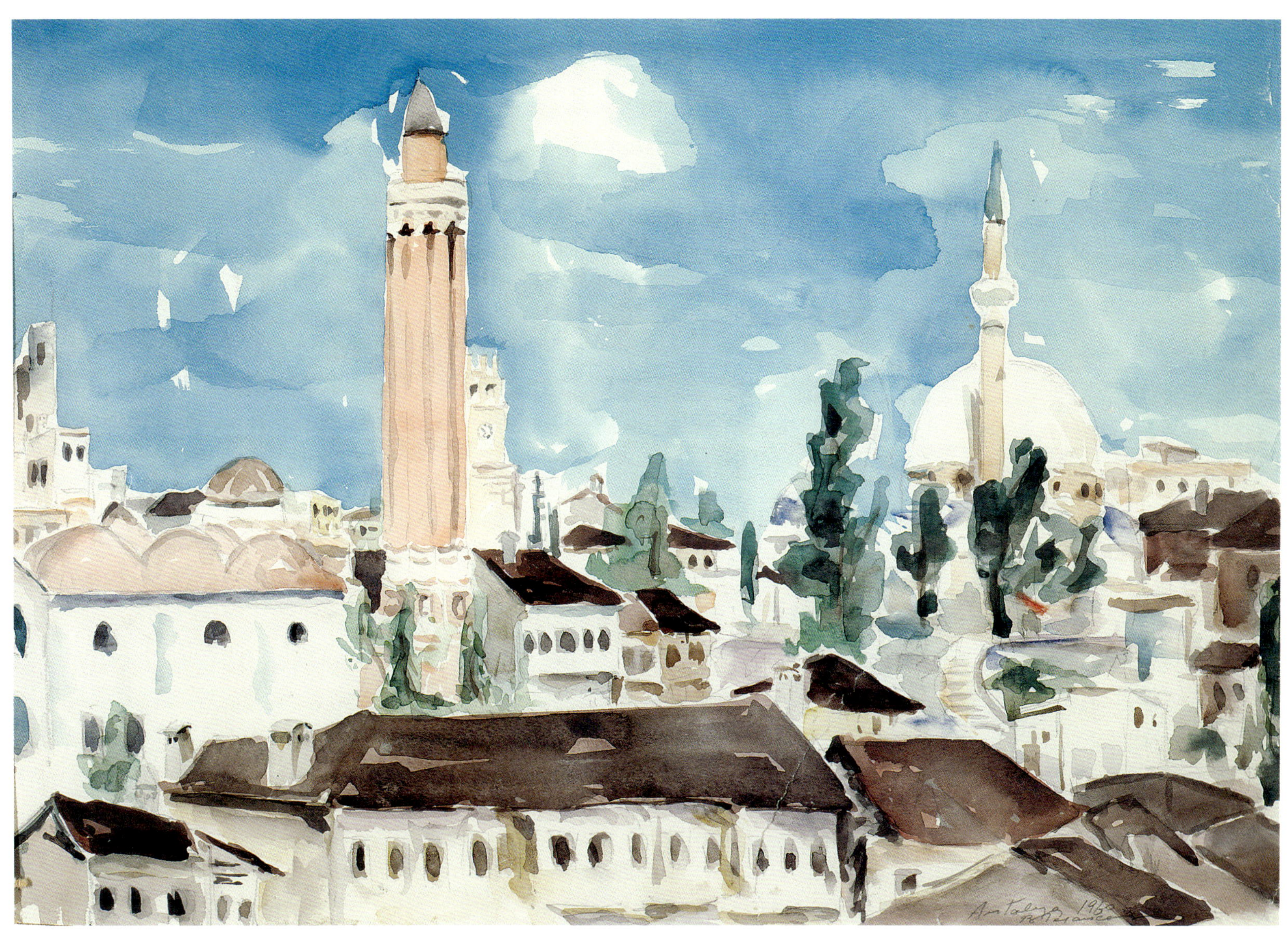

Antalya, 1960. Watercolor on paper, 12½ × 18 in. (31.8 × 45.7 cm). Collection of the artist

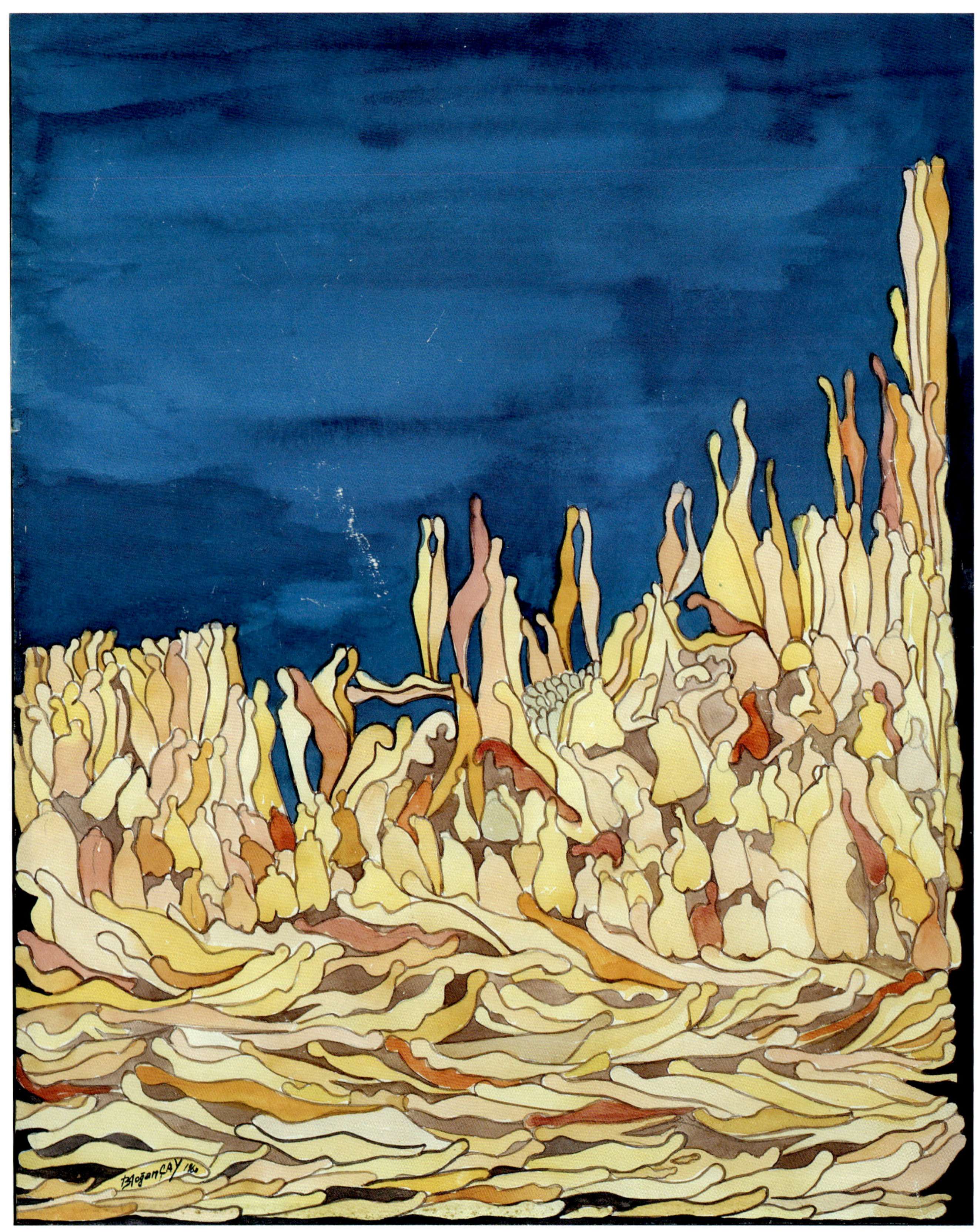

Population Explosion, 1960. Watercolor on paper, 23 × 17½ in. (58.4 × 44.5 cm). Collection of the artist

Up in the Sky, 1962. Watercolor on paper, 22 × 15 in. (55.9 × 38.1 cm). Collection of the artist

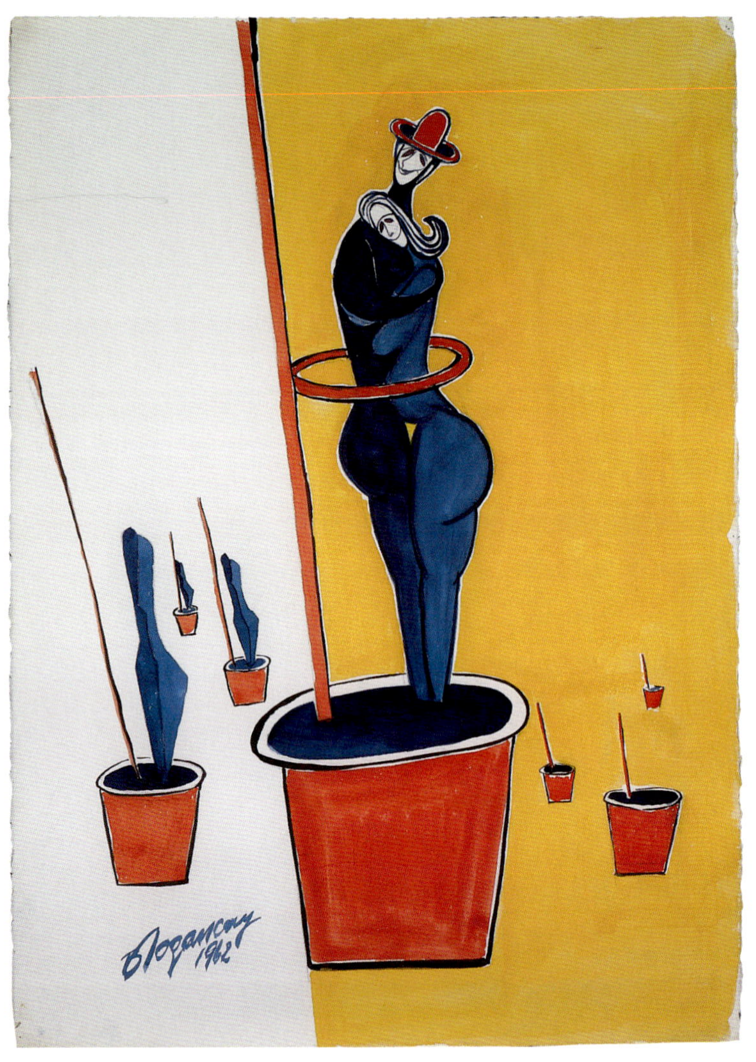

Marriage I, 1962. Watercolor on paper, 30 × 22 in. (76.2 × 55.9 cm).
Collection of the artist

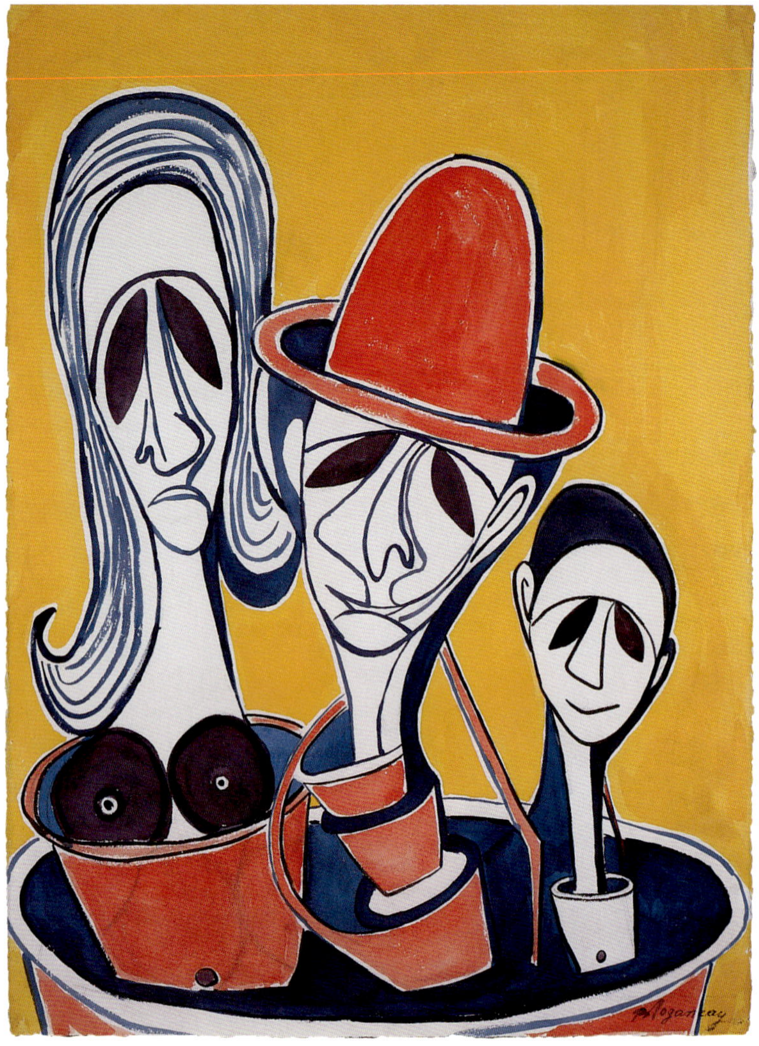

Marriage II, 1962. Watercolor on paper, 30 × 22 in. (76.2 × 55.9 cm).
Collection of the artist

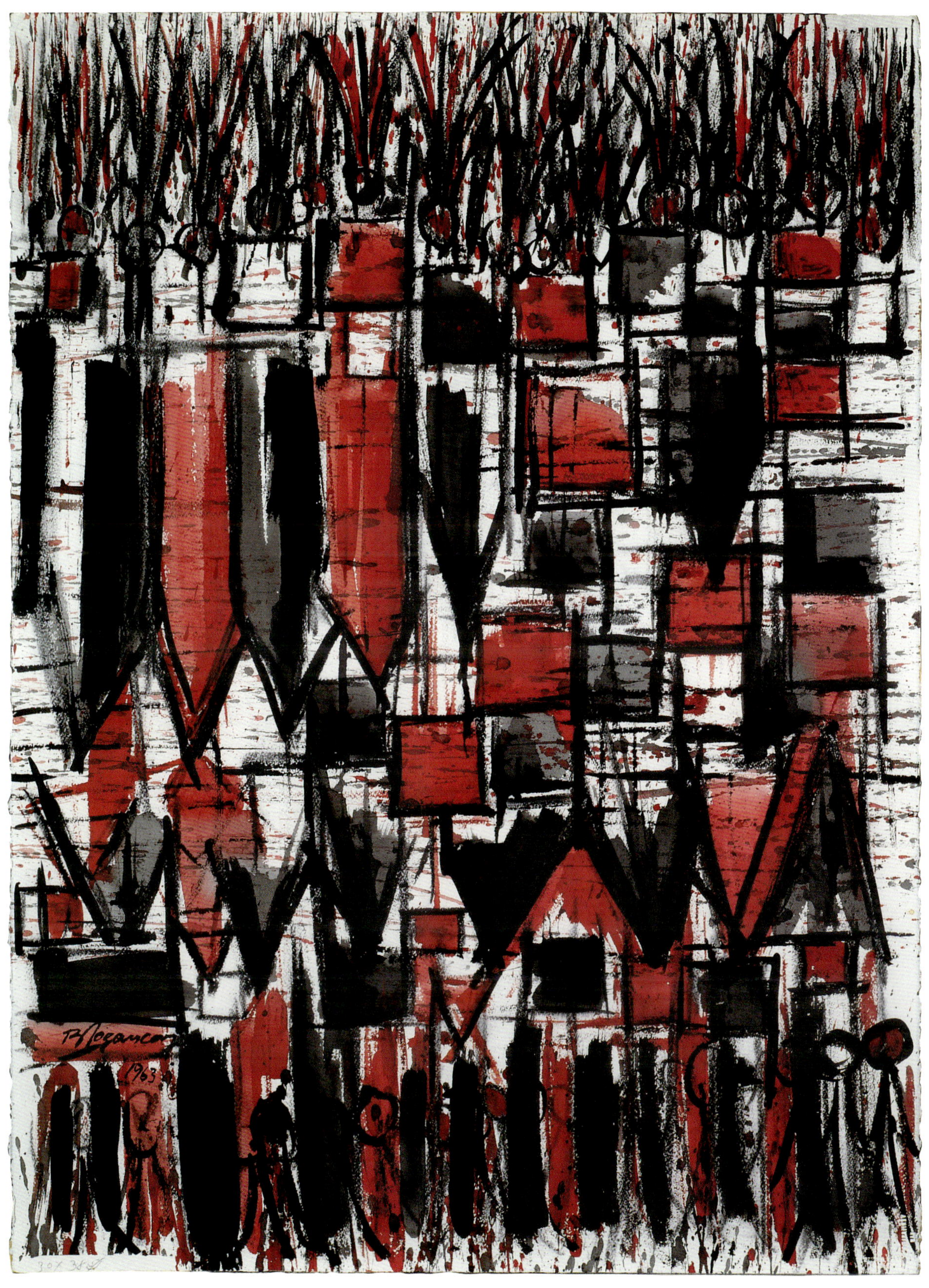

Saddlebag, 1963. Watercolor on paper, 30 × 22 in. (76.2 × 55.9 cm). Eczacıbaşı Collection, Istanbul

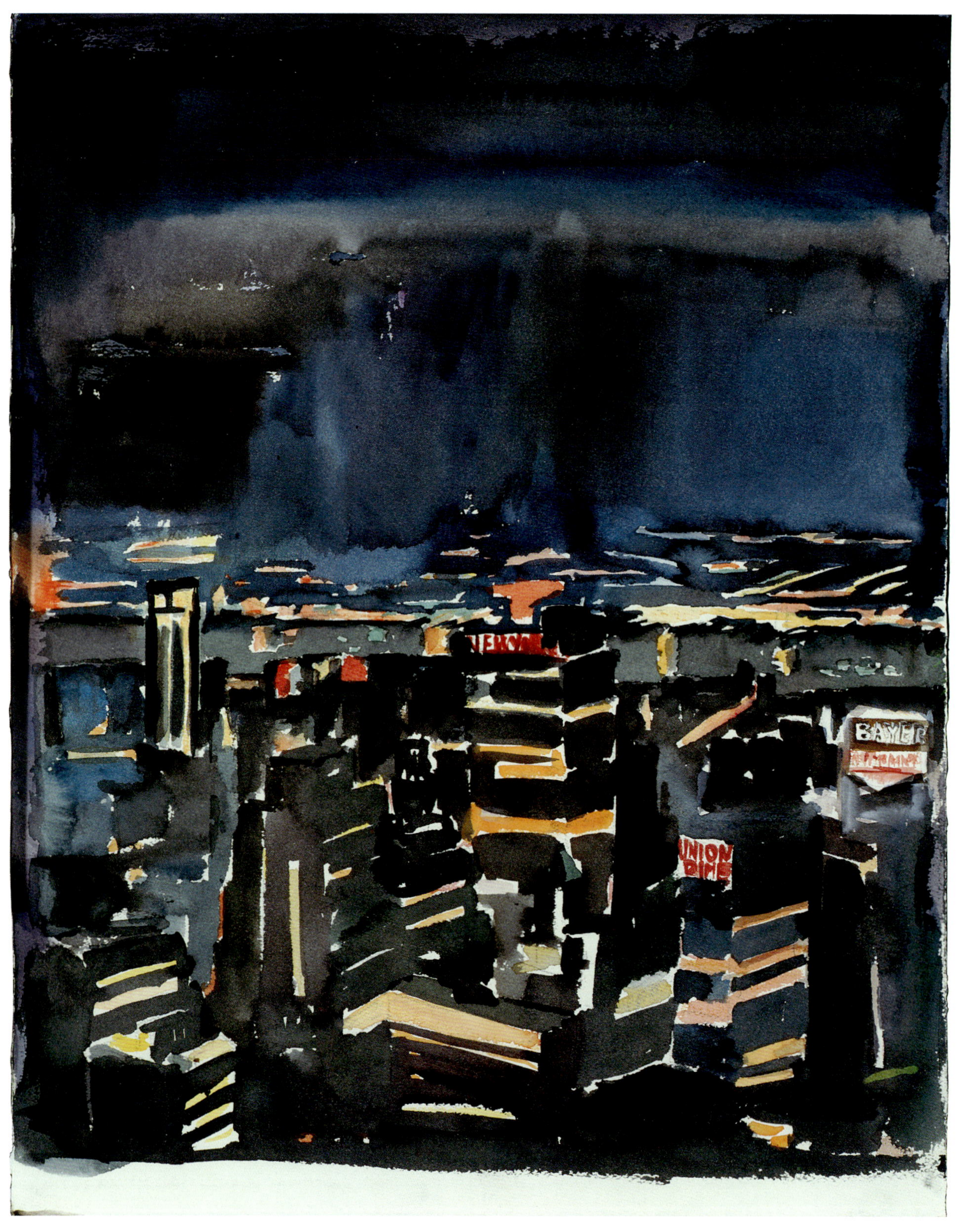

Manhattan & New Jersey at Night, 1962. Watercolor on paper, 18 × 14 in. (45.7 × 35.6 cm). Private collection

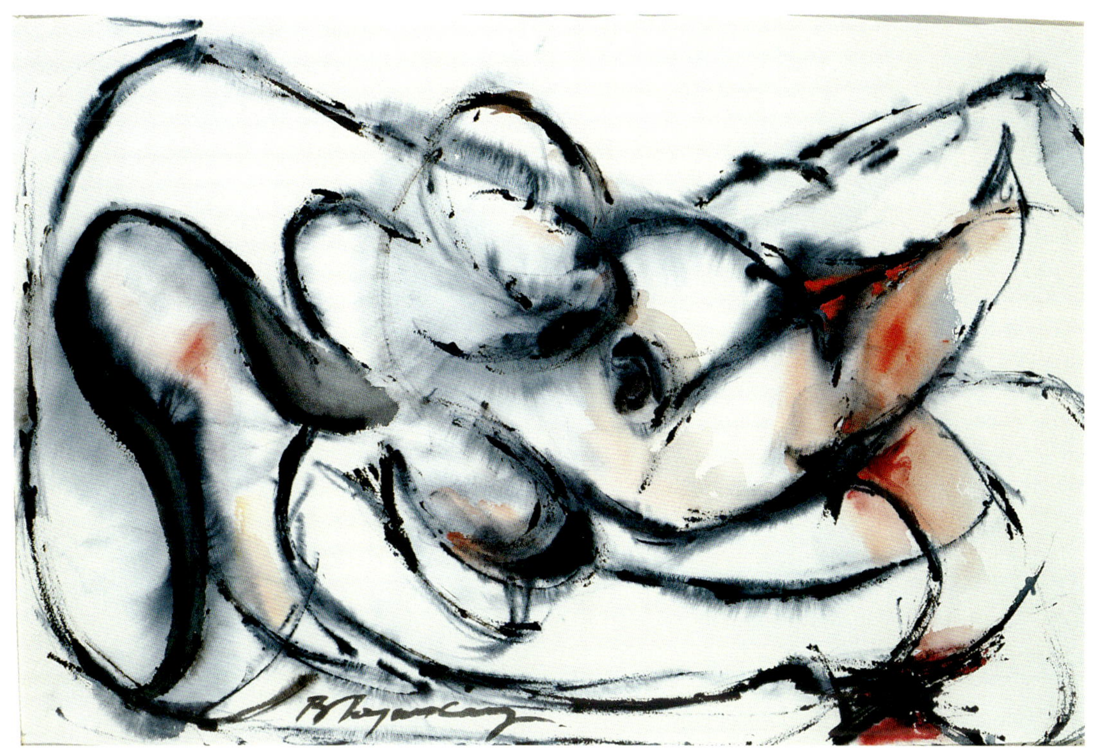

Abstract Woman, 1963. Gouache on paper, 14 × 21 in. (35.6 × 53.3 cm). Collection of the artist

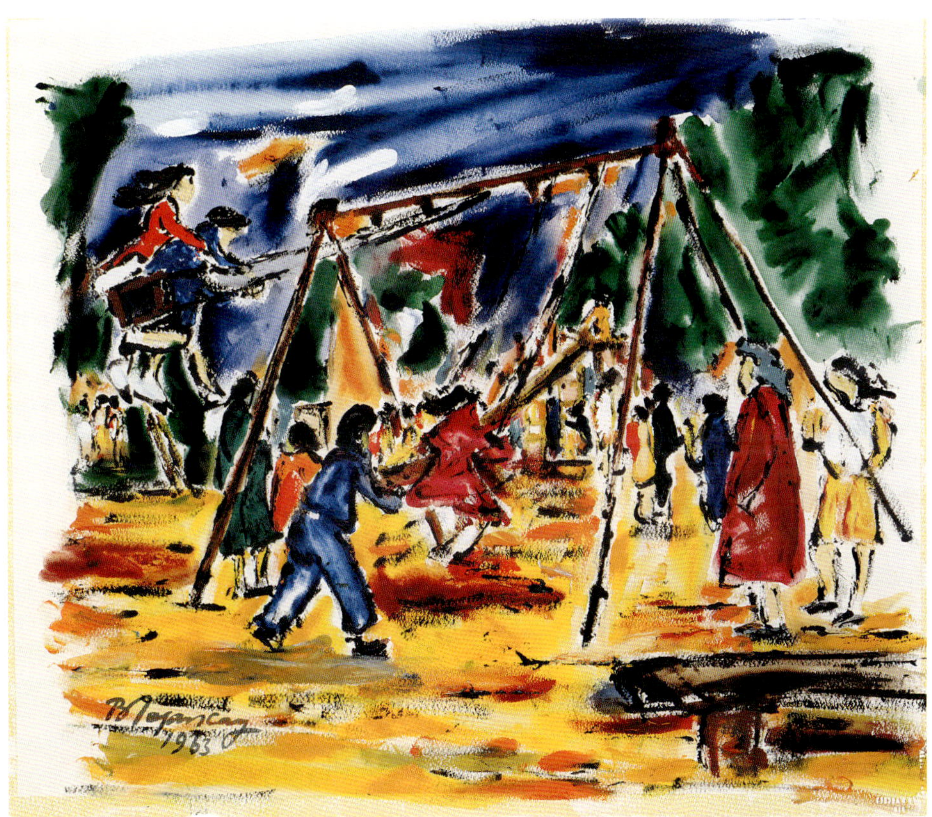

Playground, 1963. Gouache on paper, 16 × 17 in. (40.6 × 43.2 cm). Eczacıbaşı Collection, Istanbul

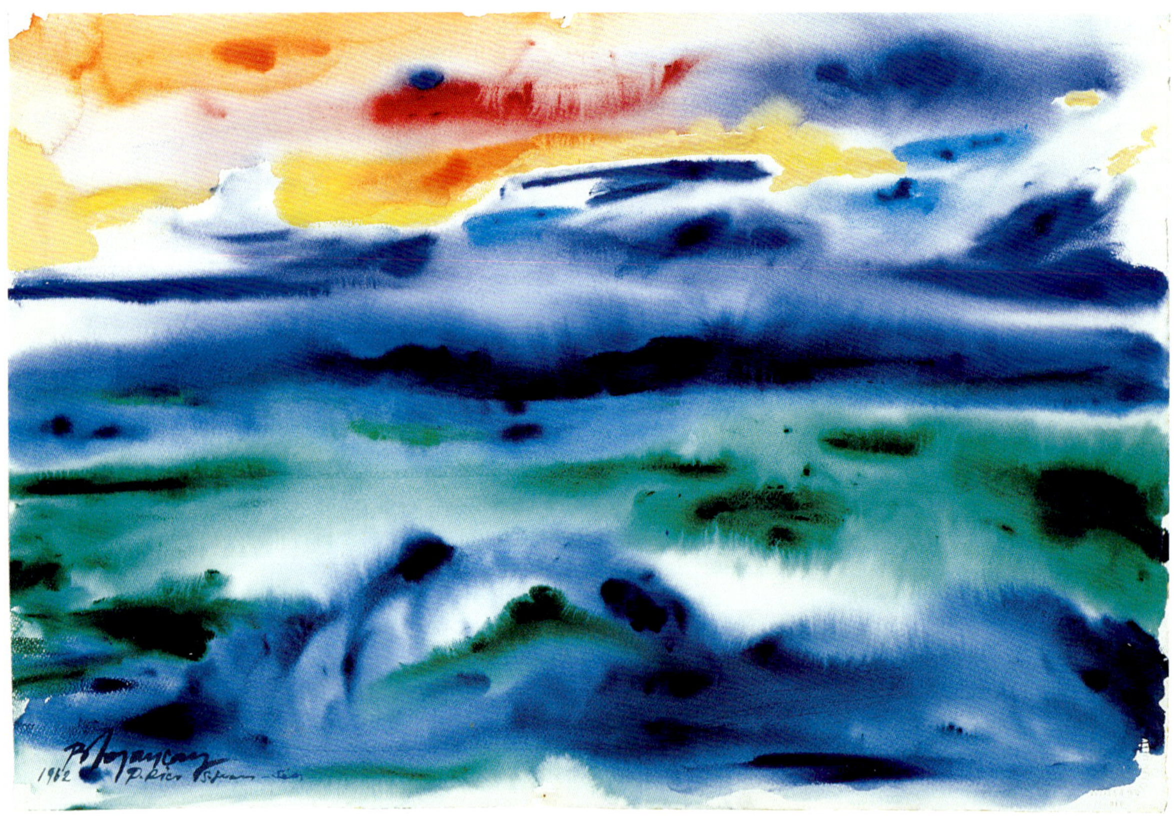

Sea in Puerto Rico, 1962. Gouache on paper, 15 × 22 in. (38.1 × 55.9 cm). Collection of the artist

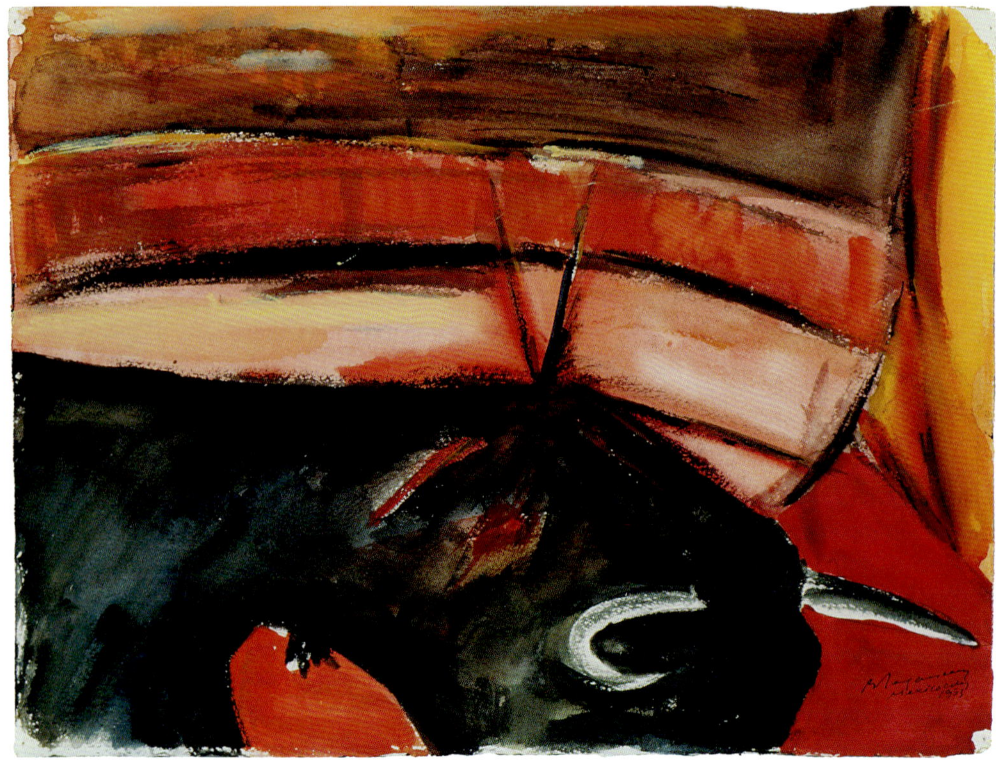

Bullfight I, 1963. Gouache on paper, 11 × 14⅞ in. (27.9 × 37.6 cm). Collection of the artist

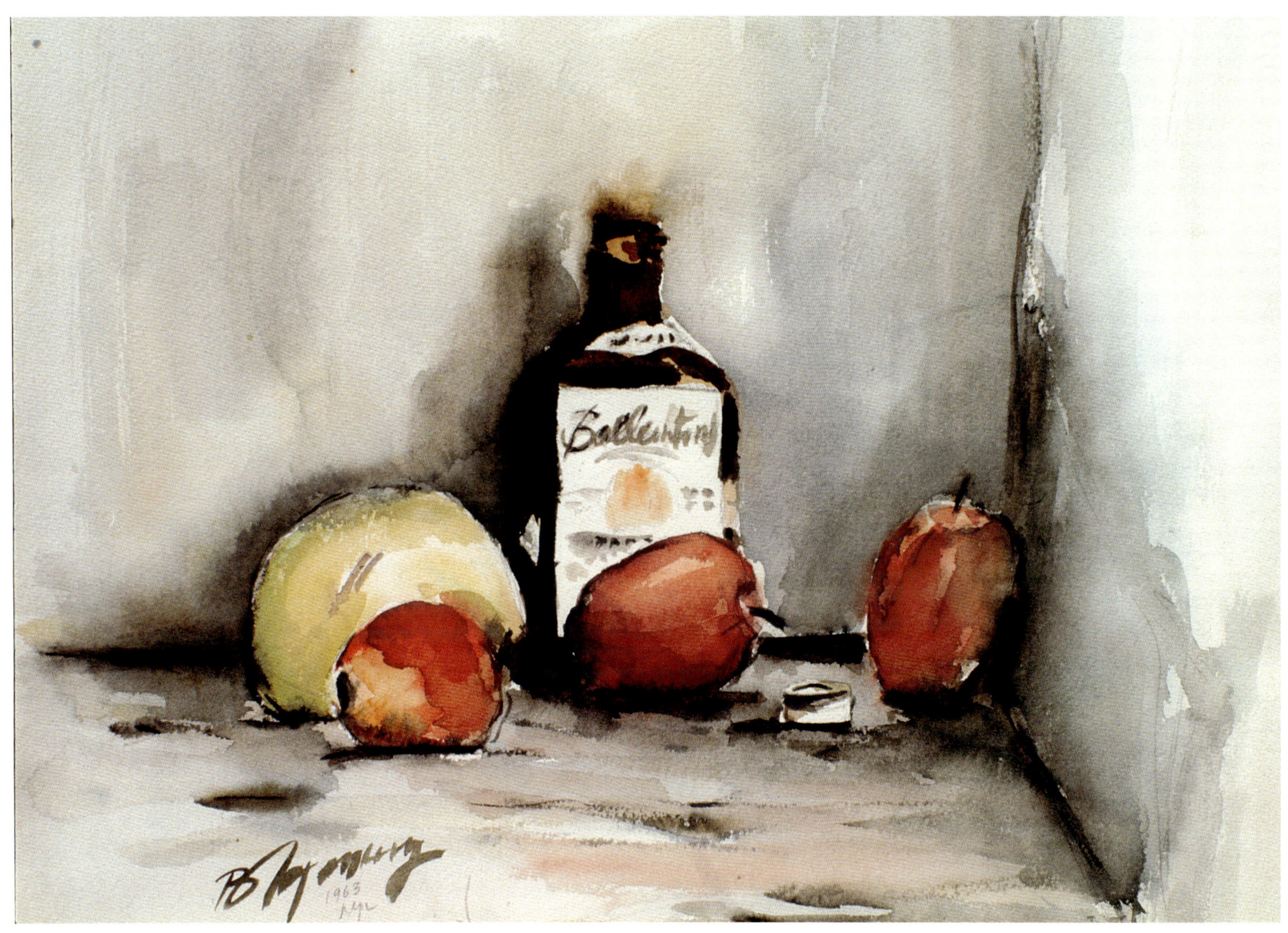

Still Life, 1963. Watercolor on paper, 15 × 18 in. (38.1 × 45.7 cm). Collection of the artist

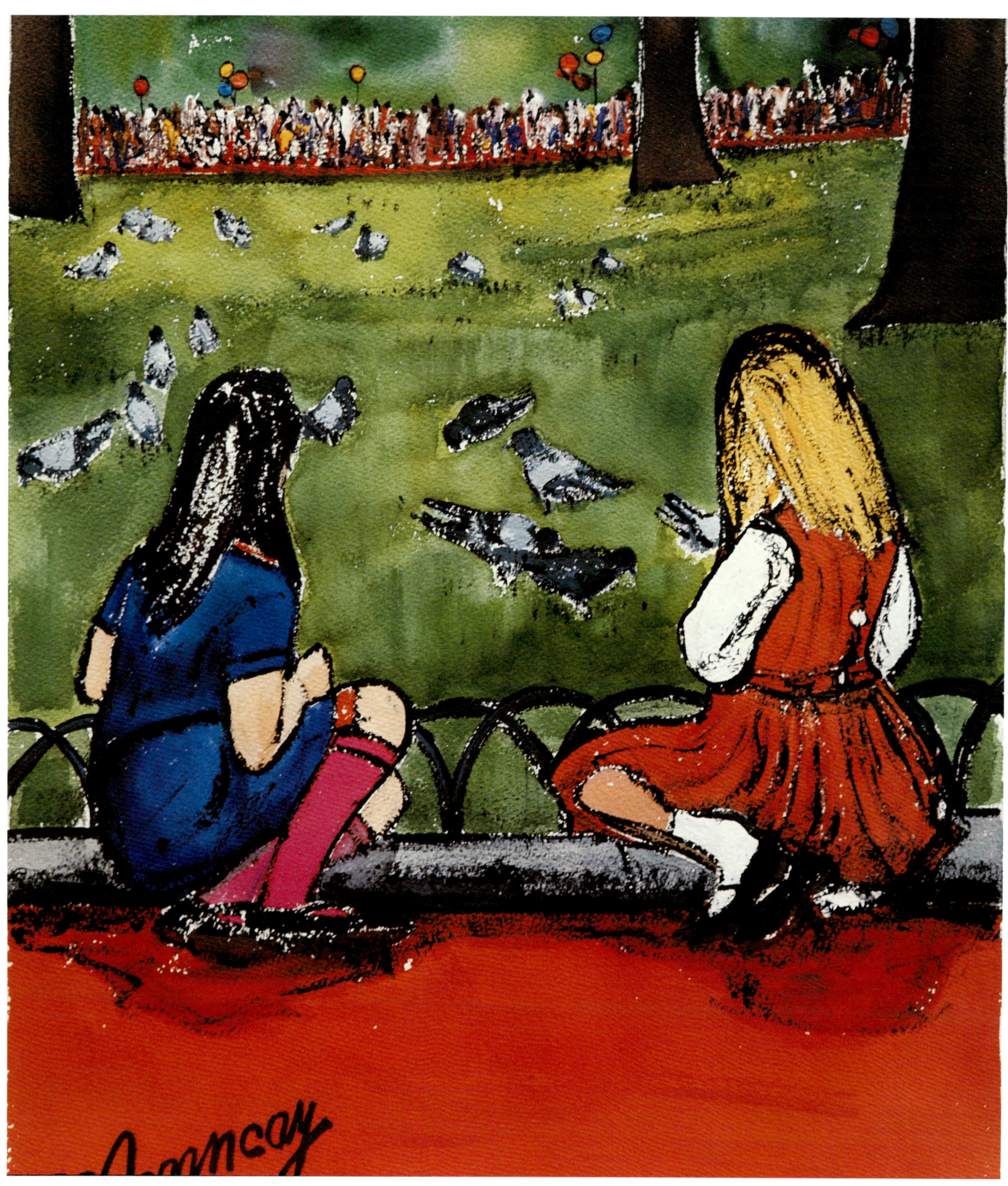

Children Feeding Pigeons, 1963. Gouache on paper, 15 × 14 in. (38.1 × 35.6 cm). Private collection

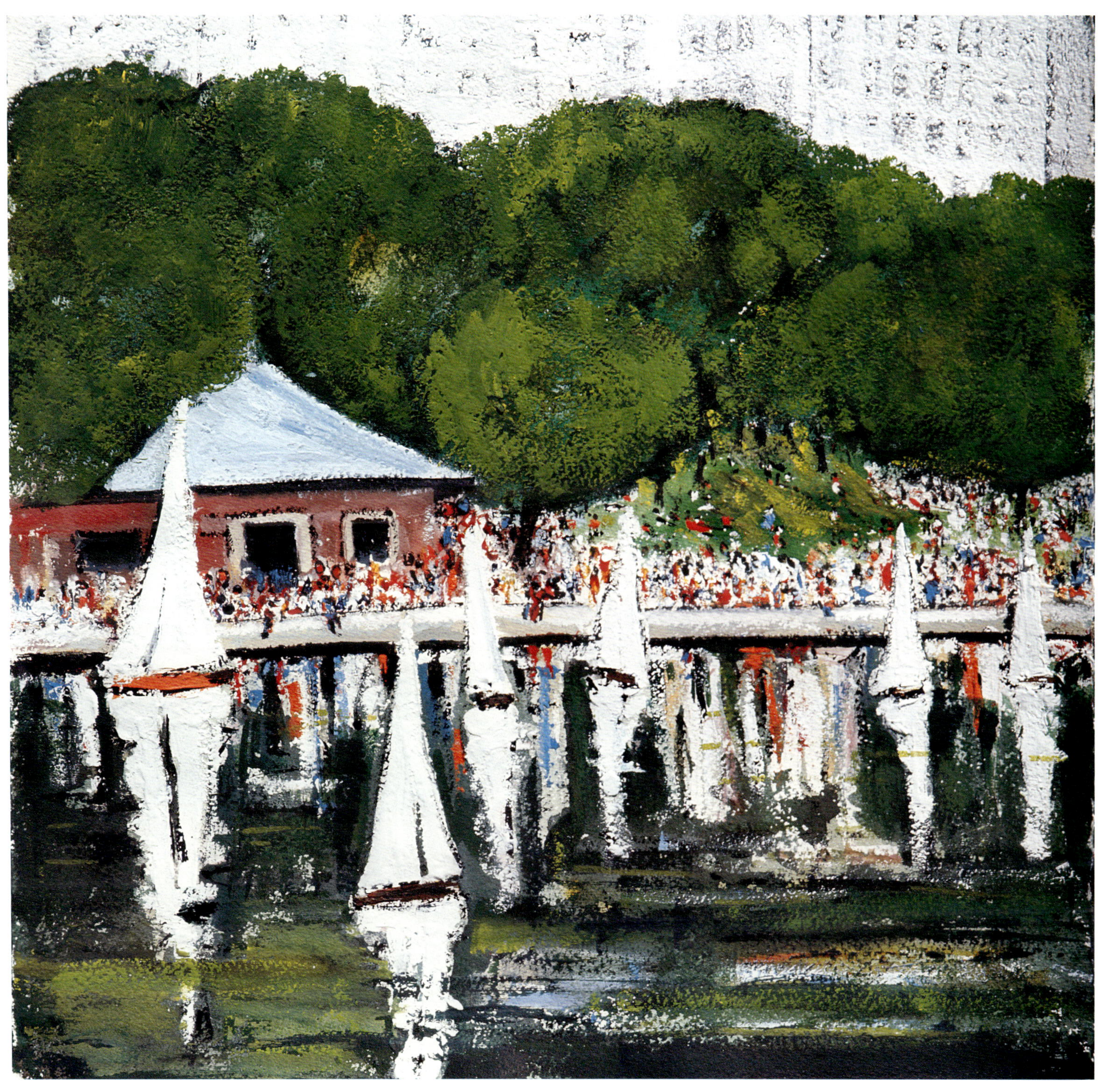

Boatlake, 1963. Gouache on paper, 15 × 15 in. (38.1 × 38.1 cm). Private collection

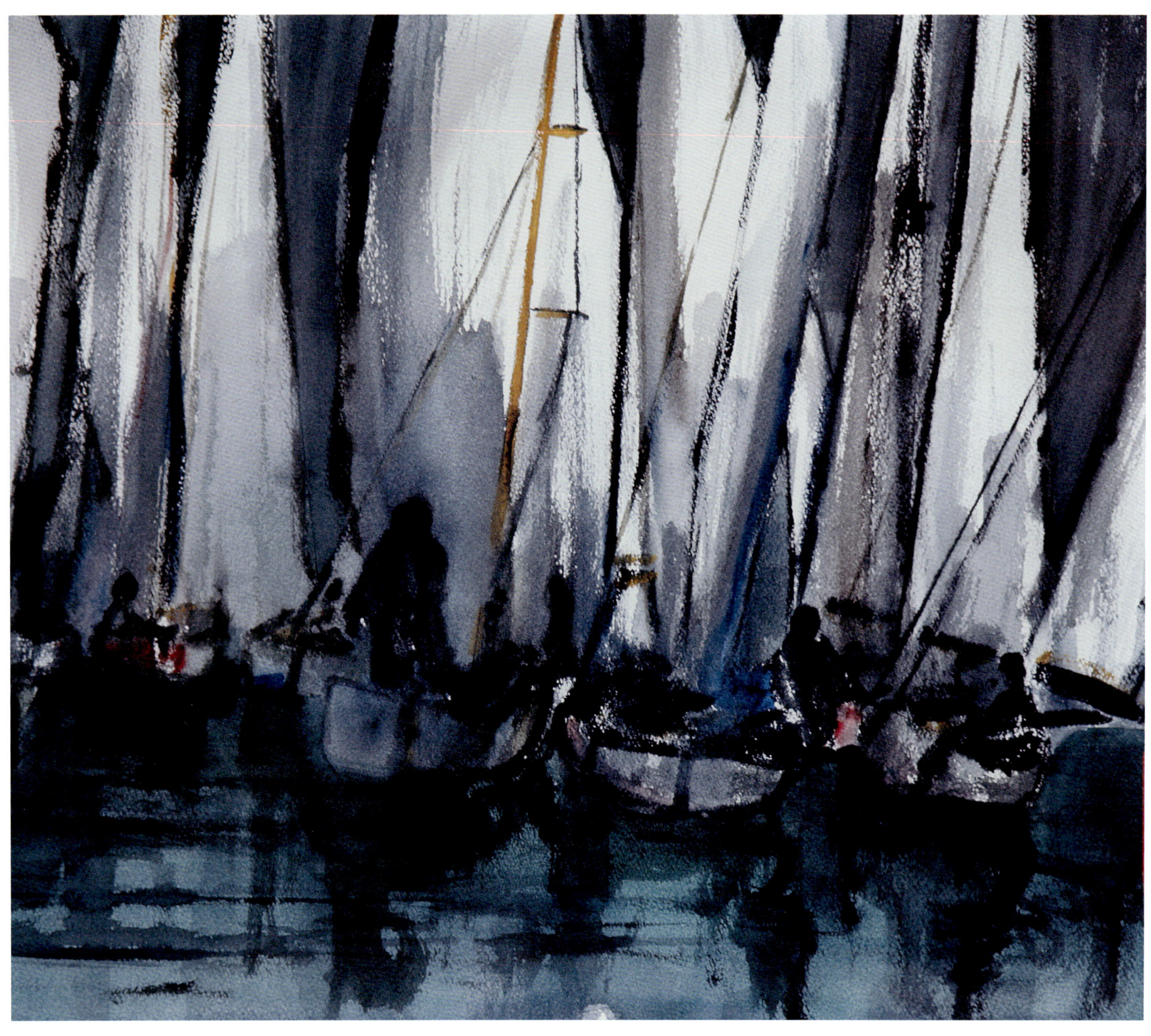

Sailing Boats, 1963. Watercolor on paper, 15 × 16½ in. (38.1 × 41.9 cm). Collection of the artist

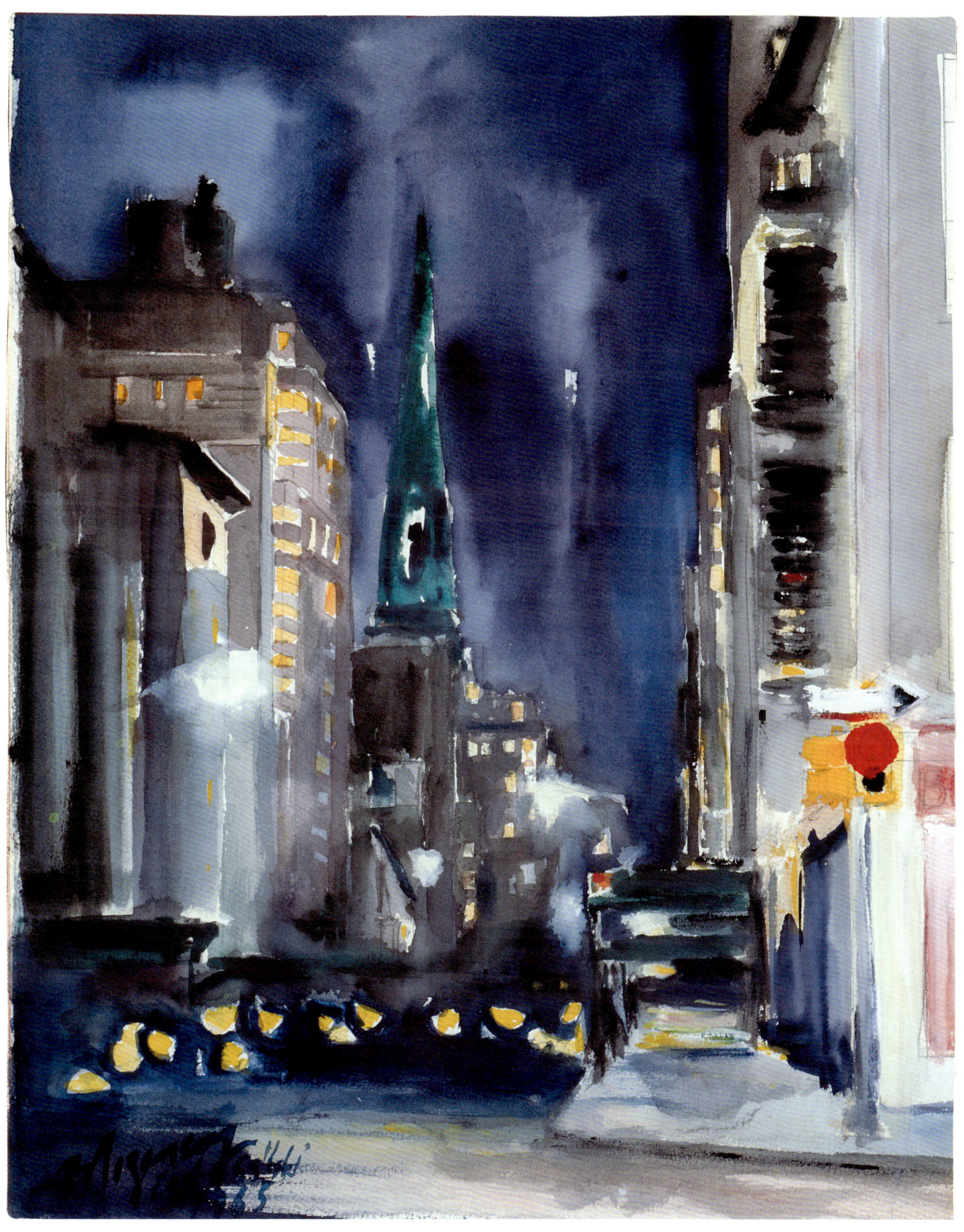

Lexington & 55th St. at Night, 1963. Watercolor on paper, 20 × 16 in. (50.8 × 40.6 cm). Private collection

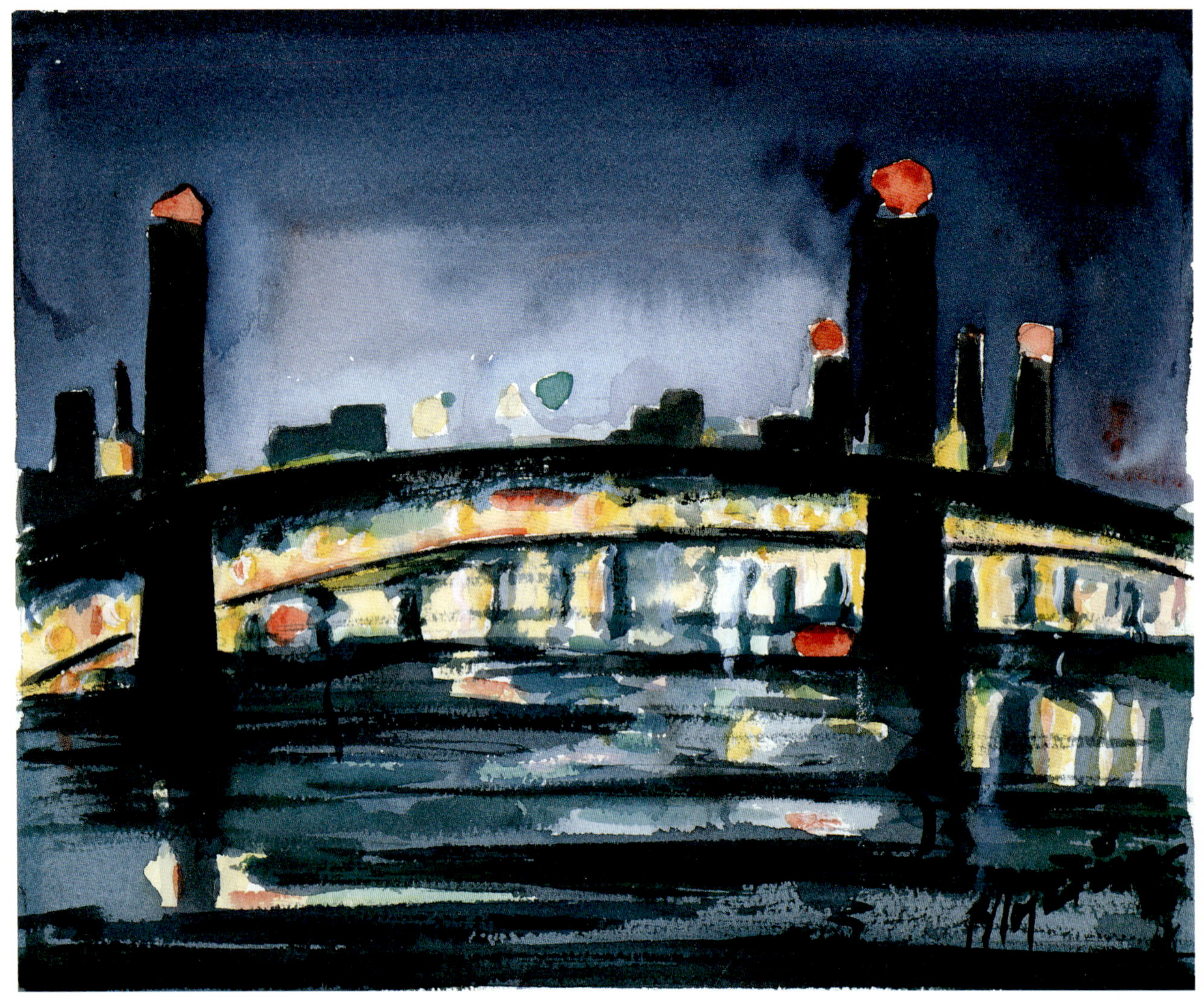

East River by Night, 1963. Watercolor on paper, 8½ × 10 in. (21.6 × 25.4 cm). Private collection

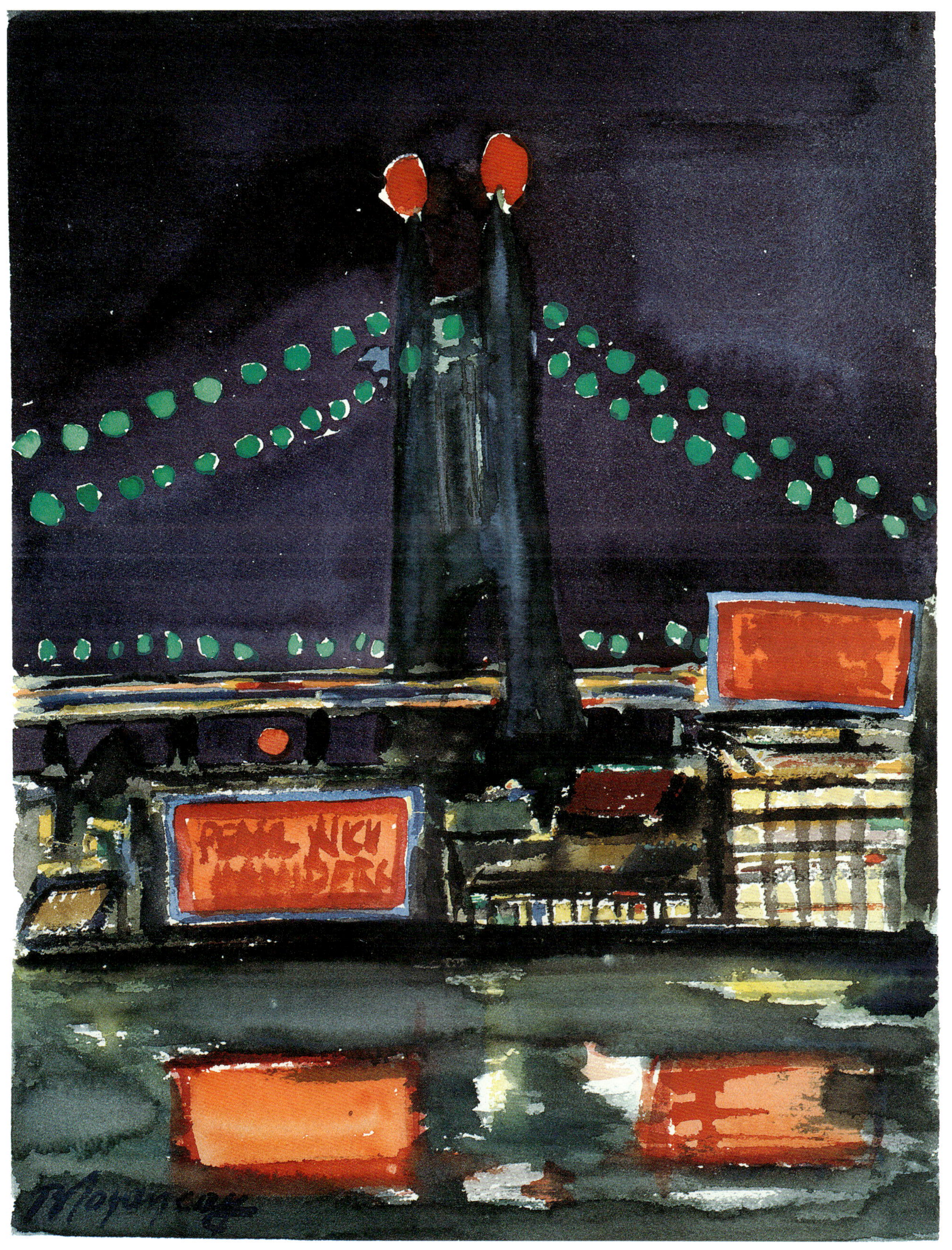

East River by Night II, 1963. Watercolor on paper, 13 × 10 in. (33 × 25.4 cm). Private collection

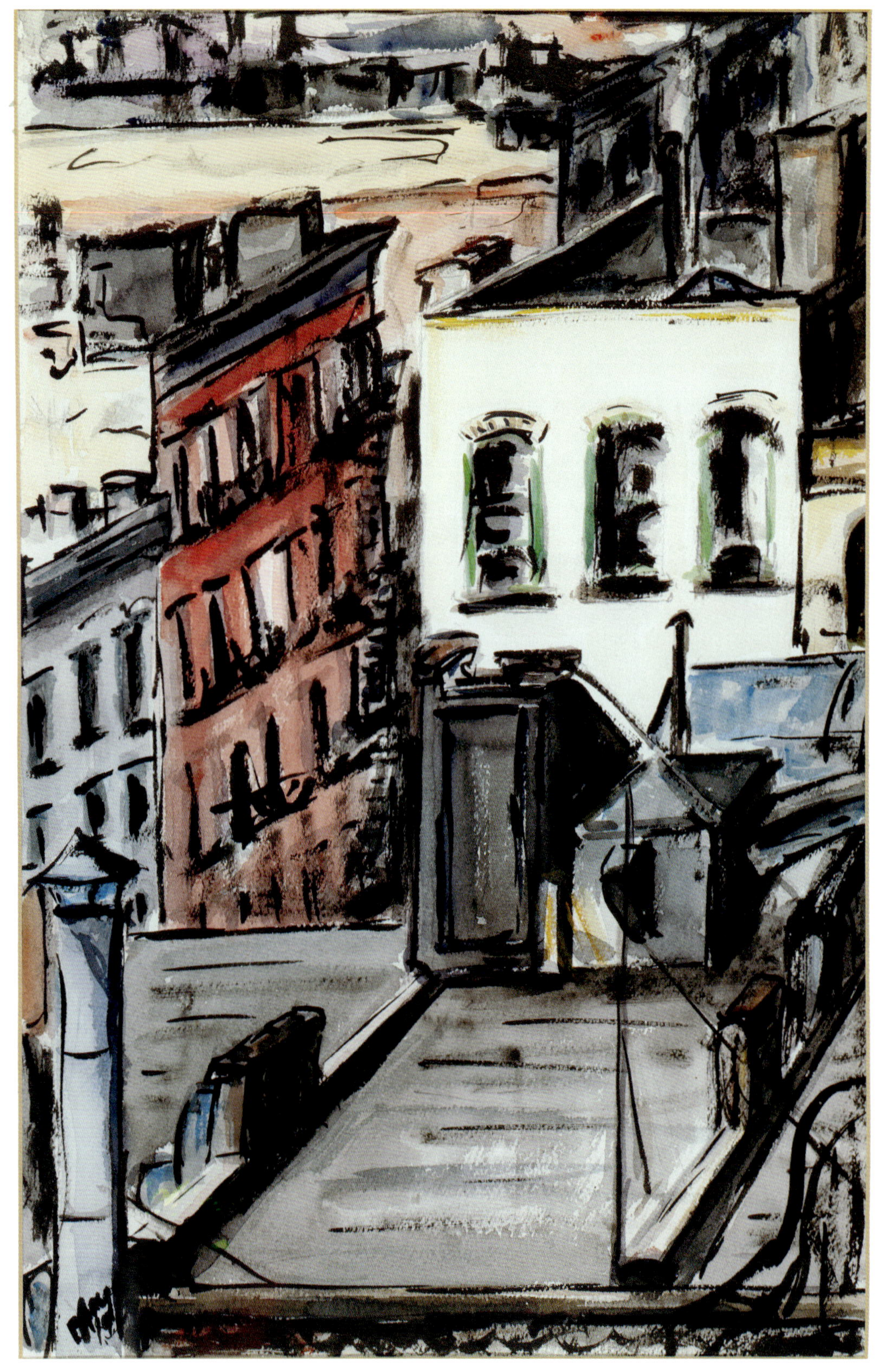

53rd Street at Third Avenue, 1963. Watercolor on paper, 18 × 12 in. (45.7 × 30.5 cm). Private collection

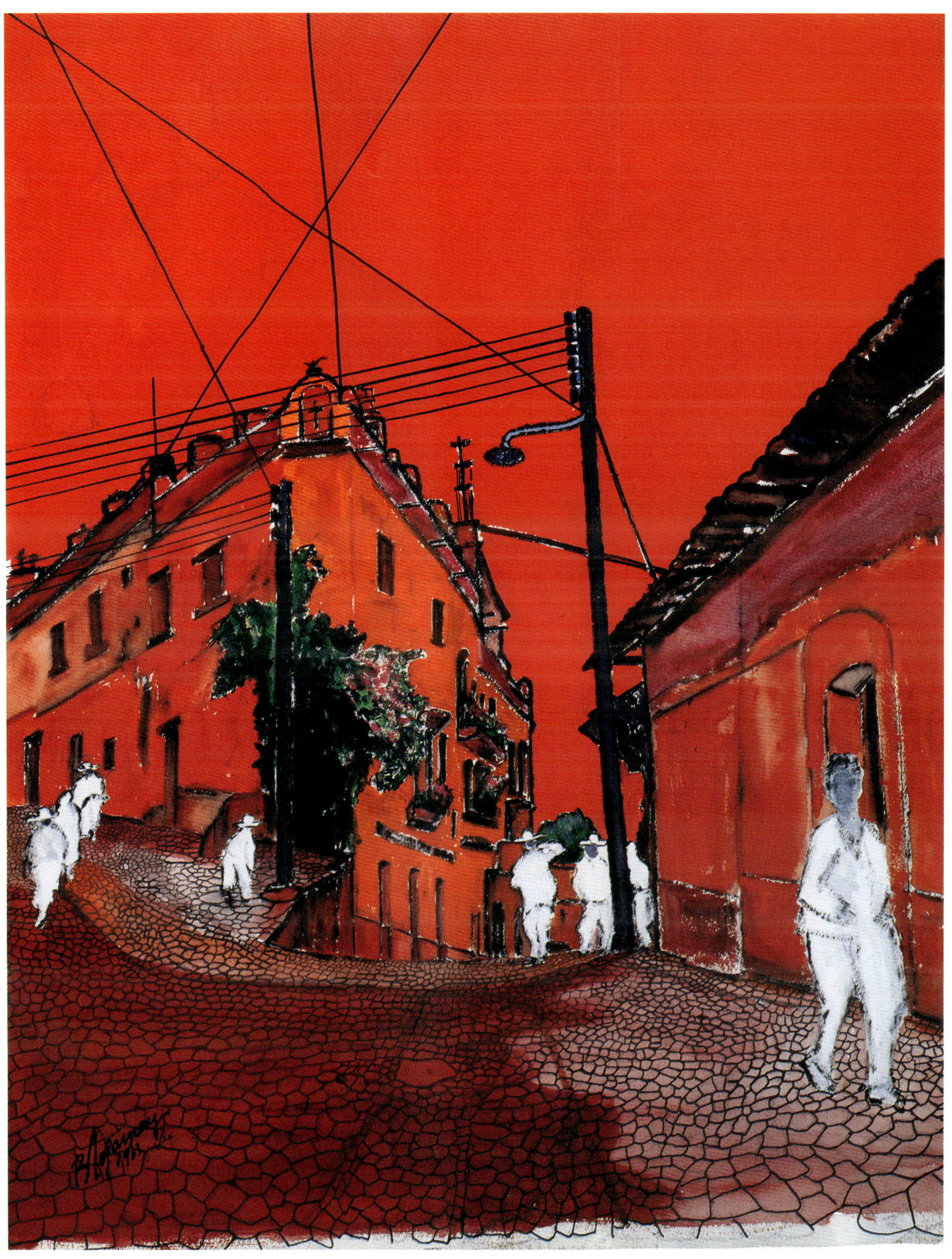

A Corner in Mexico, 1963. Gouache on paper, 30 × 22 in. (76.2 × 55.9 cm). Collection of the artist

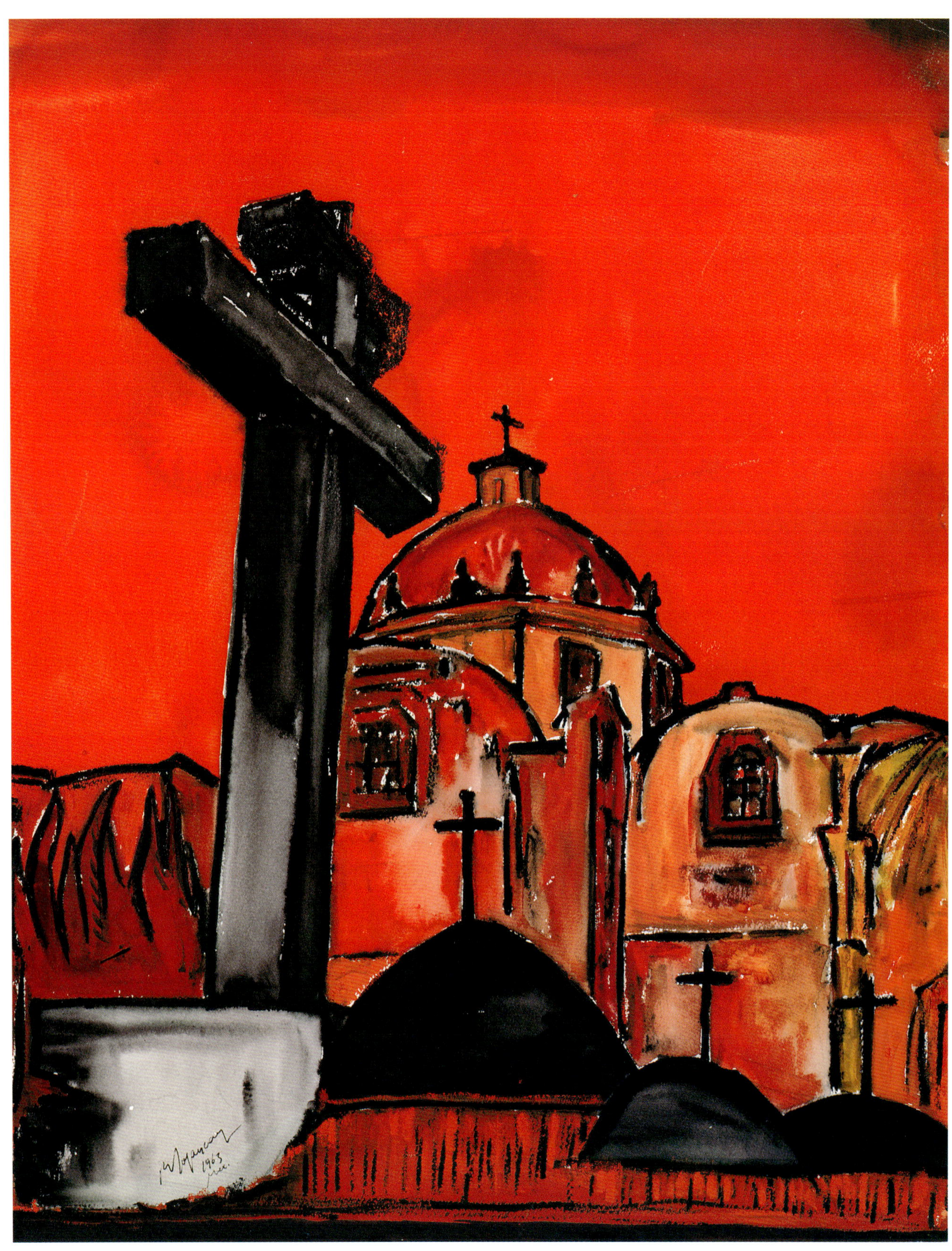

Cross, 1963. Gouache on paper, 30 × 22 in. (76.2 × 55.9 cm). Collection of the artist

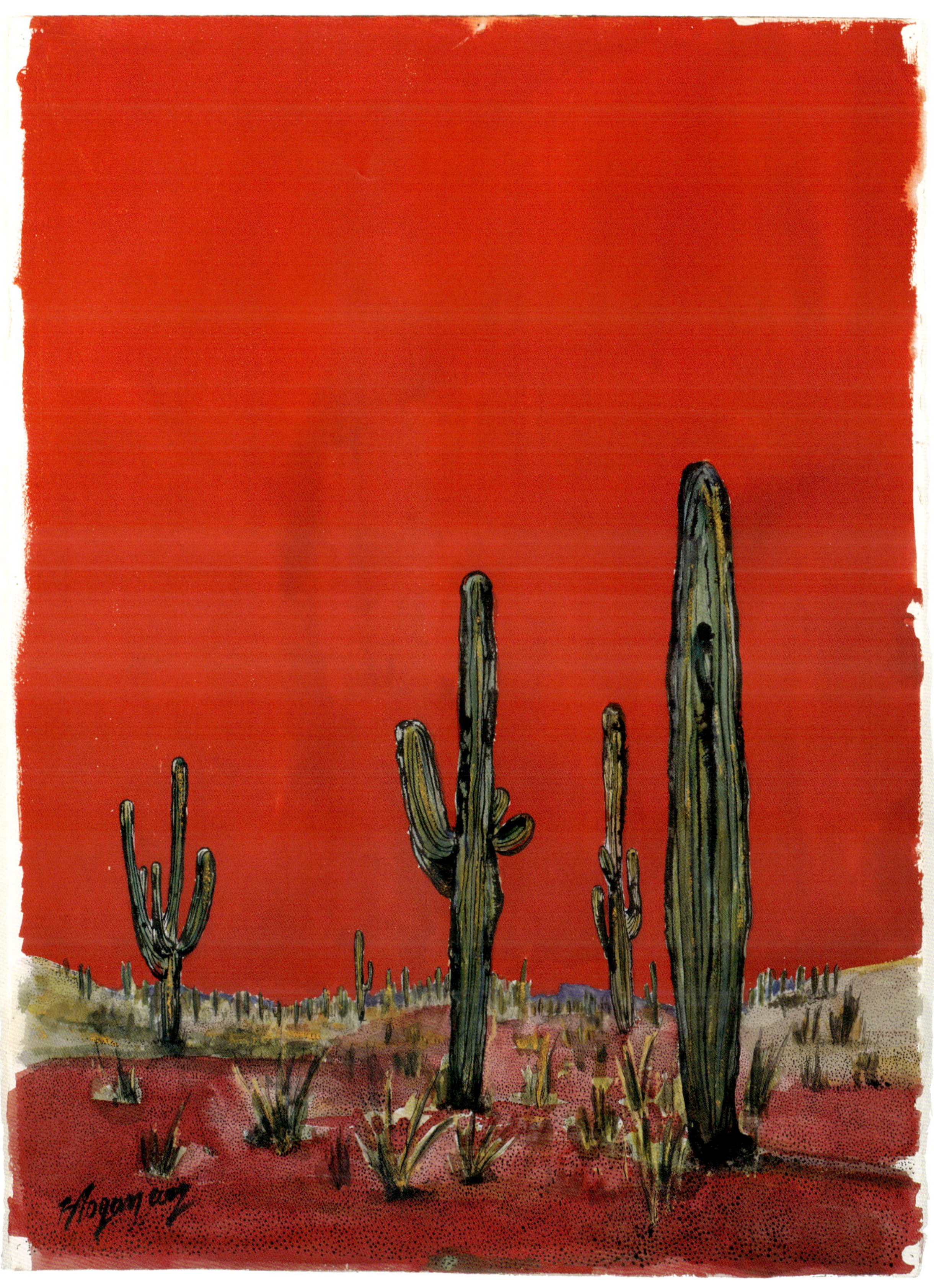

Arizona Desert, 1964. Gouache on paper, 30 × 22 in. (76.2 × 55.9 cm). Private collection

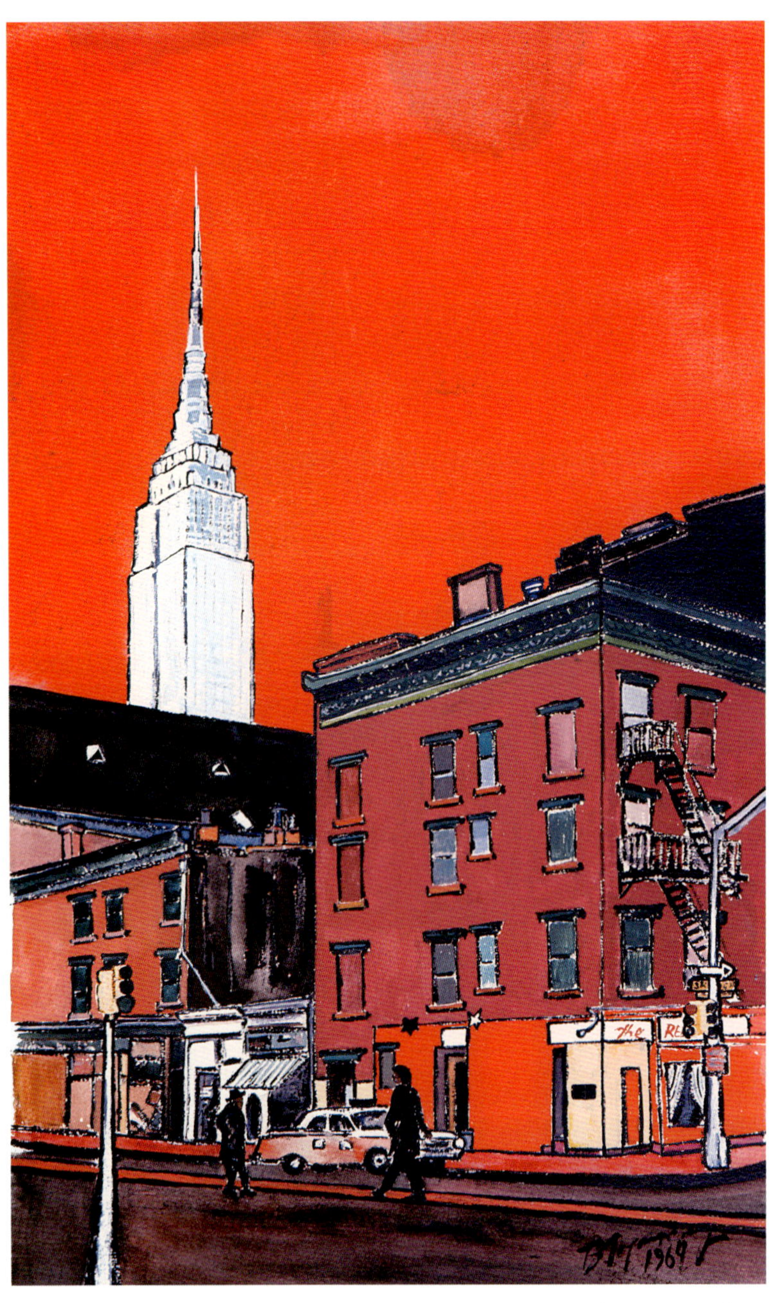

Empire State Building, 1964. Gouache on paper, 34 × 24 in. (86.4 × 61 cm). Private collection

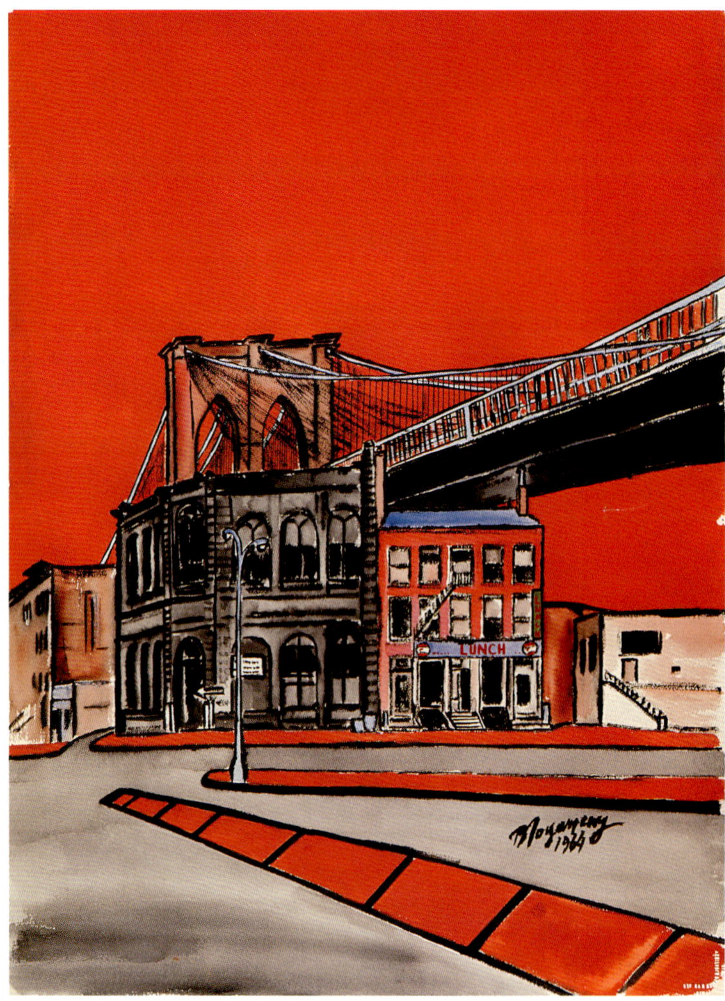

A Corner in Brooklyn, 1964. Gouache on paper, 22 × 20 in. (55.9 × 50.8 cm). Private collection

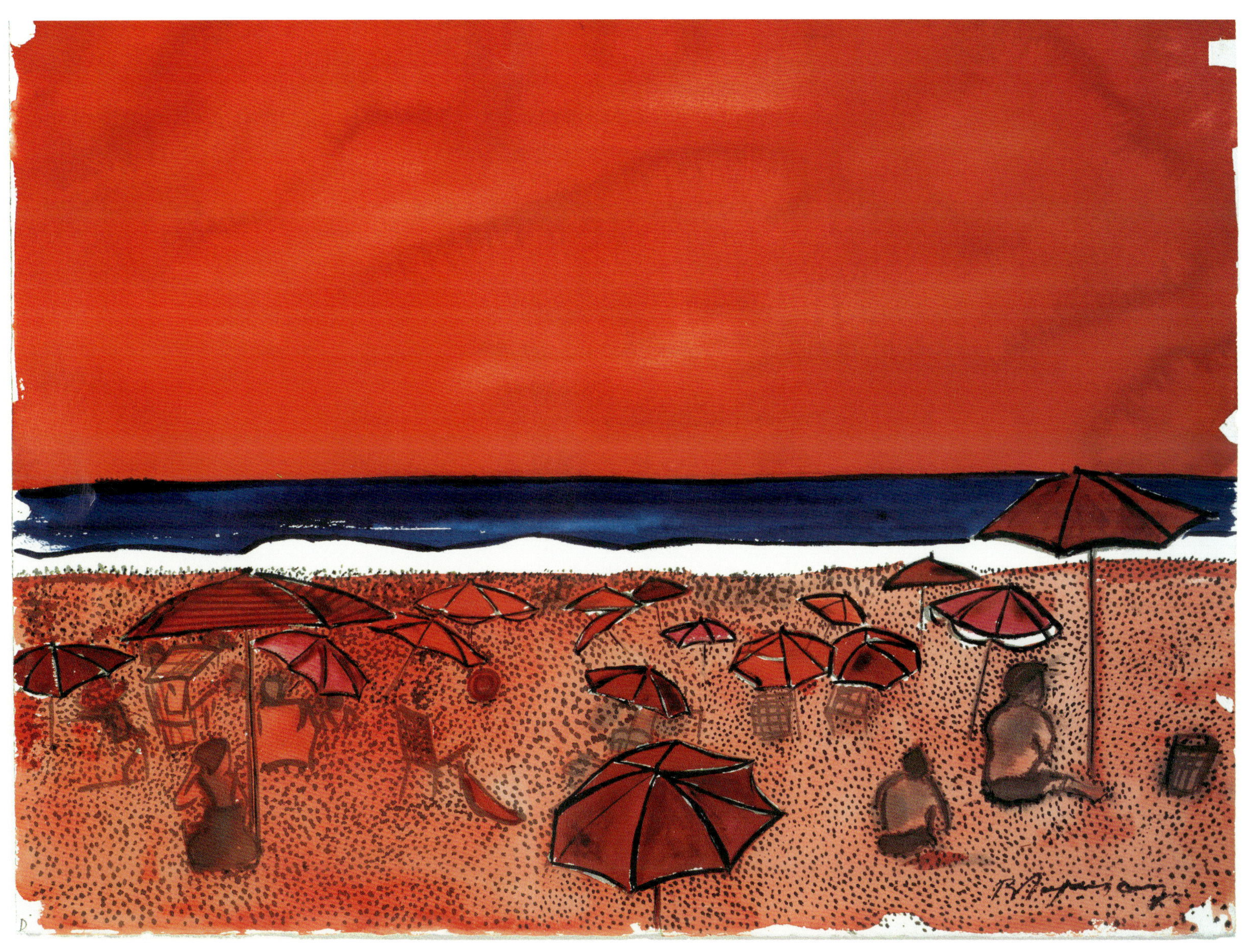

On the Beach, 1964. Gouache on paper, 22 × 30 in. (55.9 × 76.2 cm). Eczacıbaşı Collection, Istanbul

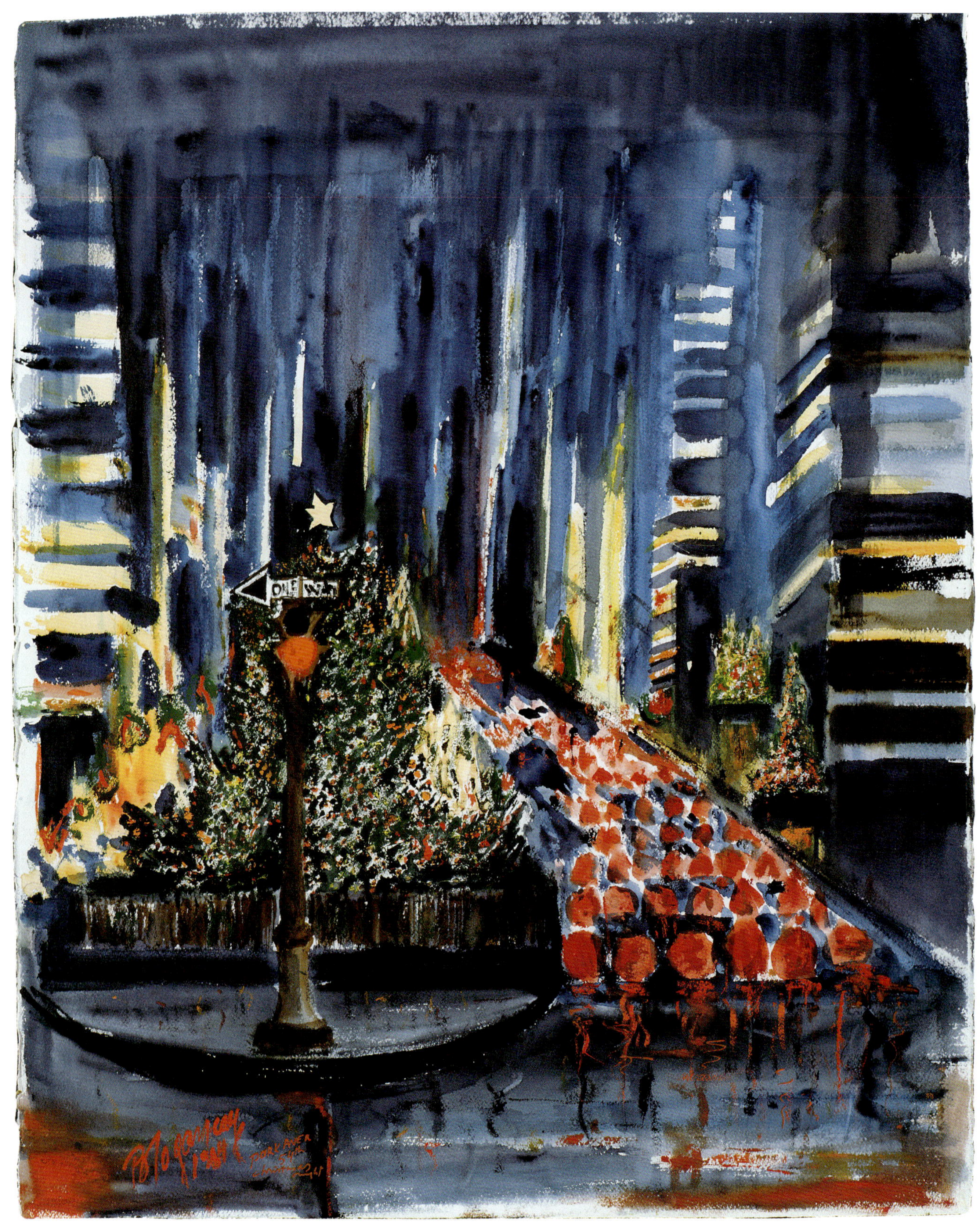

Park Avenue at 54th Street, 1964. Watercolor on paper, 18½ × 15 in. (47 × 38.1 cm). Private collection

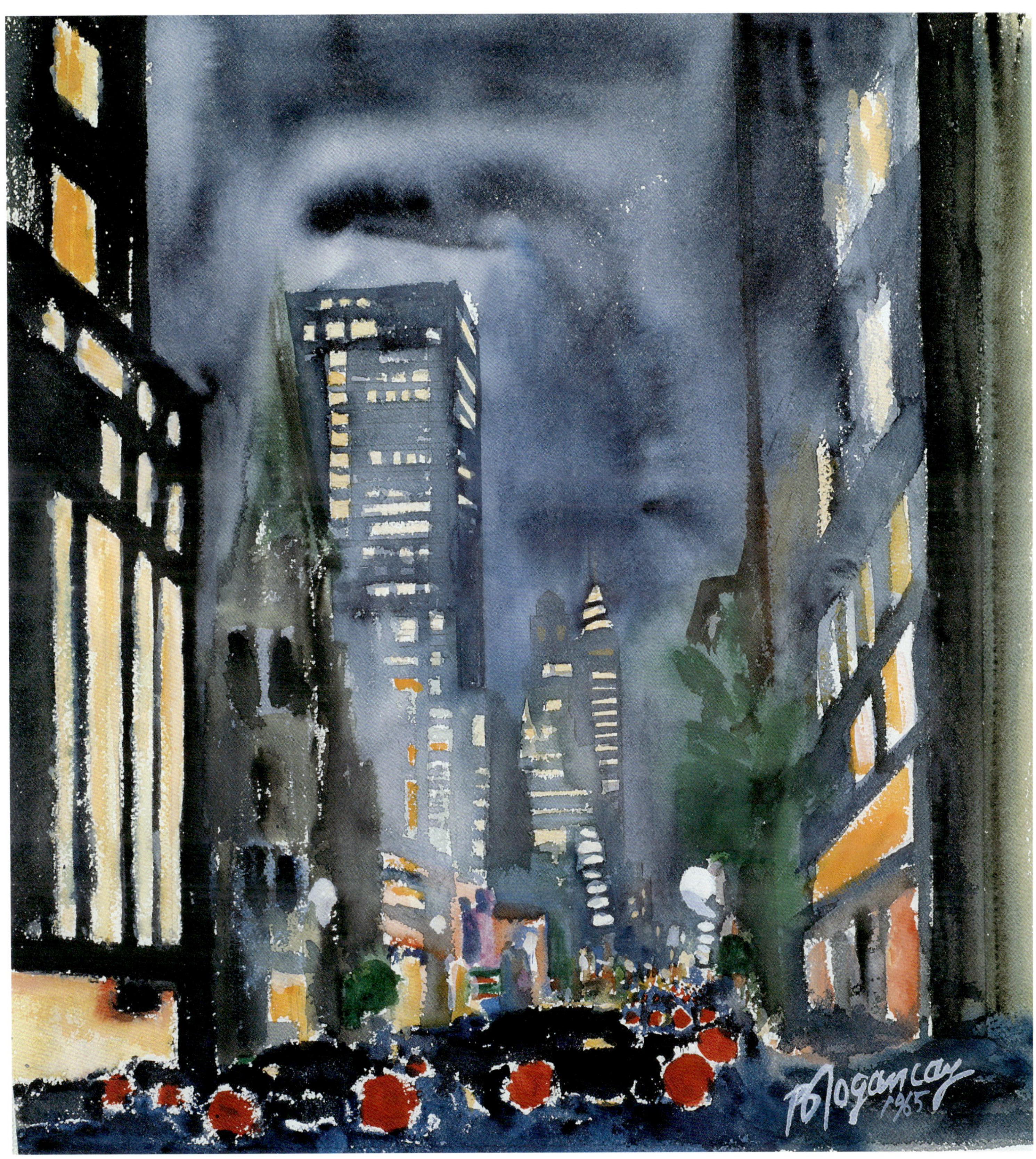

Lexington Avenue by Night, 1965. Watercolor on paper, 21 × 19 in. (53.3 × 48.3 cm). Collection of the artist

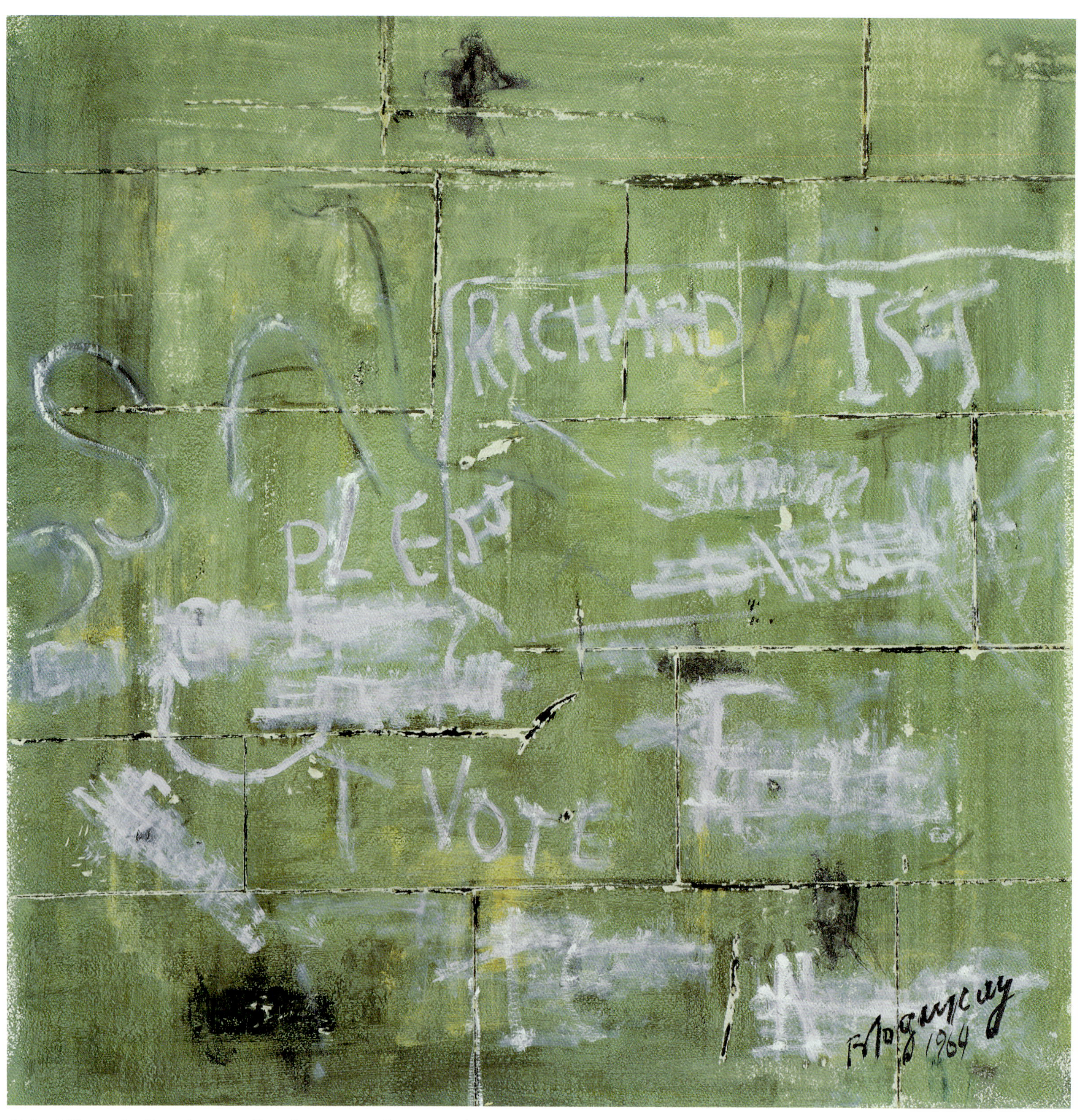

Richard First, 1964. Gouache on cardboard, 26 × 26 in. (66 × 66 cm). Eczacıbaşı Collection, Istanbul

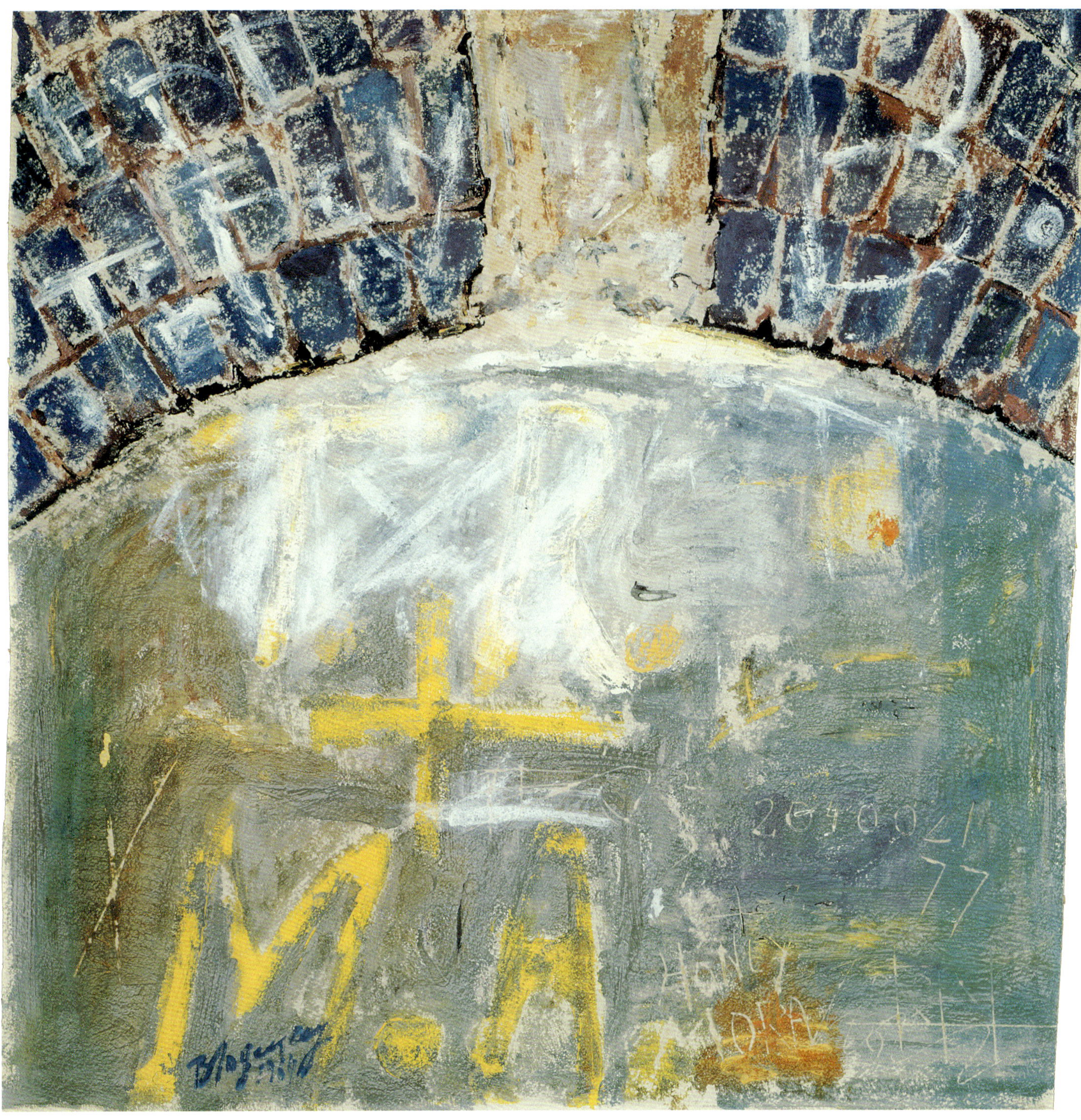

Honey Lora, 1964. Gouache on cardboard, 24 × 24 in. (61 × 61 cm). Private collection

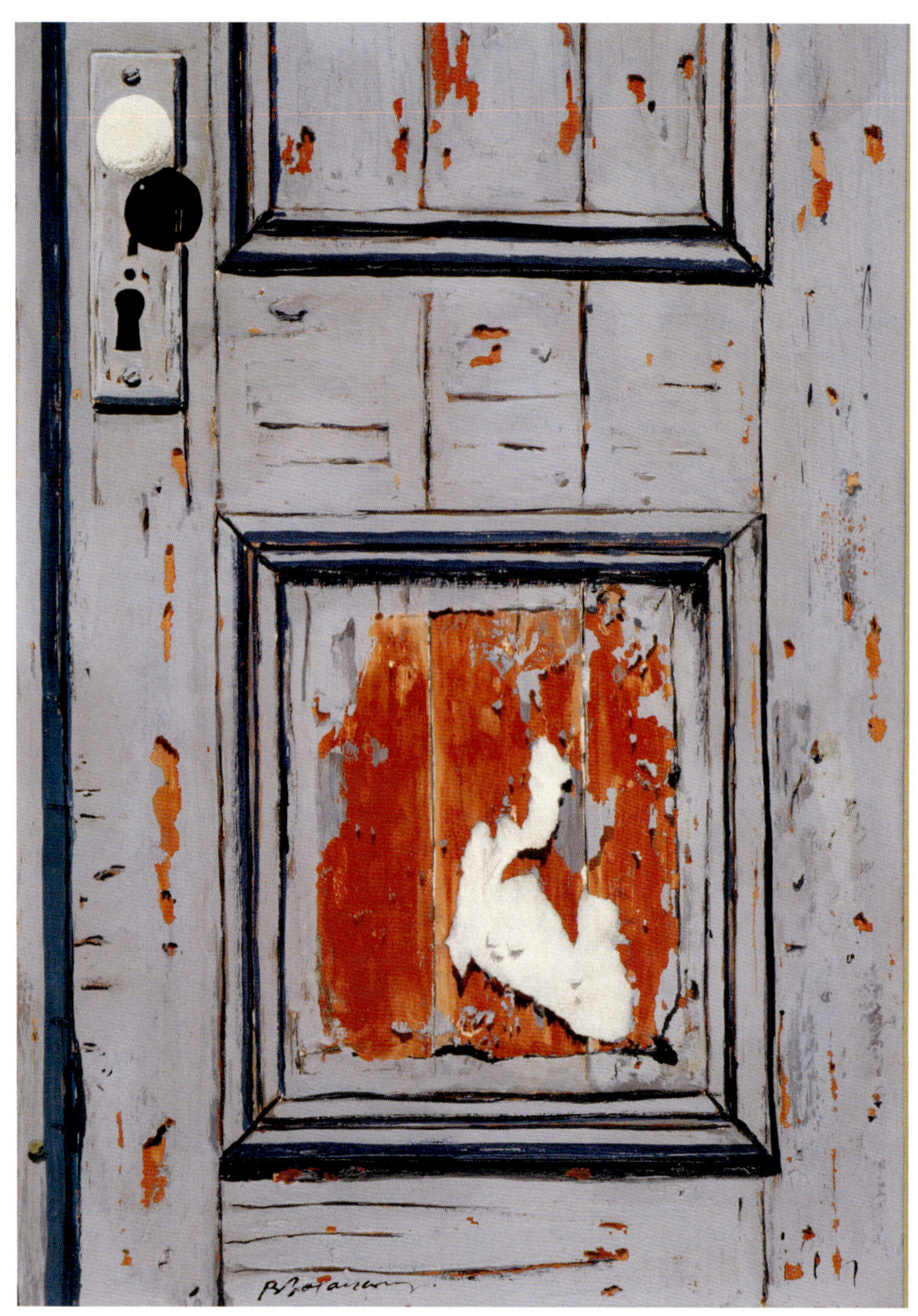

Door in Need of Fresh Paint, 1966. Gouache on cardboard, 16 × 11½ in. (40.6 × 29.2 cm).
Collection of the artist

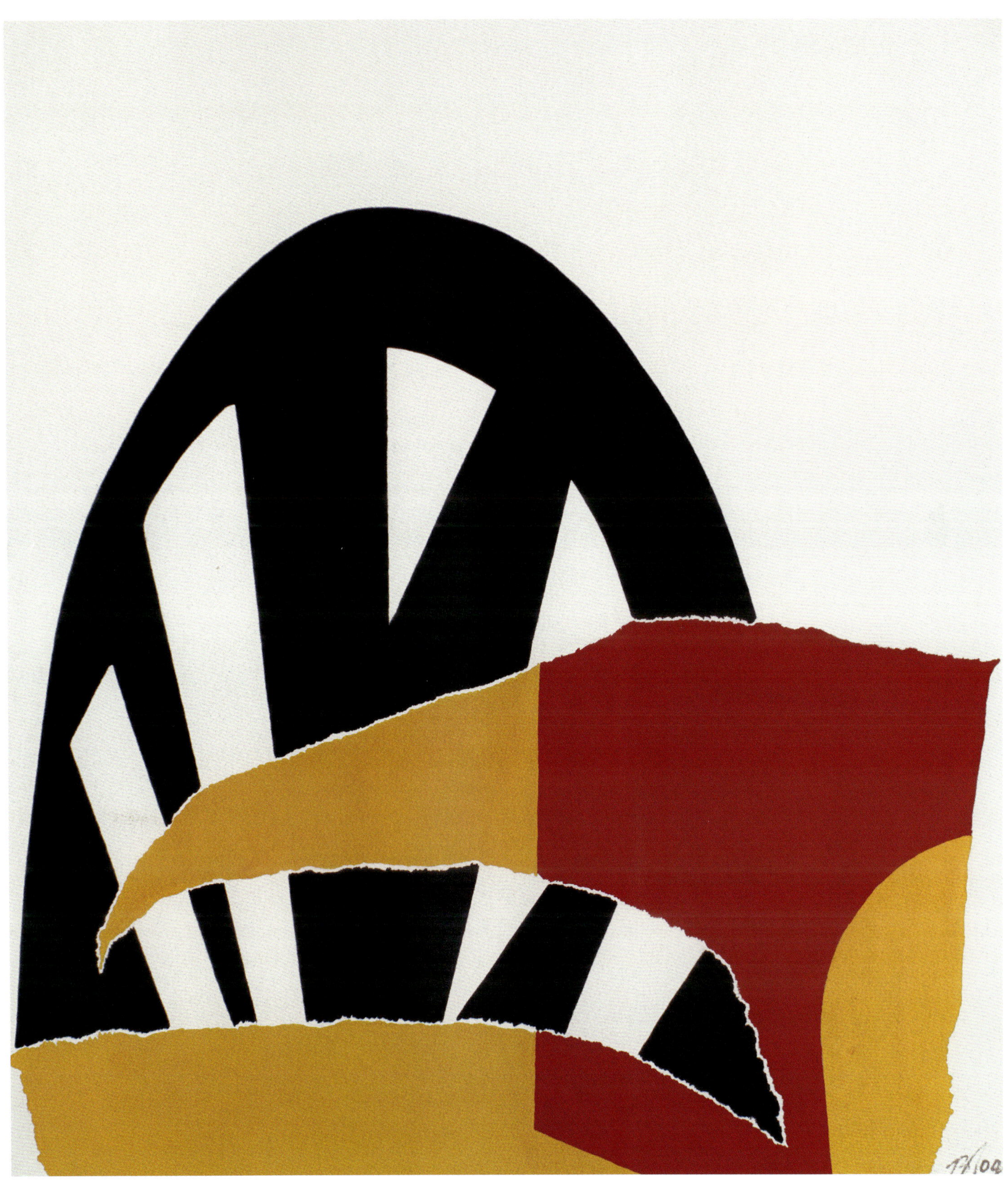

Sundial, 1968. Gouache on paper, 30 × 22 in. (76.2 × 55.9 cm). Private collection

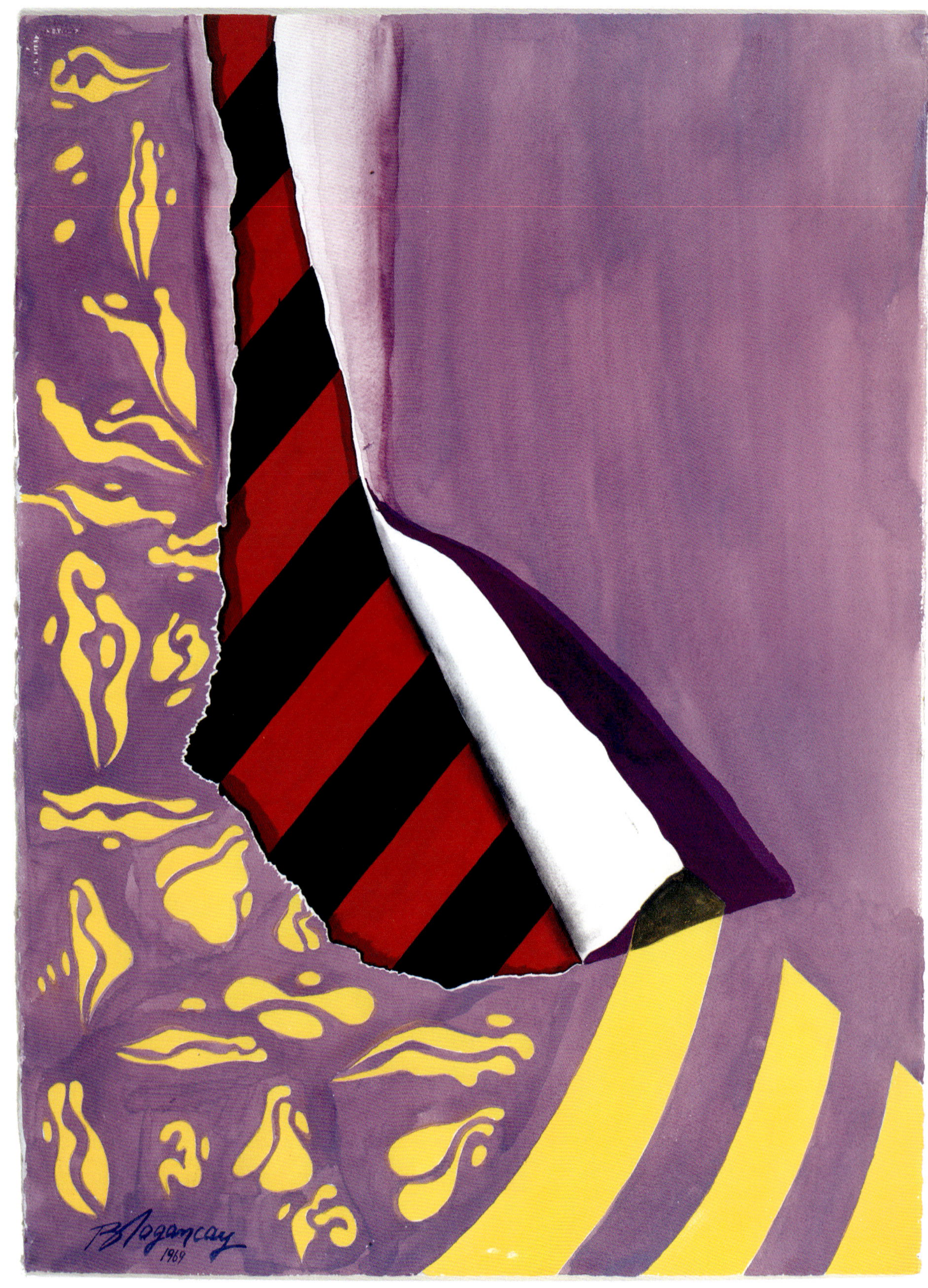

Residue of Human Beings, 1969. Gouache on paper, 30 × 22 in. (76.2 × 55.9 cm). Collection of the artist

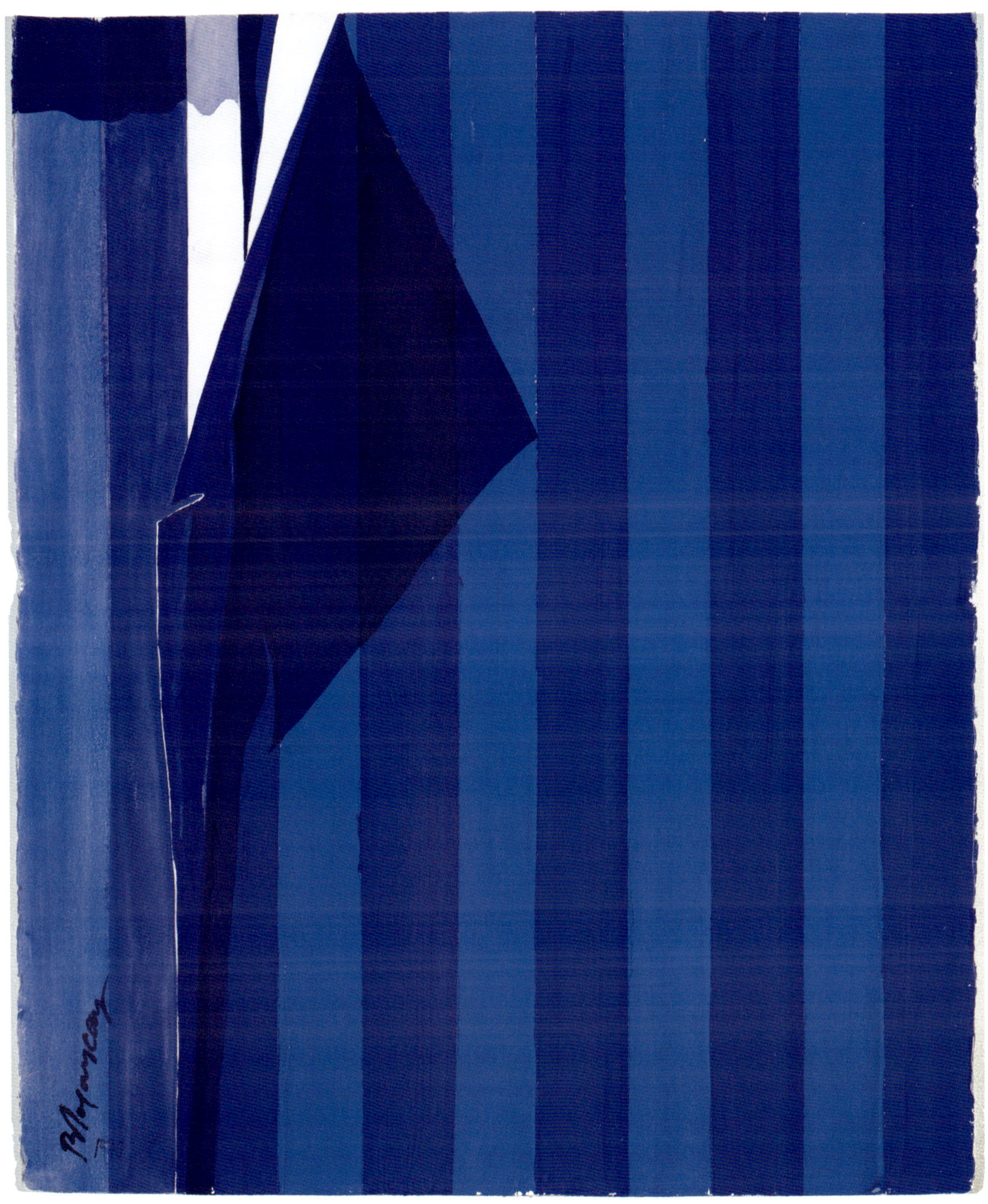

Blues, 1970. Gouache on paper, 26¾ × 22 in. (67.9 × 55.9 cm). Collection of the artist

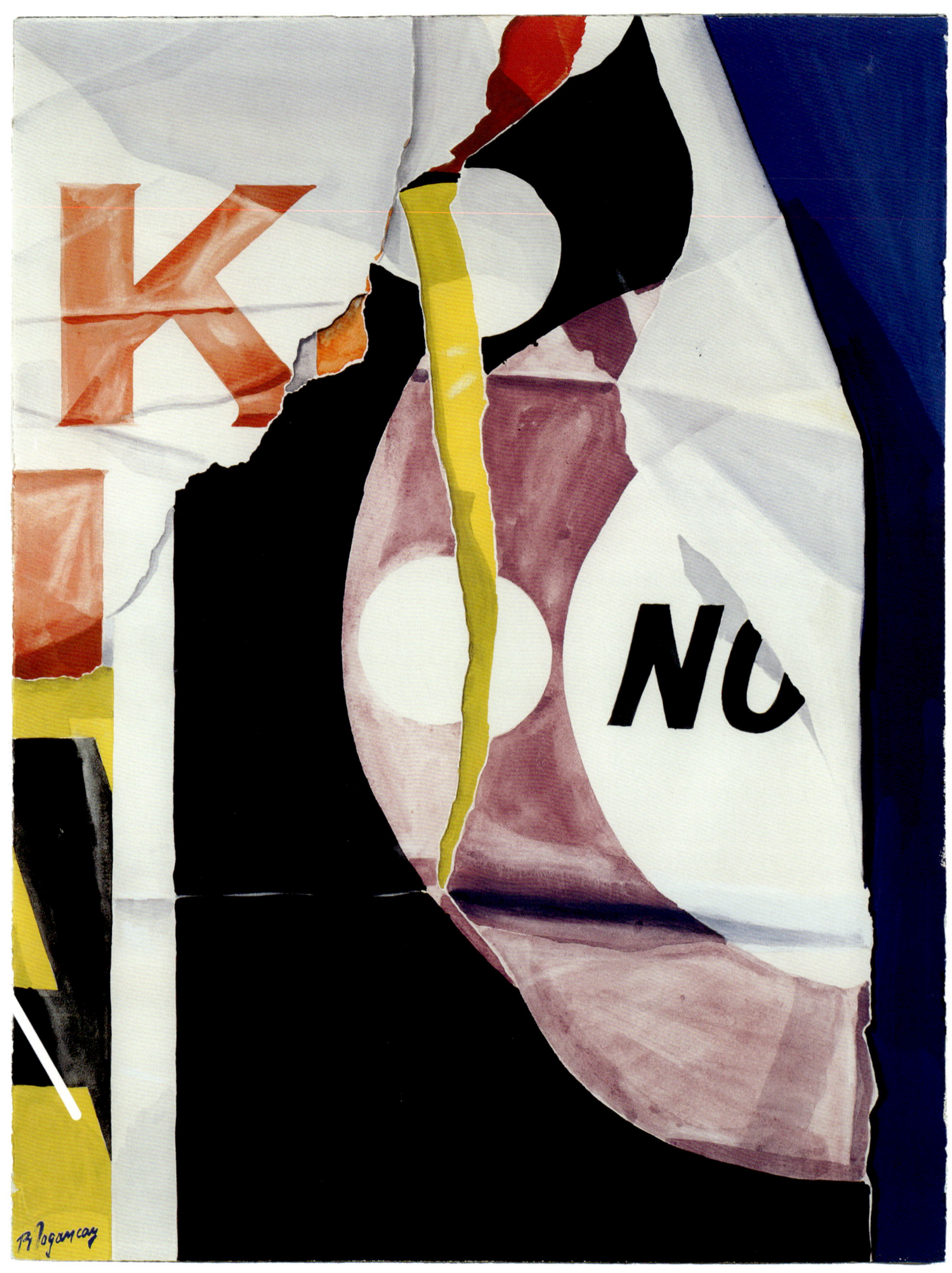

Simply No, 1971. Gouache on paper, 32 × 25 in. (81.3 × 63.5 cm). Collection of the artist

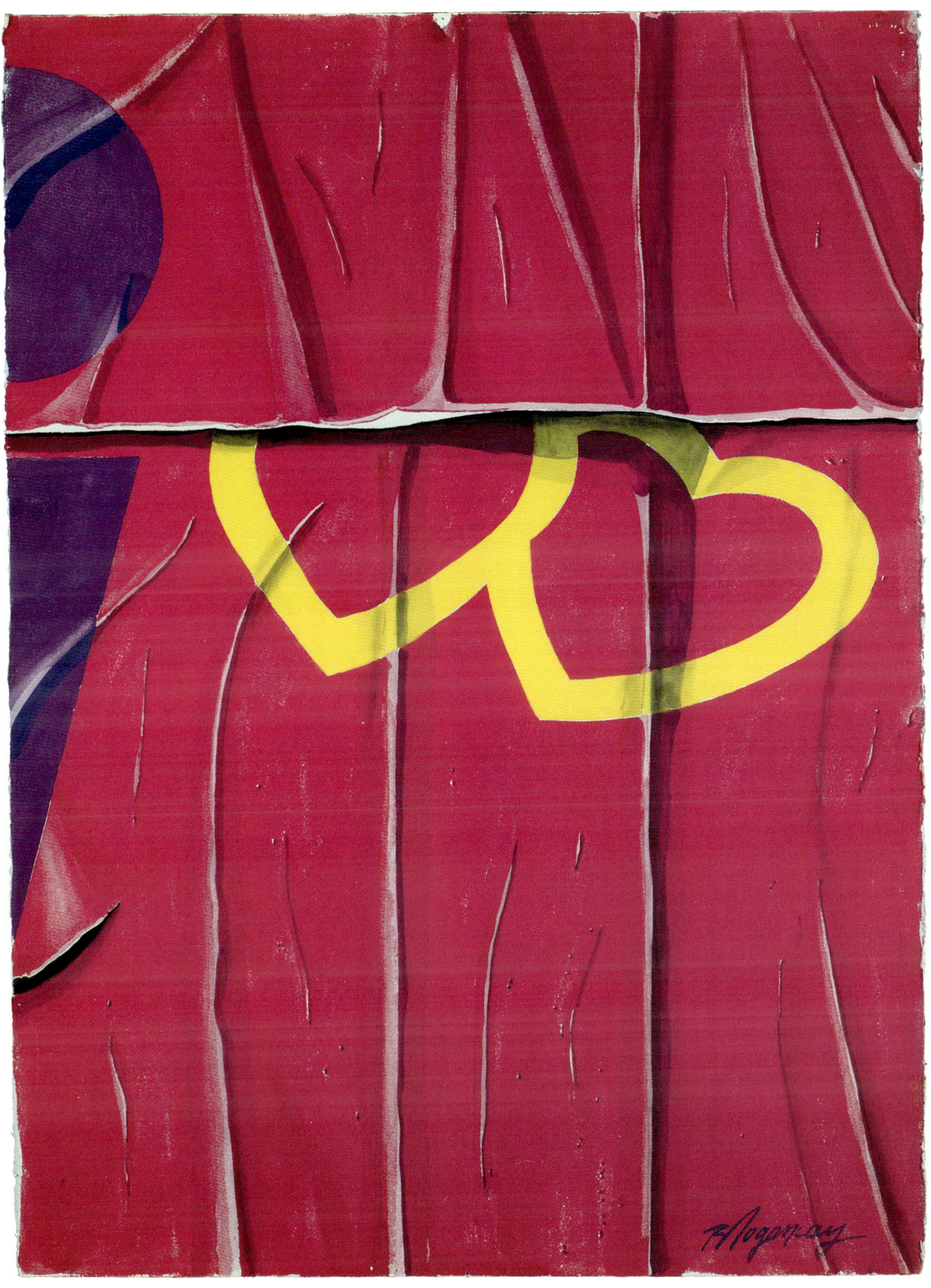

Sweet Hearts, 1972. Gouache on paper, 30 × 22 in. (76.2 × 55.9 cm). Private collection, Paris

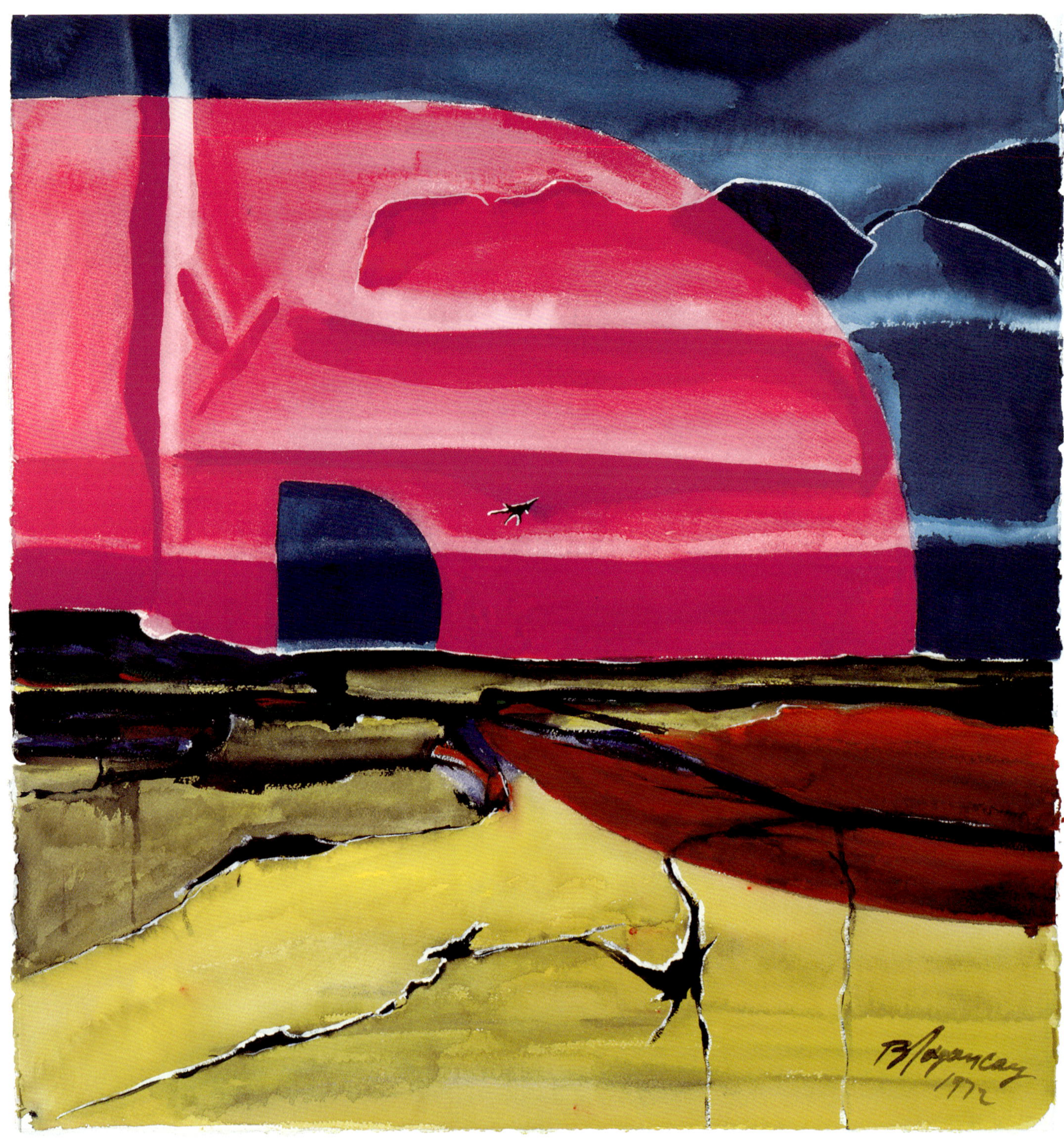

Magic Mountain, 1972. Gouache on paper, 23 × 22½ in. (58.4 × 57.2 cm). Private collection

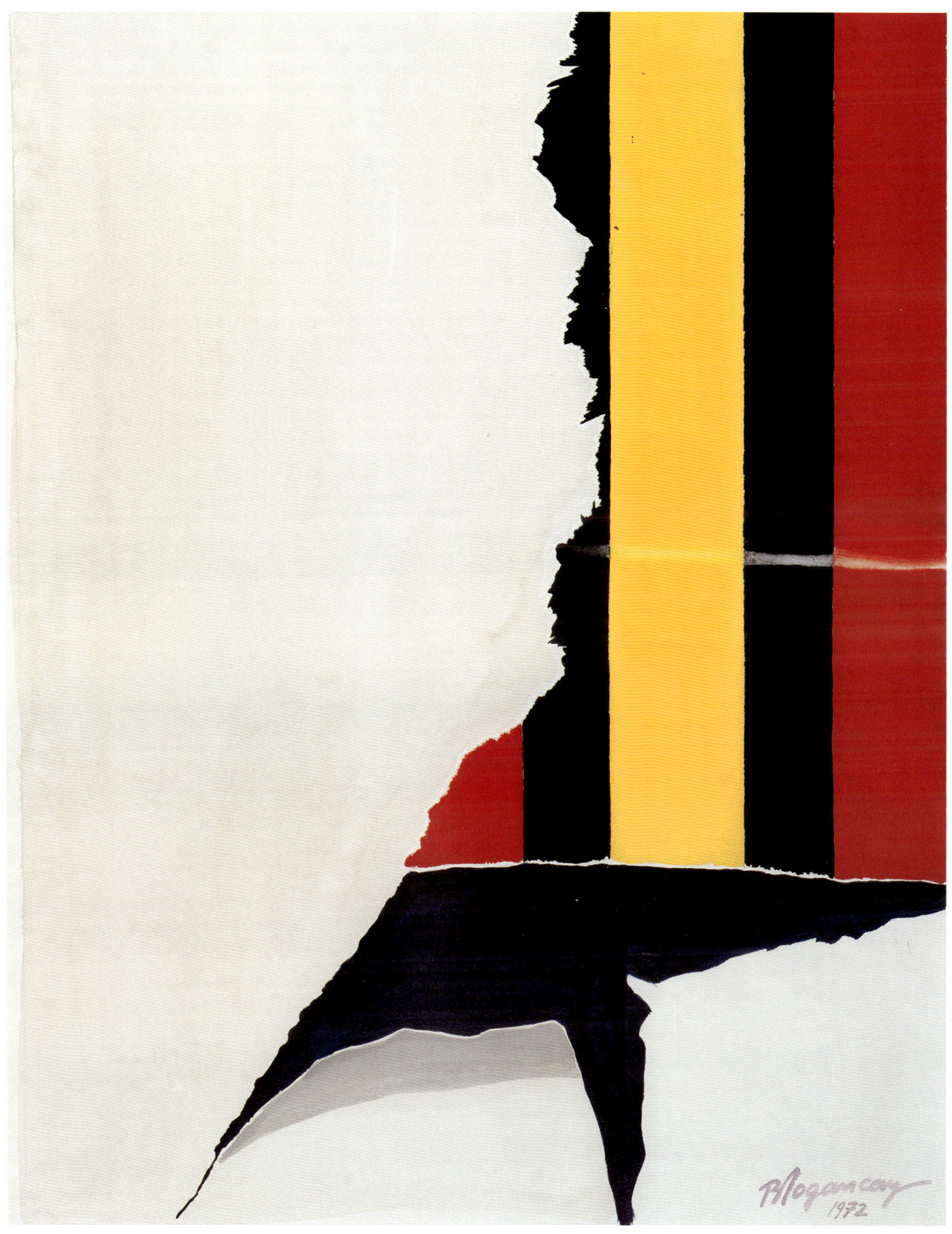

Plain Vanilla, 1972. Gouache on paper, 26 × 20¼ in. (66 × 51.4 cm). Collection of the artist

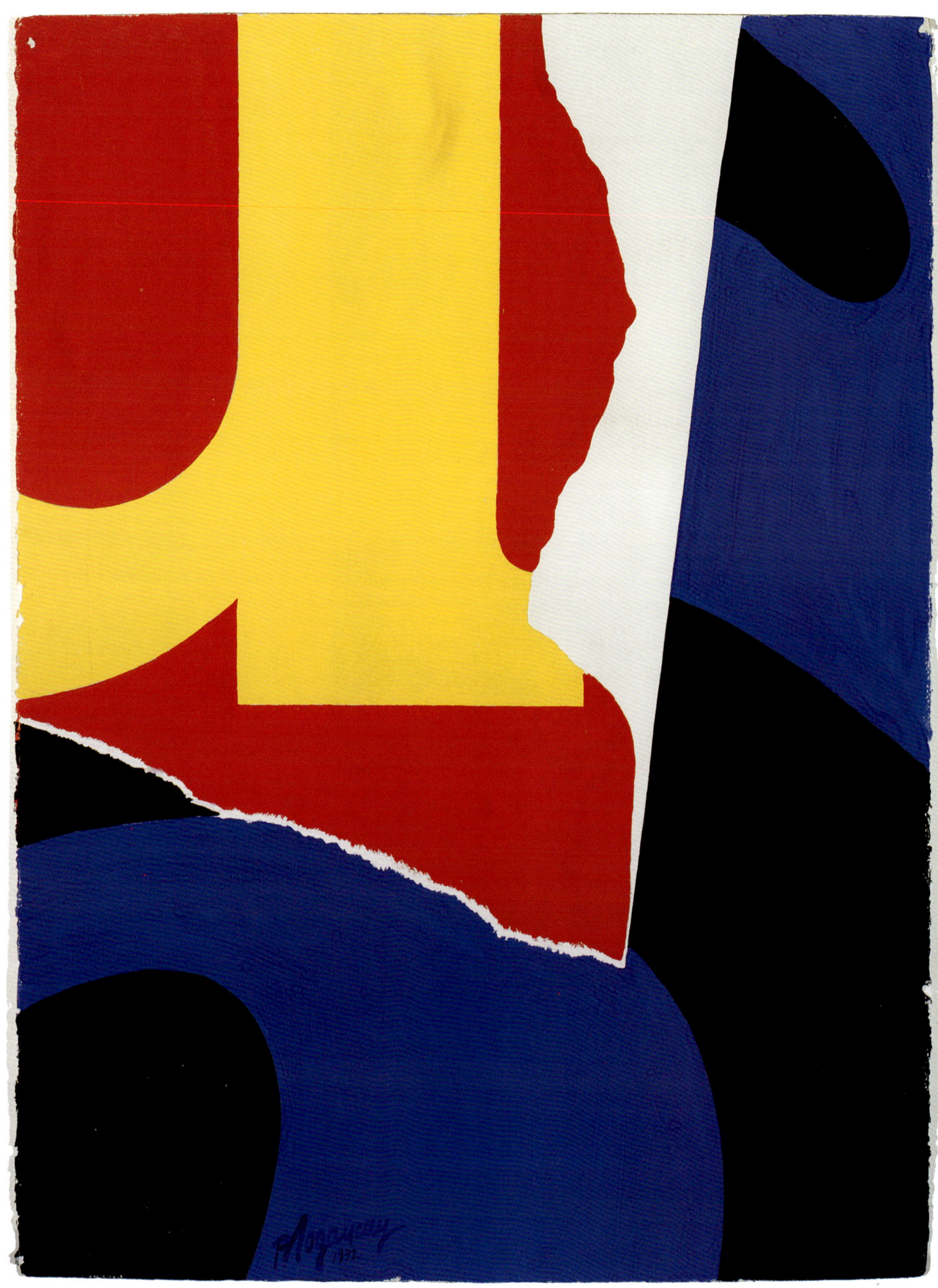

Miro Colors, 1972. Gouache on paper, 30 × 22 in. (76.2 × 55.9 cm). Collection of the artist

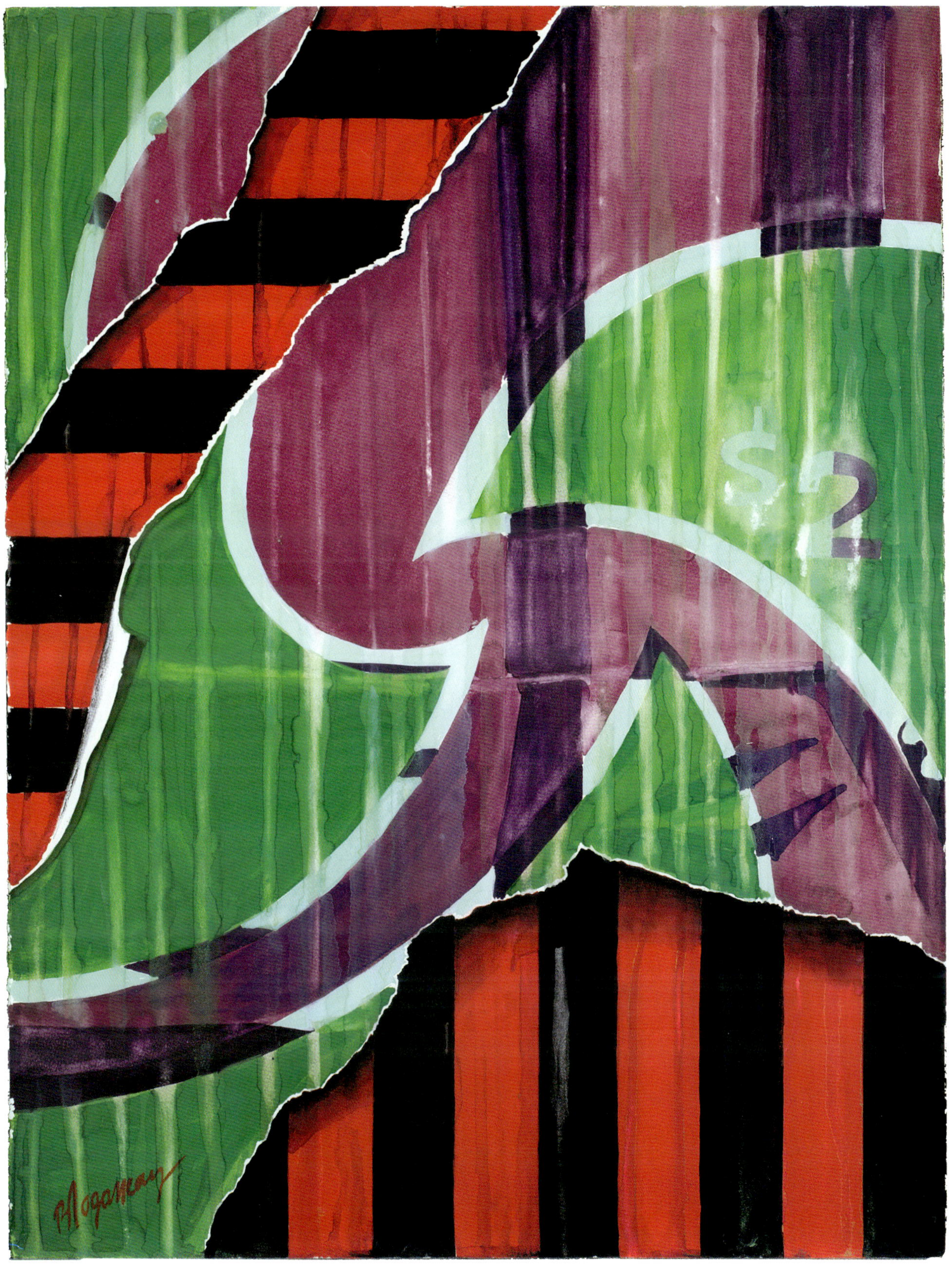

Two Dollars, 1972. Gouache on paper, 30 × 22 in. (76.2 × 55.9 cm). Private collection

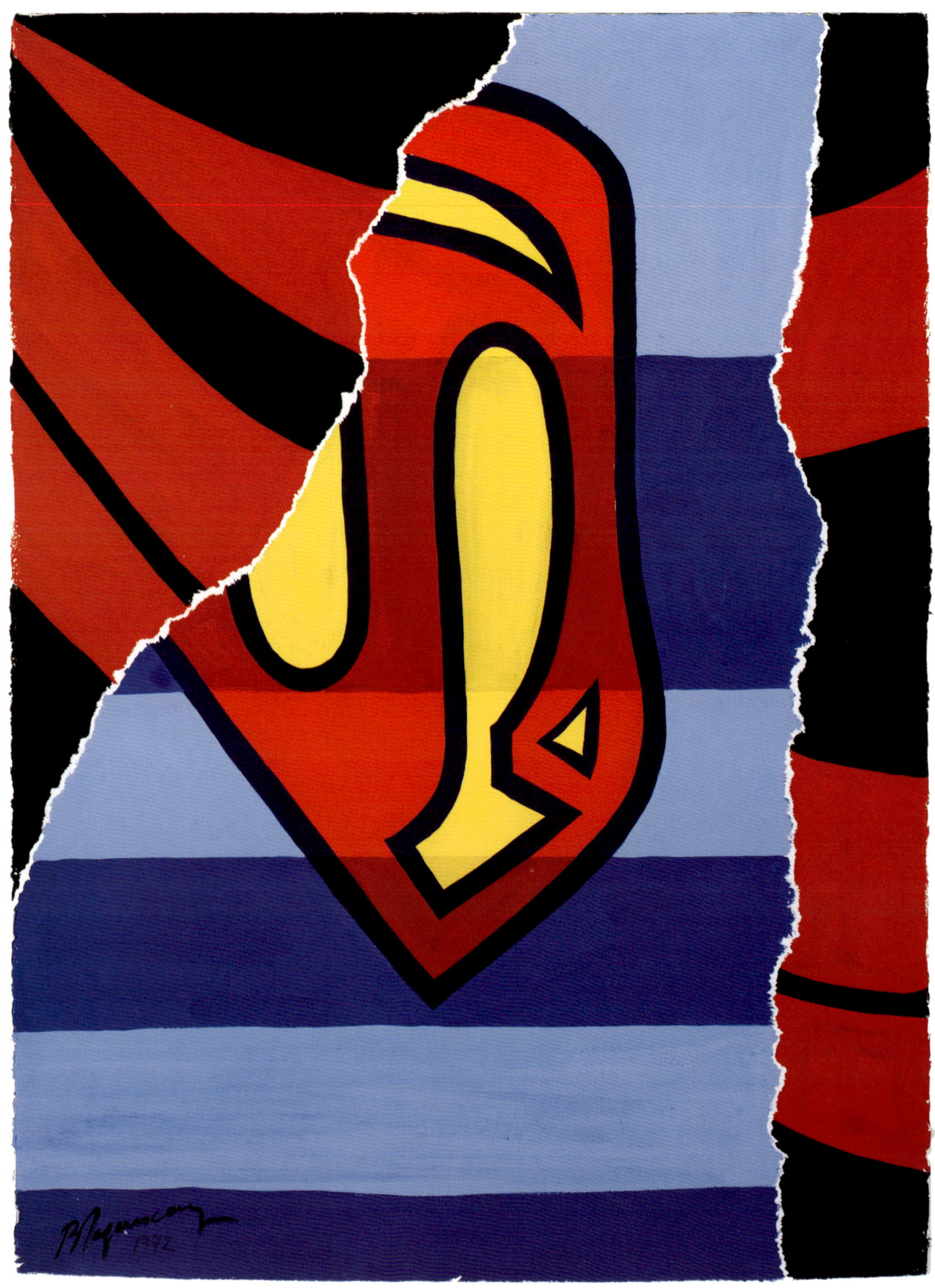

Superman, 1972. Gouache on paper, 30 × 22 in. (76.2 × 55.9 cm). Collection of the artist

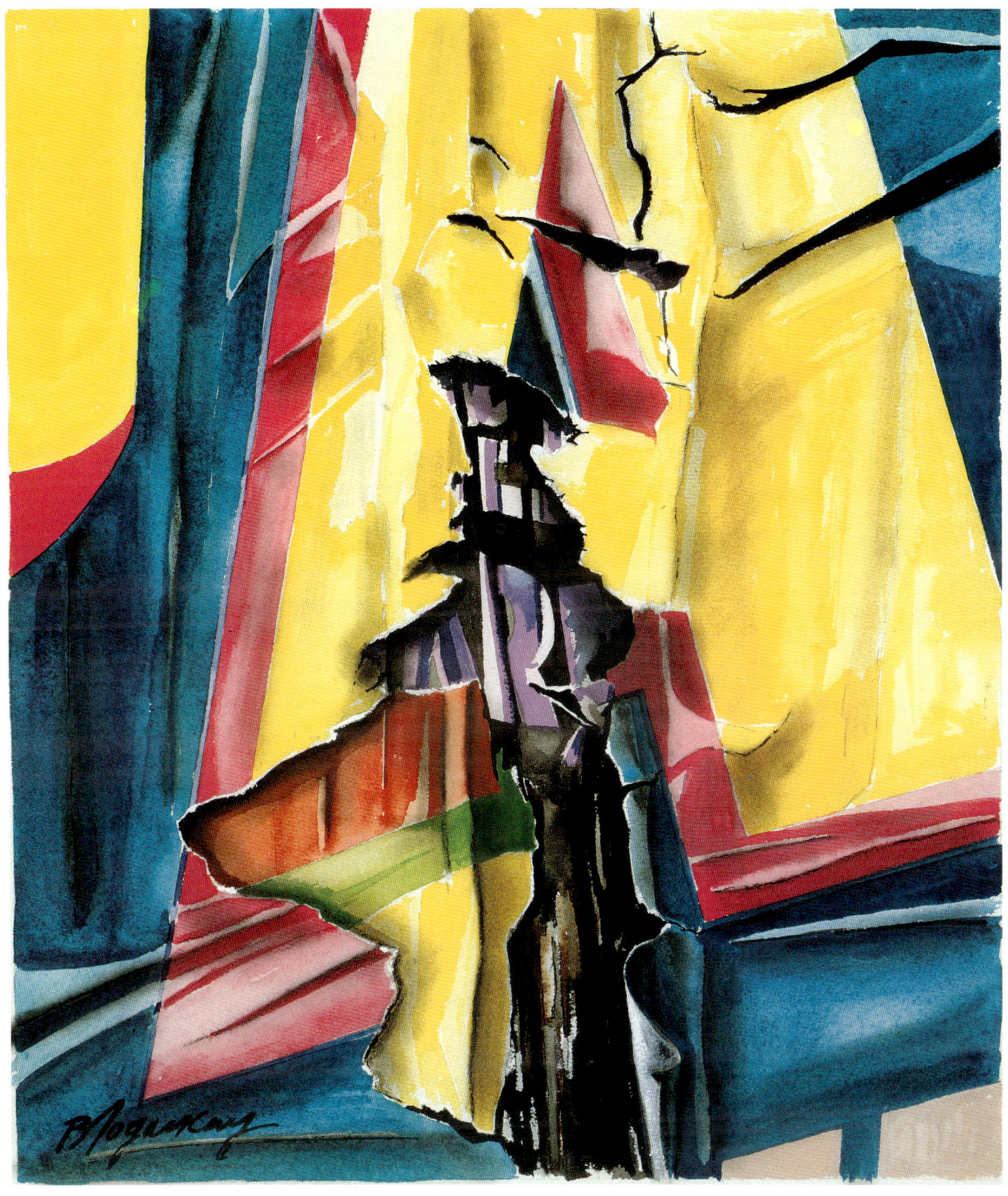

A as in Amour, 1972. Gouache on paper, 17 × 14 in. (43.2 × 35.6 cm). Private collection, Germany

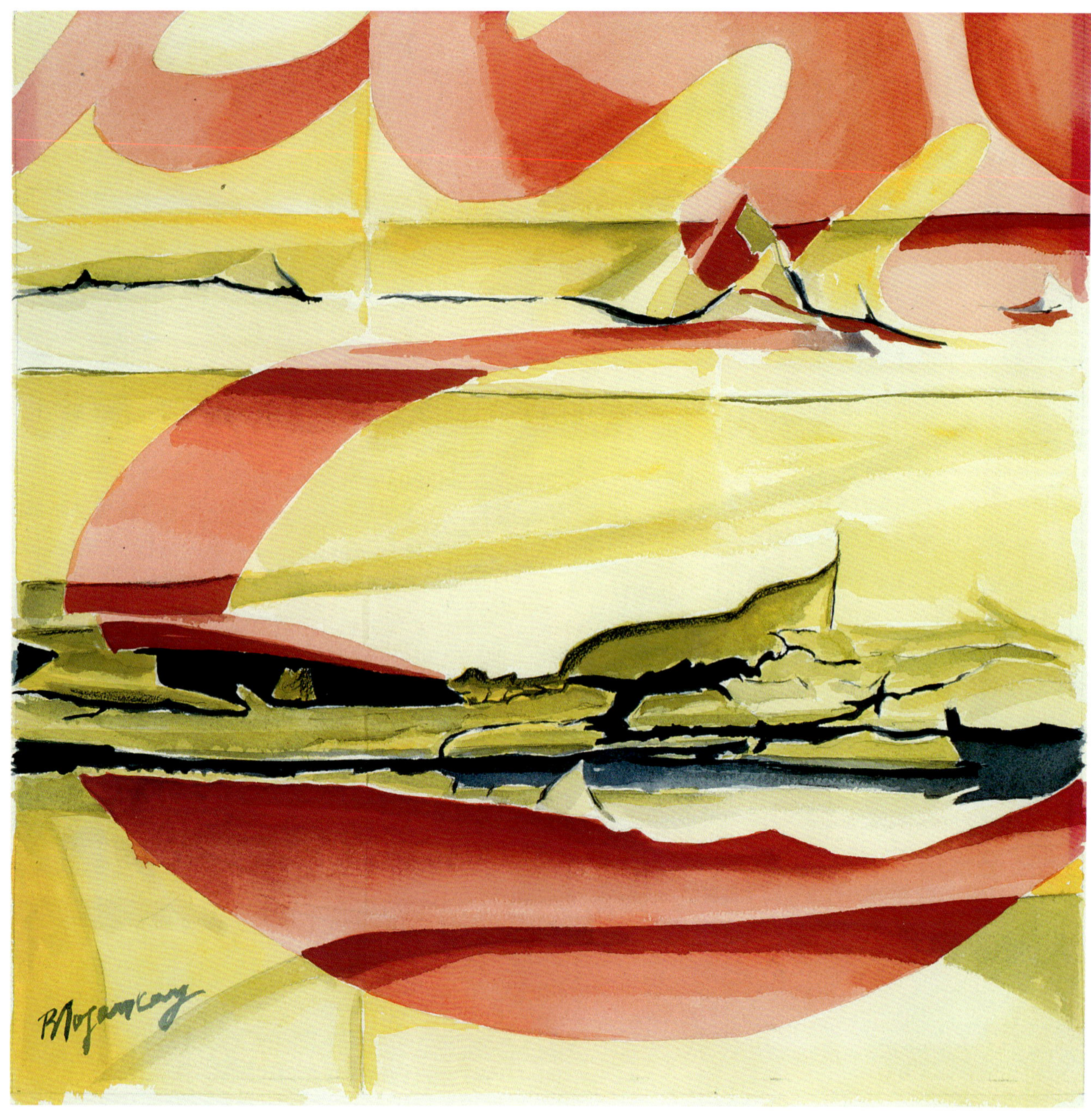

Composition: Yellow and Pink, 1973. Gouache on paper, 17 × 17 in. (43.2 × 43.2 cm). Private collection

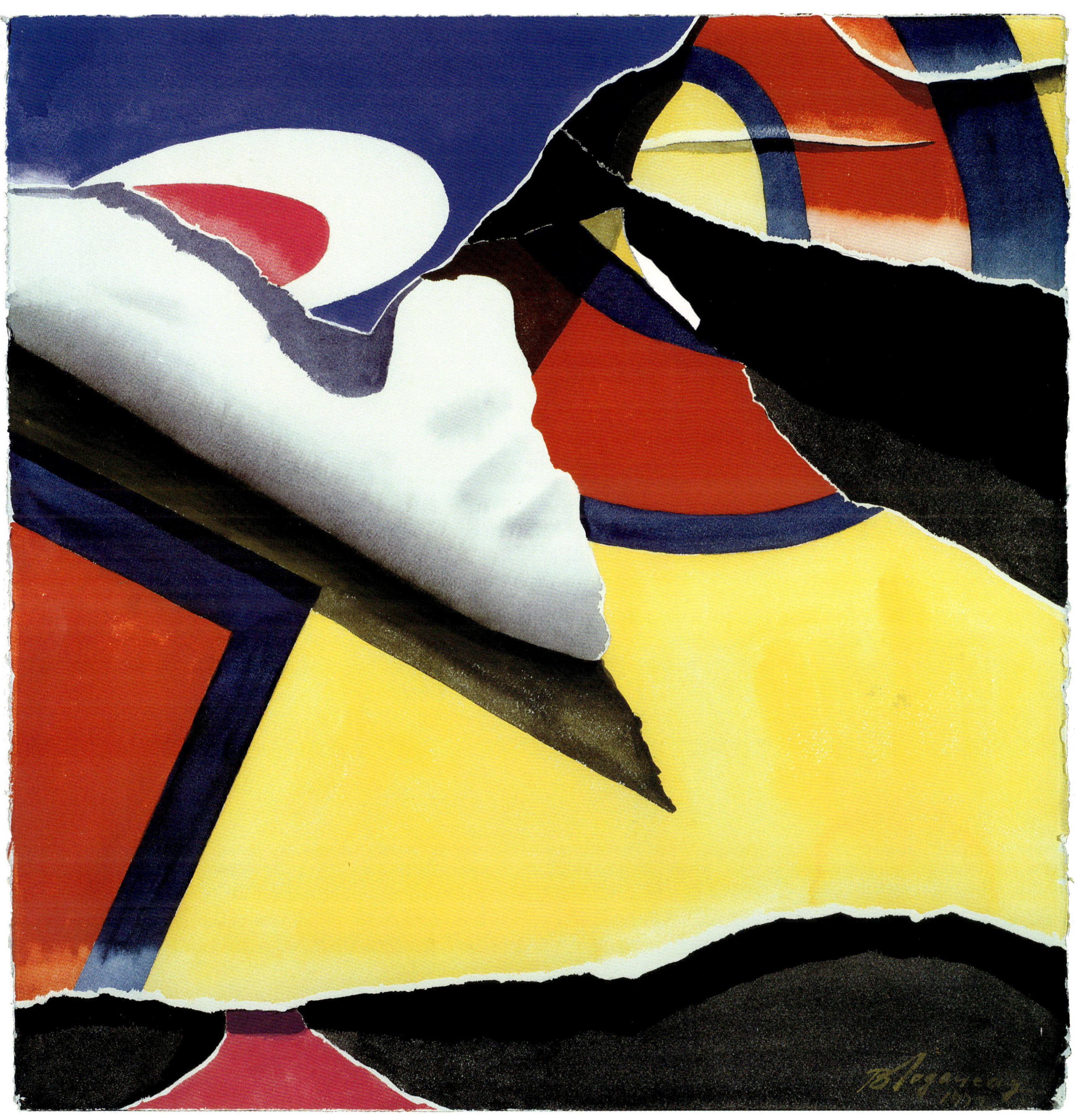

Wave, 1973. Gouache on paper, 22½ × 22½ in. (57.2 × 57.2 cm). Private collection, New Jersey

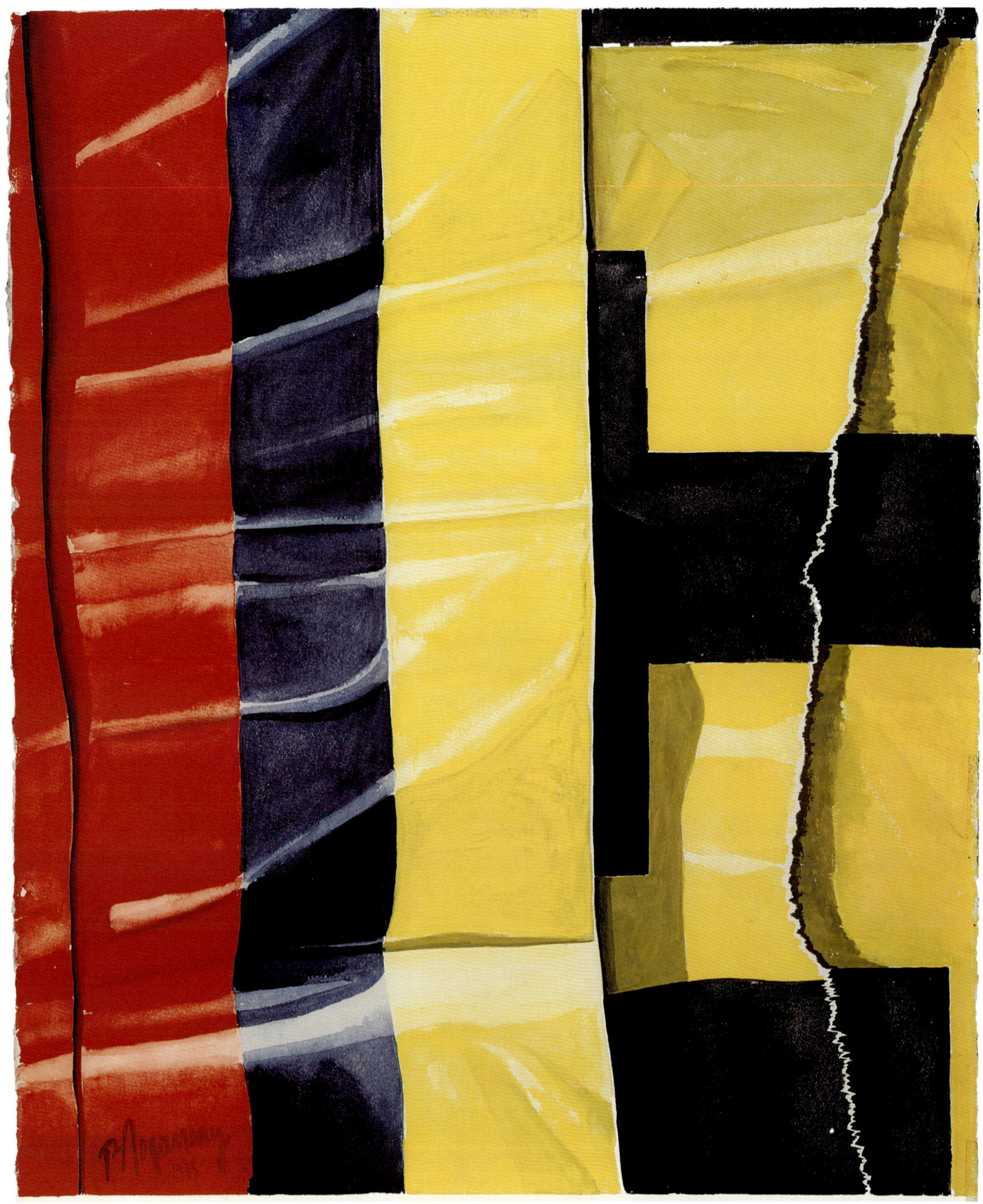

White Wrinkles, 1973. Gouache on paper, 26½ × 22 in. (67.3 × 55.9 cm). Collection of the artist

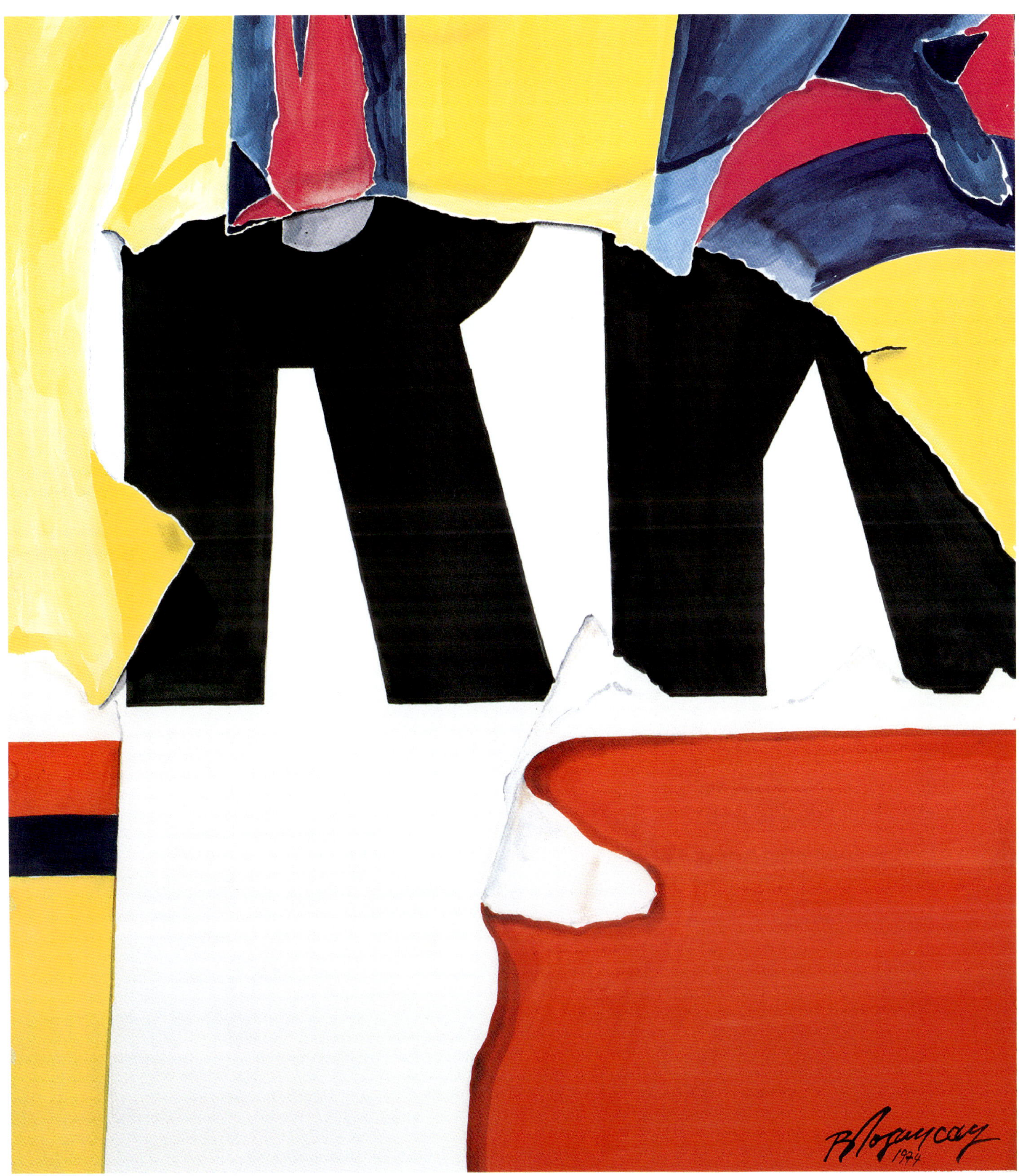

Ark, 1974. Gouache on paper, 30 × 22 in. (76.2 × 55.9 cm). Collection of the artist

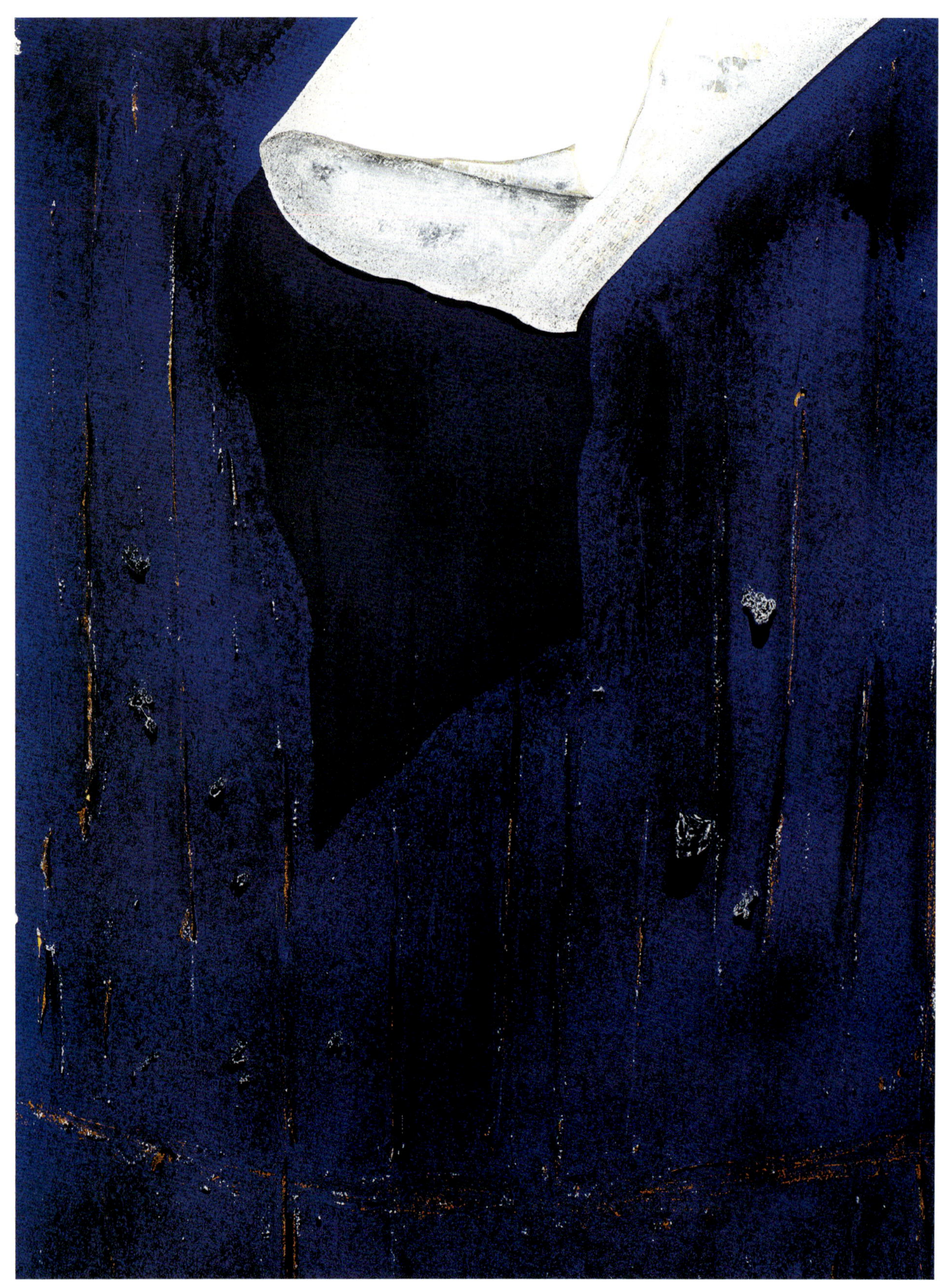

A Piece of Paper, 1974. Gouache on paper, 30 × 22 in. (76.2 × 55.9 cm). Collection of the artist

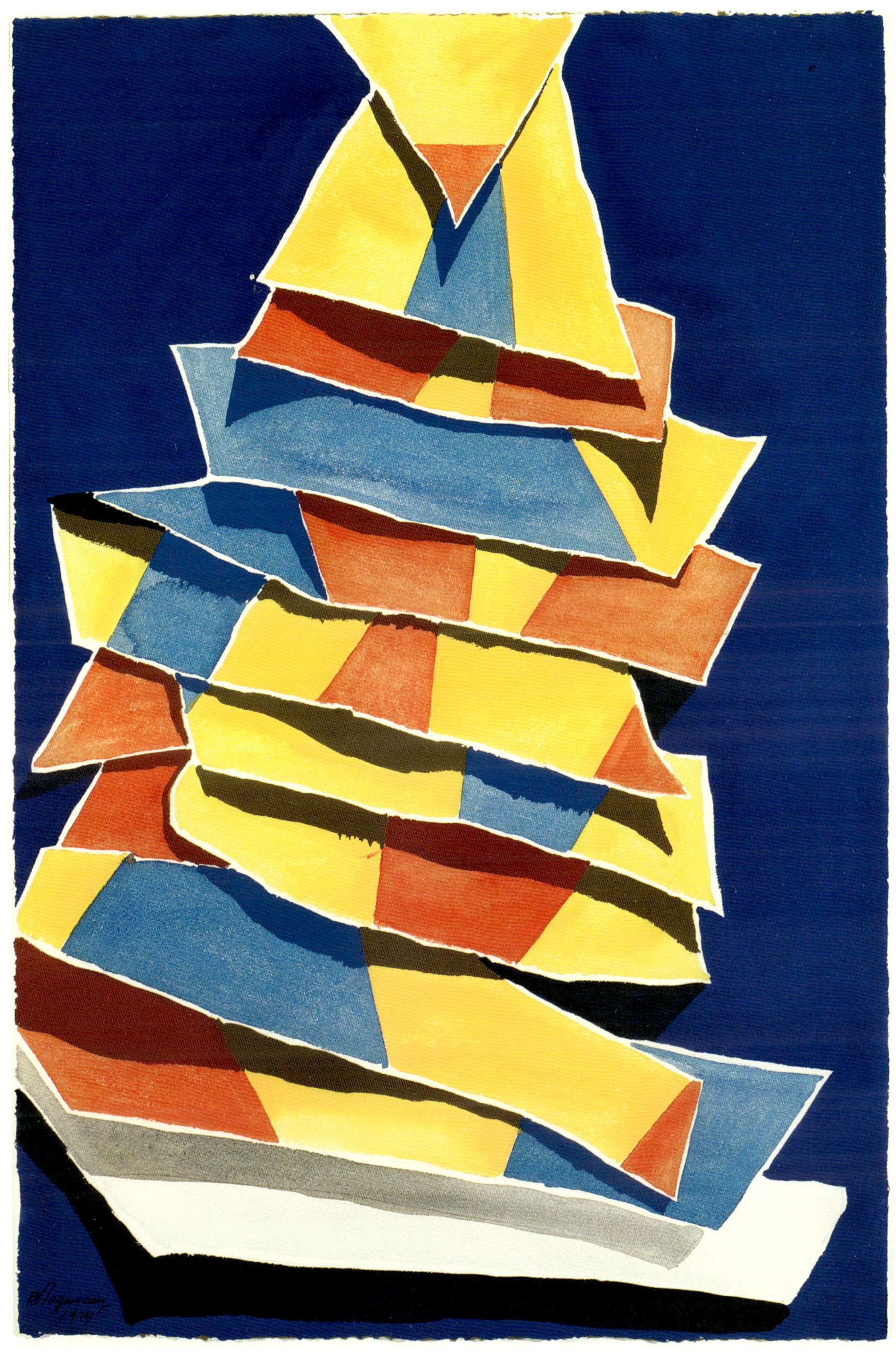

Up Wind, 1974. Gouache on paper, 22 × 15 in. (55.9 × 38.1 cm). The Solomon R. Guggenheim Museum, New York

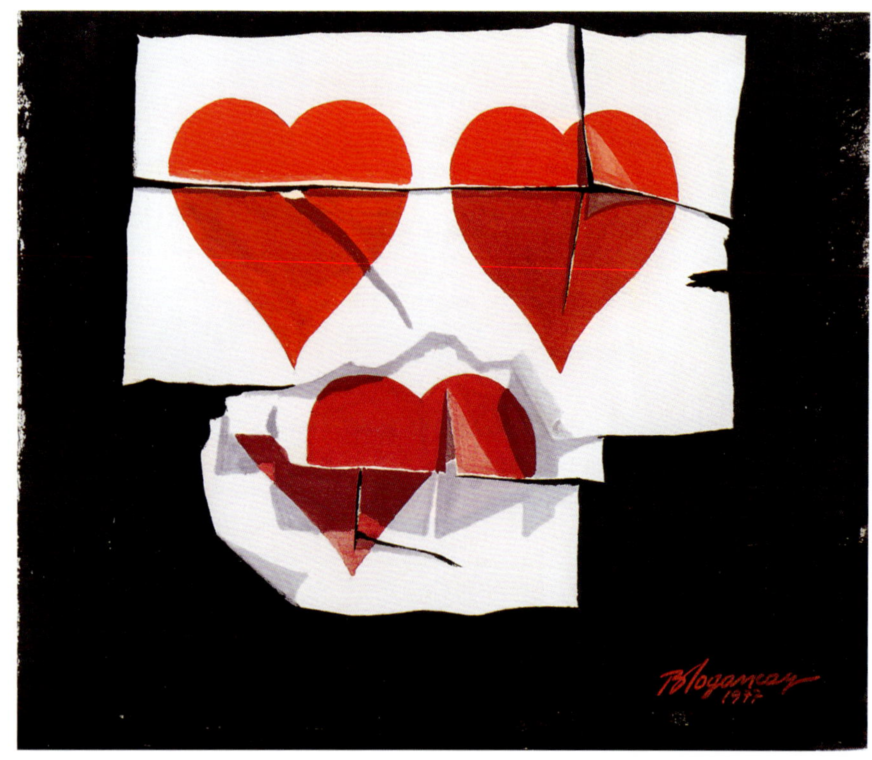

Three Break-ups, 1977. Gouache on paper, 10½ × 11 in. (26.7 × 27.9 cm).
Collection of the artist

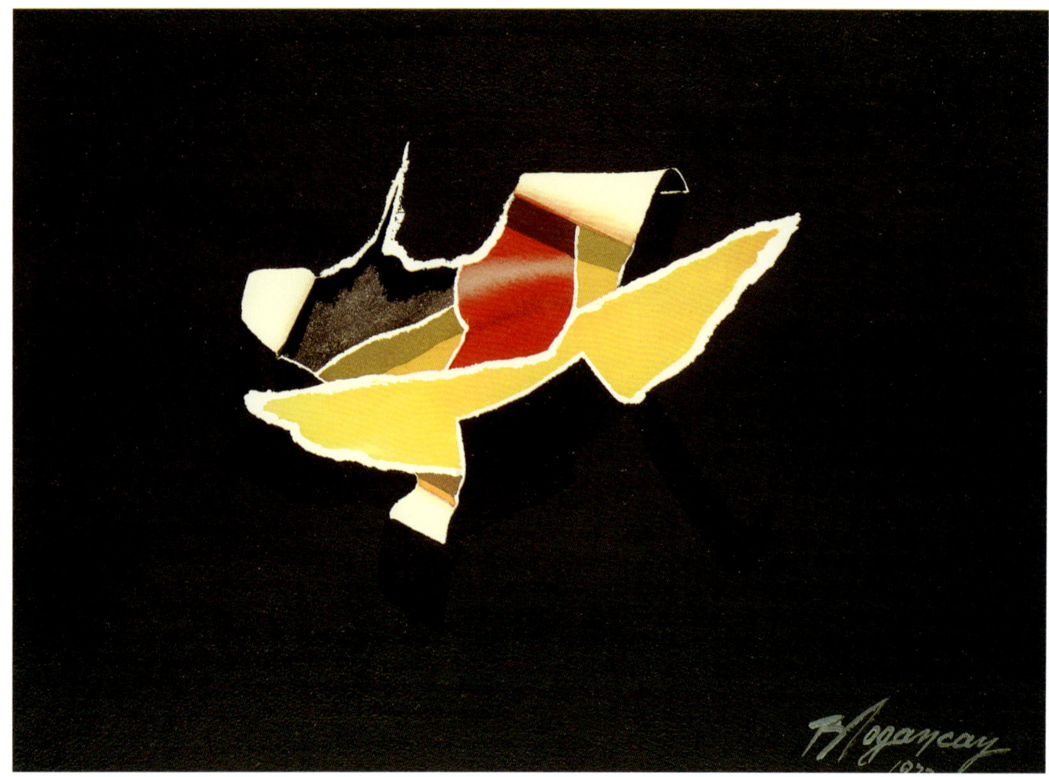

Untitled, 1977. Gouache on paper, 11¼ × 15 in. (28.6 × 38.1 cm). The Solomon R. Guggenheim Museum,
New York

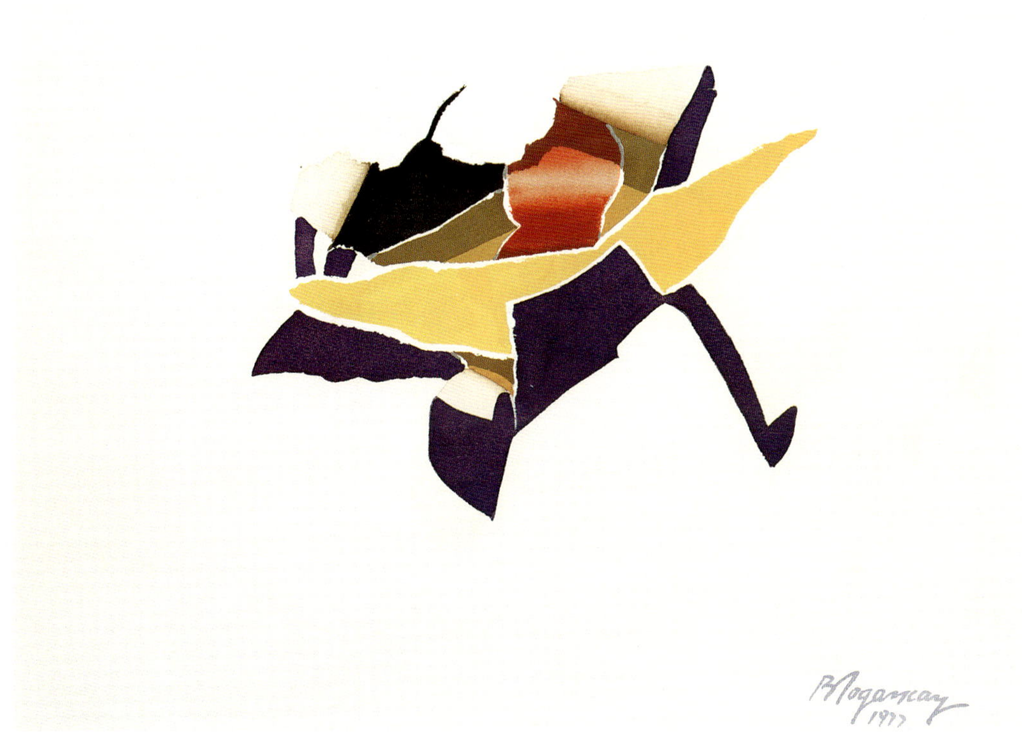

Untitled, 1977. Gouache on paper, 11¼ × 15 in. (28.6 × 38.1 cm). The Solomon R. Guggenheim Museum, New York

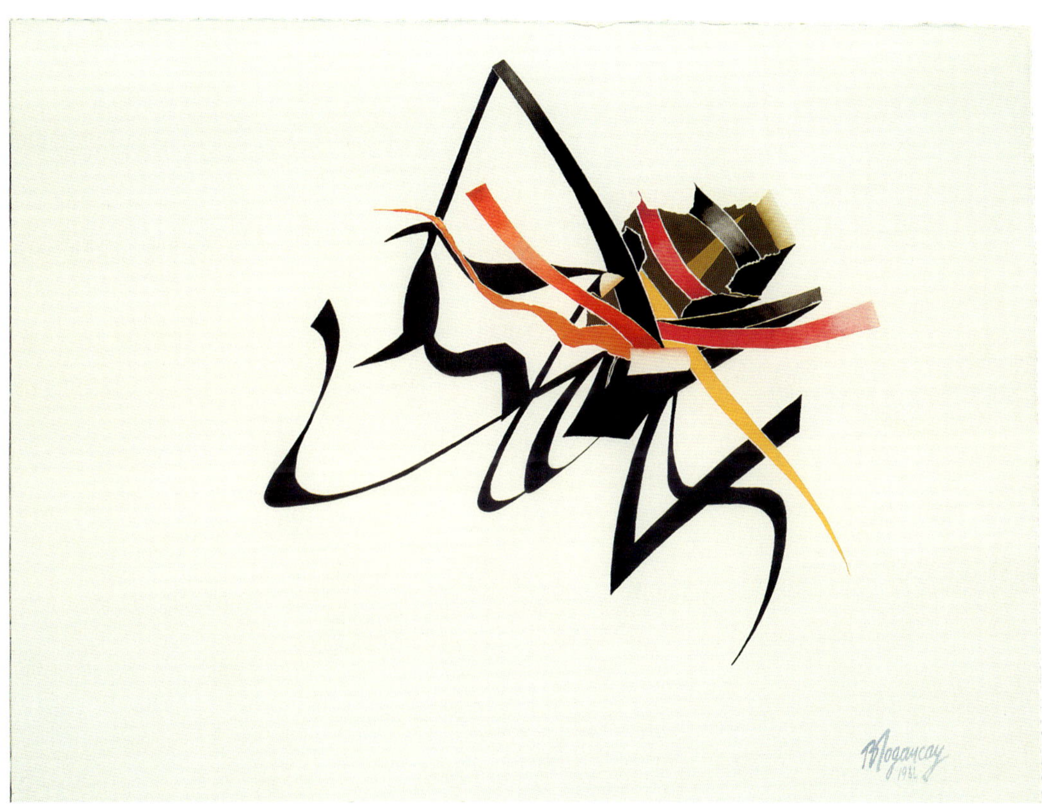

Spiderweb, 1982. Gouache on paper, 22 × 30 in. (55.9 × 76.2 cm). Private collection, Dusseldorf

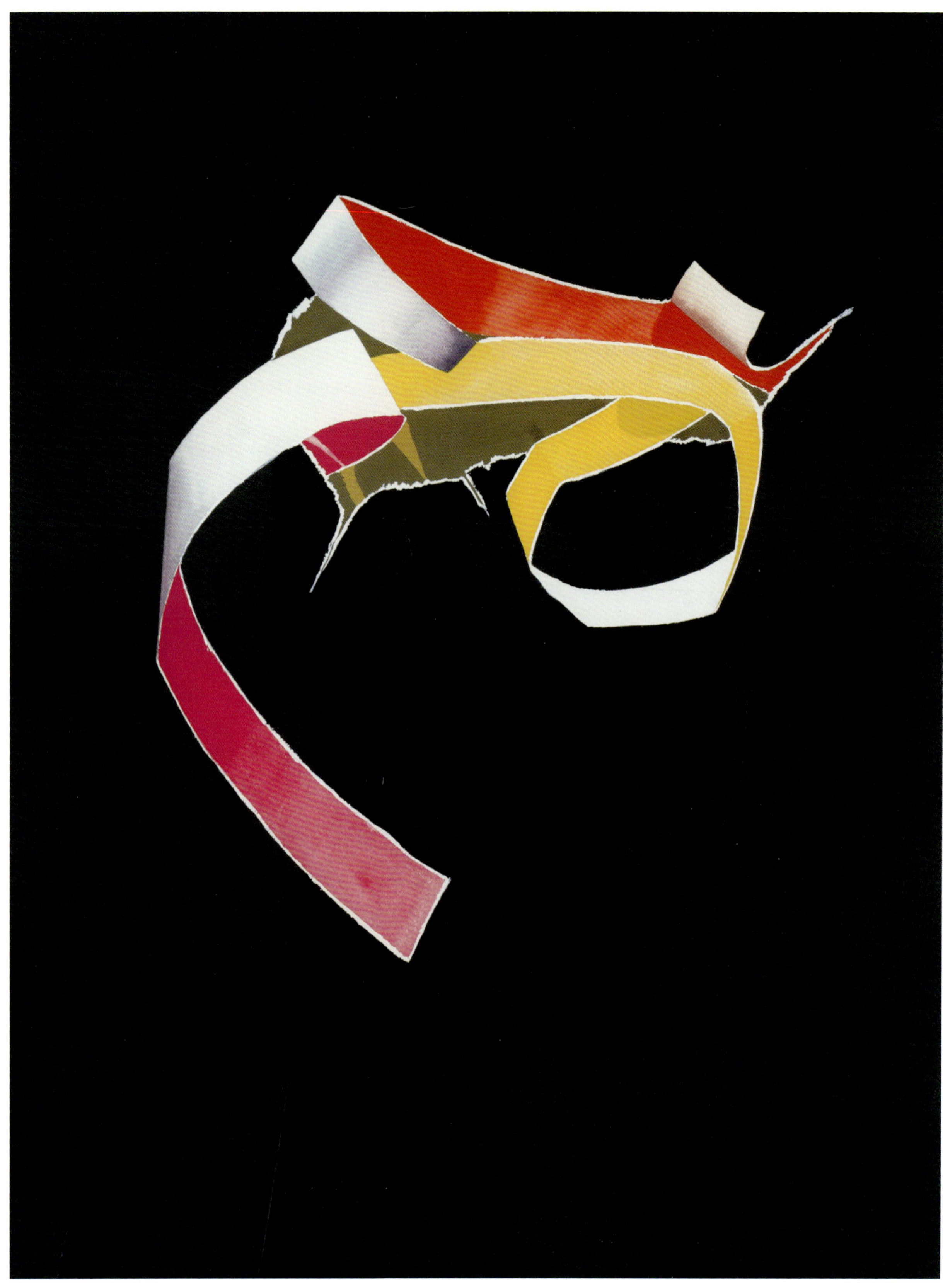

Pirouette, 1983. Gouache on paper, 30 × 22 in. (76.2 × 55.9 cm). Private collection, New York

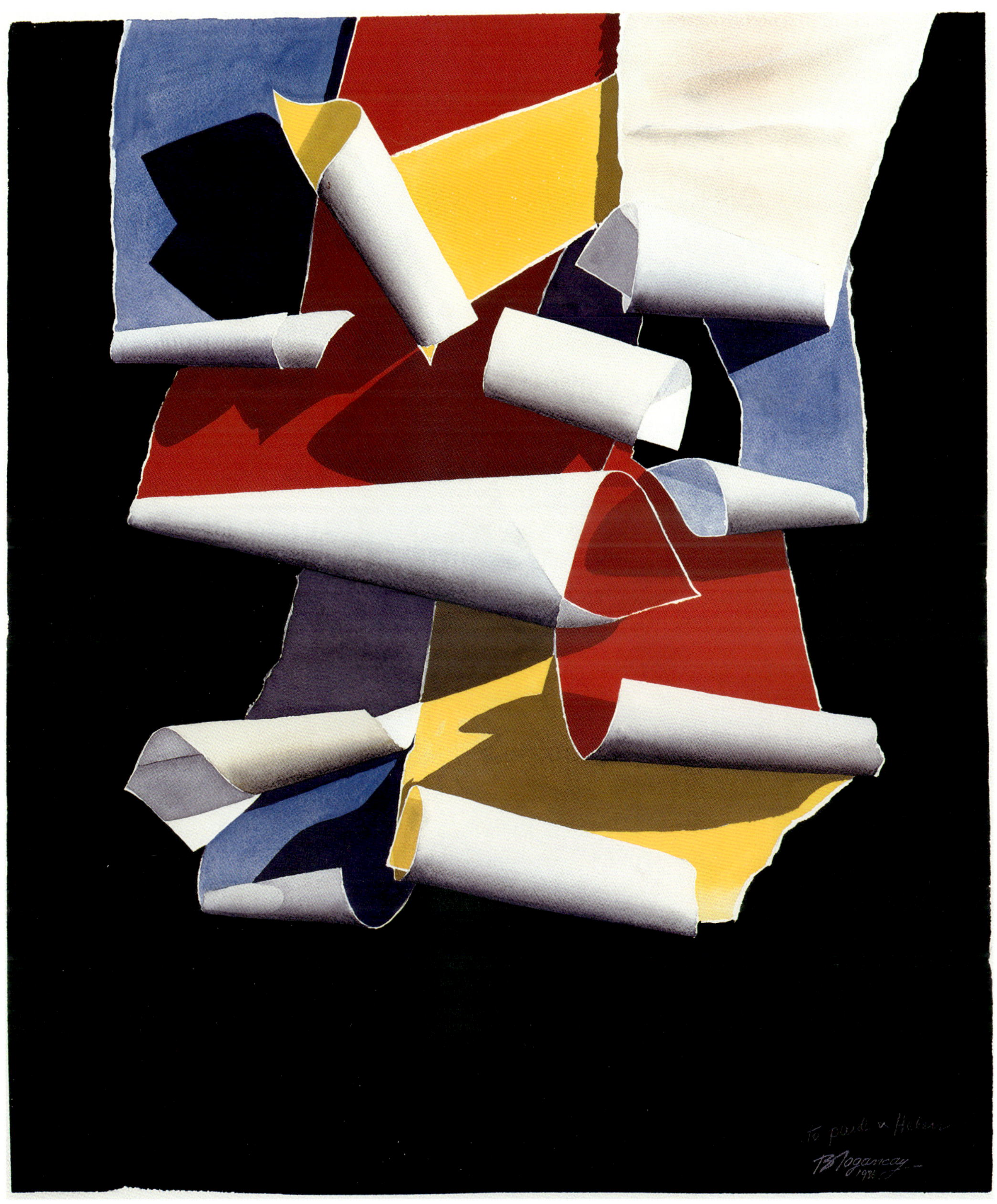

Sailing on the Hudson, 1986. Gouache on paper, 24½ × 20 in. (62.2 × 50.8 cm). Collection Helen and Paul Anbinder, New York

III

Fumages

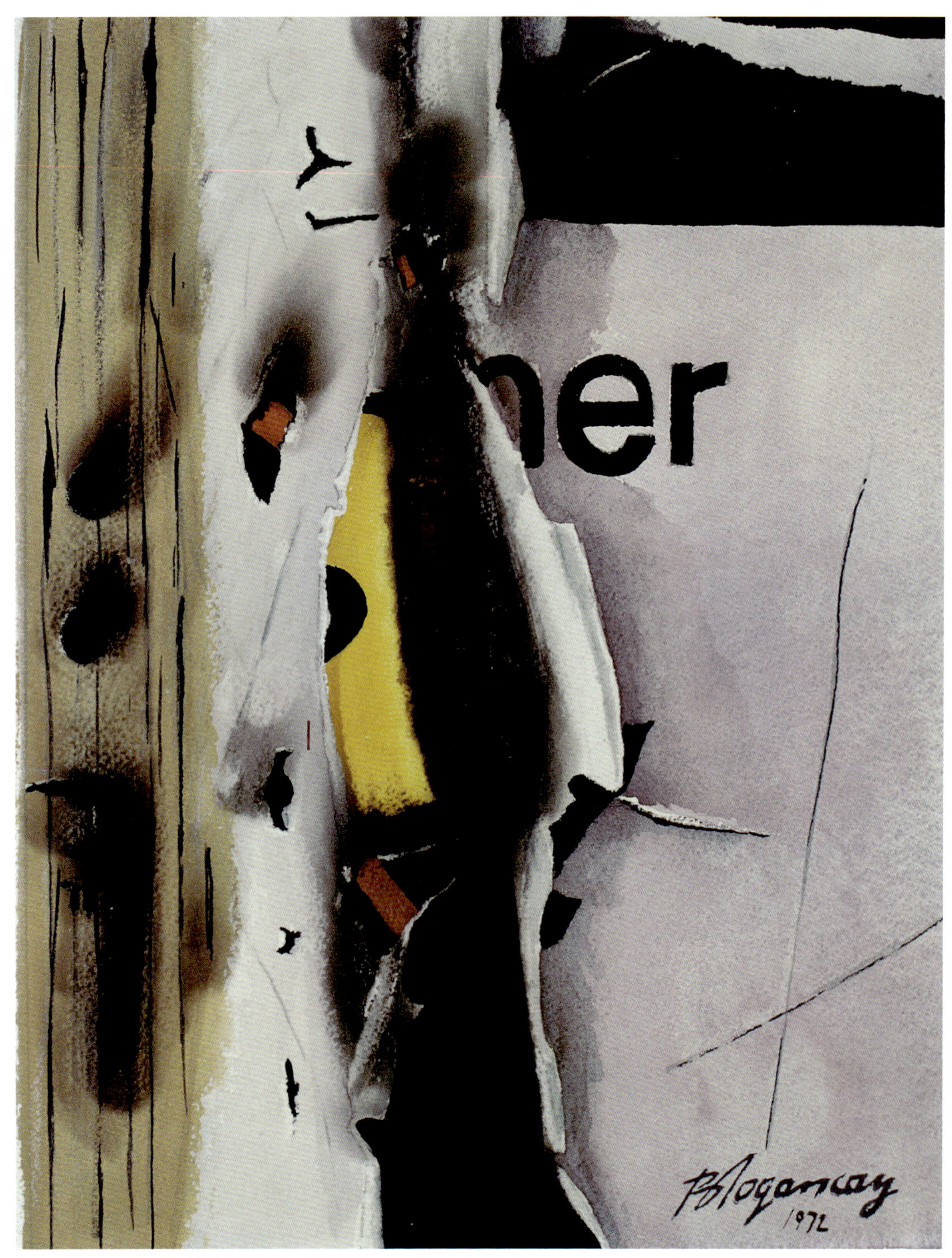

Corner, 1972. Fumage on paper, 15 × 12 in. (38.1 × 30.5 cm). Collection of the artist

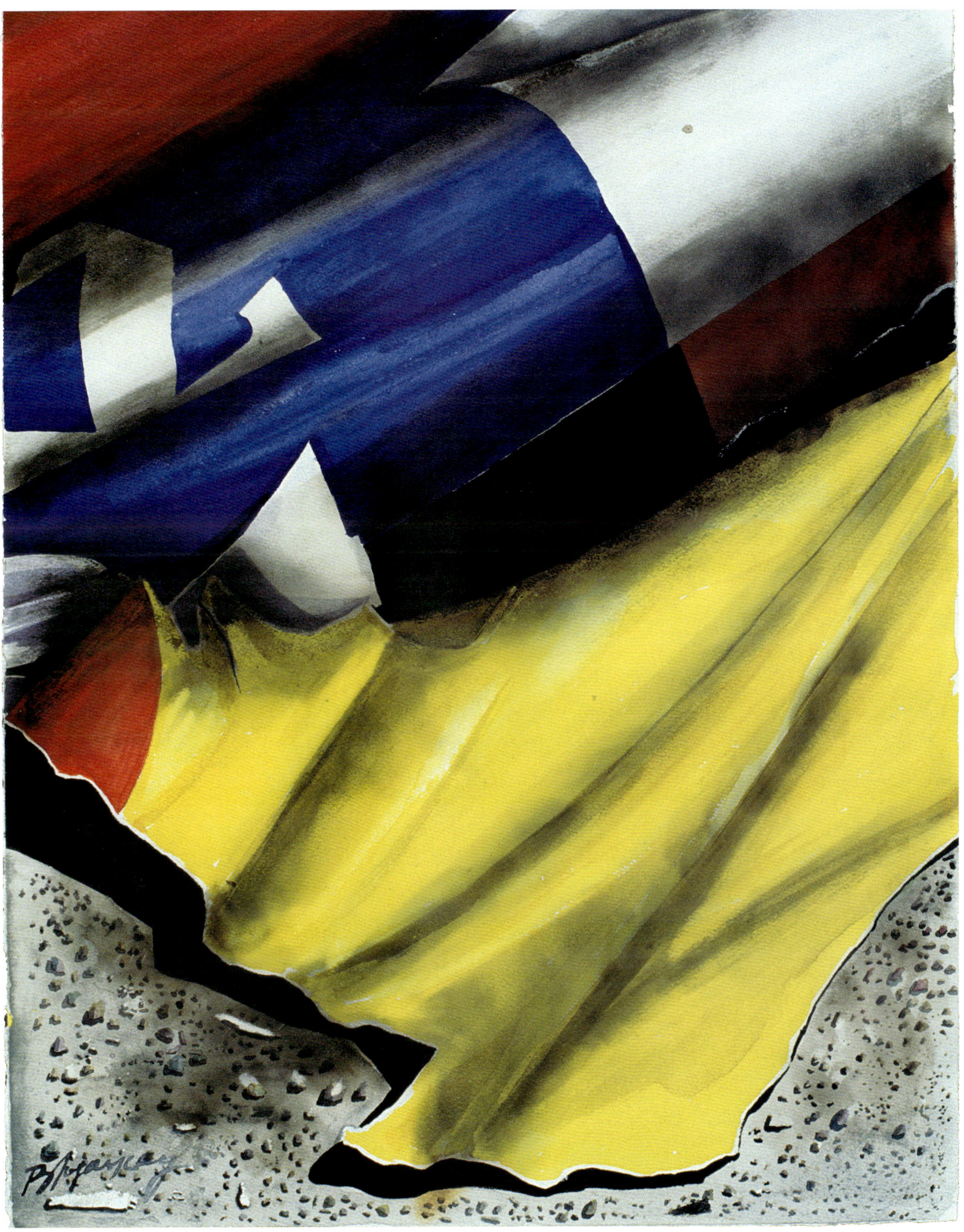

Like Pebbles on the Sand, 1972. Fumage on paper, 19 × 15 in. (48.3 × 38.1 cm). Collection of the artist

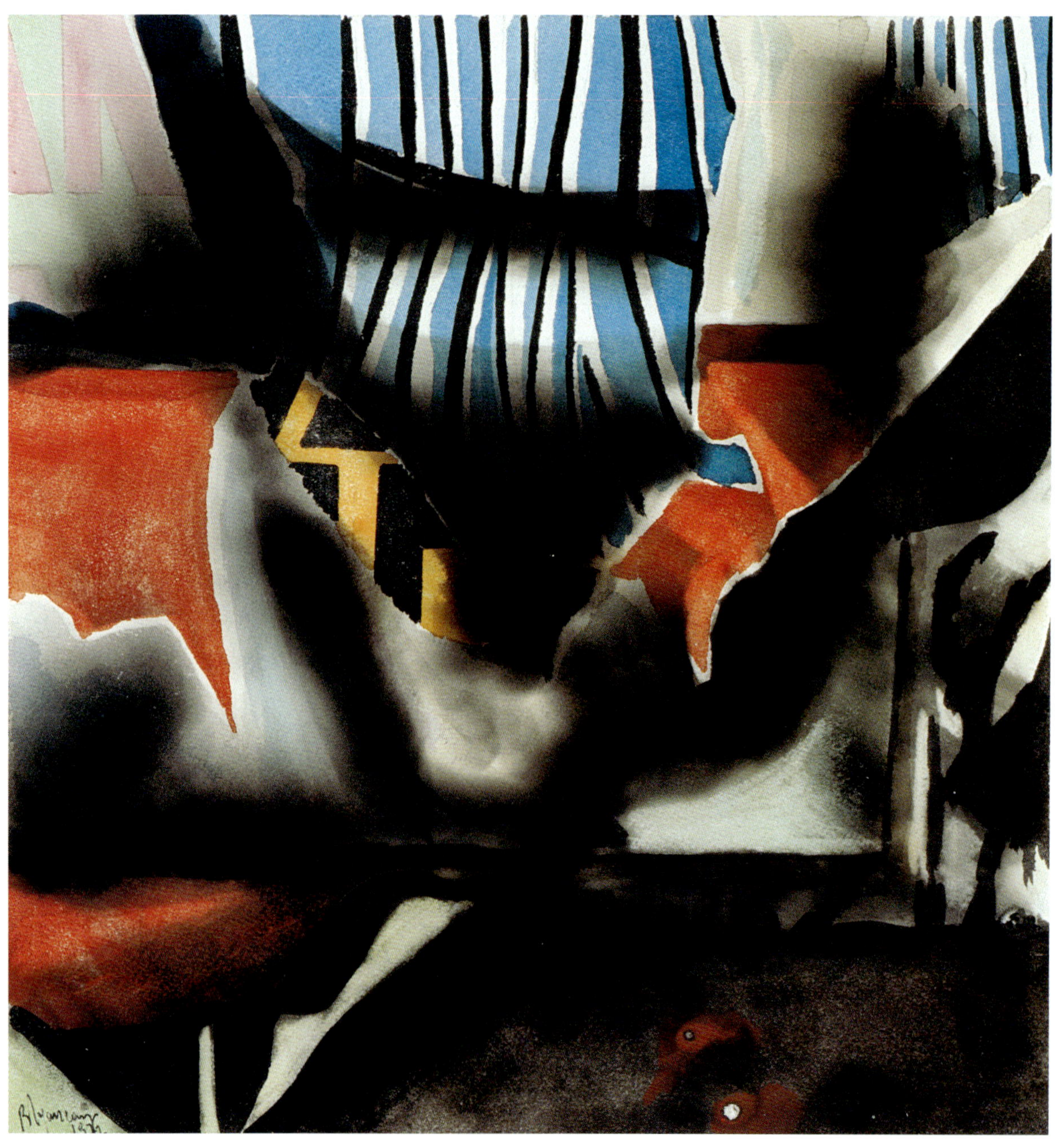

Smoke All Over, 1972. Fumage on paper, 11¾ × 11¼ in. (29.8 × 28.6 cm). Collection of the artist

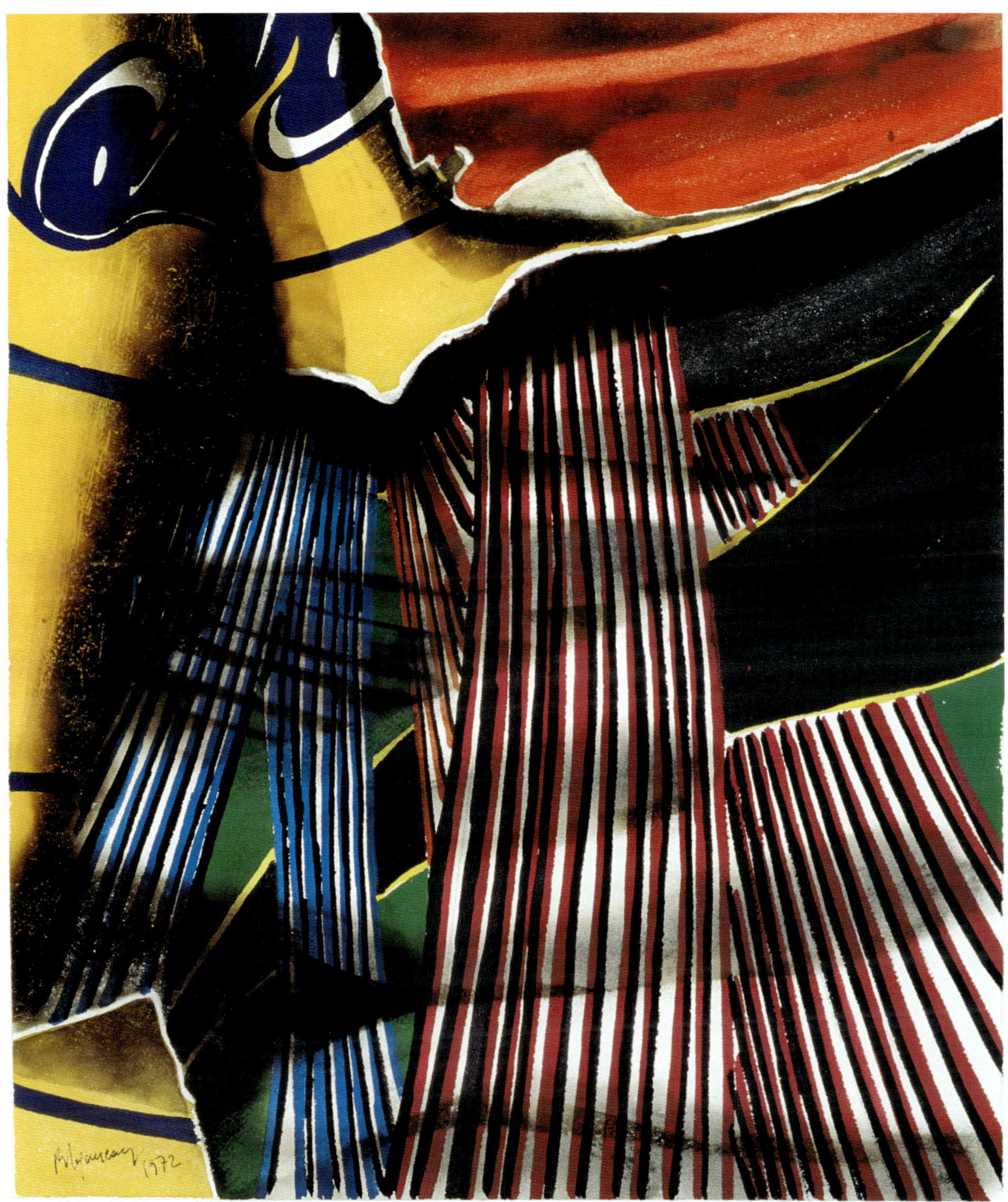

Spying Eyes, 1972. Fumage on paper, 14 × 12 in. (35.6 × 30.5 cm). Collection of the artist

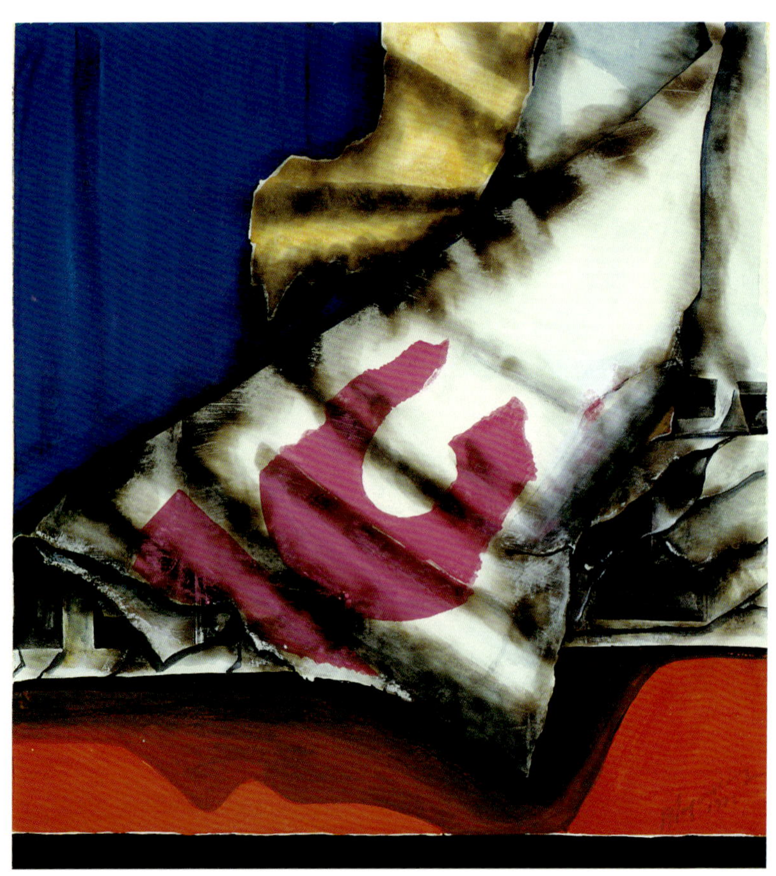

IC as in Terrific, 1972. Fumage on paper, 22 × 20 in. (55.9 × 50.8 cm). Private collection, New York

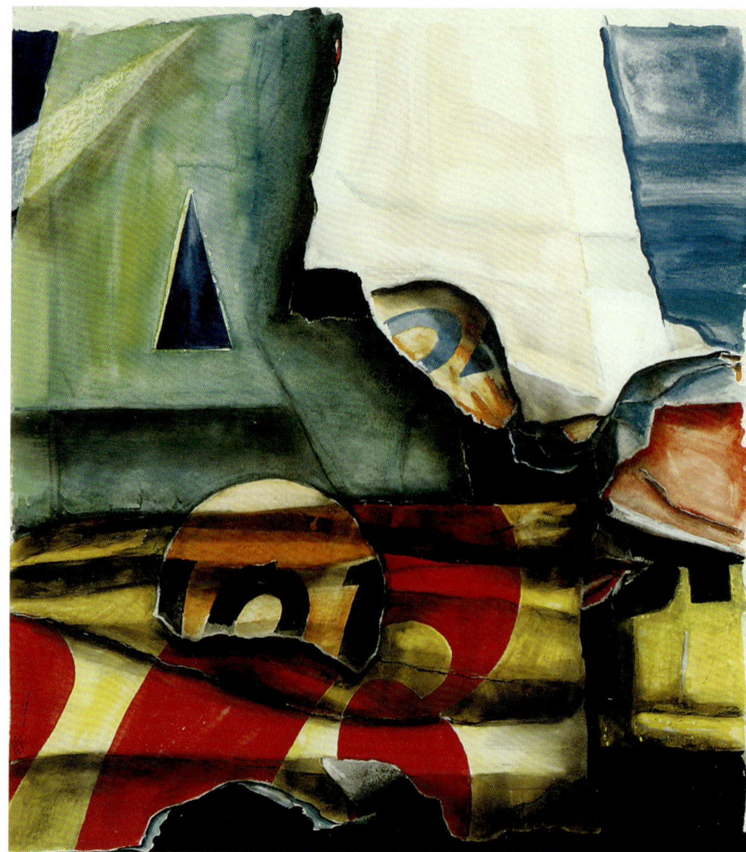

A as in Angel, 1972. Fumage on paper, 23¼ × 20 in. (59.1 × 50.8 cm). Collection of the artist

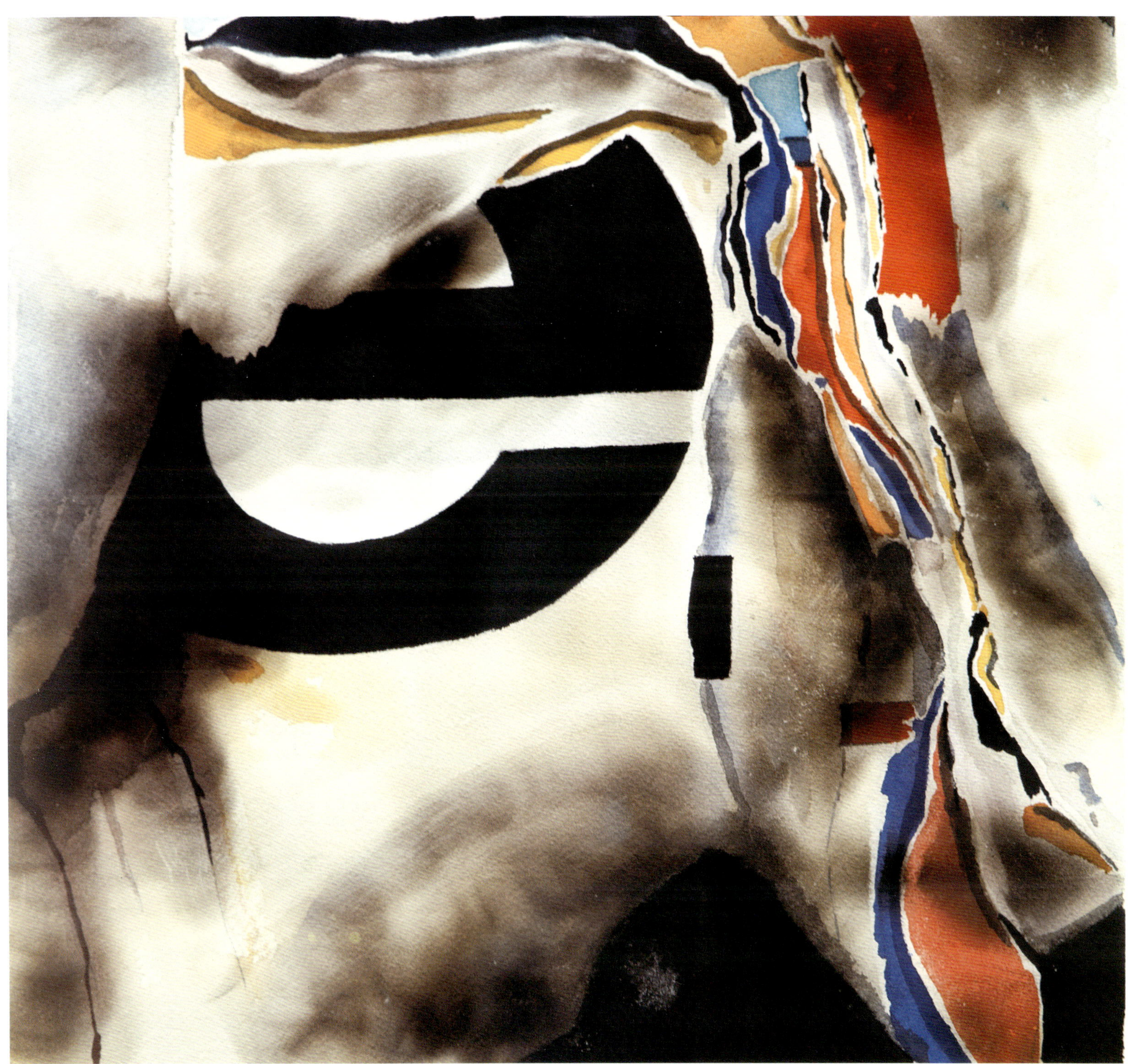

Big Small e, 1973. Fumage on paper, 22 × 28 in. (55.9 × 71.1 cm). Private collection, Istanbul

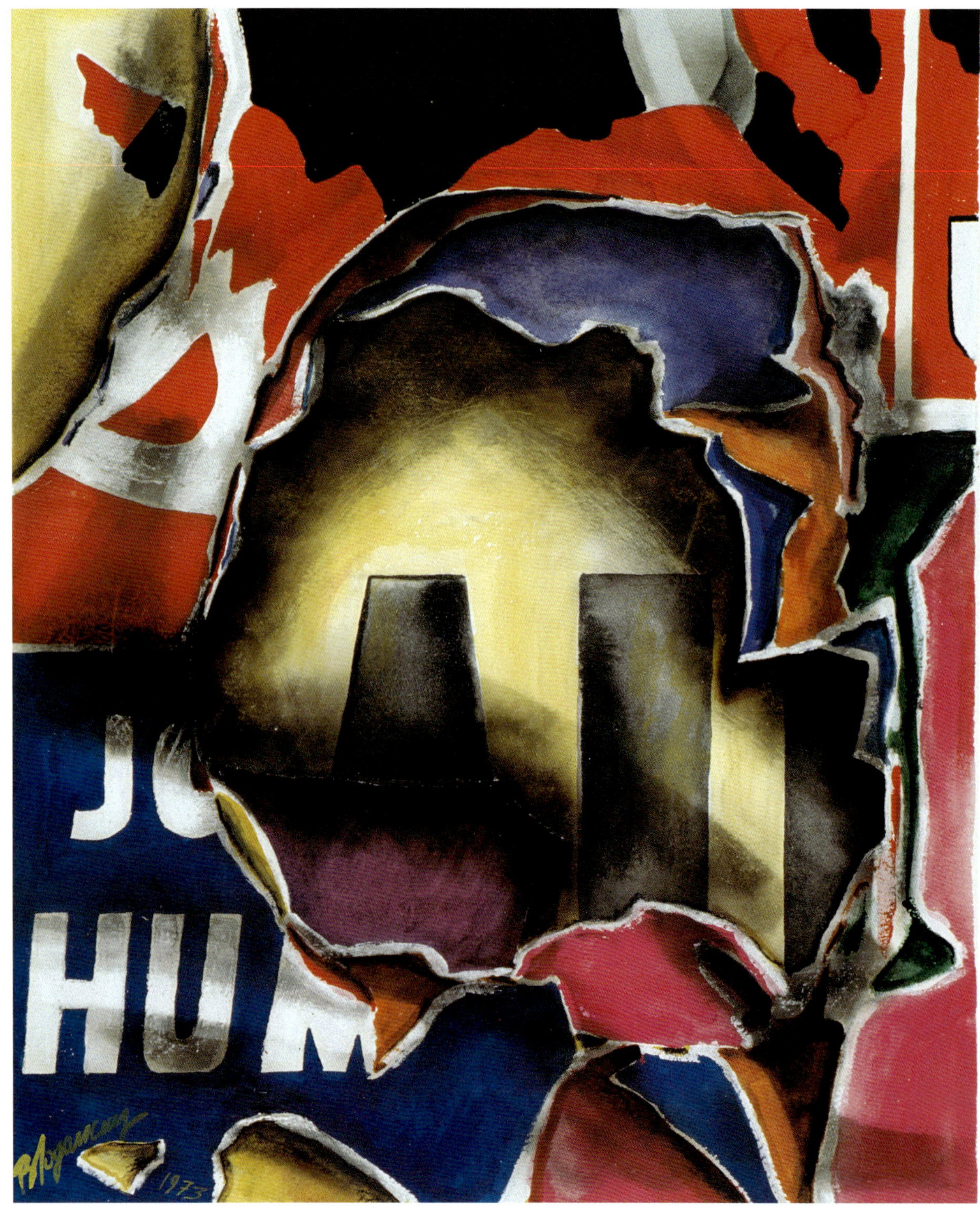

Hum, 1973. Fumage on paper, 16 × 13 in. (40.6 × 33 cm). Collection of the artist

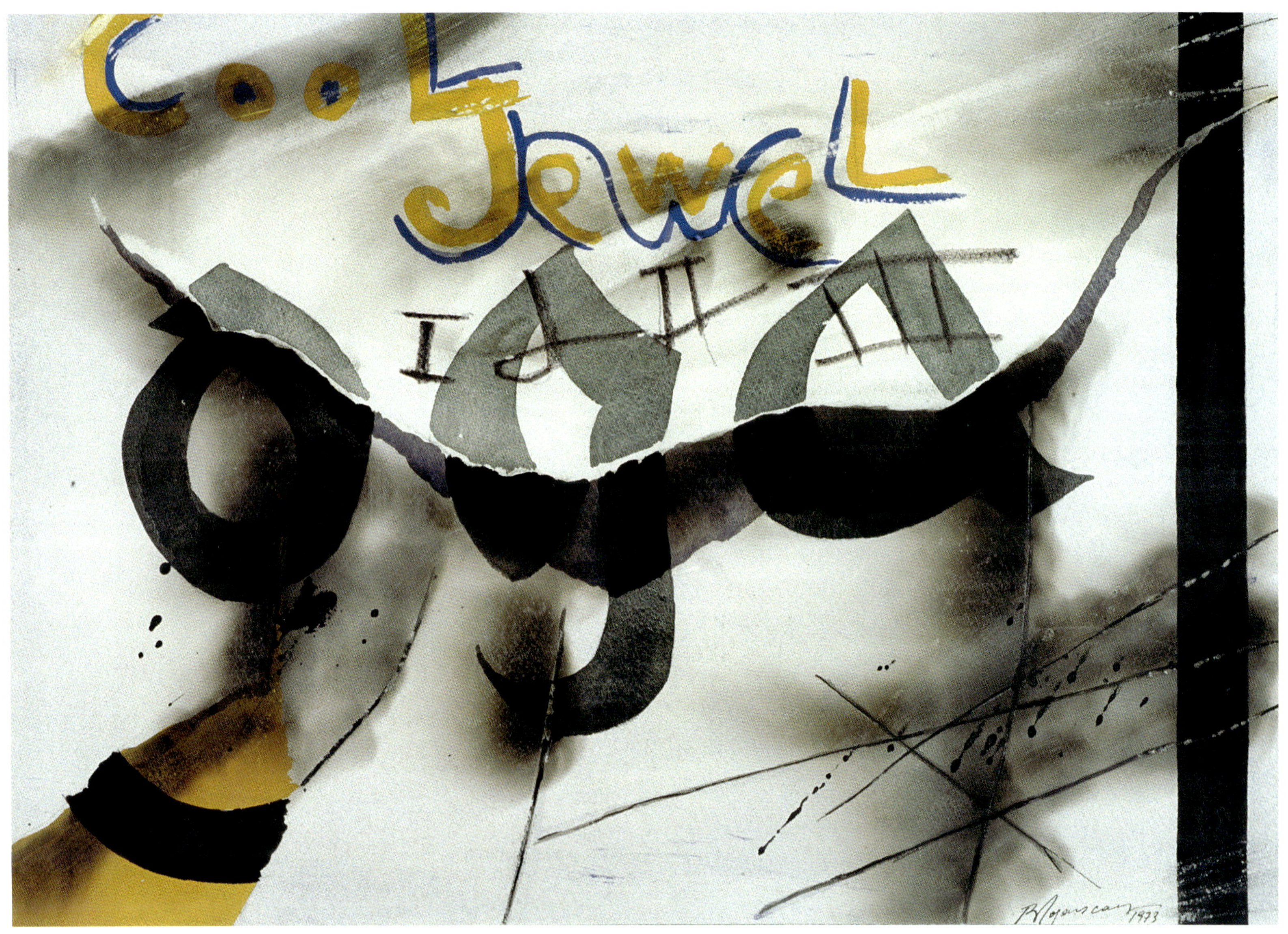

Jewel, 1973. Fumage on paper, 10½ × 15 in. (25.4 × 38.1 cm). Collection of the artist

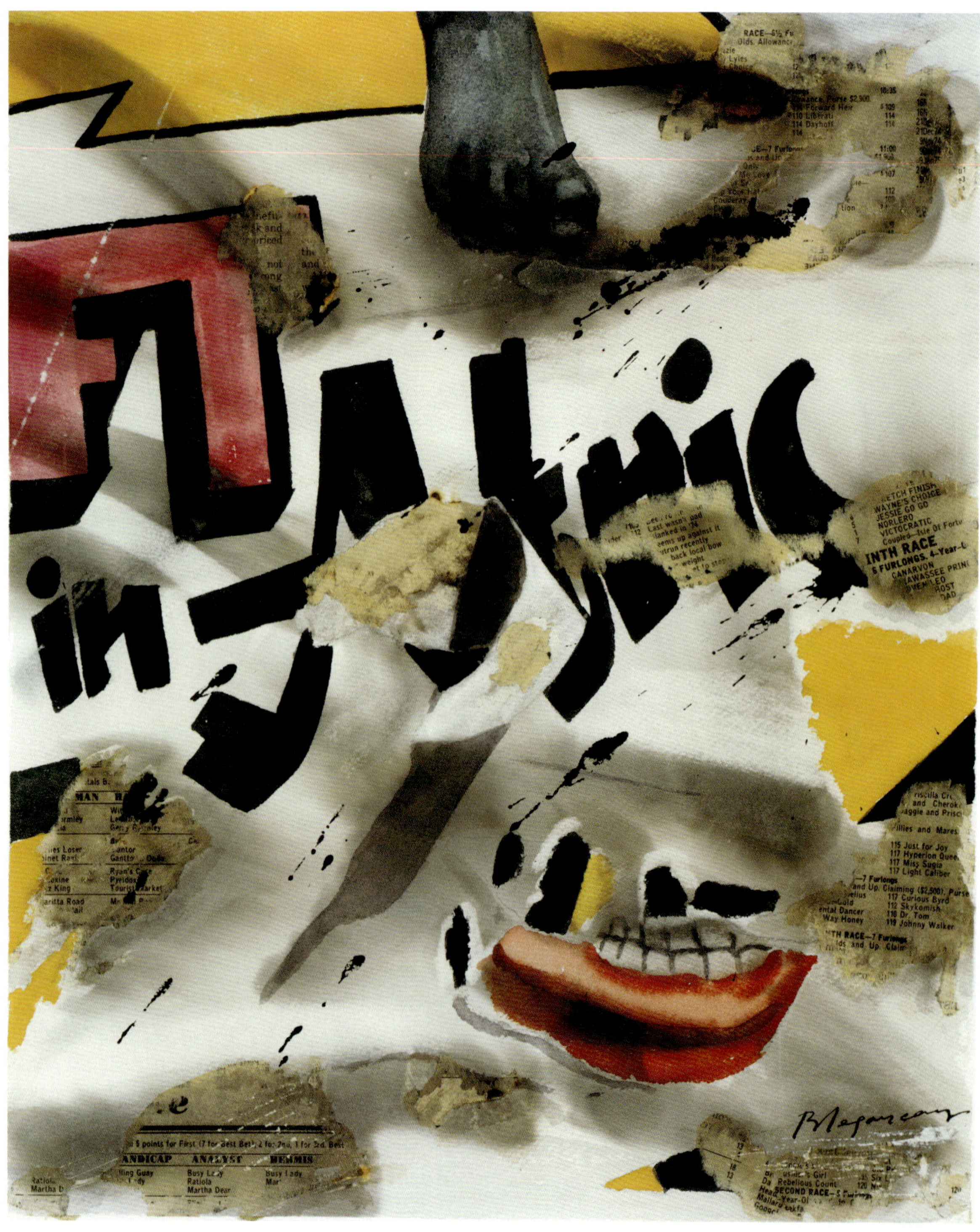

La Grande Bouffe, 1973. Fumage on paper, 13¾ × 11¼ in. (35 × 28.6 cm). Private collection, New York

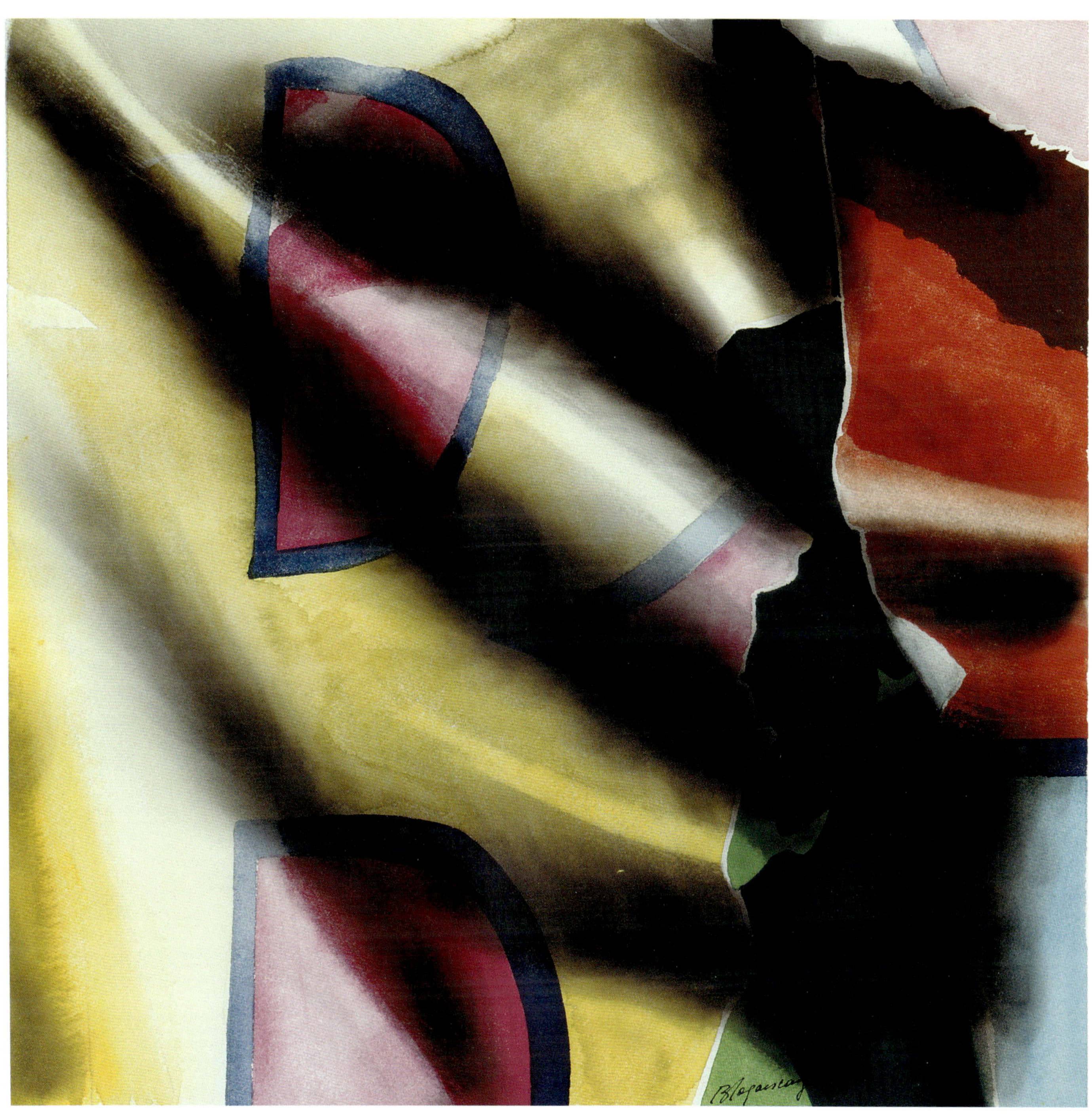

Letter Fragmentation, 1973. Fumage on paper, 11¾ × 11¾ in. (29.8 × 29.8 cm). Private collection

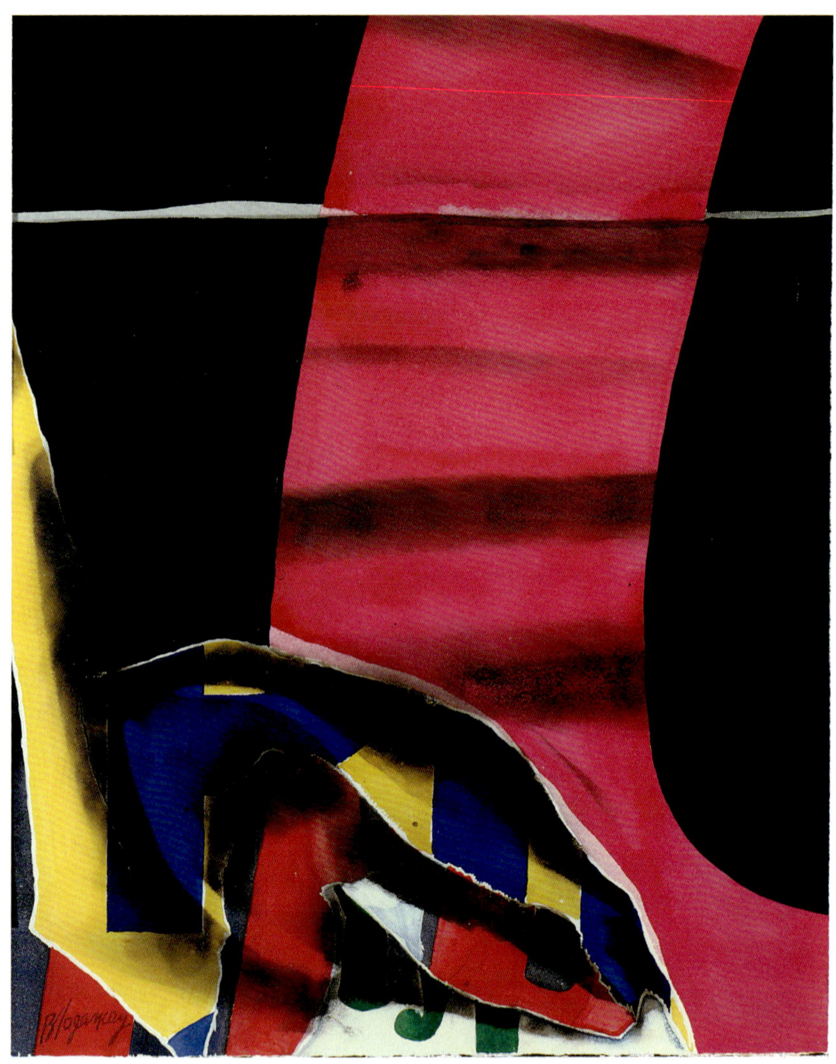

Red Verticality, 1973. Fumage on paper, 47 × 39 in. (119.4 × 99.1 cm).
Collection of the artist

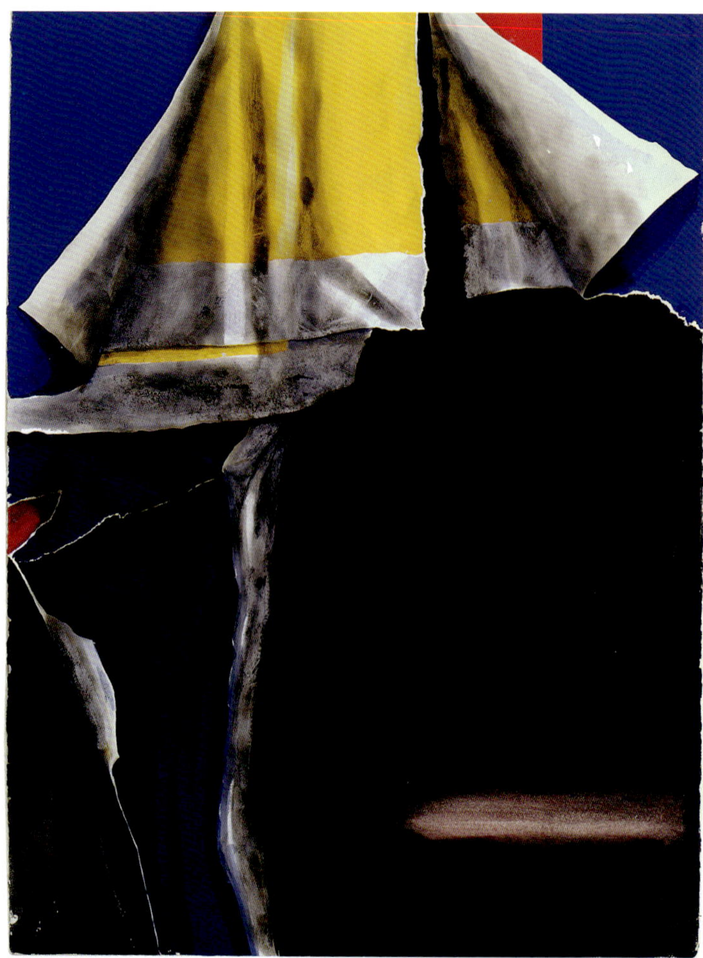

Black Hole, 1973. Fumage on paper, 30 × 22 in. (76.2 × 55.9 cm).
Collection of the artist

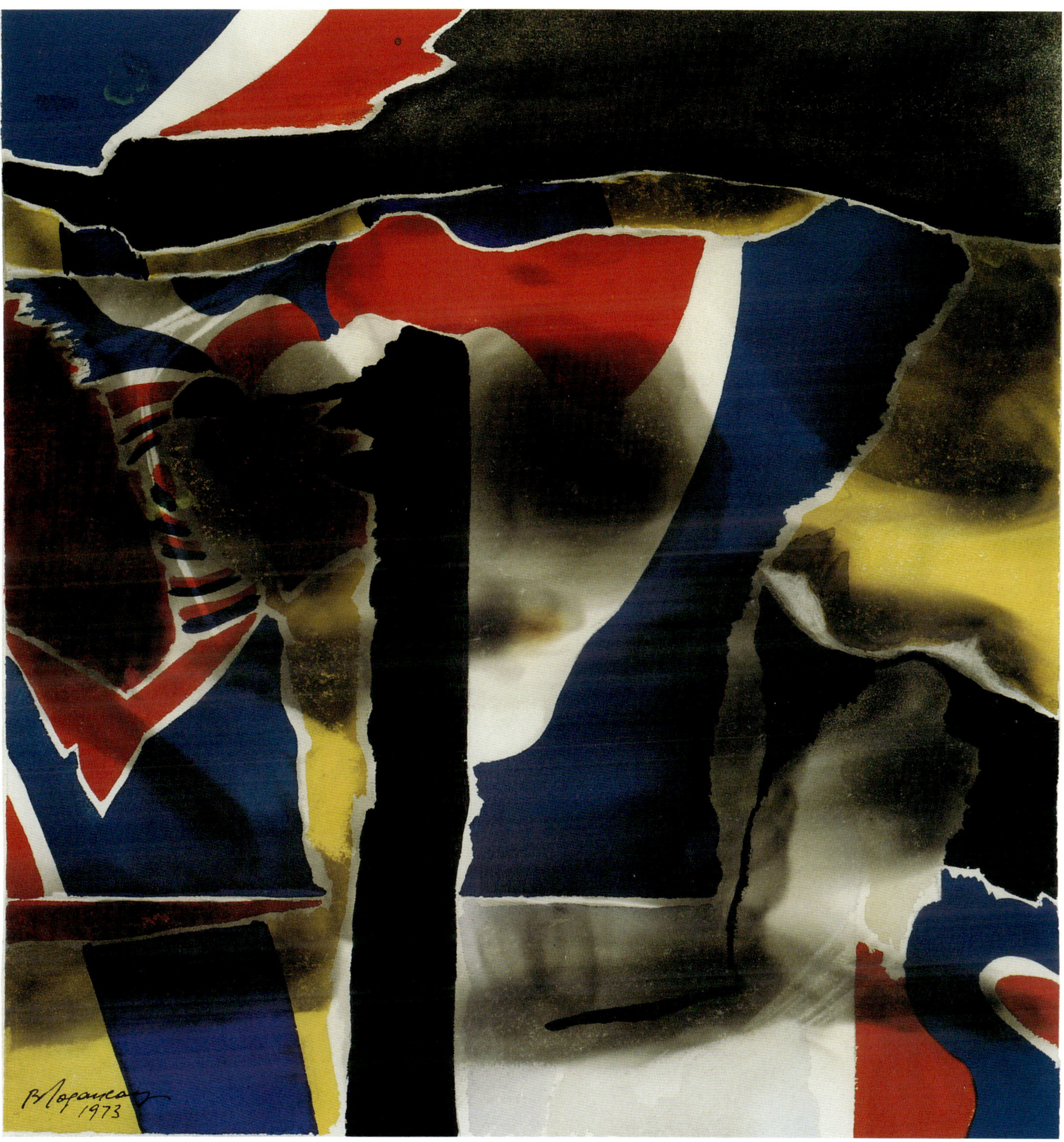

X-Ray in Color, 1973. Fumage on paper, 12 × 11 in. (30.5 × 27.9 cm). Private collection, Düsseldorf

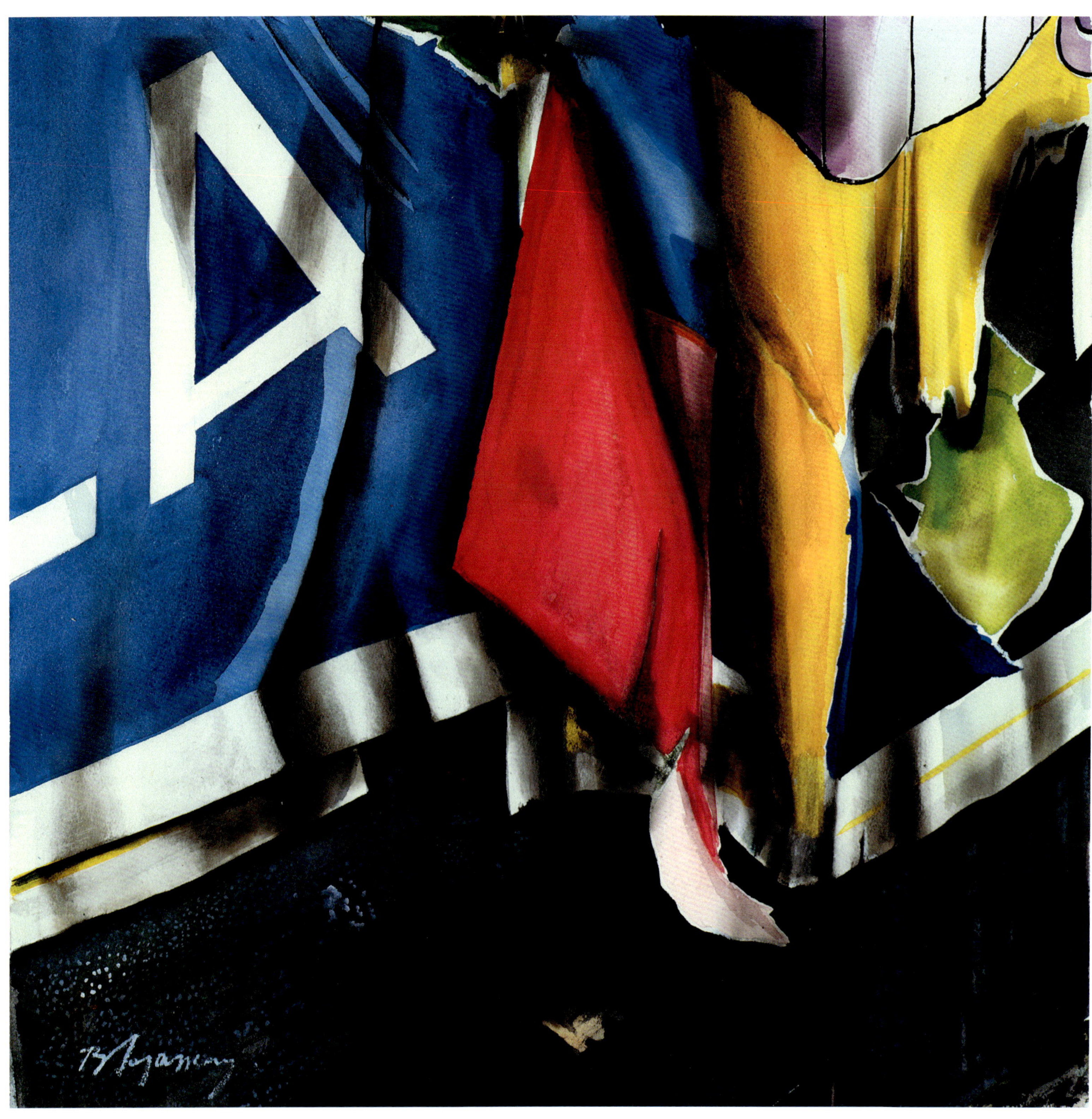

Turning the Corner, 1973. Fumage on paper, 17½ × 17½ in. (44.5 × 44.5 cm). Private collection, Paris

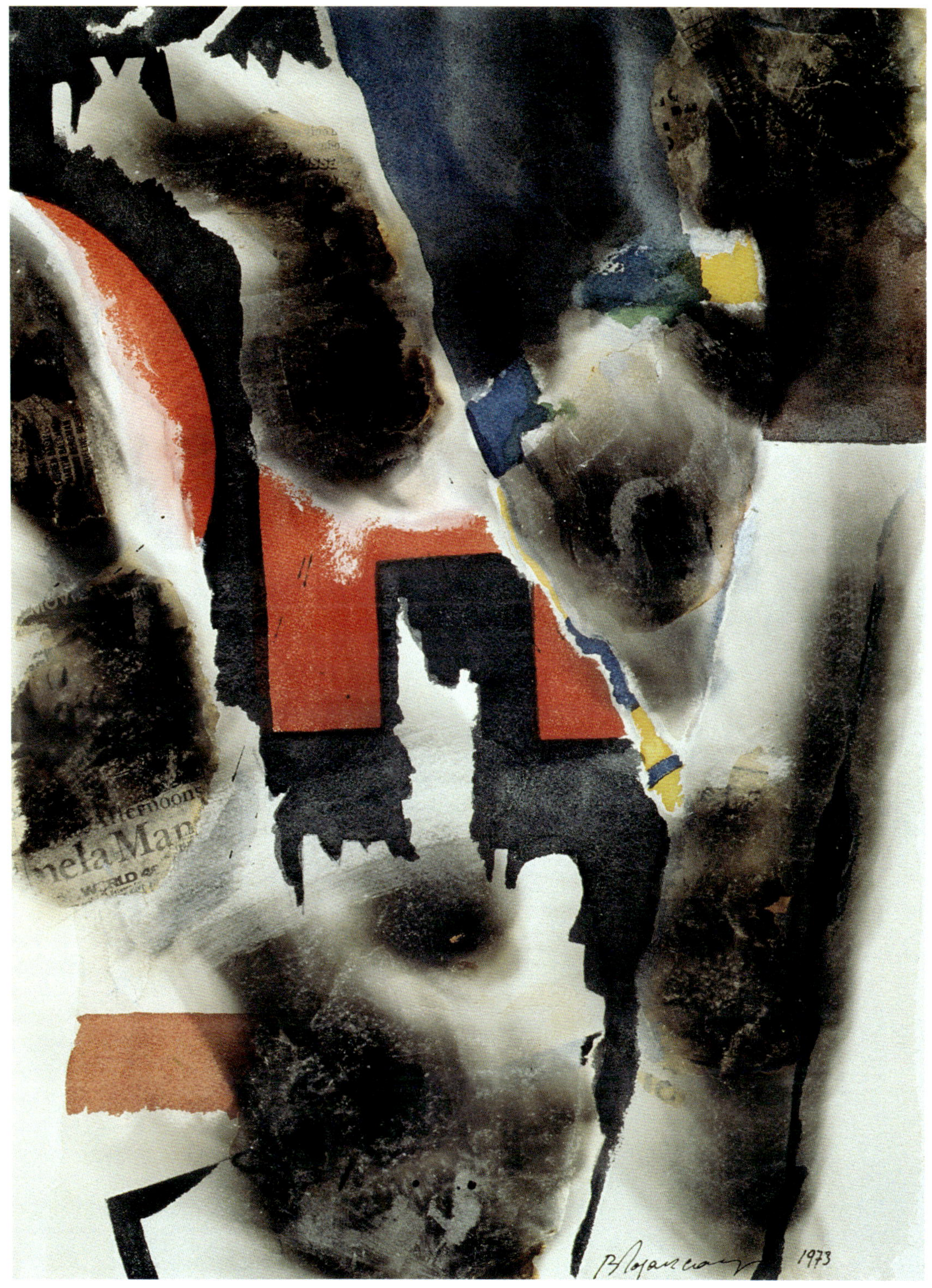

Mela Man, 1973. Fumage on paper, 14 × 10 in. (35.6 × 25.4 cm). Collection of the artist

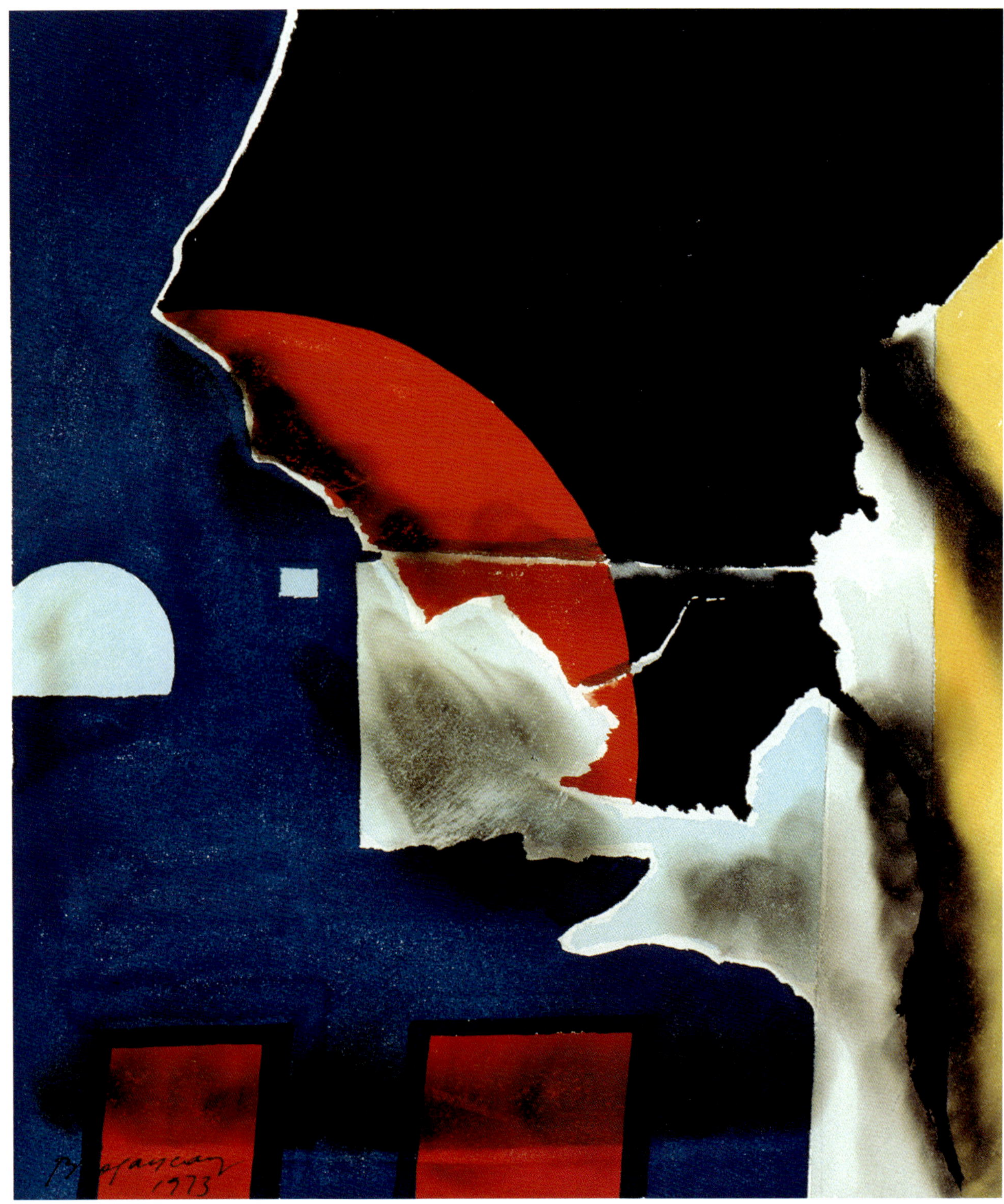

Red Moon, 1973. Fumage on paper, 12¼ × 10½ in. (31.1 × 26.7 cm). Collection of the artist

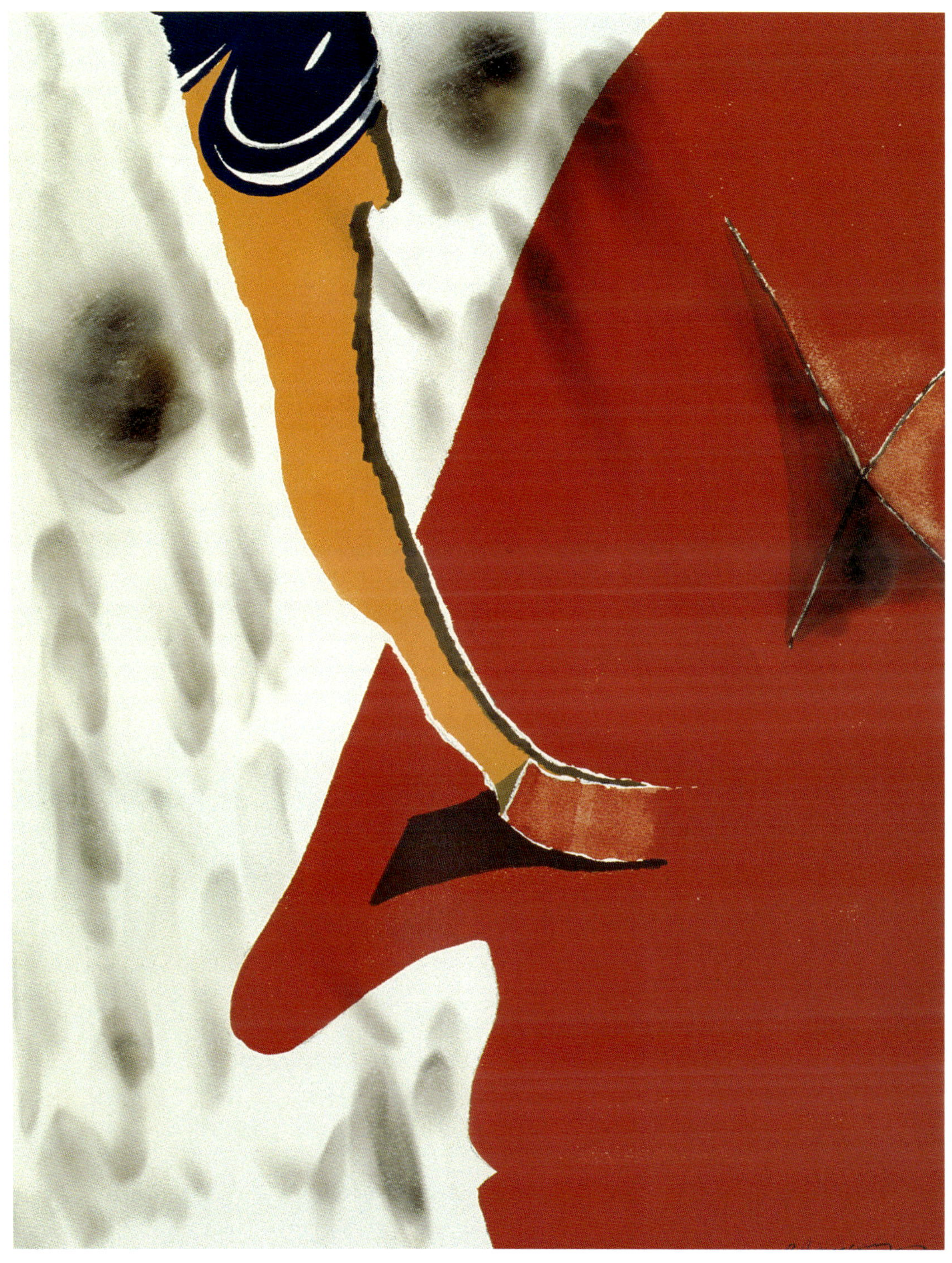

Long Red-Nosed Face, 1973. Fumage on paper, 14½ × 11¼ in. (36.8 × 28.6 cm). Collection of the artist

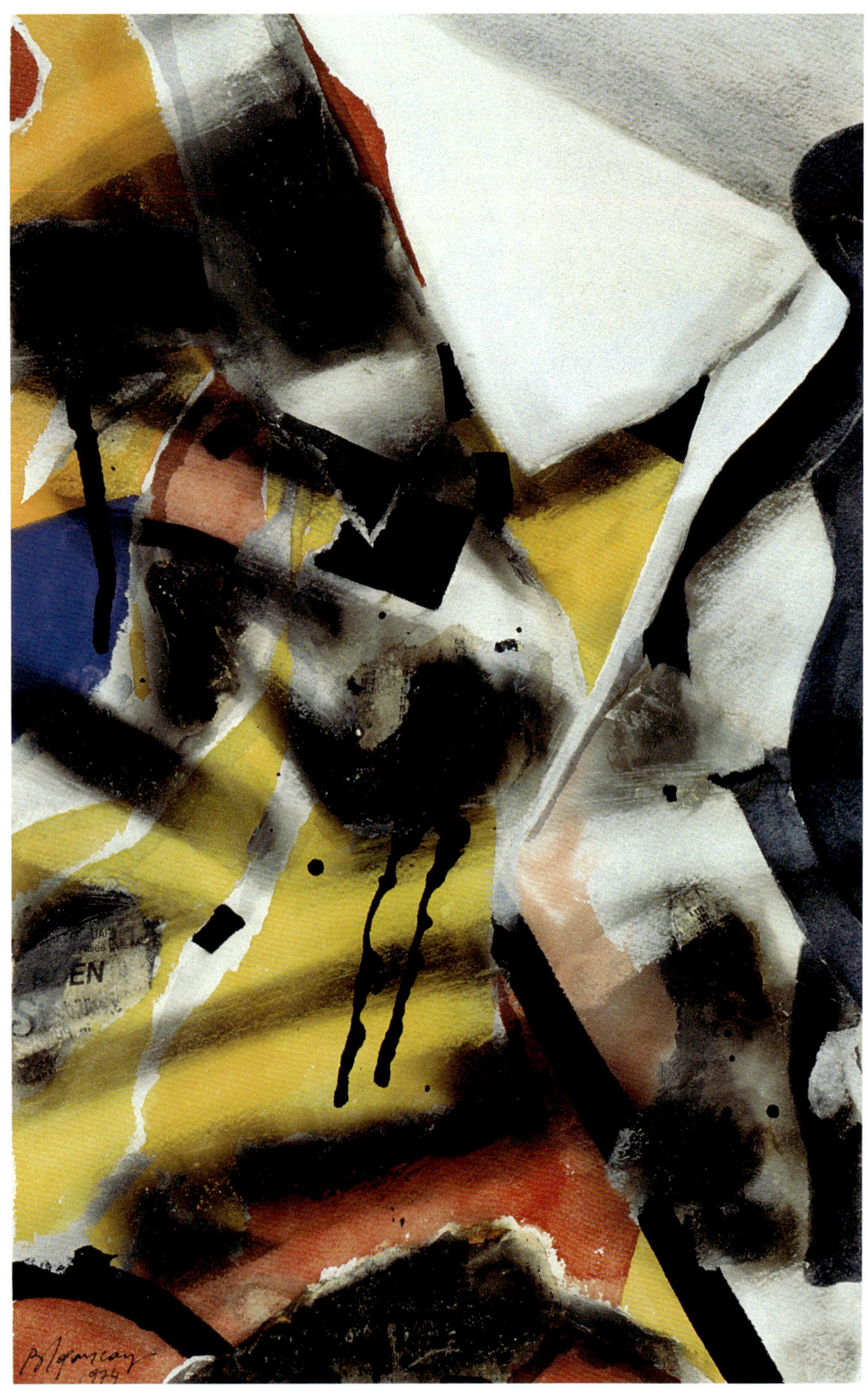

Collapsing Poster, 1974. Fumage on paper, 14½ × 9½ in. (36.8 × 24.1 cm).
Collection of the artist

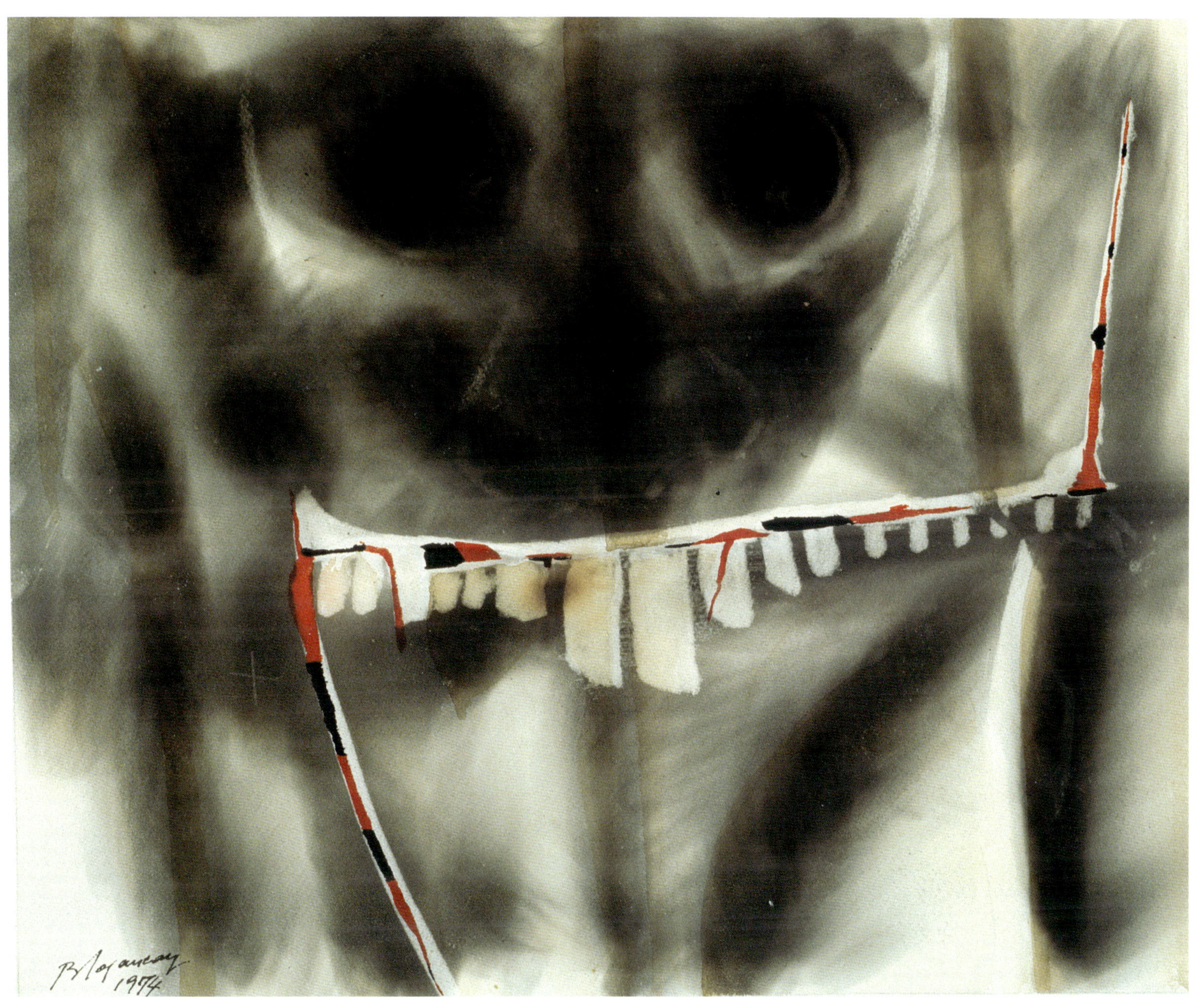

Friendly Ghost, 1974. Fumage on paper, 11¾ × 14 in. (29.8 × 35.6). Collection of the artist

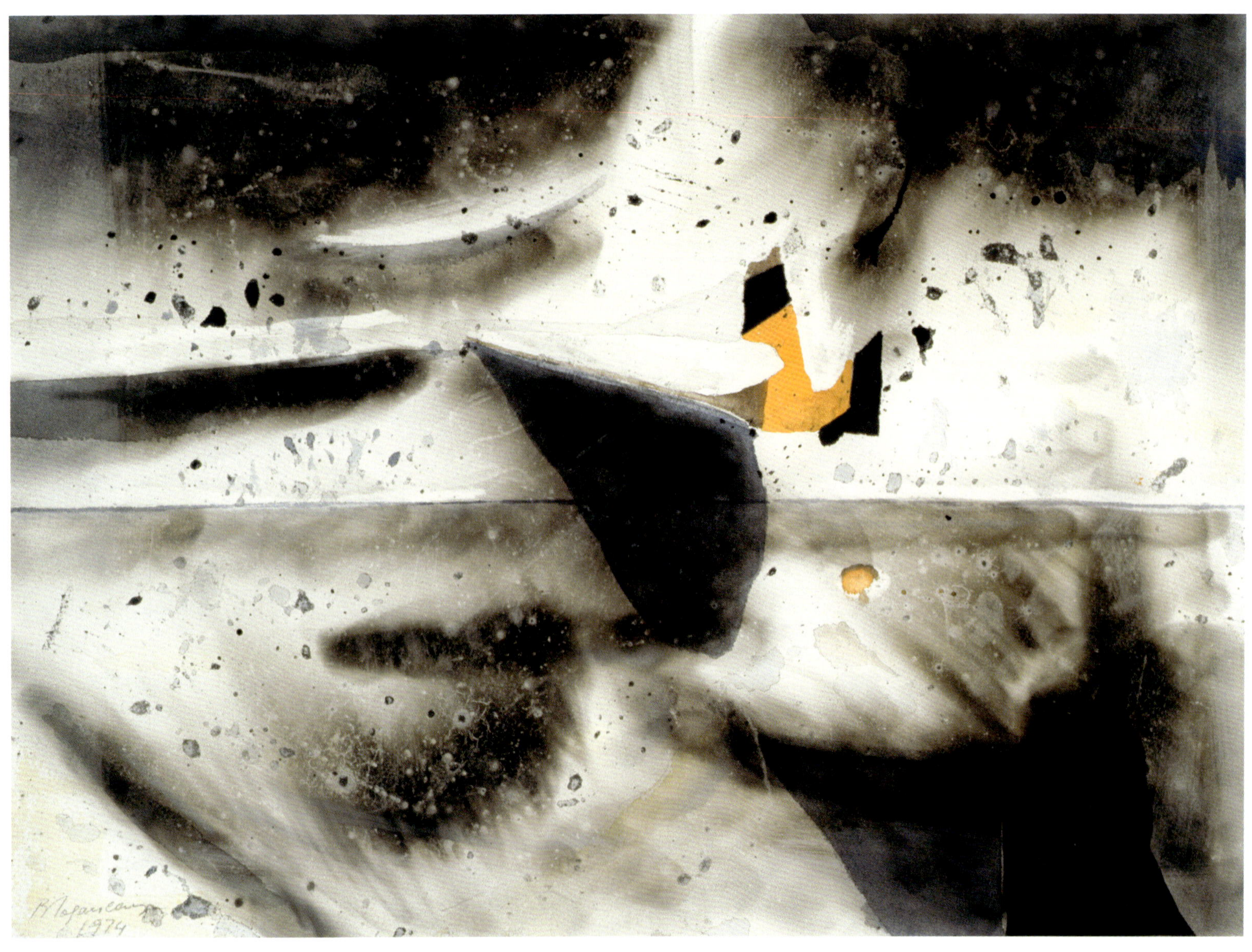

Smoking Orange, 1974. Fumage on paper, 21 × 16½ in. (30.5 × 41.9 cm). Kennedy Museum of Art, Athens, Ohio

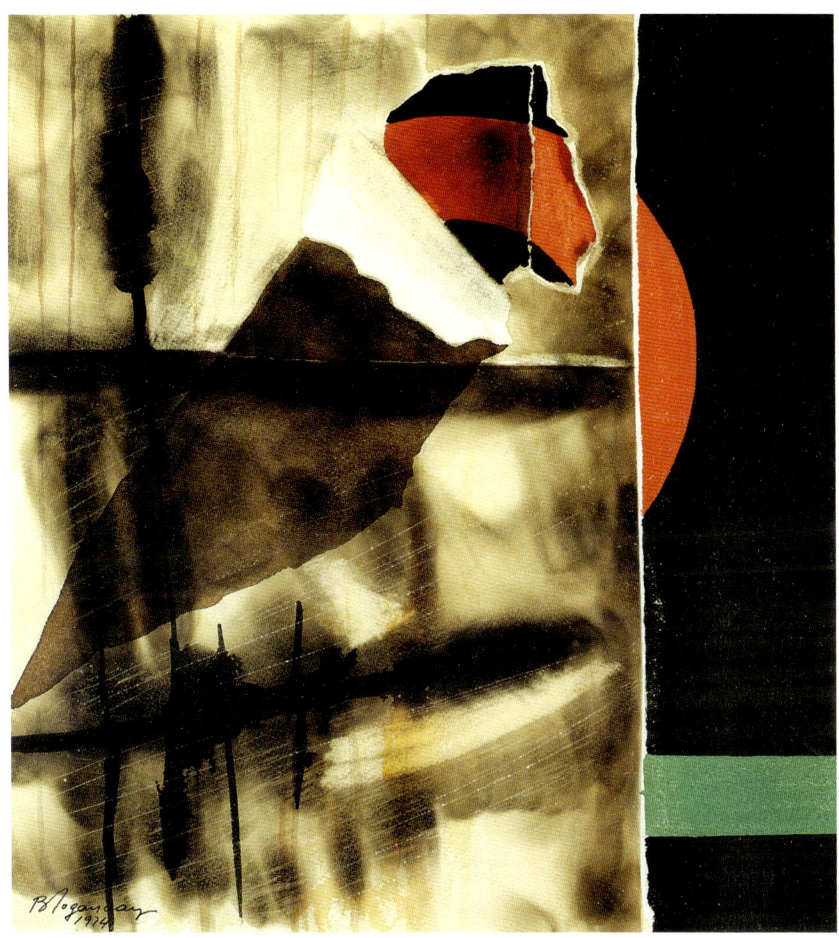

With Smoke (Dumanlı), 1974. Fumage on paper, 14 × 13 in. (35.6 × 33 cm).
The Solomon R. Guggenheim Museum, New York

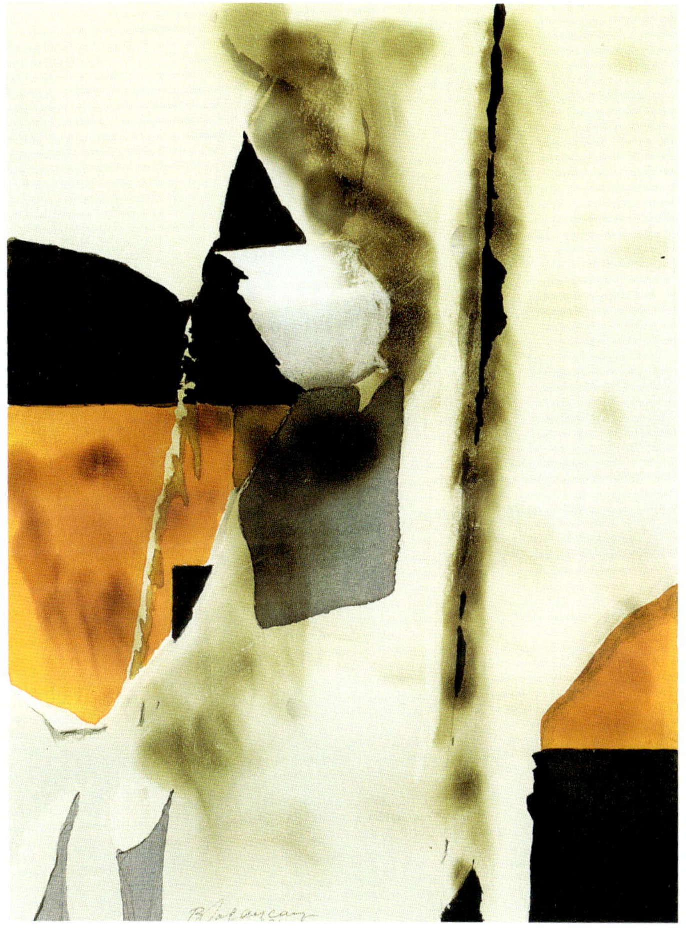

Isle, 1974. Fumage on paper, 14 × 11 in. (35.6 × 27.9 cm).
The Solomon R. Guggenheim Museum, New York

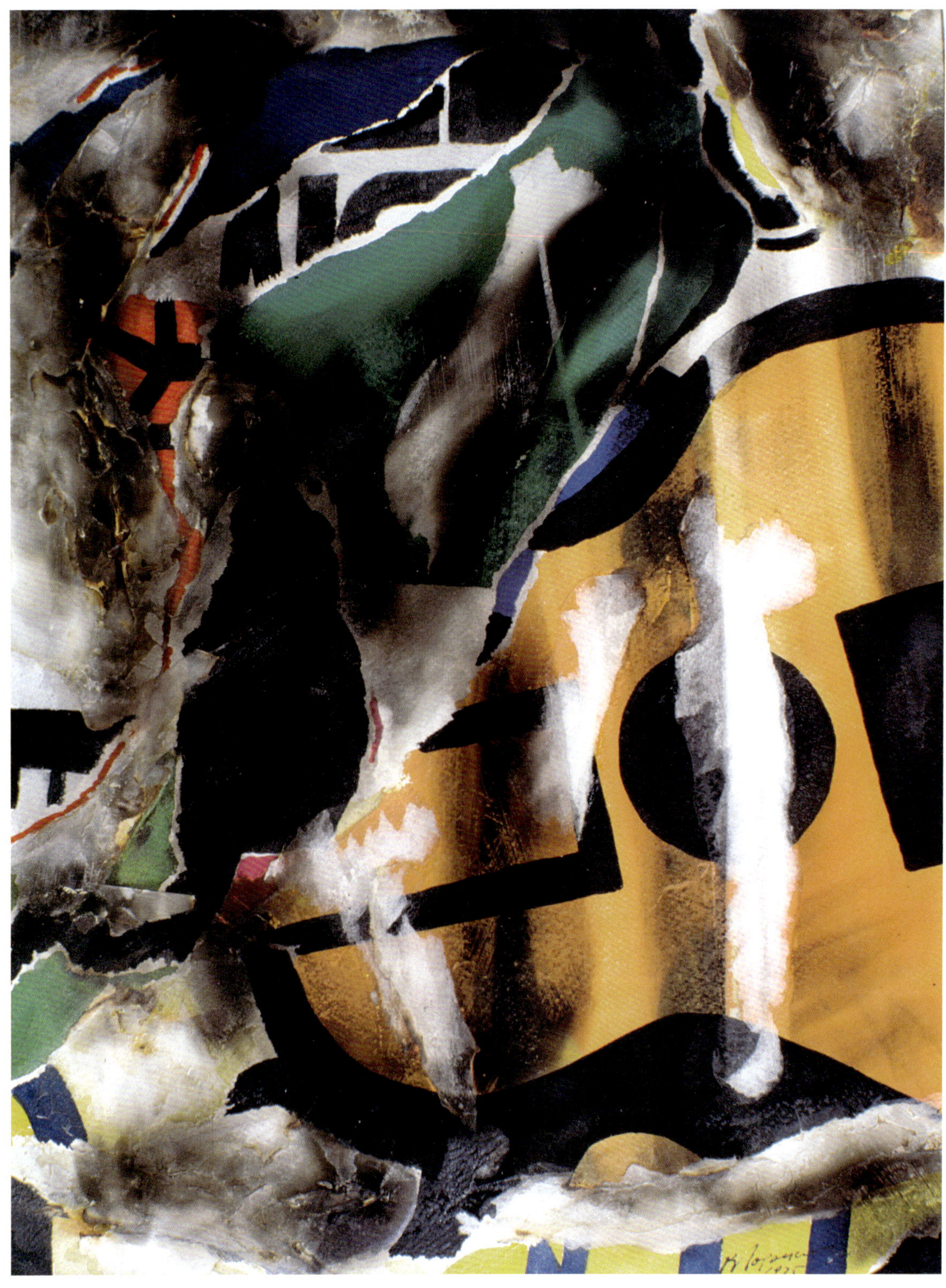

Broken Guitar, 1975. Fumage on paper, 14 × 10 in. (35.6 × 25.4 cm). Collection of the artist

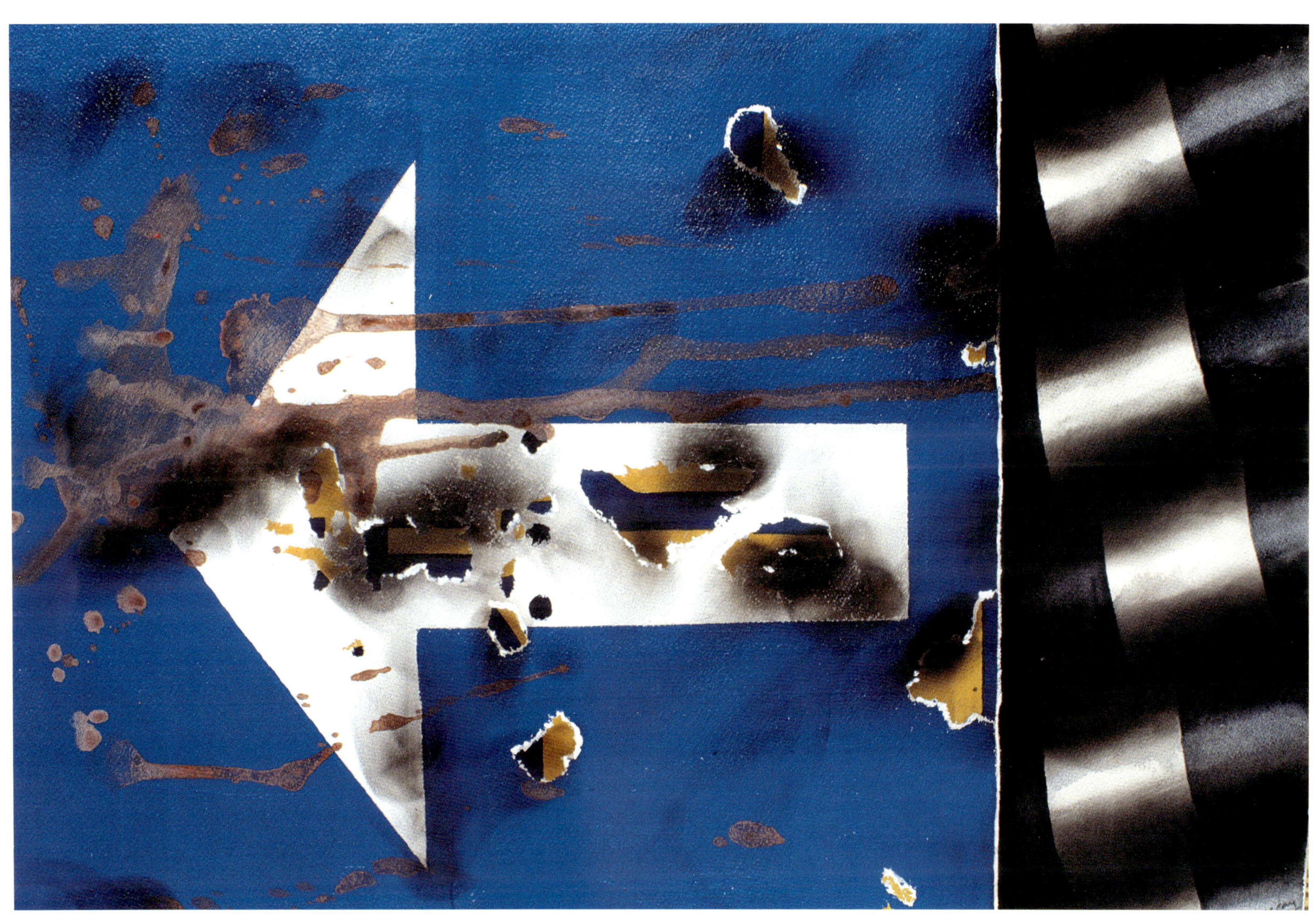

A Wall in Tel Aviv, 1975. Fumage on paper, 14½ × 20½ in. (36.8 × 52.1 cm). Collection of the artist

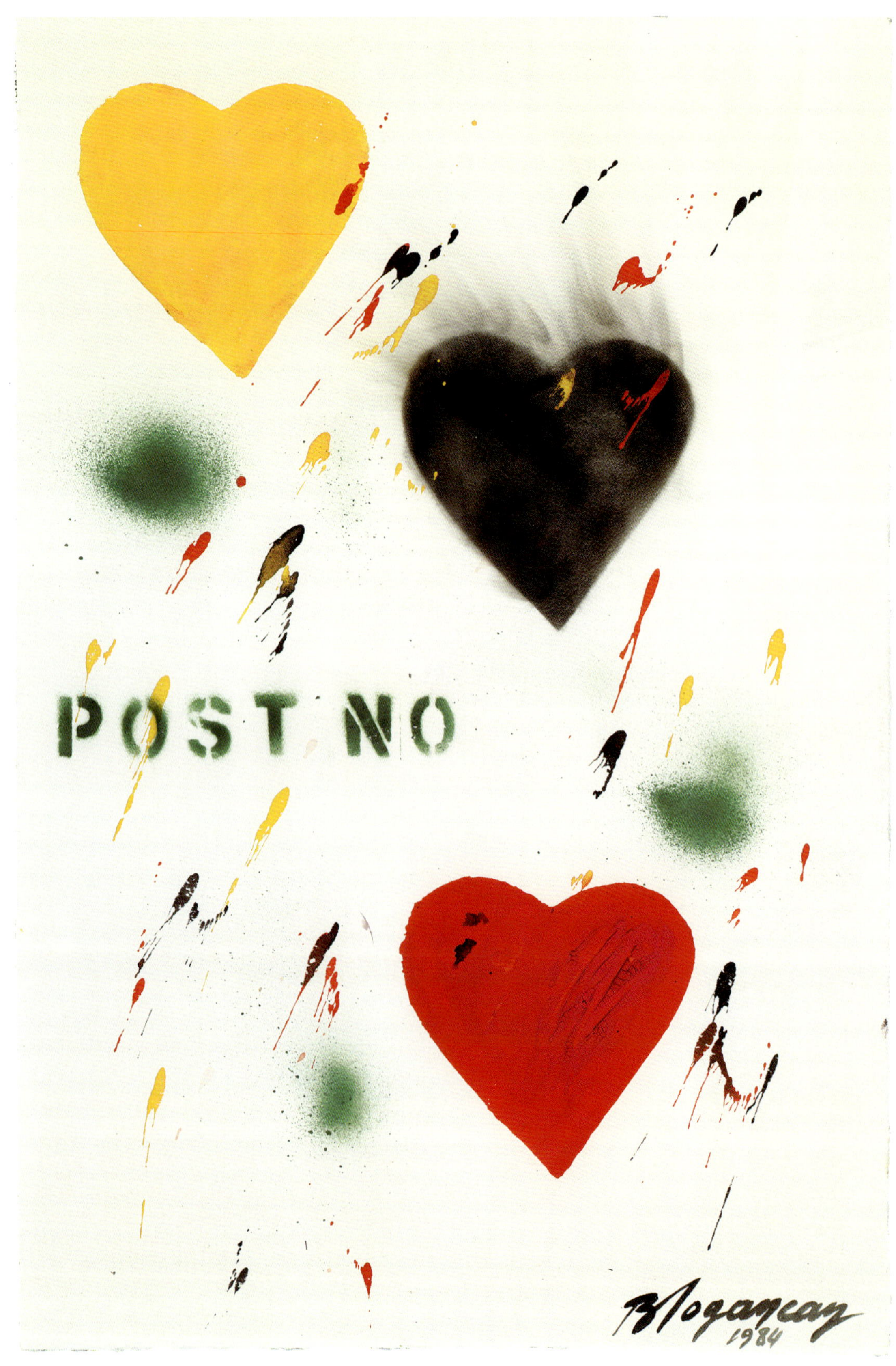

Post No Hearts, 1984. Fumage on paper, 22 × 15 in. (55.9 × 38.1 cm). Collection of the artist

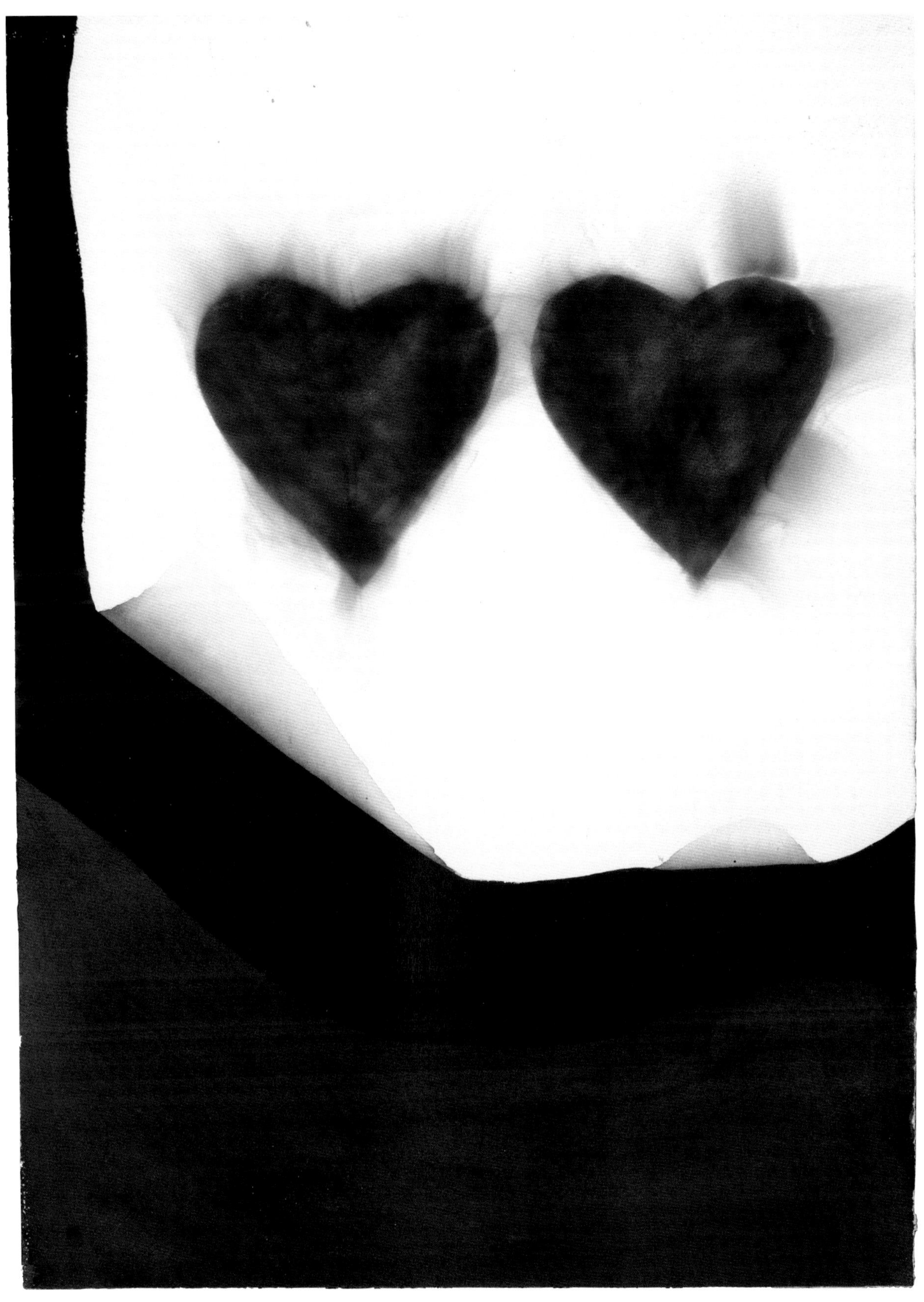

Burning Hearts, 1984. Fumage on paper, 22 × 15 in. (55.9 × 38.1 cm). Collection of the artist

IV

Collages

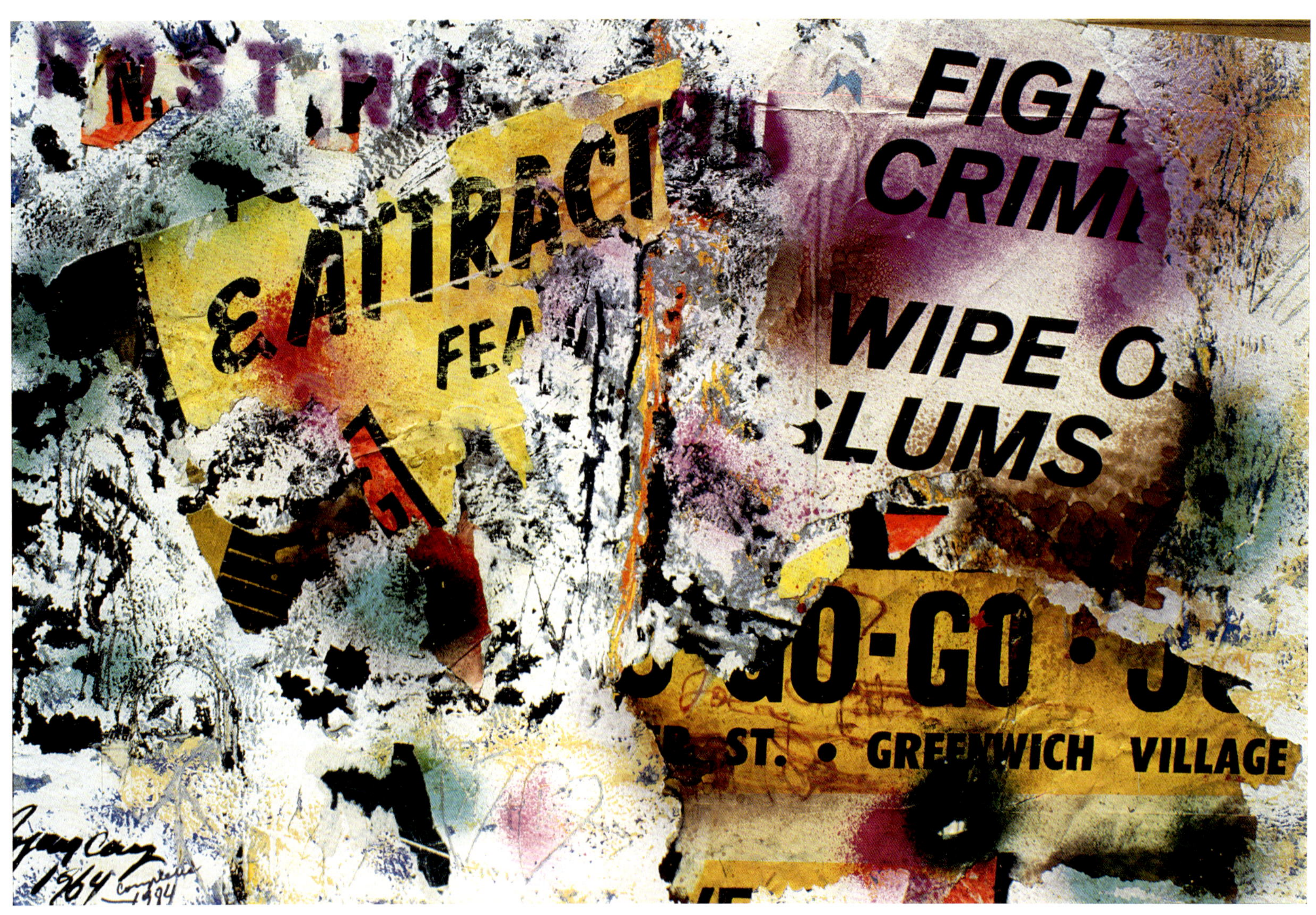

Wipe Out Slums, 1964 (completed 1984). Collage, acrylic, and gouache on paper, 15½ × 24½ in. (39.4 × 62.2 cm). Collection of the artist

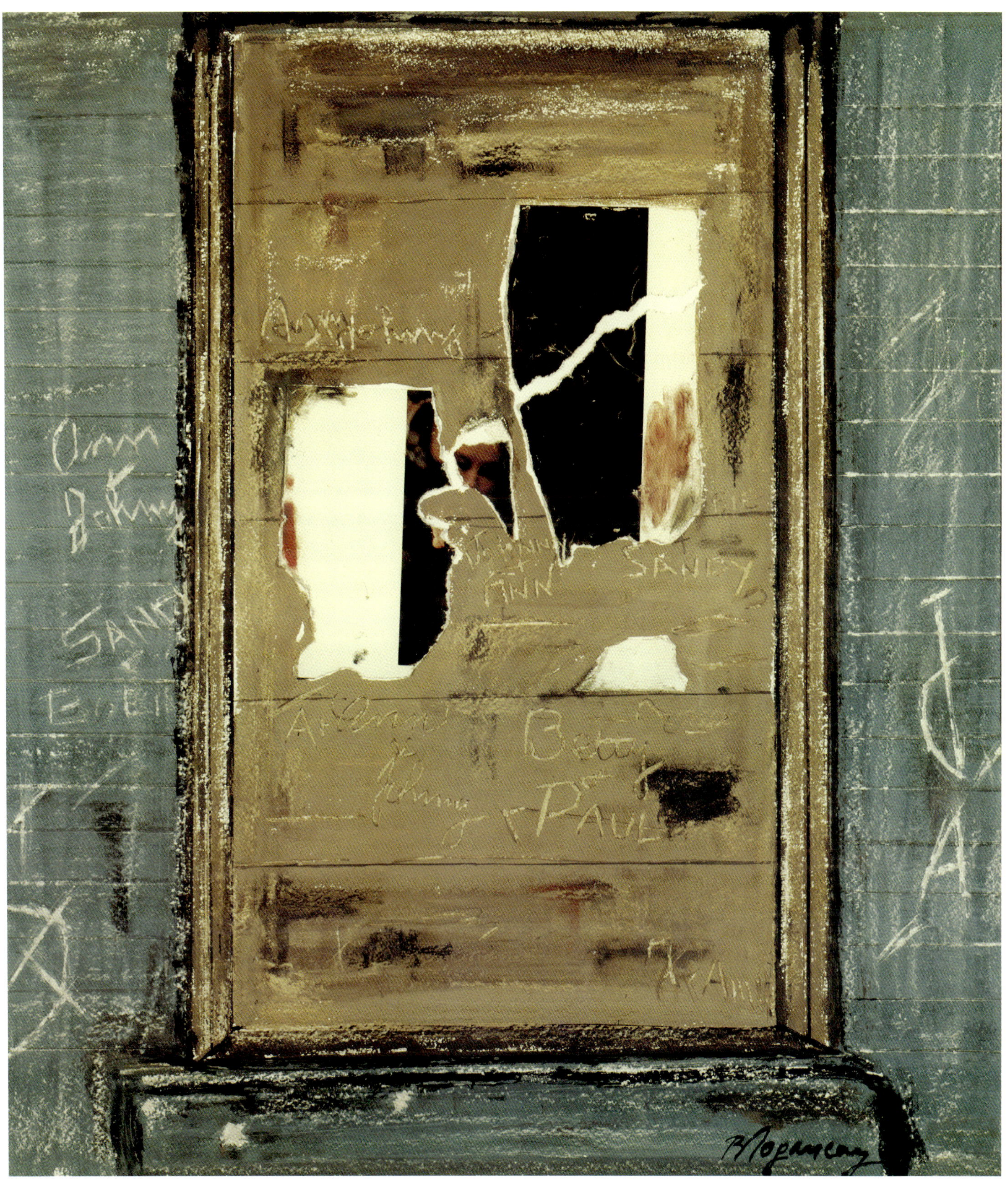

Billboard, 1964. Collage and gouache on cardboard, 22 1/16 × 19 3/4 in. (56.2 × 50.2 cm). The Solomon R. Guggenheim Museum, New York

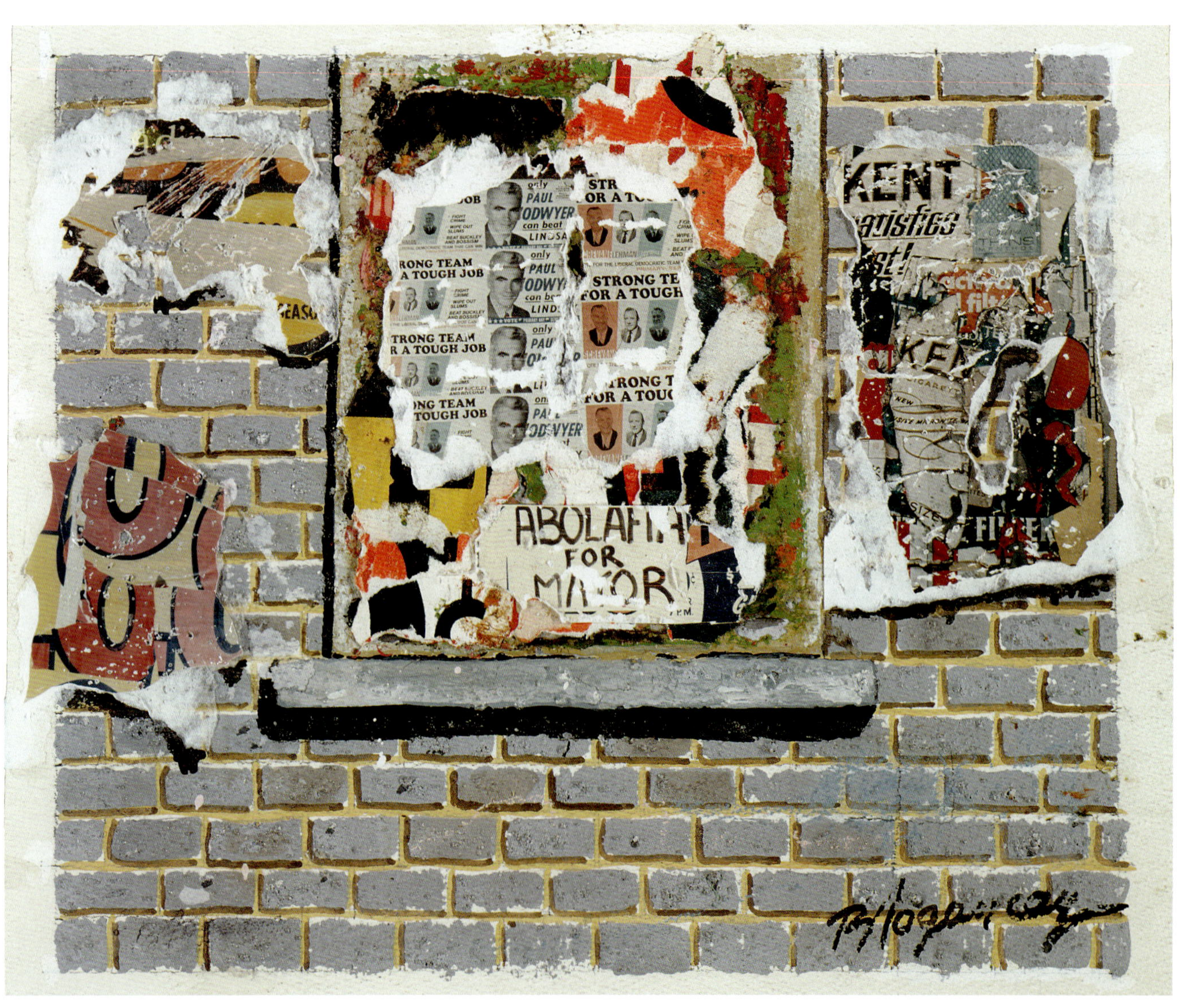

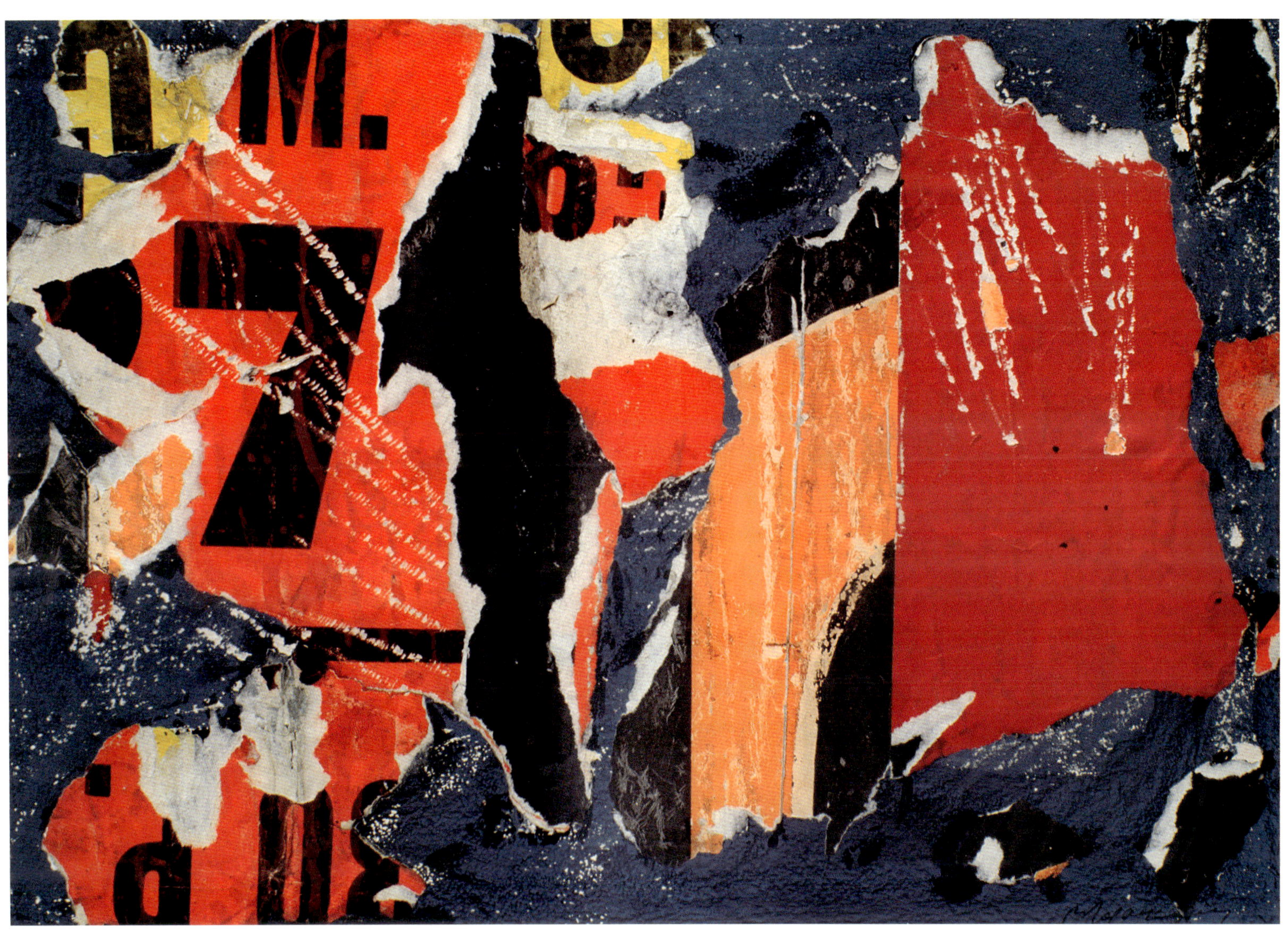

Black 7, 1970. Collage and acrylic on paper, 13½ × 20½ in. (34.3 × 52.1 cm). Collection of the artist

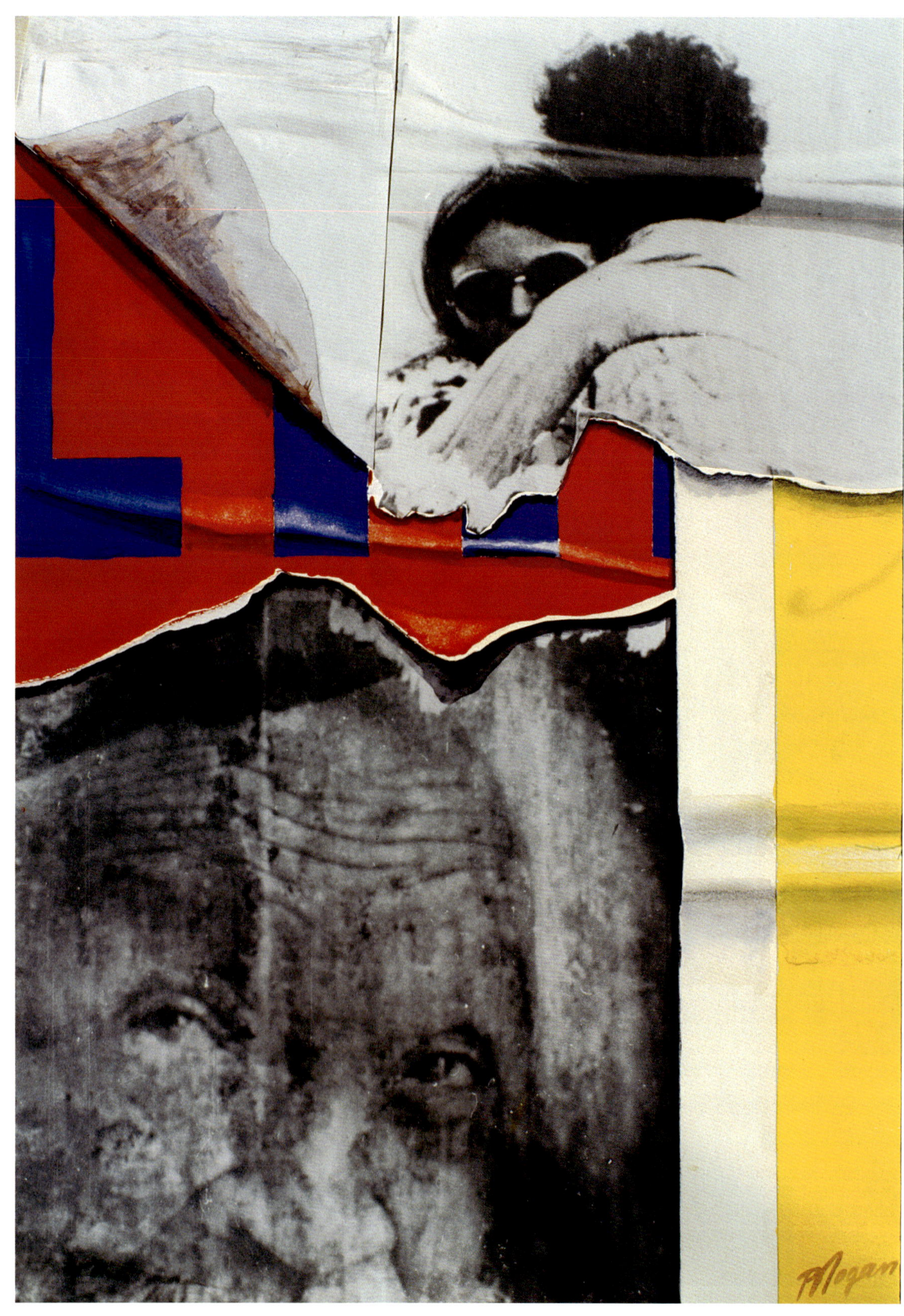

Souvenirs, 1973. Collage and gouache on paper, 30 × 22 in. (76.2 × 55.9 cm). Collection of the artist

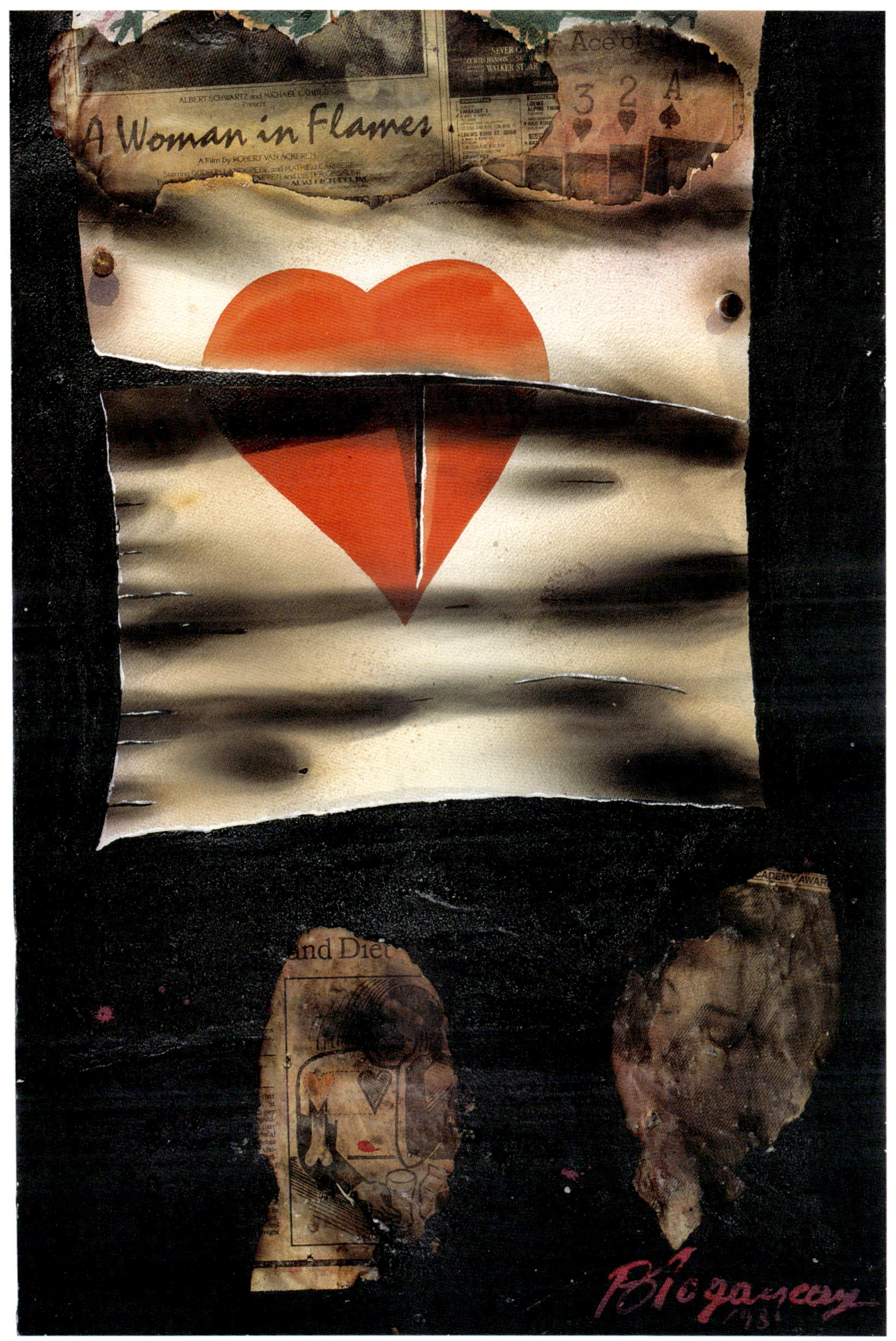

Woman in Flames, 1981. Collage, acrylic, and gouache on paper, 22 × 15 in. (55.9 × 38.1 cm).
Collection of the artist

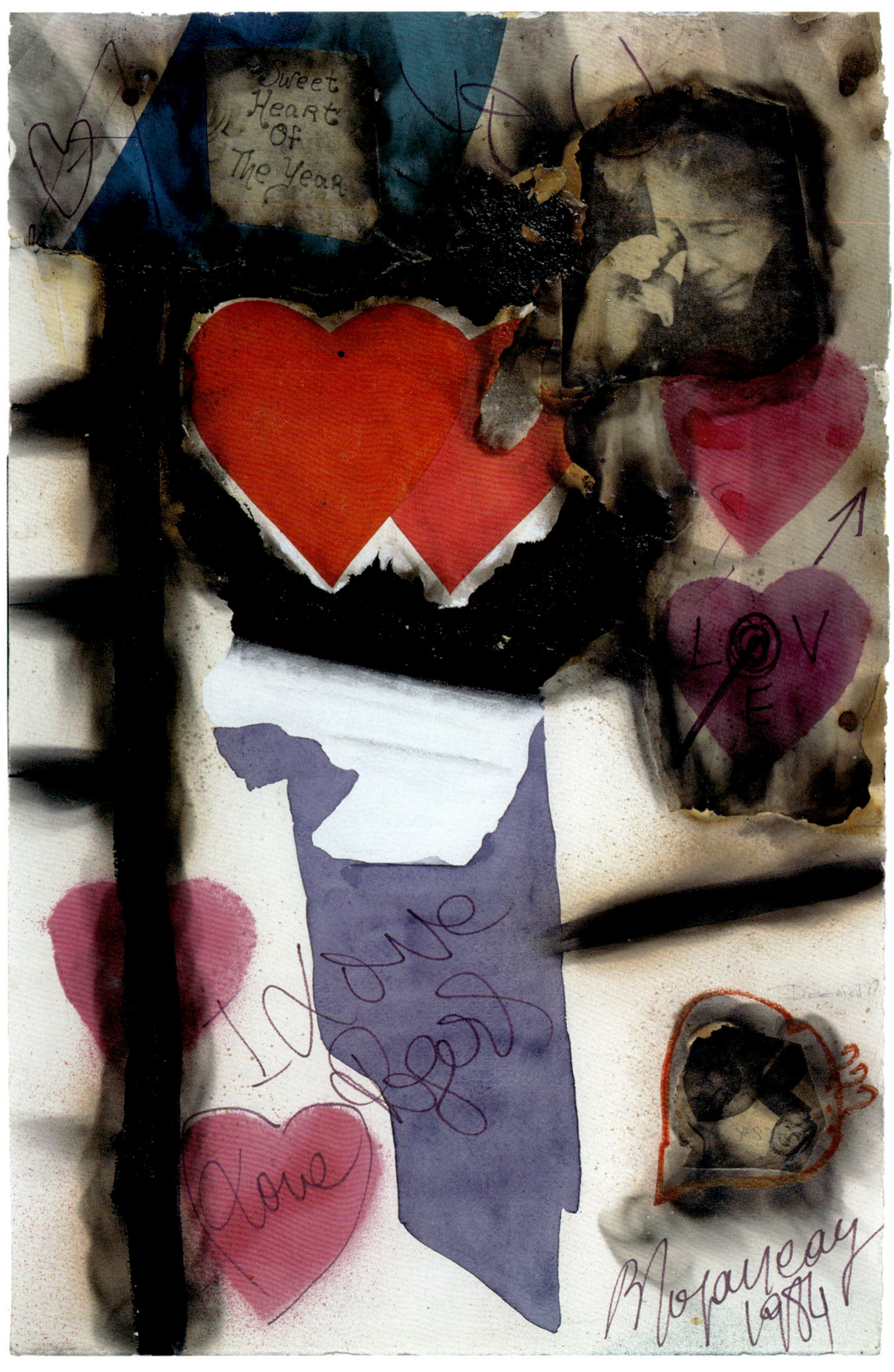

Sweetheart of the Year, 1984. Collage, acrylic, and gouache on paper, 22 × 15 in. (55.9 × 38.1 cm). Collection of the artist

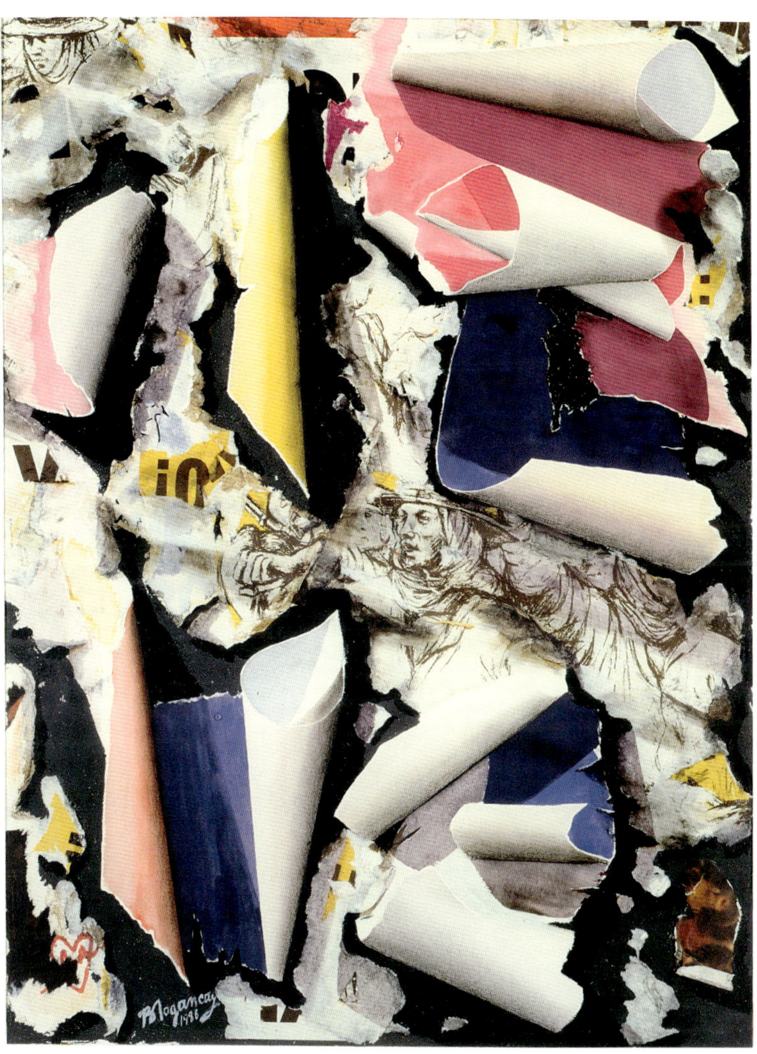

Freedom Fighters, 1986. Collage and gouache on paper, 30 × 22 in. (76.2 × 55.9 cm). Private collection

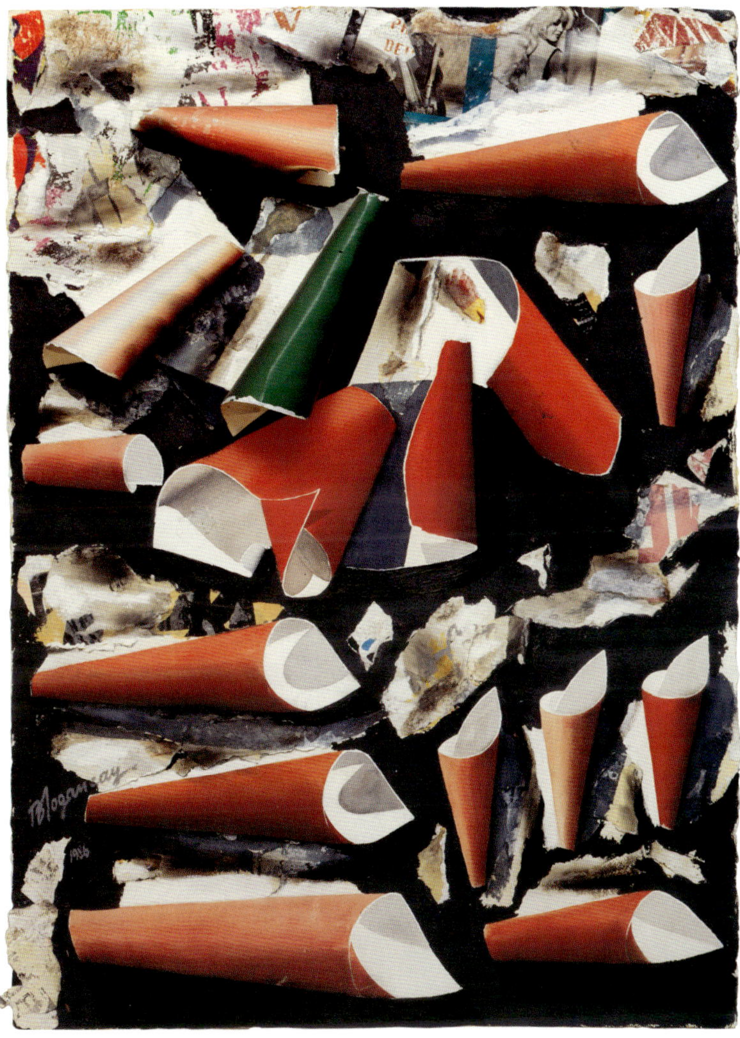

Cones in a Box, 1986. Collage and gouache on paper, 30 × 22 in. (76.2 × 55.9 cm). Collection of the artist

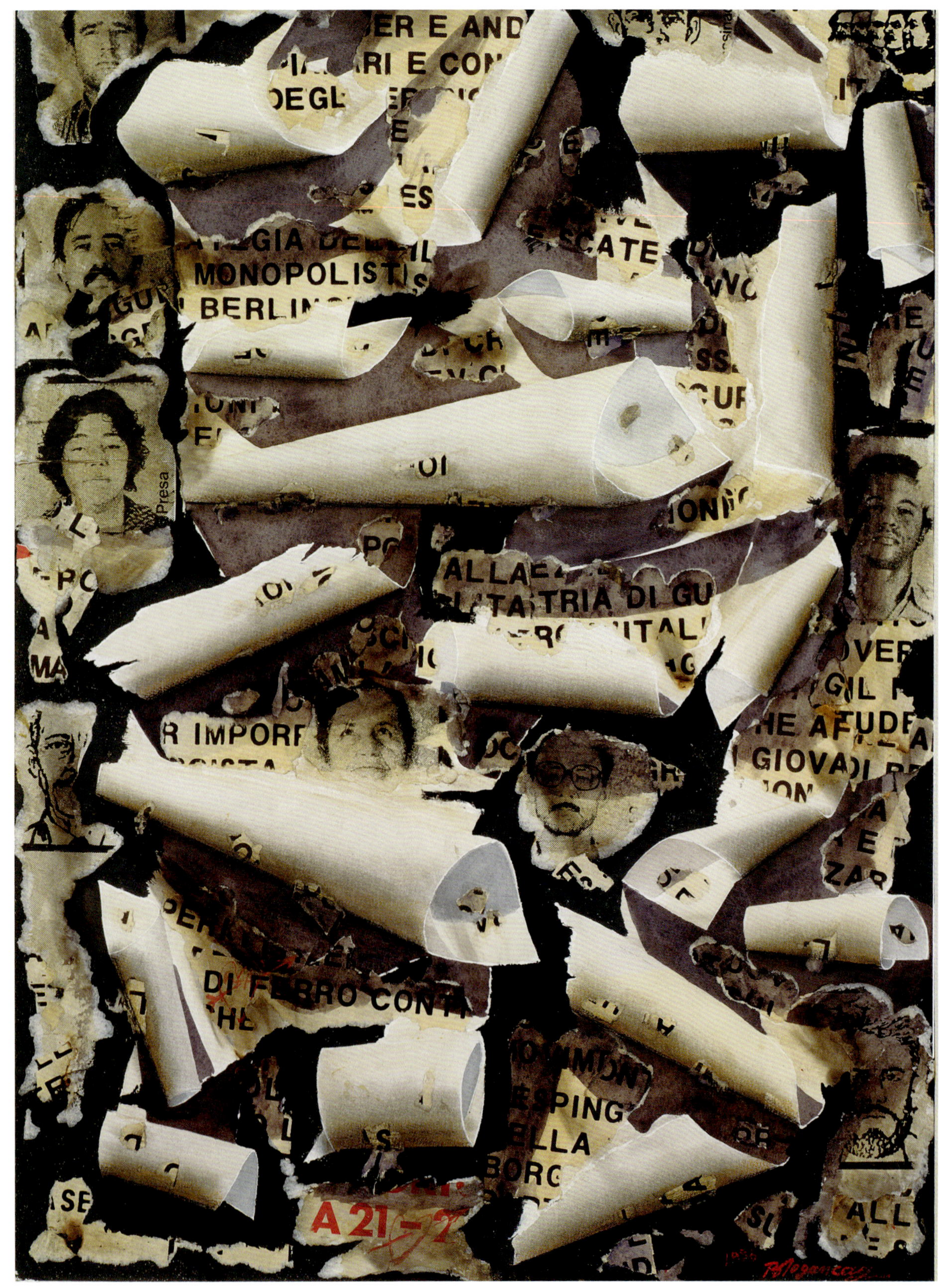

Newsprint, 1986. Collage, acrylic, and gouache on paper, 30 × 22 in. (76.2 × 55.9 cm). Collection of the artist

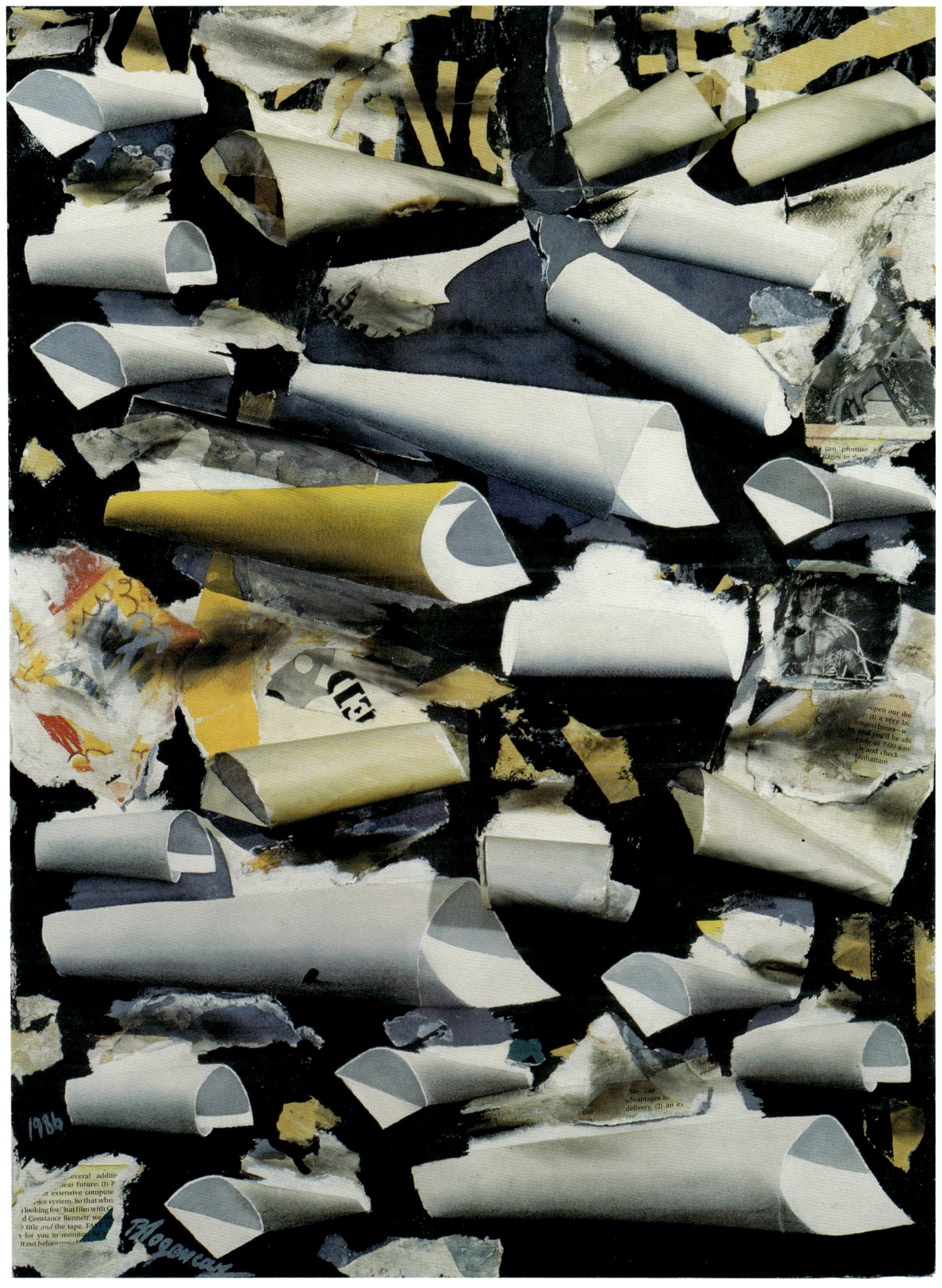

Yellow ED, 1986. Collage, acrylic, and gouache on paper, 30 × 22 in. (76.2 × 55.9 cm). Collection of the artist

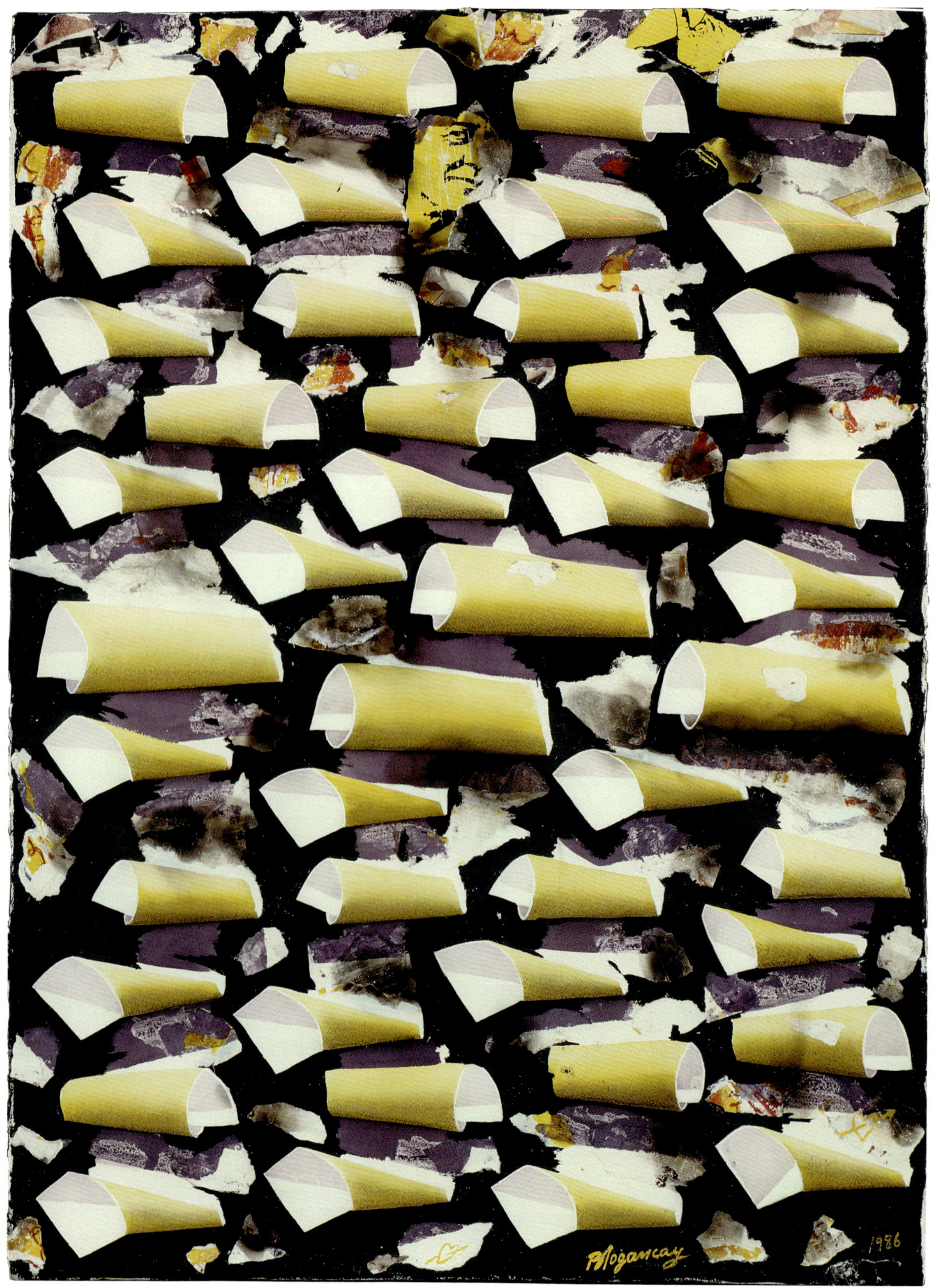

Yellow Curls, 1986. Collage, acrylic, and gouache on paper, 30 × 22 in. (76.2 × 55.9 cm). Collection of the artist

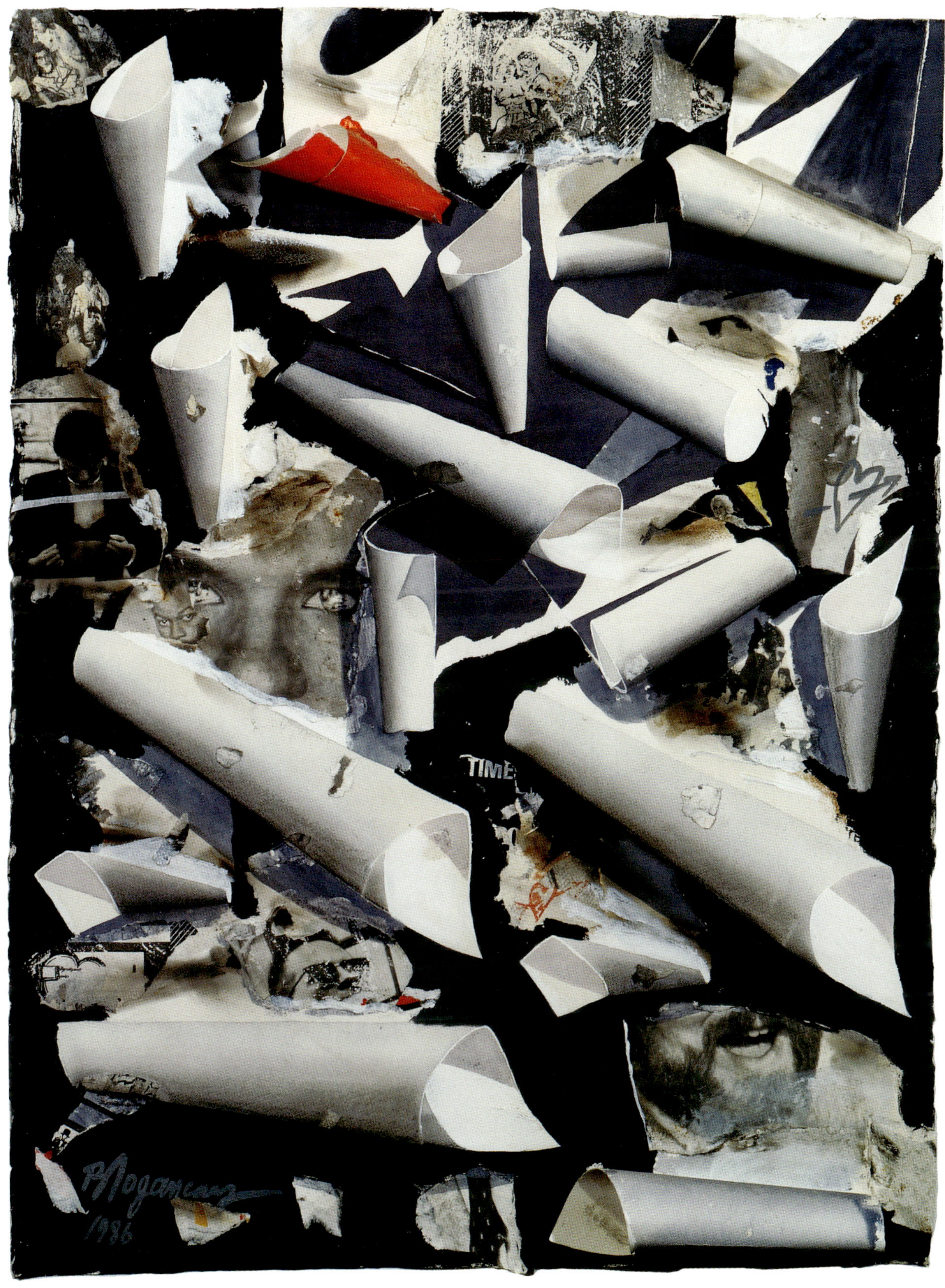

Real vs. Unreal, 1986. Collage and gouache on paper, 30 × 22 in. (76.2 × 55.9 cm). Collection of the artist

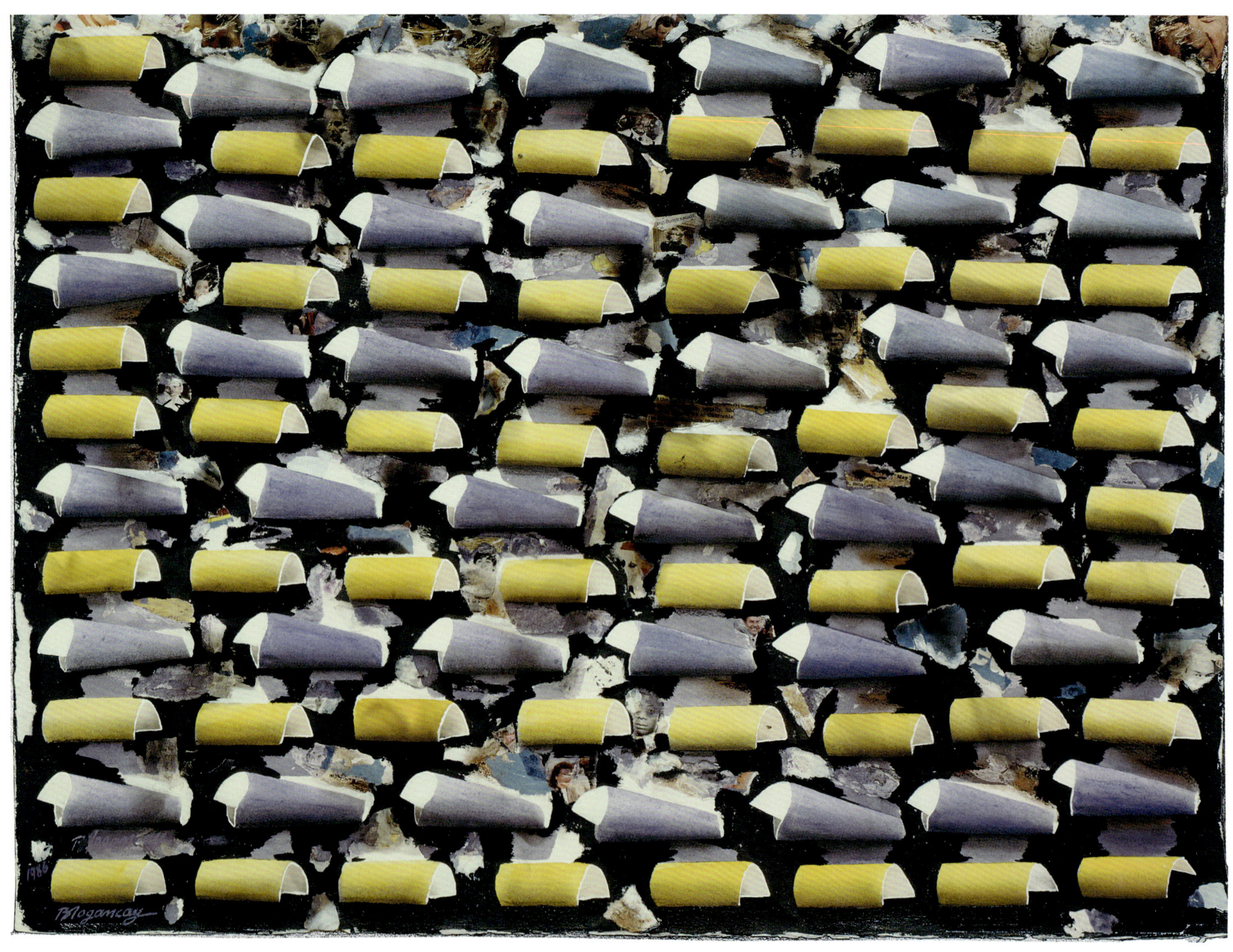

Yellow and Blue Scrolls, 1986. Collage and gouache on paper, 22 × 30 in. (55.9 × 76.2 cm). Private collection

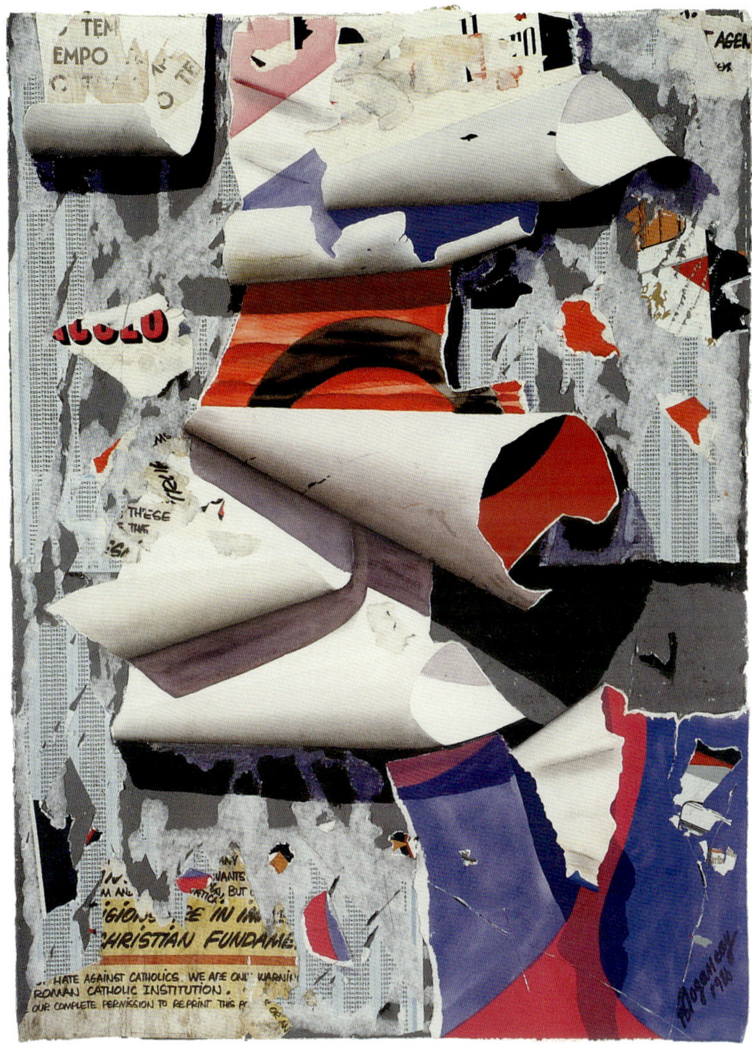

Target, 1986. Collage, acrylic, and gouache on paper, 30 × 22 in.
(76.2 × 55.9 cm). Private collection

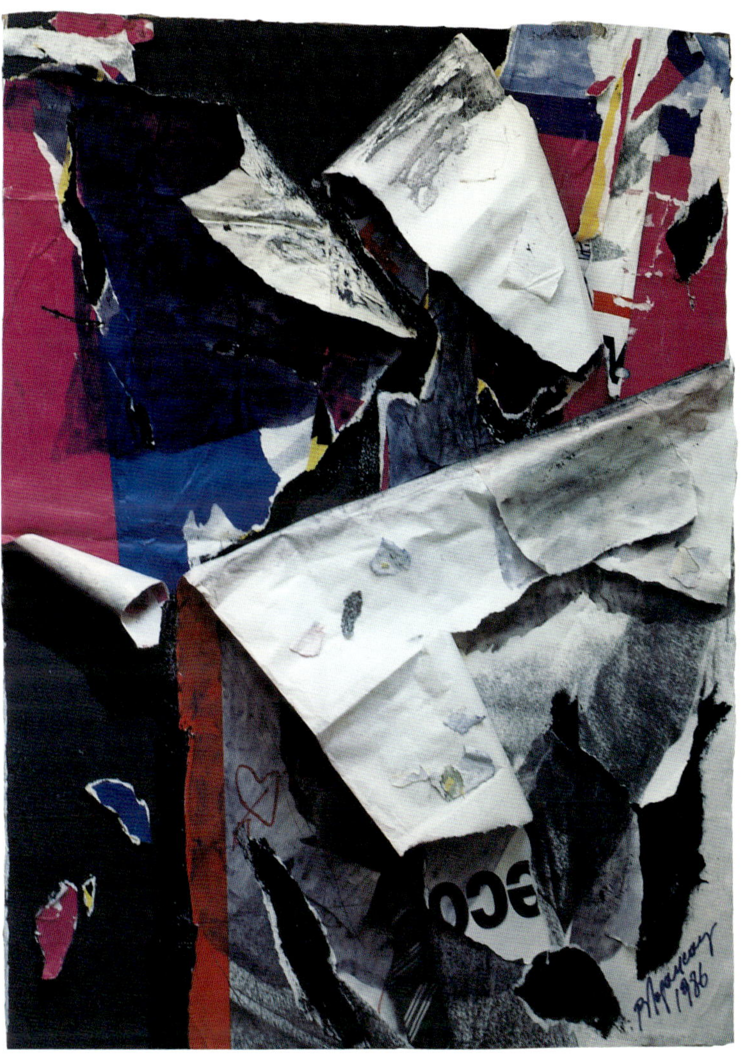

Above Our TV, 1986. Collage and gouache on paper, 30 × 22 in.
(76.2 × 55.9 cm). Collection of the artist

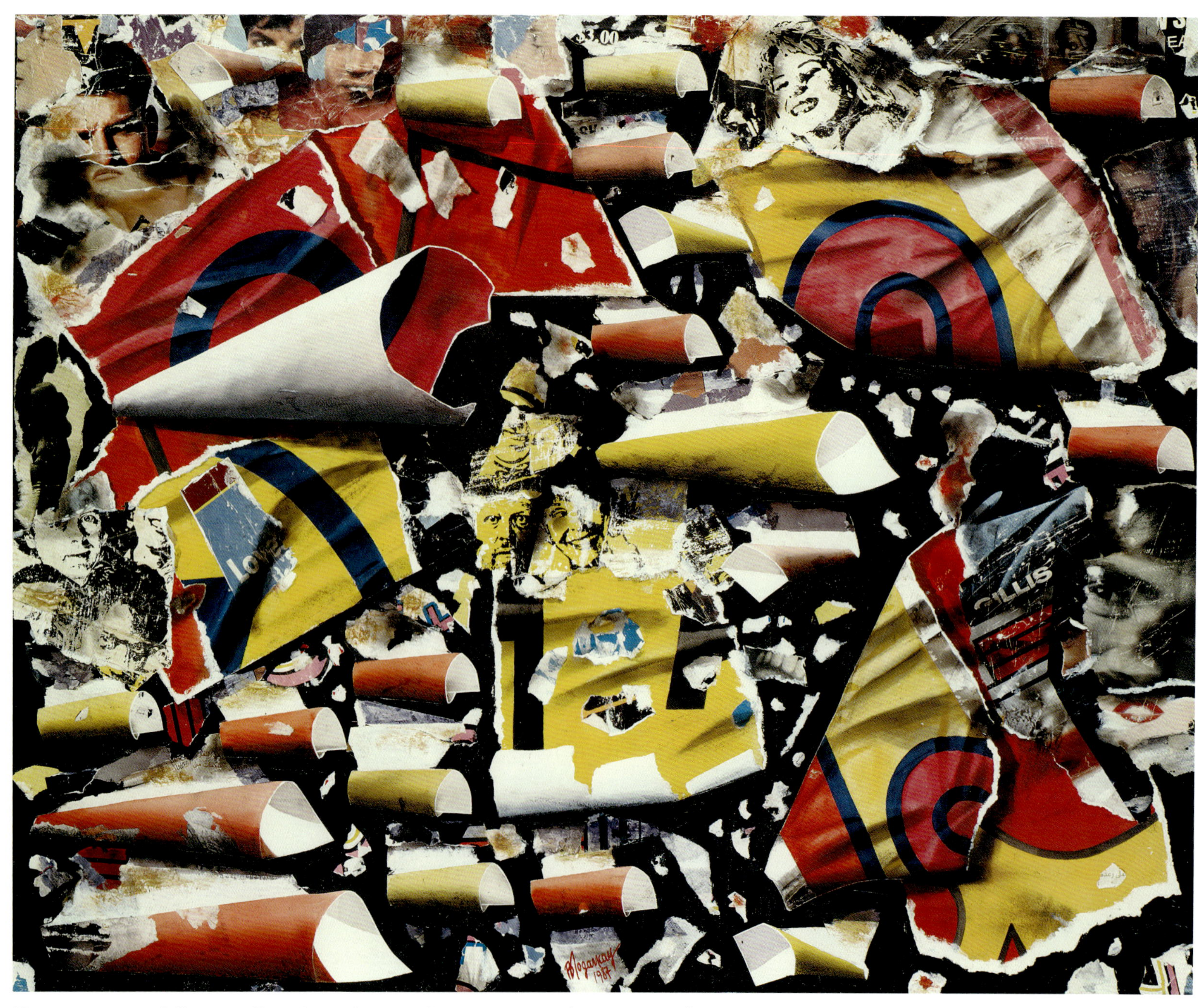

Kaleidoscope, 1987. Collage, acrylic, and gouache on cardboard, 30 × 42 in. (76.2 × 106.7 cm). Private collection

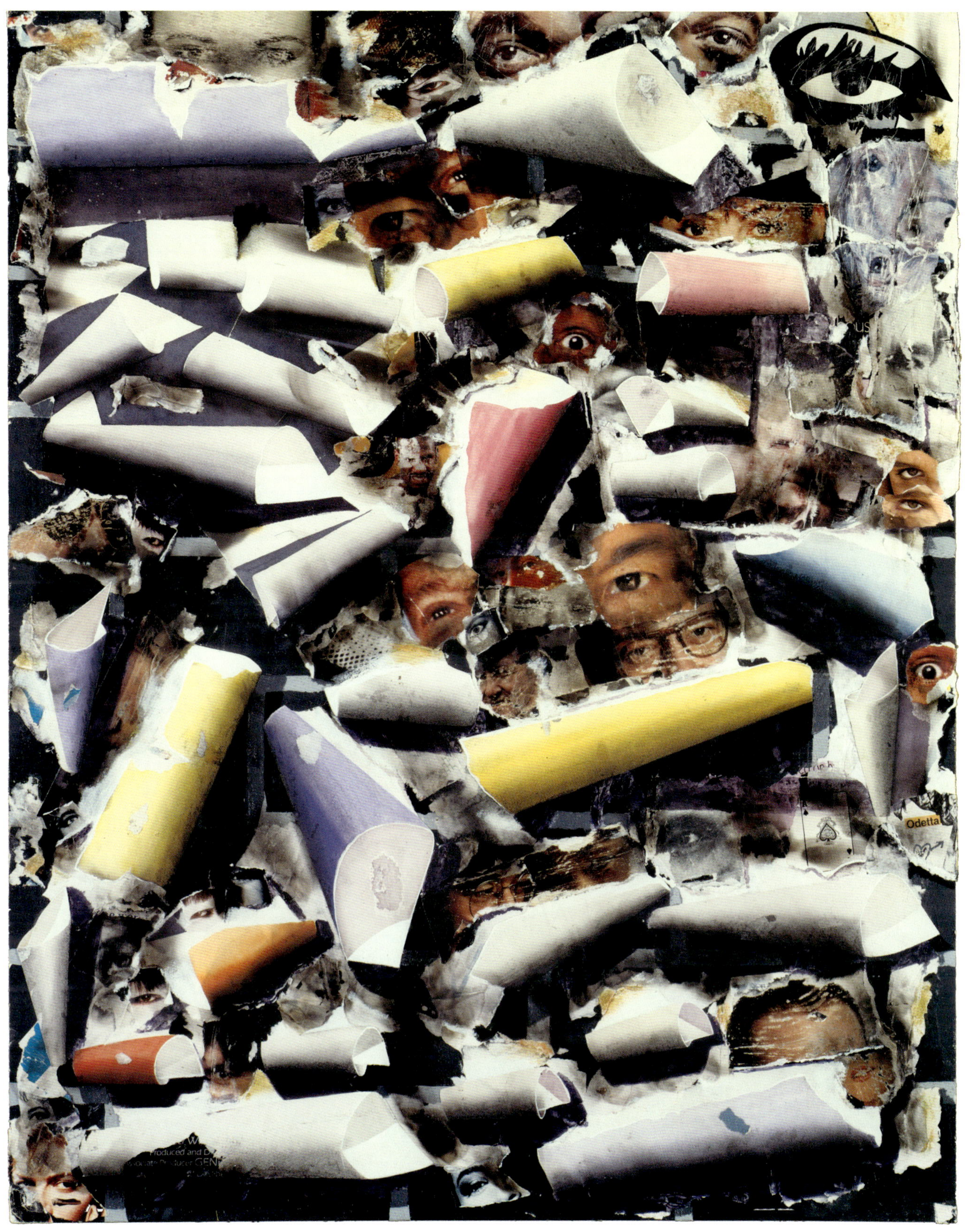

Famous Eyes, 1987. Collage, acrylic, and gouache on paper, 30 × 22 in. (76.2 × 55.9 cm). Collection of the artist

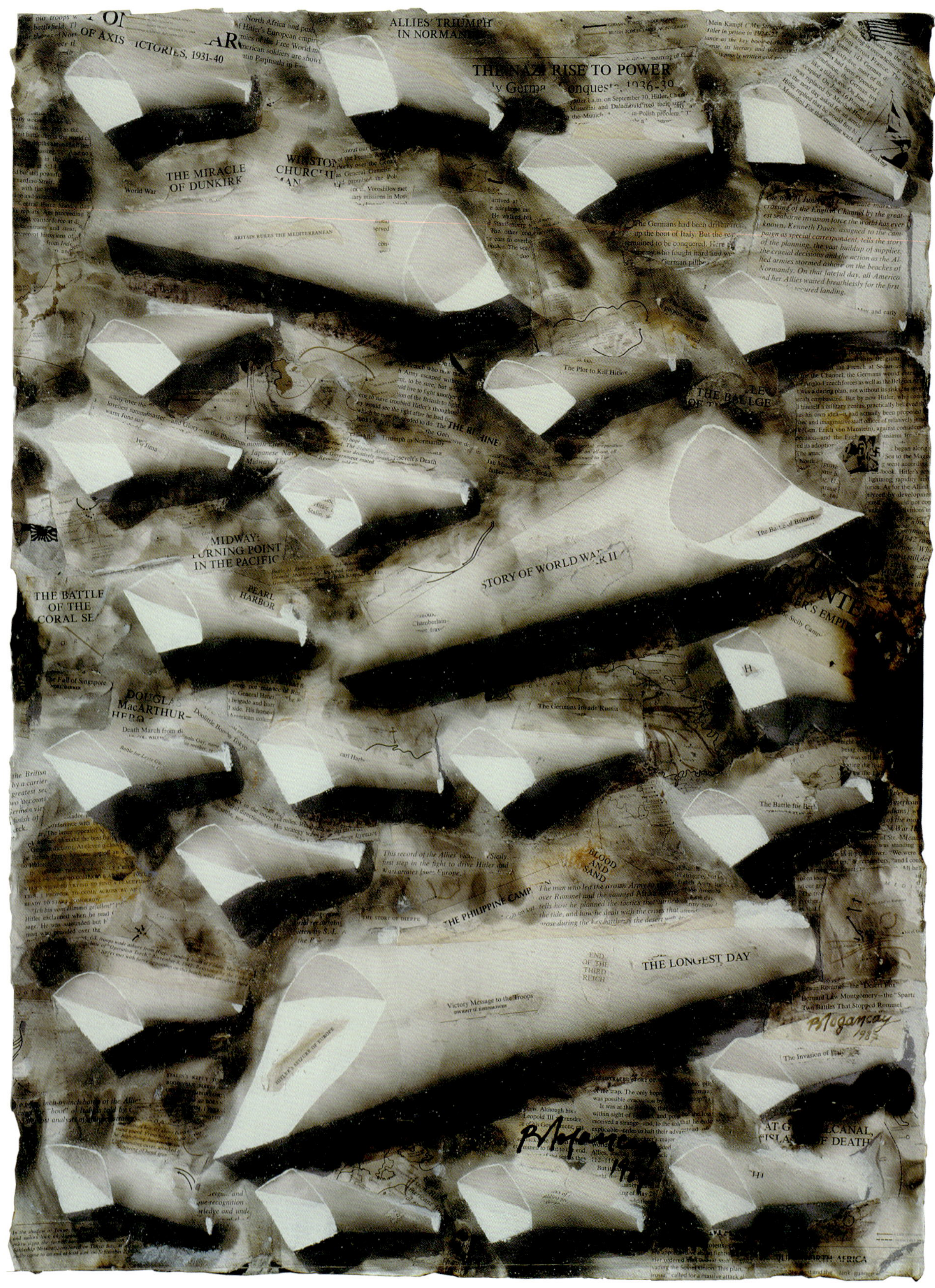

The Story of WW II, 1987. Collage, acrylic, and gouache on paper, 30 × 22 in. (76.2 × 55.9 cm). Collection of the artist

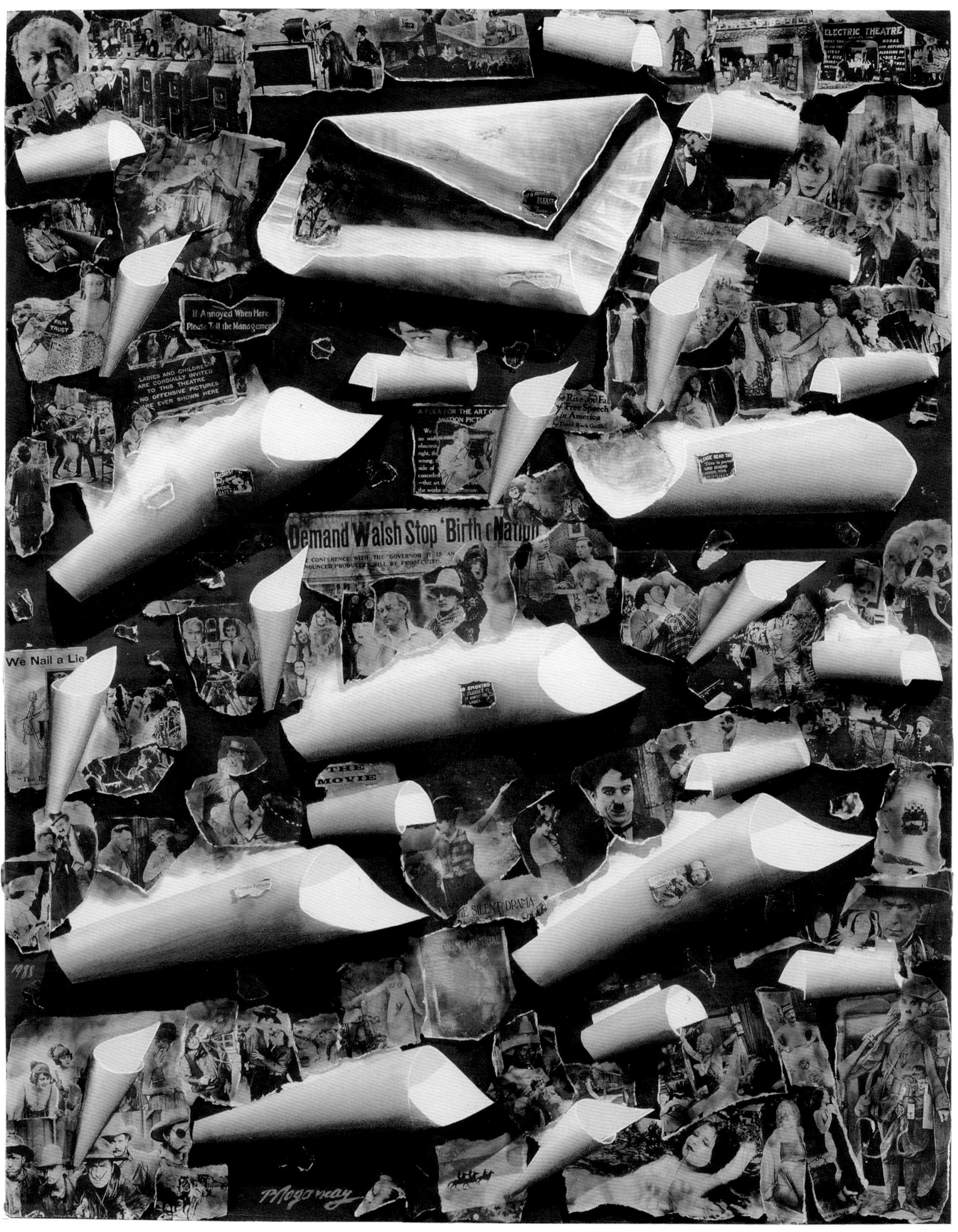

Electric Theatre, 1988. Collage, acrylic, and gouache on cardboard, 40 × 32 in. (101.6 × 81.3 cm). Collection of the artist

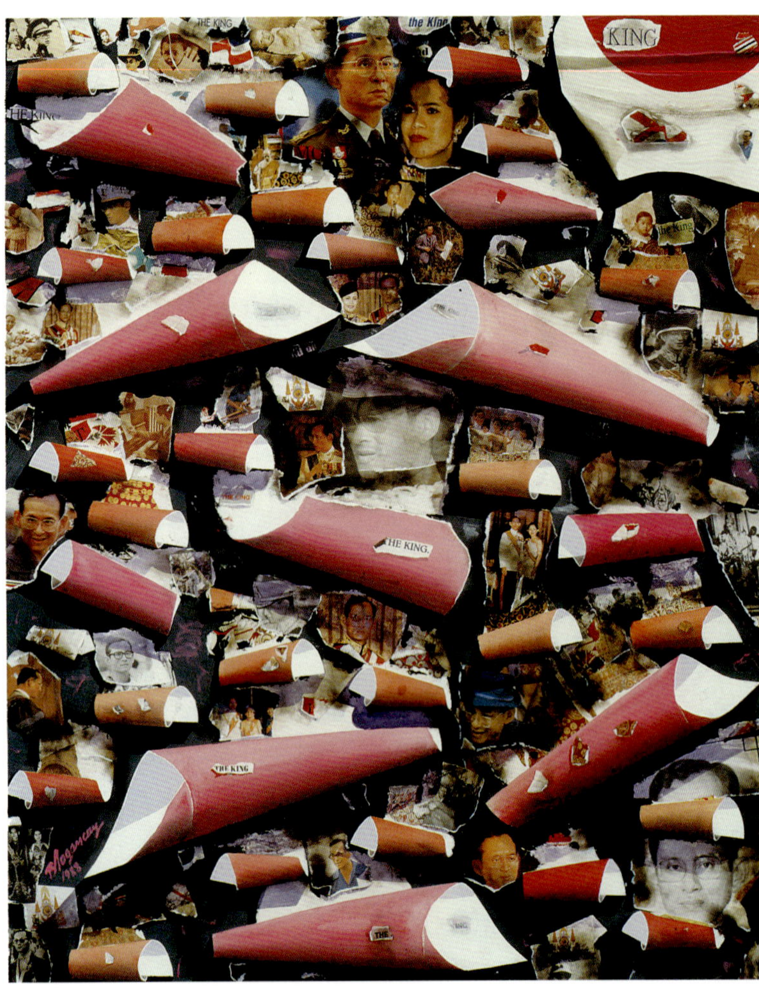 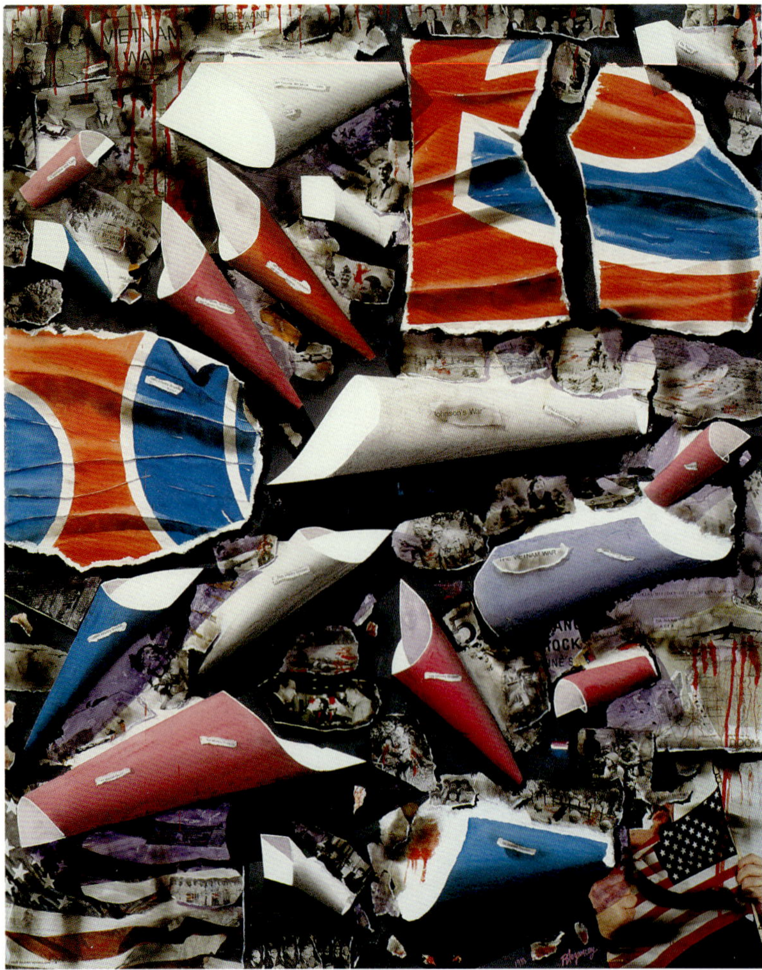

The King and I, 1988. Collage, acrylic, and gouache on cardboard, 40 × 32 in. (101.6 × 81.3 cm). Collection of the artist

The Vietnam War, 1988. Collage, acrylic, and gouache on cardboard, 40 × 32 in. (101.6 × 81.3 cm). Collection of the artist

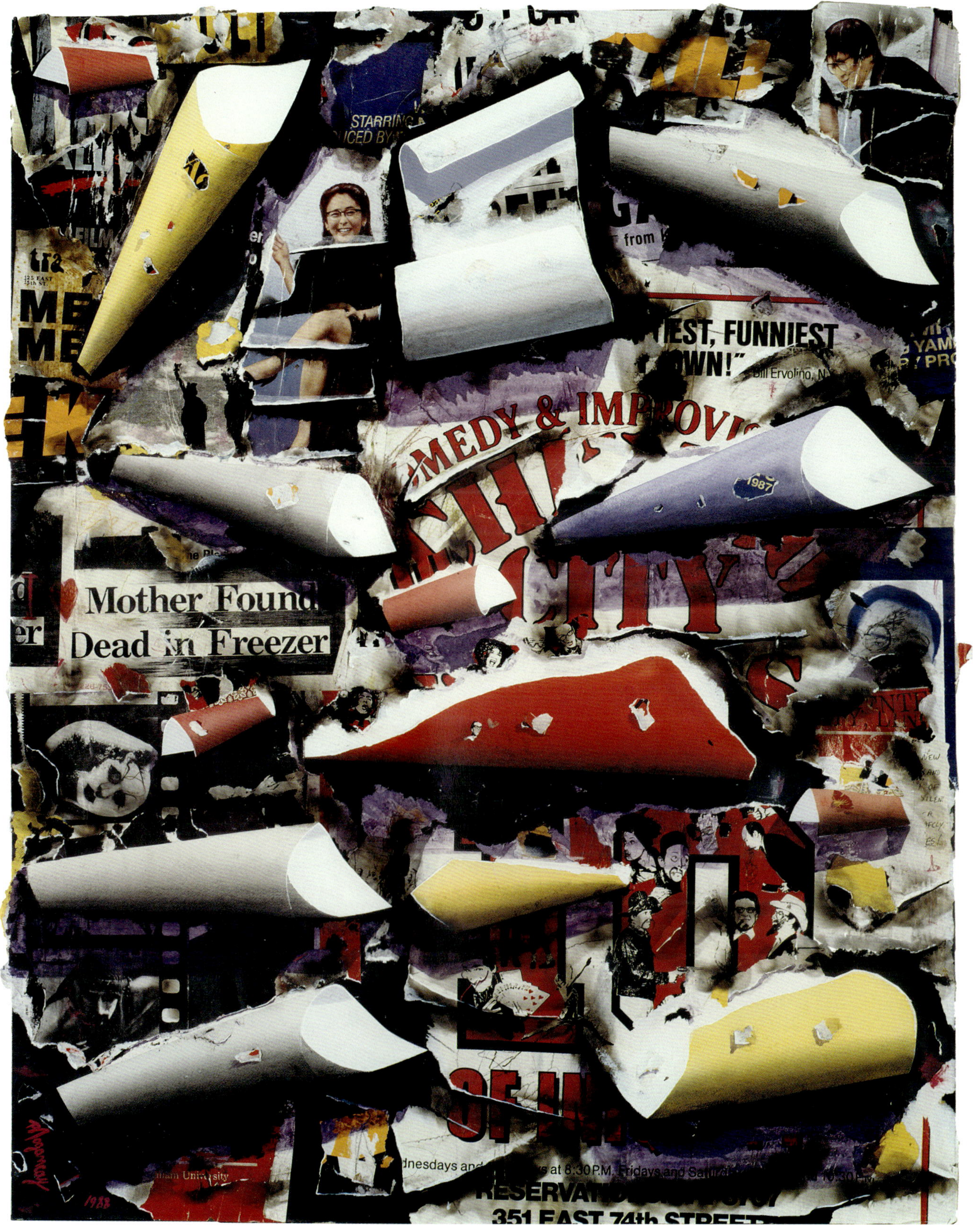

Gloomy News, 1988. Collage, acrylic, and gouache on cardboard, 40 × 32 in. (101.6 × 81.3 cm). Collection of the artist

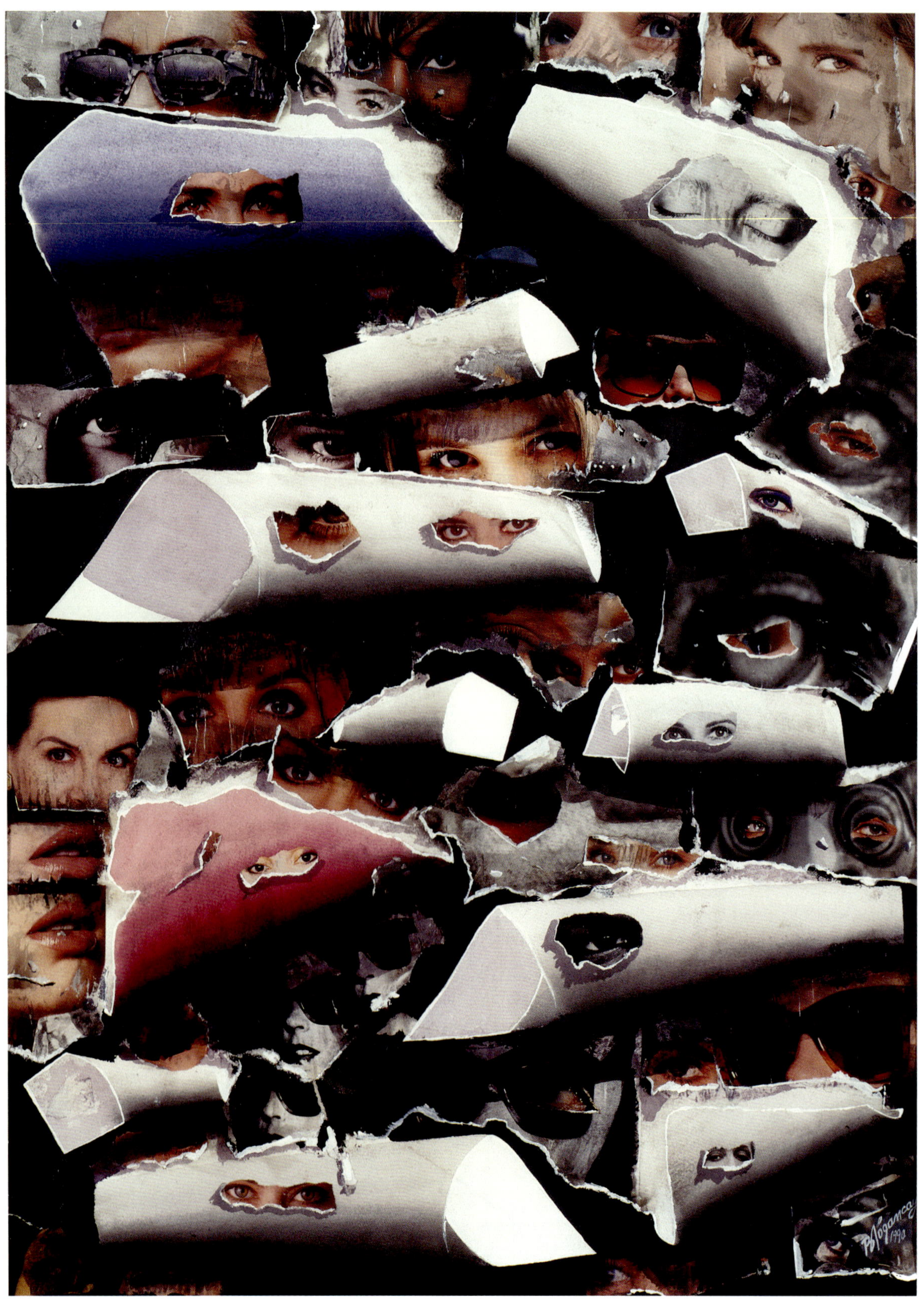

Mysterious Eyes, 1990. Collage, acrylic, and gouache on paper, 30 × 22 in. (76.2 × 55.9 cm). Collection of the artist

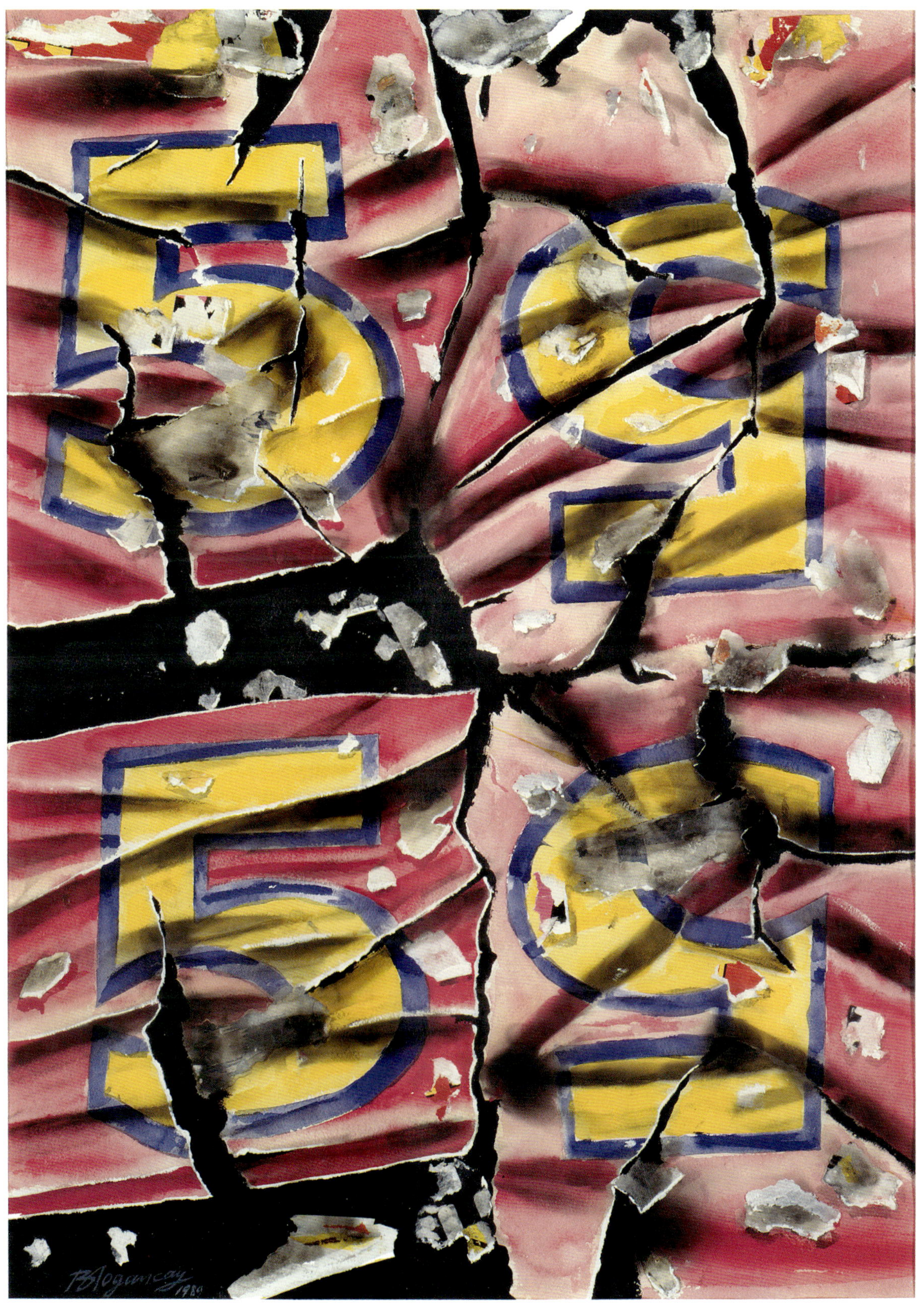

A Couple of Fives, 1989. Collage, acrylic, and gouache on paper, 30 × 22 in. (76.2 × 55.9 cm). Collection of the artist

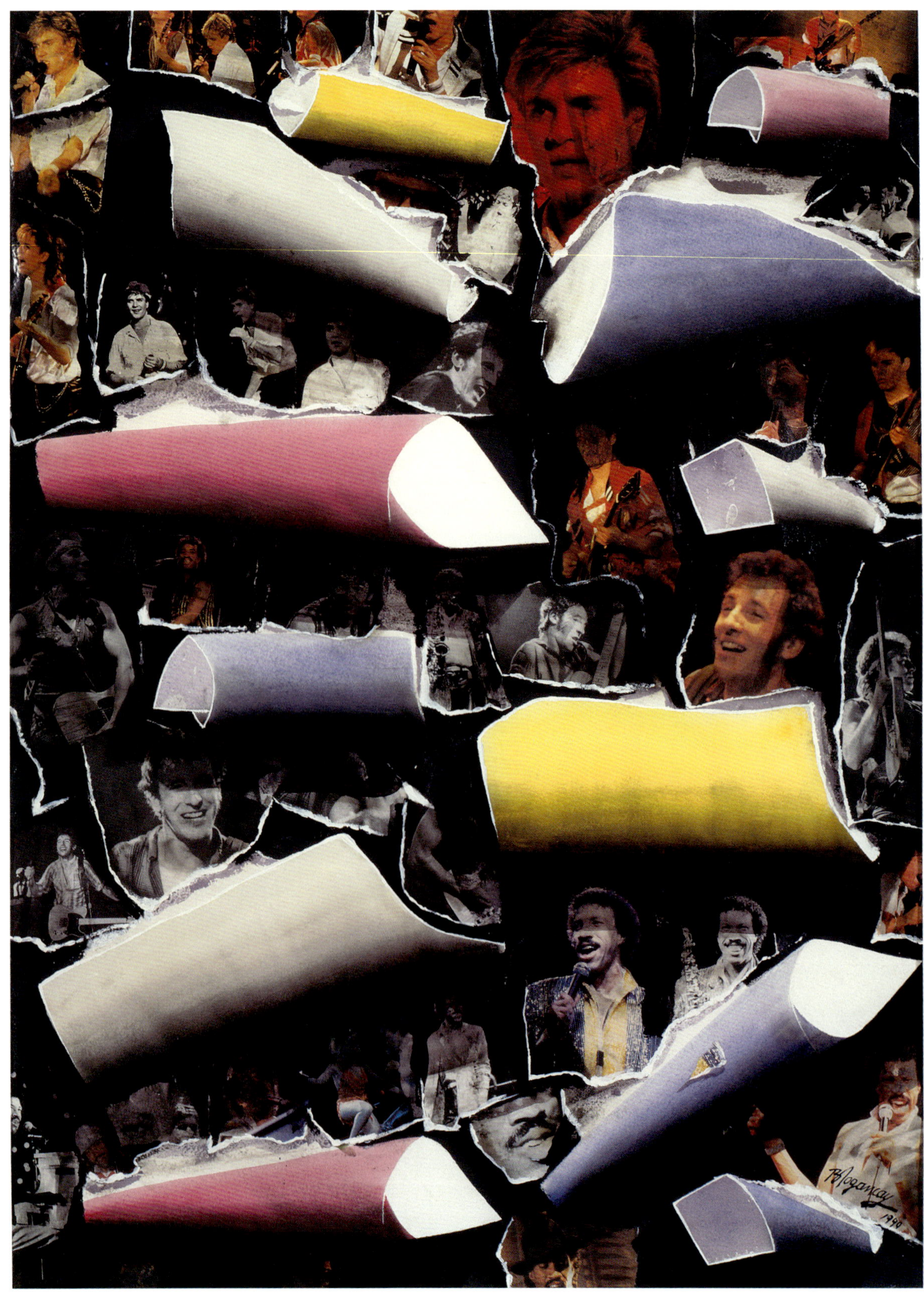

Rockstars, 1990. Collage, acrylic, and gouache on paper, 30 × 22 in. (76.2 × 55.9 cm). Collection of the artist

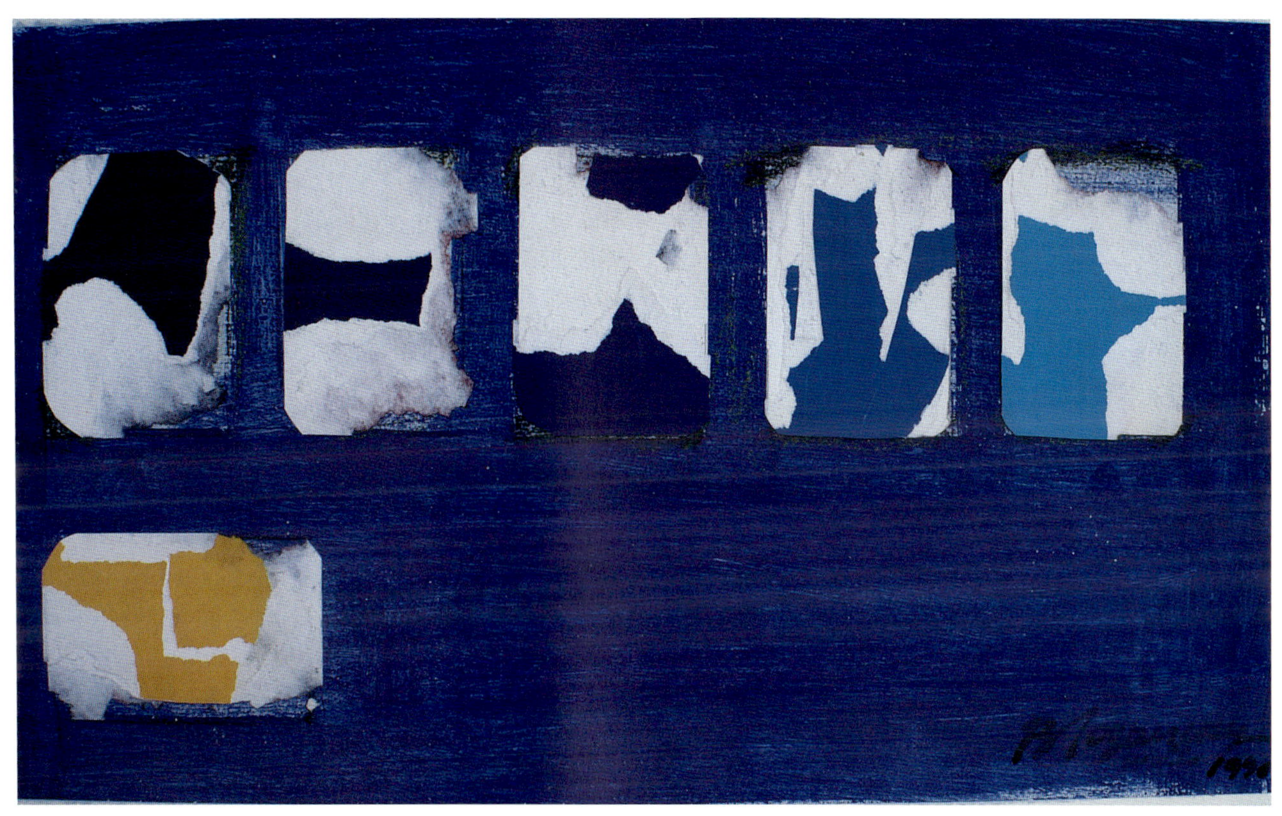

Study for Housepainter Series, 1990. Collage and acrylic on paper, 8 × 14 in. (20.3 × 35.6 cm). Collection of the artist

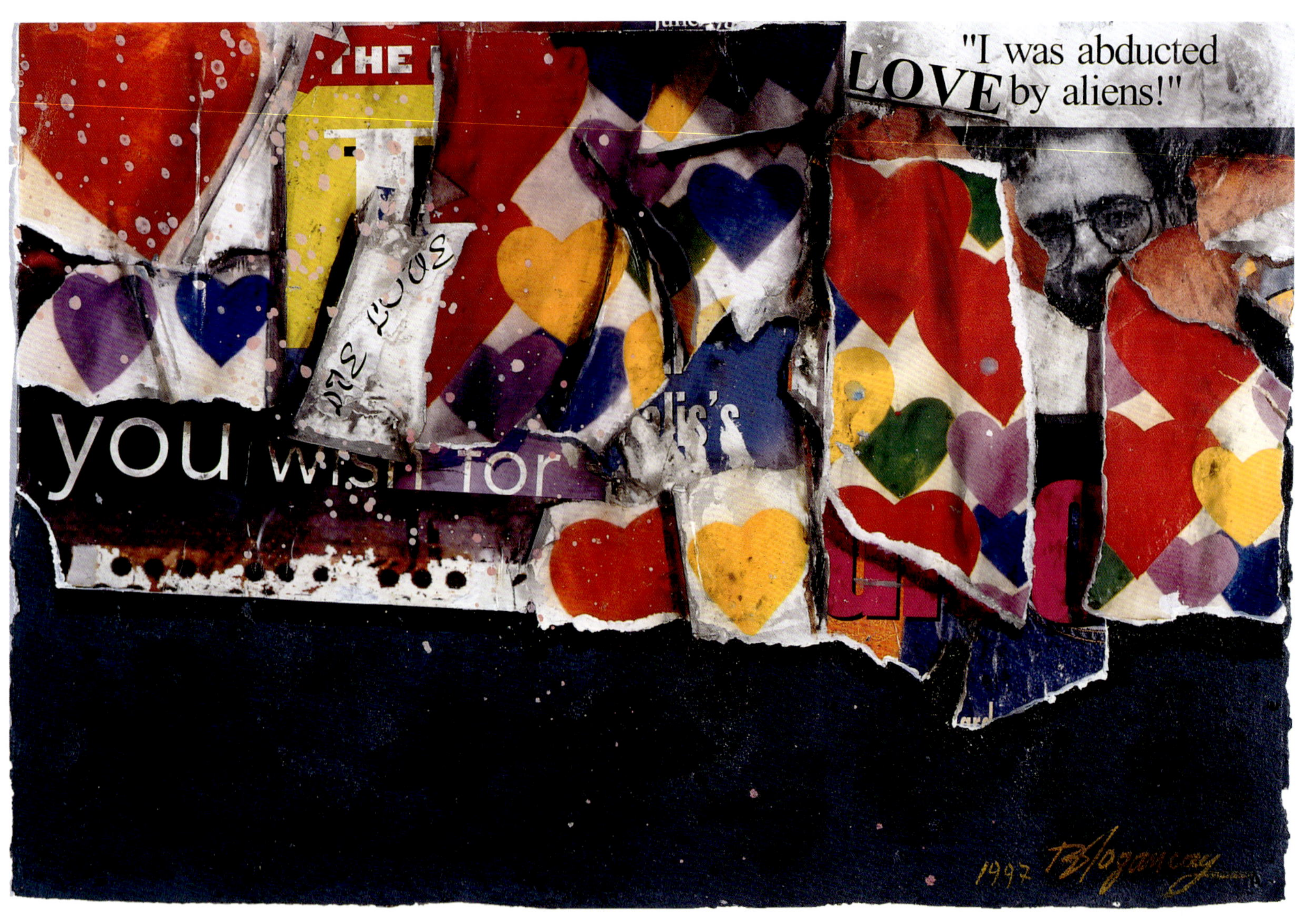

I Was Abducted by Aliens, 1997. Collage, acrylic, and gouache on paper, 15 × 22 in. (38.1 × 55.9 cm). Collection of the artist

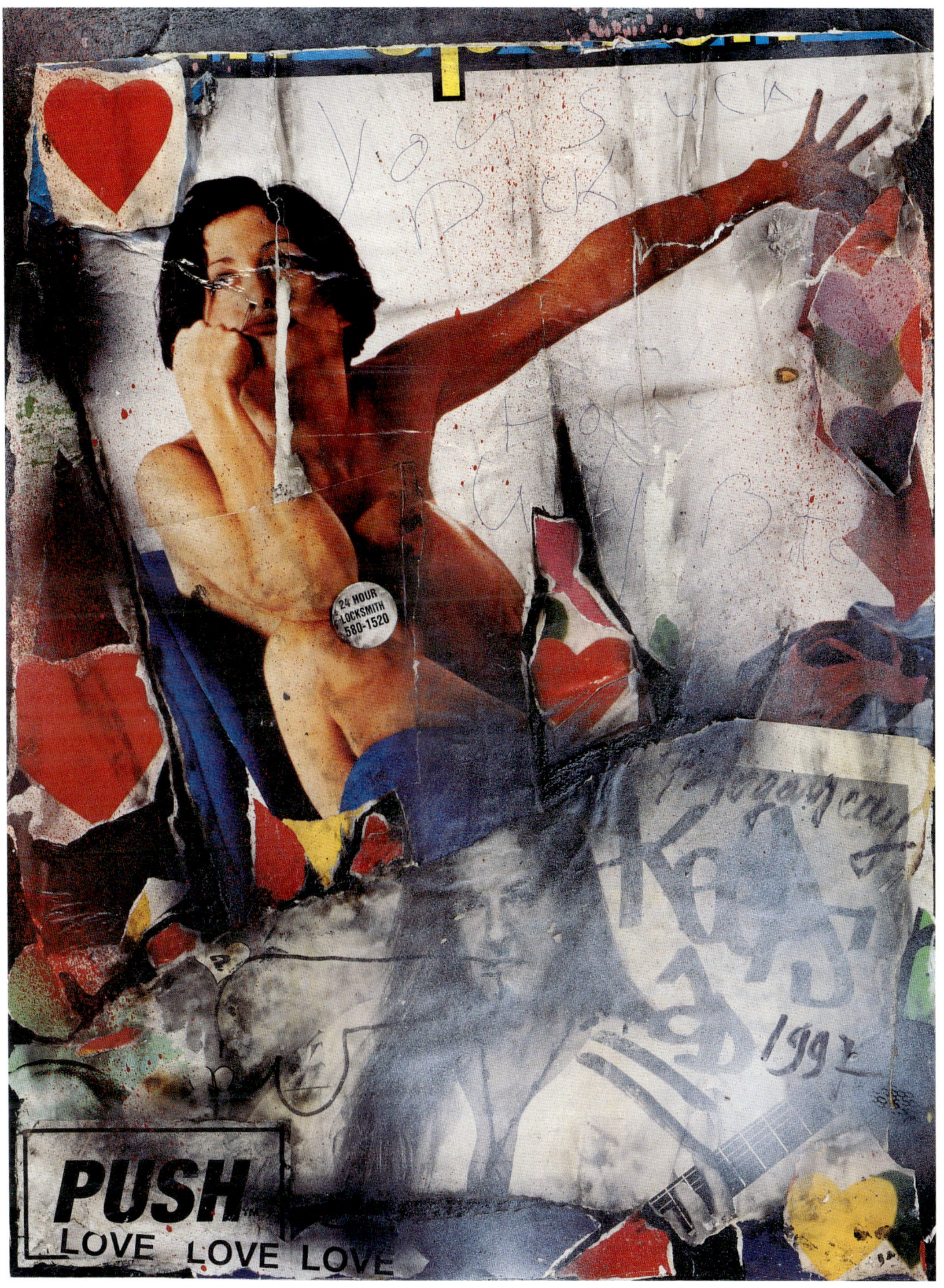

Push Love, 1997. Collage, acrylic, and gouache on paper, 22 × 15 in. (55.9 × 38.1 cm). Collection of the artist

V

Mixed Media

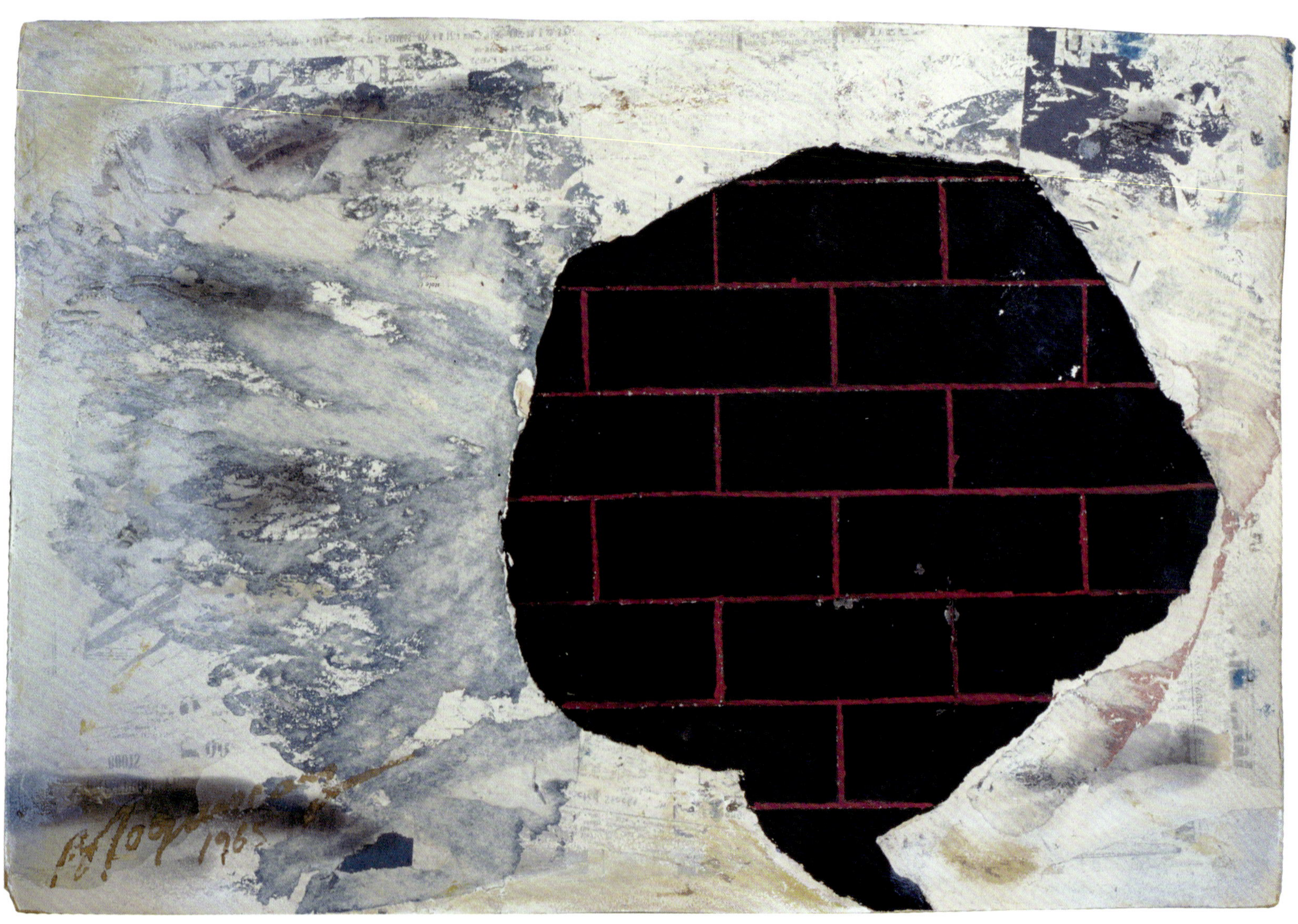

Black Bricks, 1965. Mixed media on paper, 15 × 25⅝ in. (38.1 × 65 cm). Collection of the artist

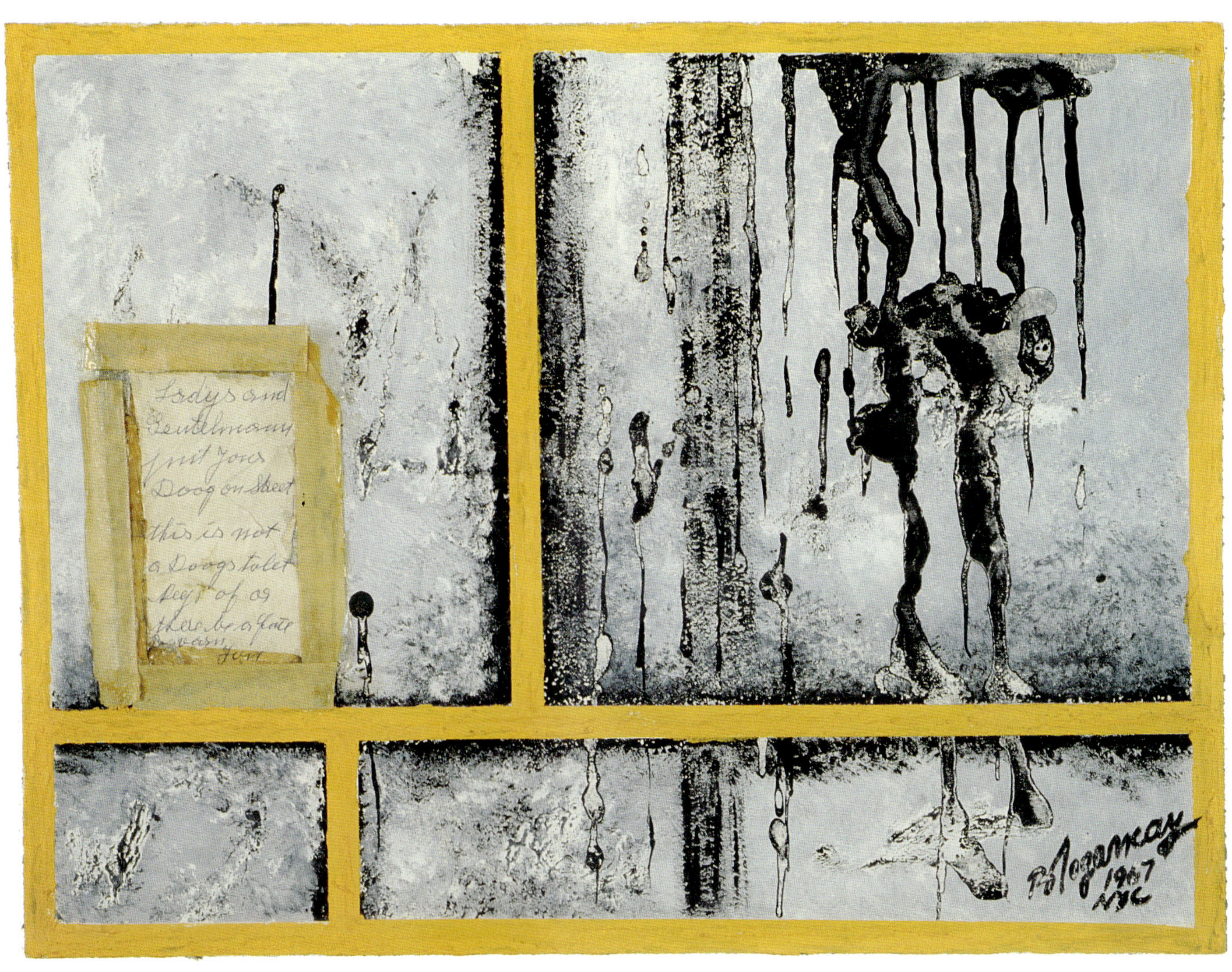

Ladys and Gentilmen, 1967. Mixed media on cardboard, 15 × 20 in. (38.1 × 50.8 cm). Collection of the artist

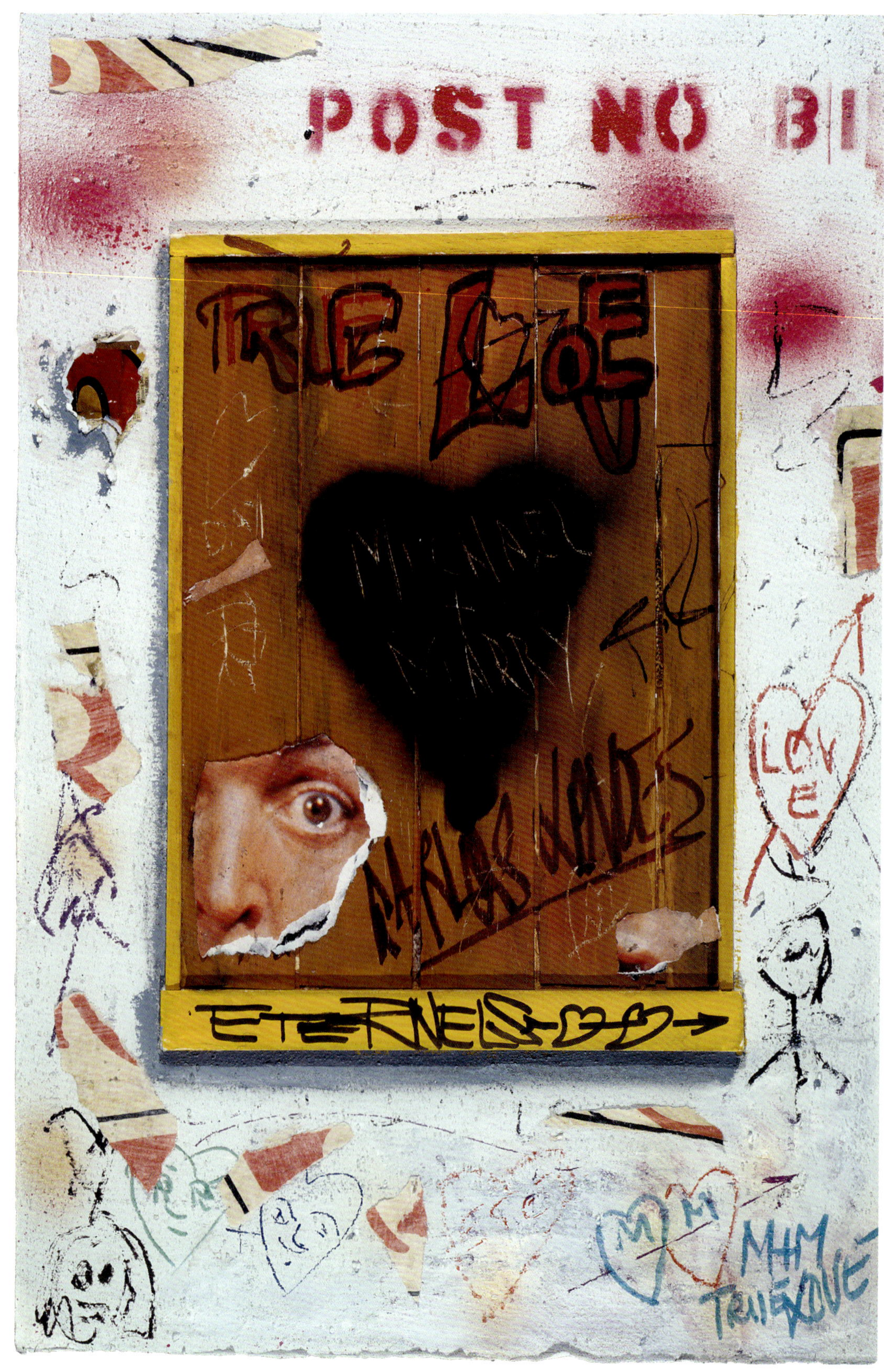

True Love, 1984. Mixed media on paper, 22 × 15 in. (55 × 38 cm). Collection of the artist

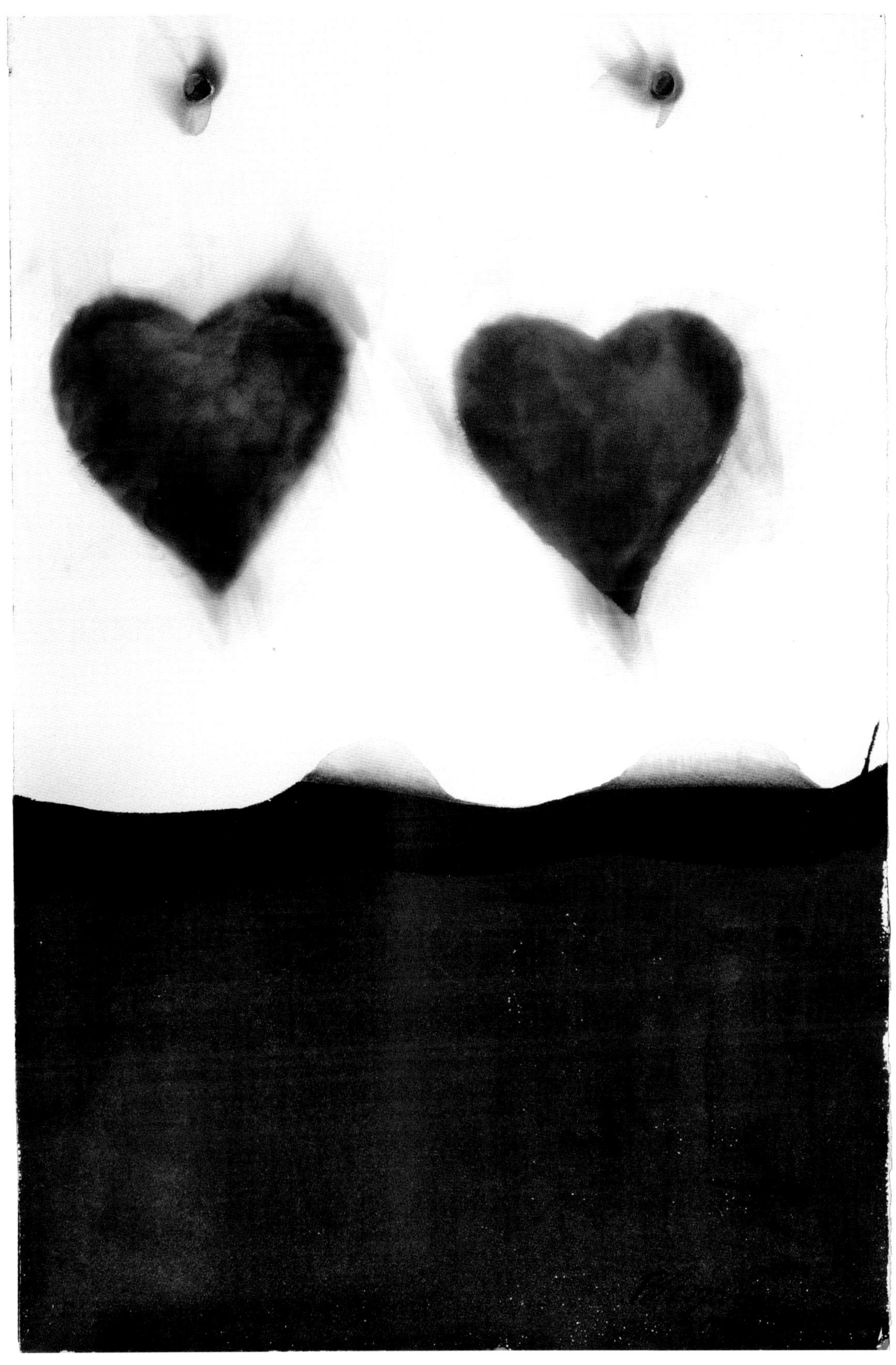

Twins, 1984. Mixed media on paper, 22 × 15 in. (55 × 38 cm). Collection of the artist

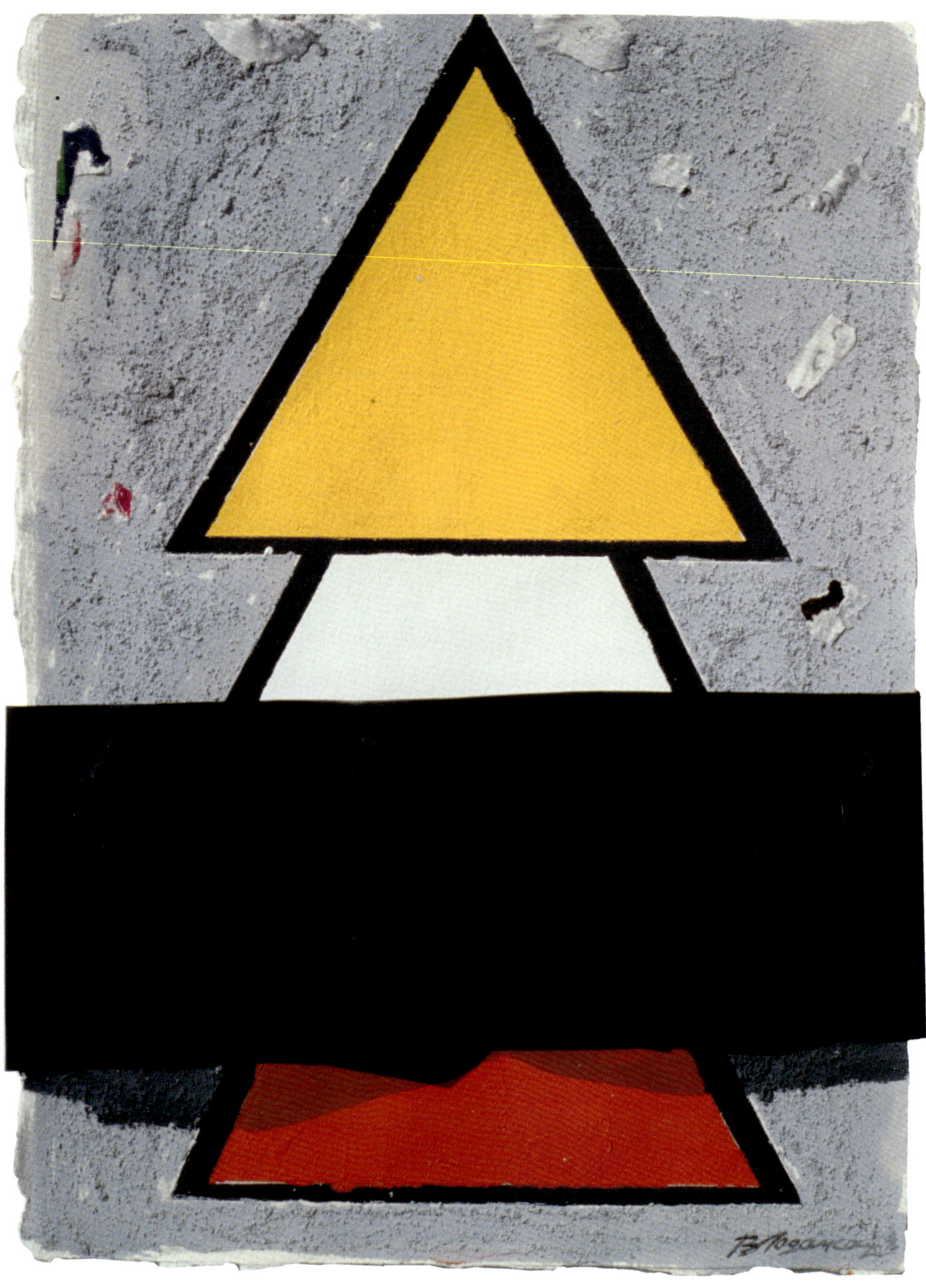

Yellow Arrow, 1990. Mixed media on paper, 15 × 11⅜ in. (38.1 × 29 cm). Collection of the artist

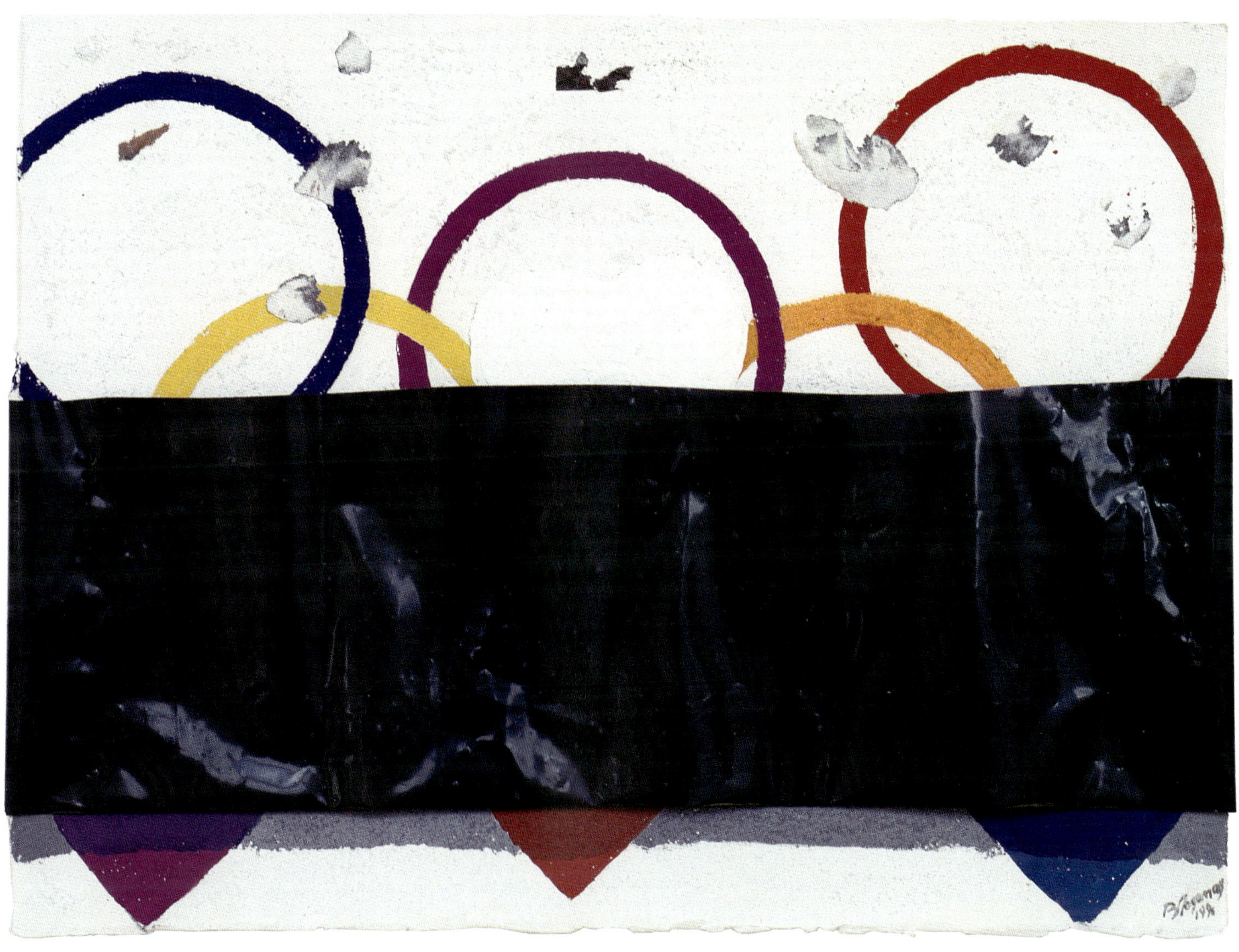

Olympic Rings, 1990. Mixed media on paper, 11⅜ × 15 in. (29 × 38.1 cm). Collection of the artist

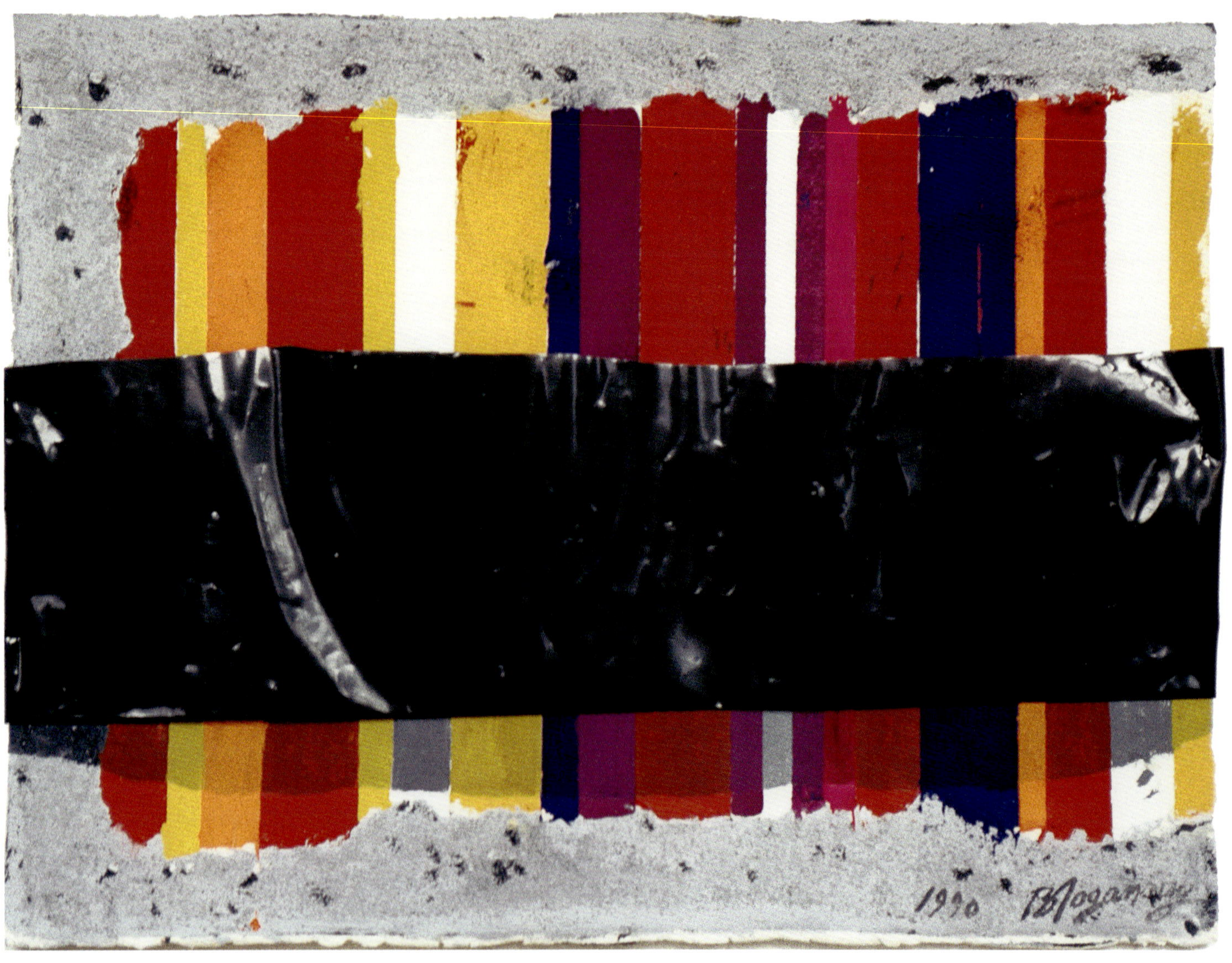

Rainbow, 1990. Mixed media on paper, 11⅜ × 15 in. (29 × 38.1 cm). Collection of the artist

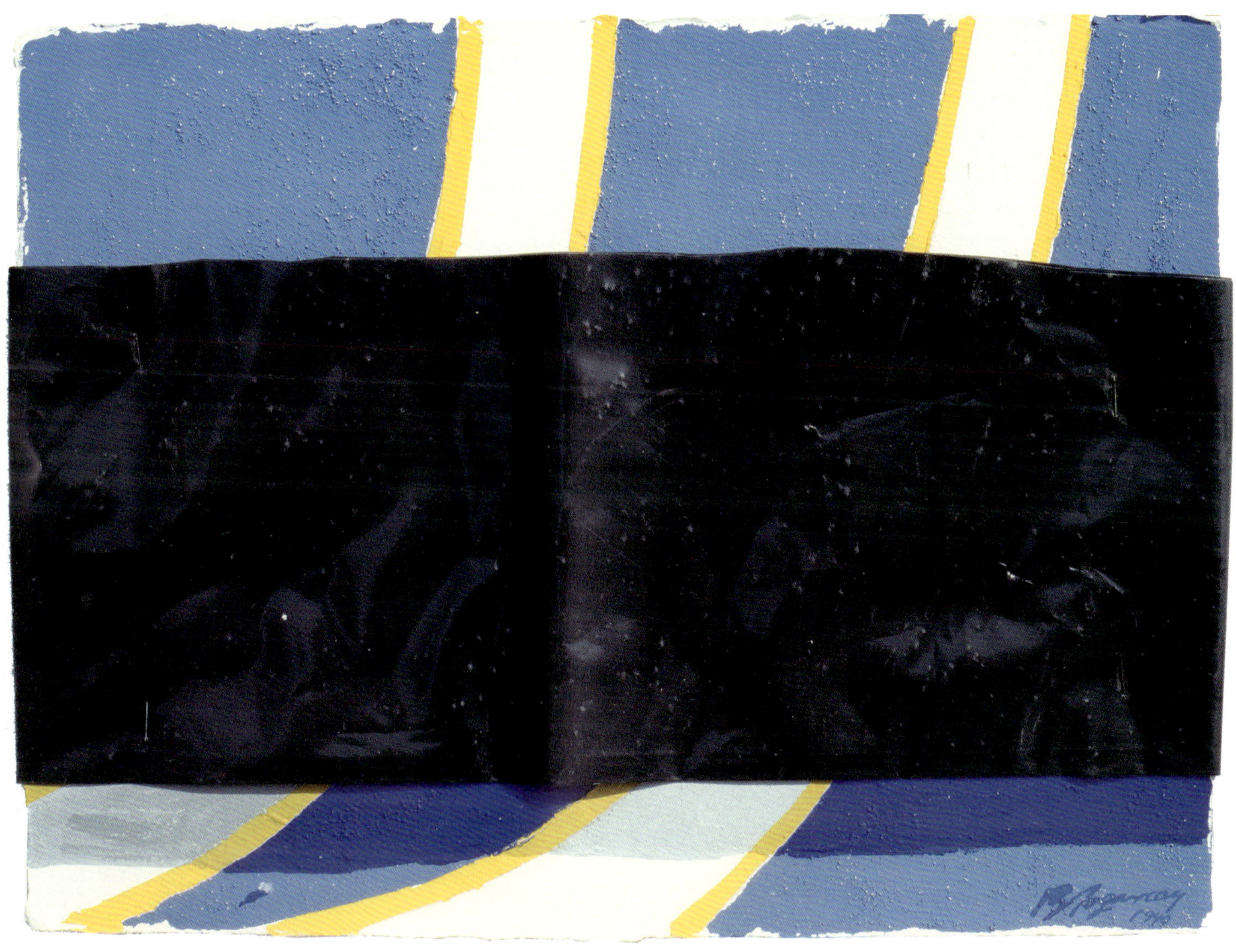

Two White Tracks, 1990. Mixed media on paper, 11⅜ × 15 in. (29 × 38.1 cm). Collection of the artist

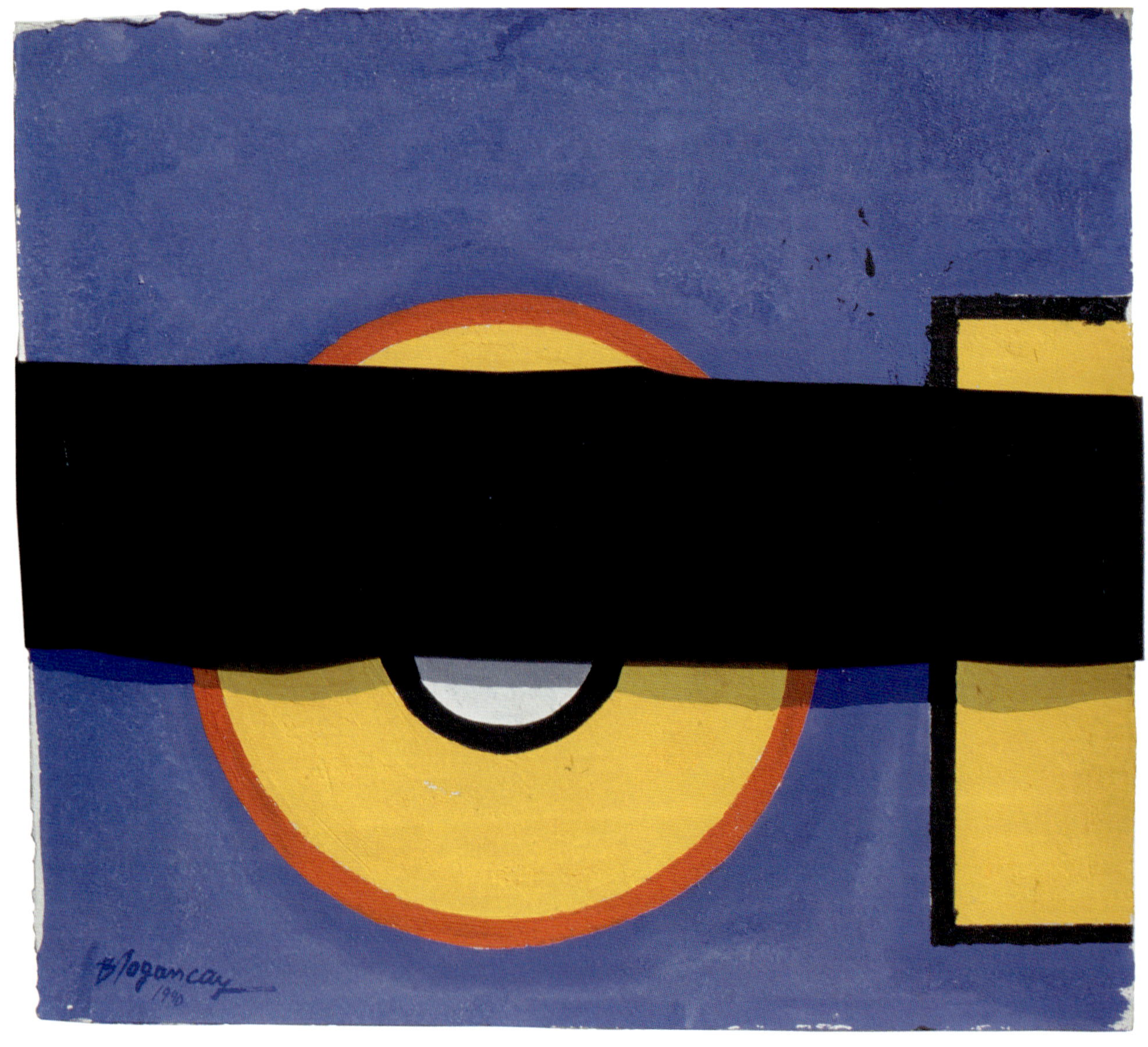

Yellow O, 1990. Mixed media on paper, 13⅜ × 15 in. (34 × 38.1 cm). Collection of the artist

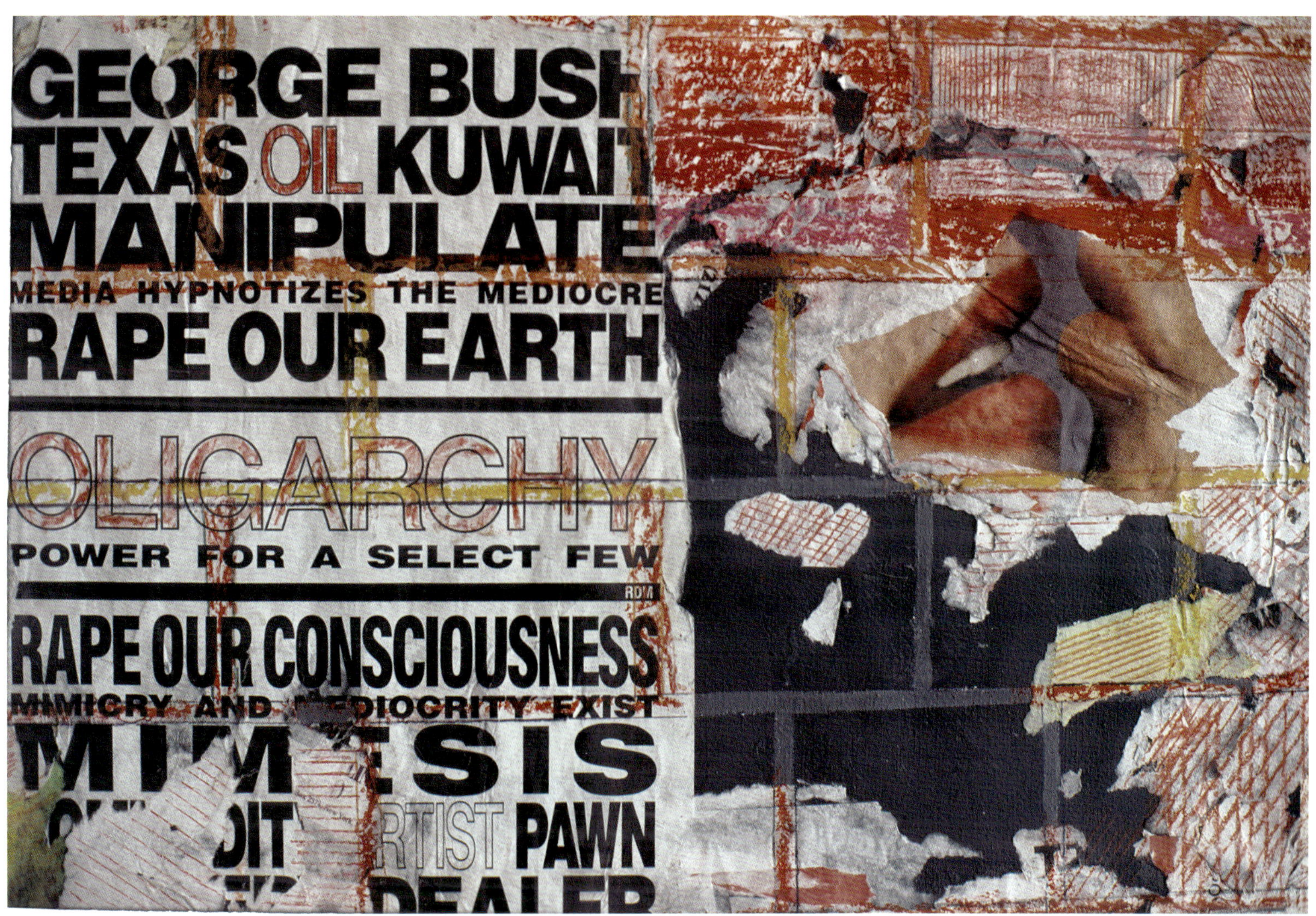

Oligarchy, 1992. Mixed media on paper, 15 × 22 in. (38.1 × 55.9 cm). Collection of the artist

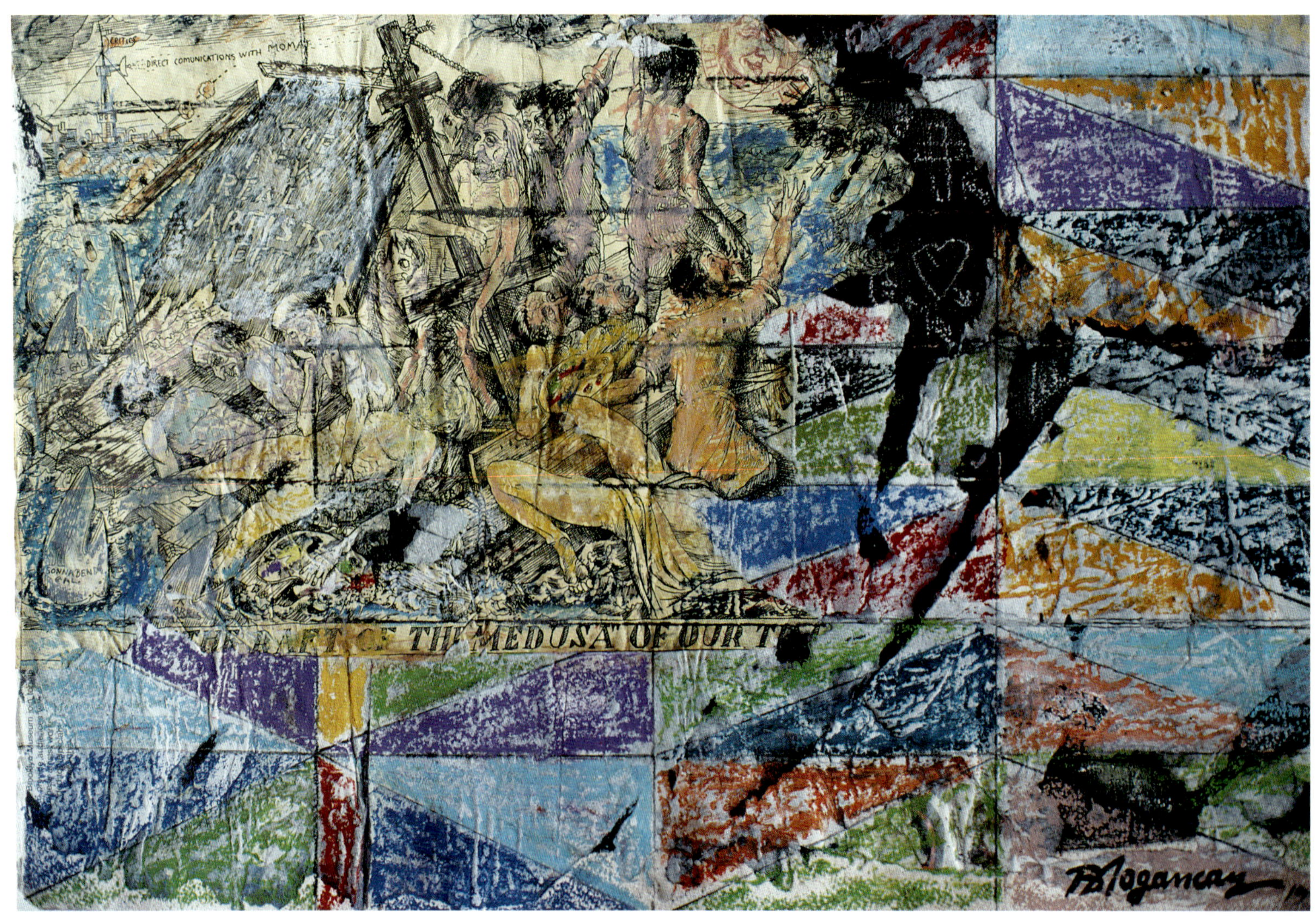

Medusa, 1992. Mixed media on paper, 15 × 22 in. (38.1 × 55.9 cm). Collection of the artist

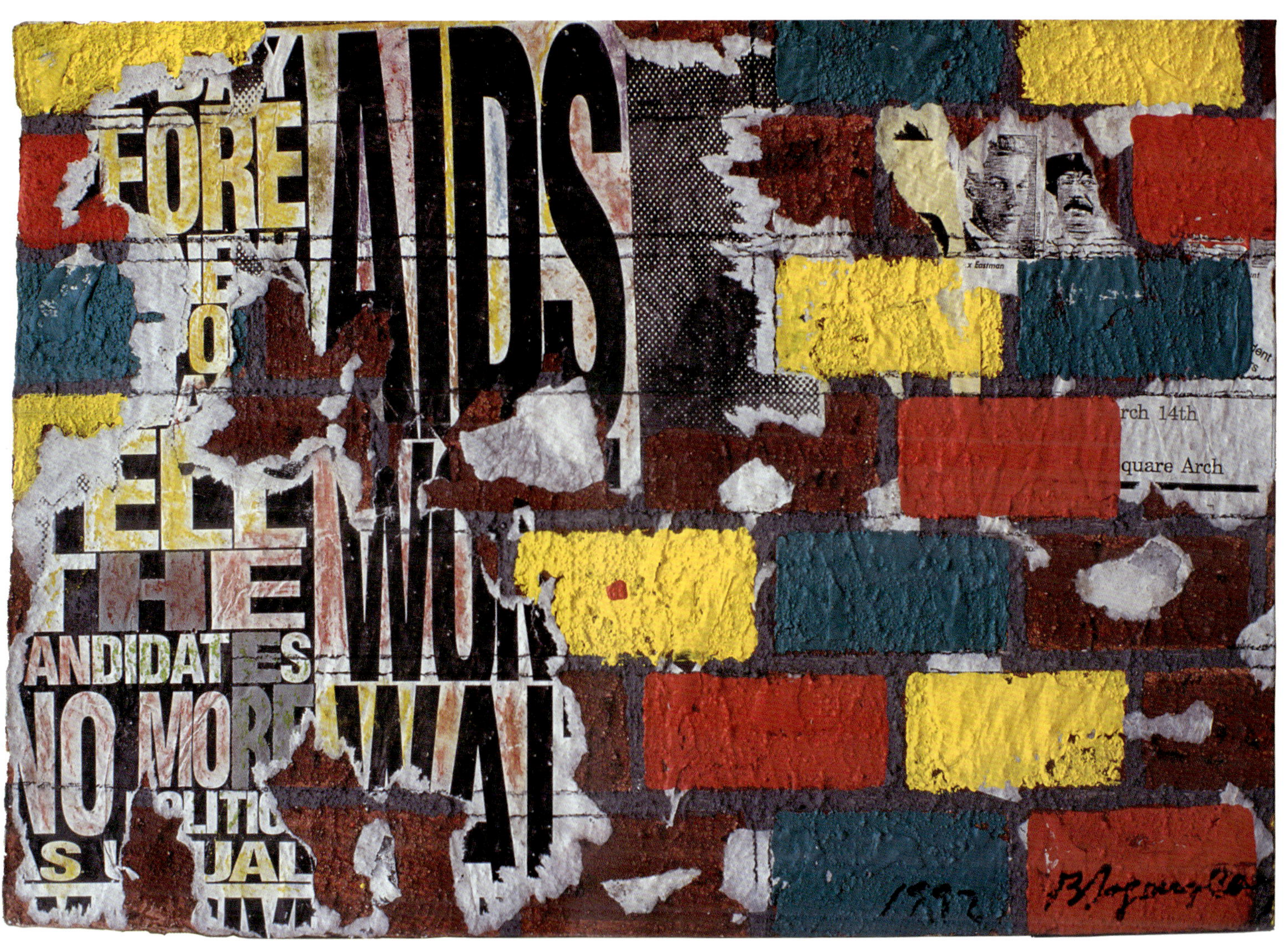

Grego's Wall, 1992. Mixed media on paper, 15 × 22 in. (38.1 × 55.9 cm). Collection of the artist

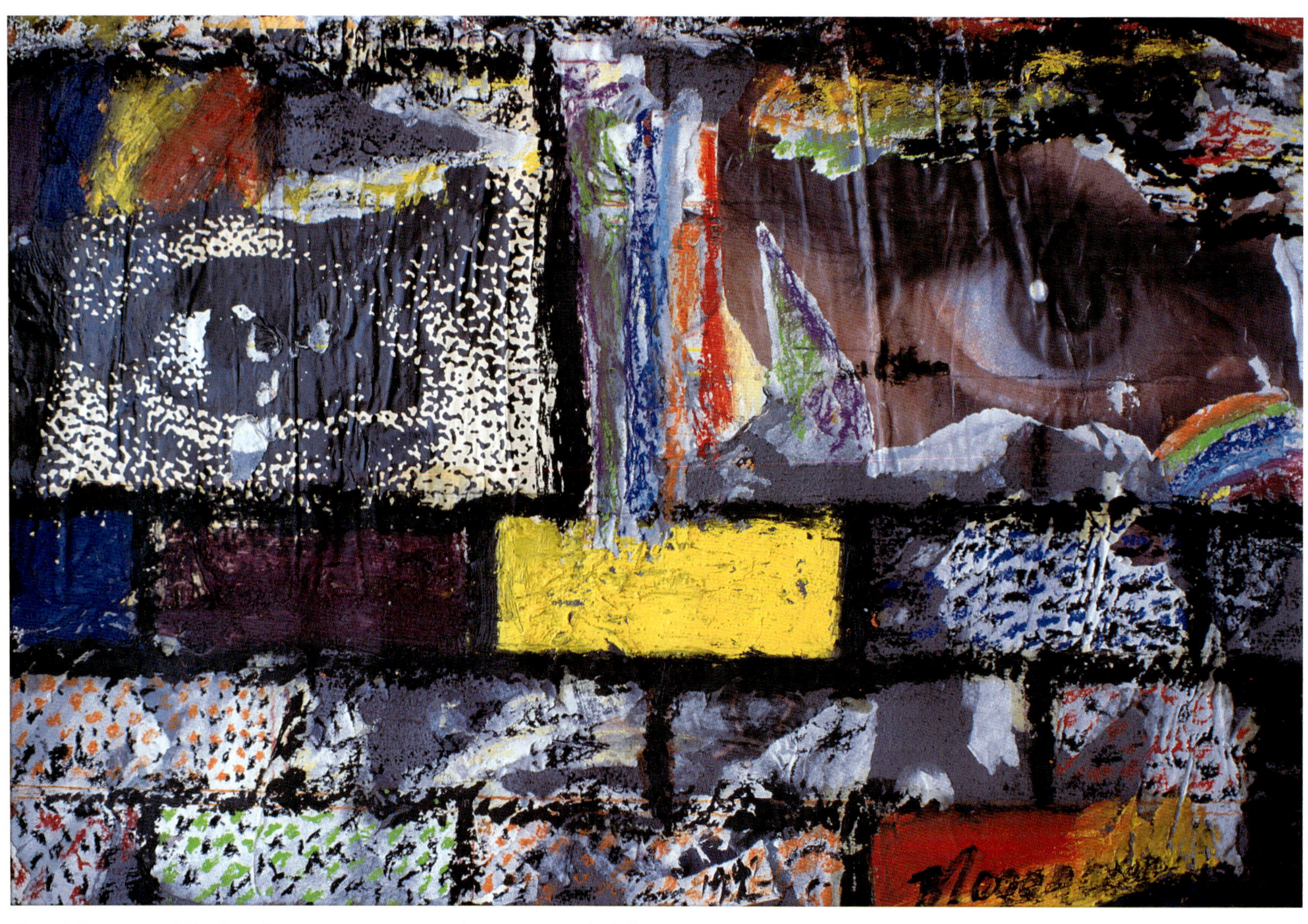

Grego's Eyes, 1992. Mixed media on paper, 15 × 22 in. (38.1 × 55.9 cm). Collection of the artist

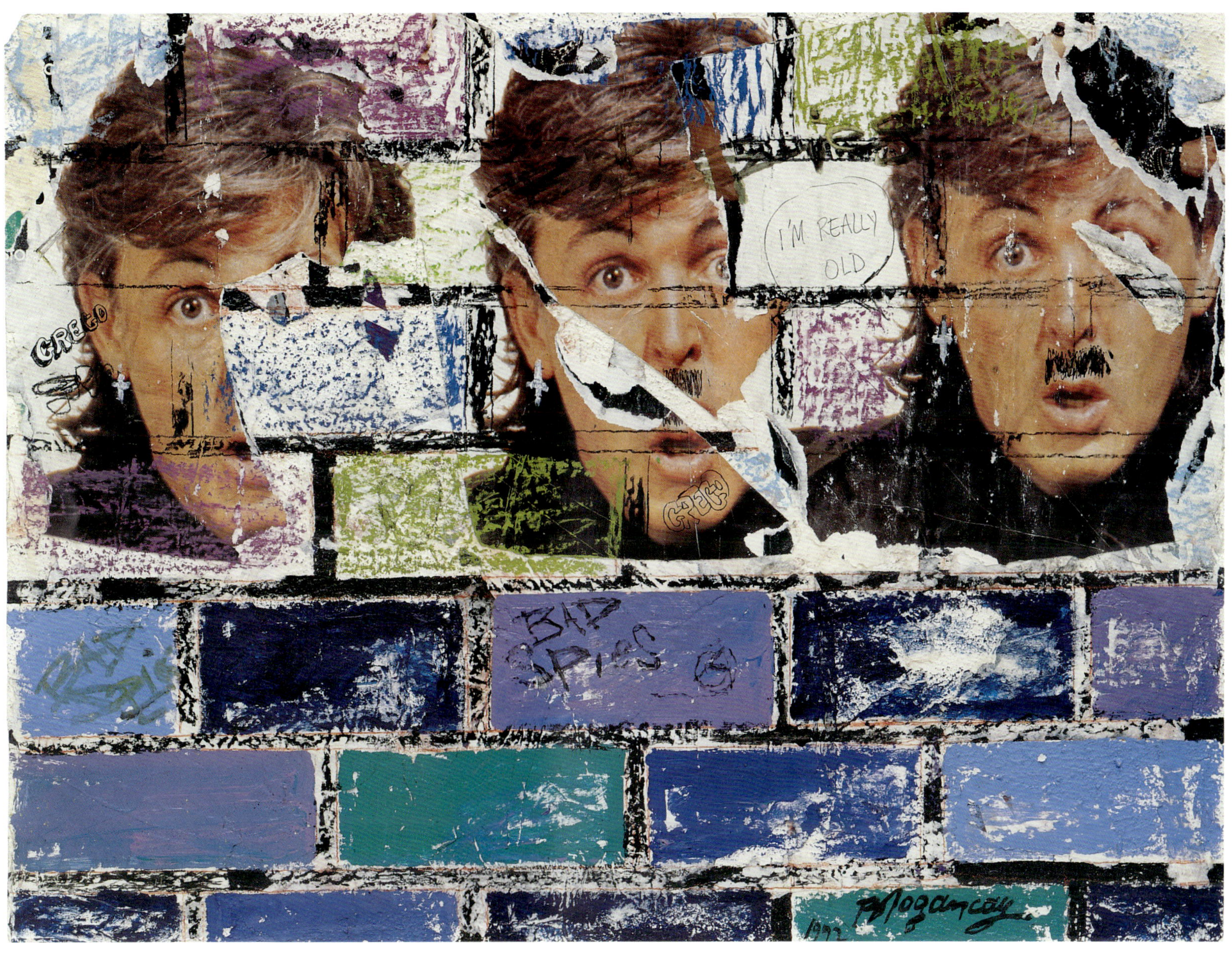

I'm Really Old, 1992. Mixed media on paper, 22 × 30 in. (55.9 × 76.2 cm). Collection of the artist

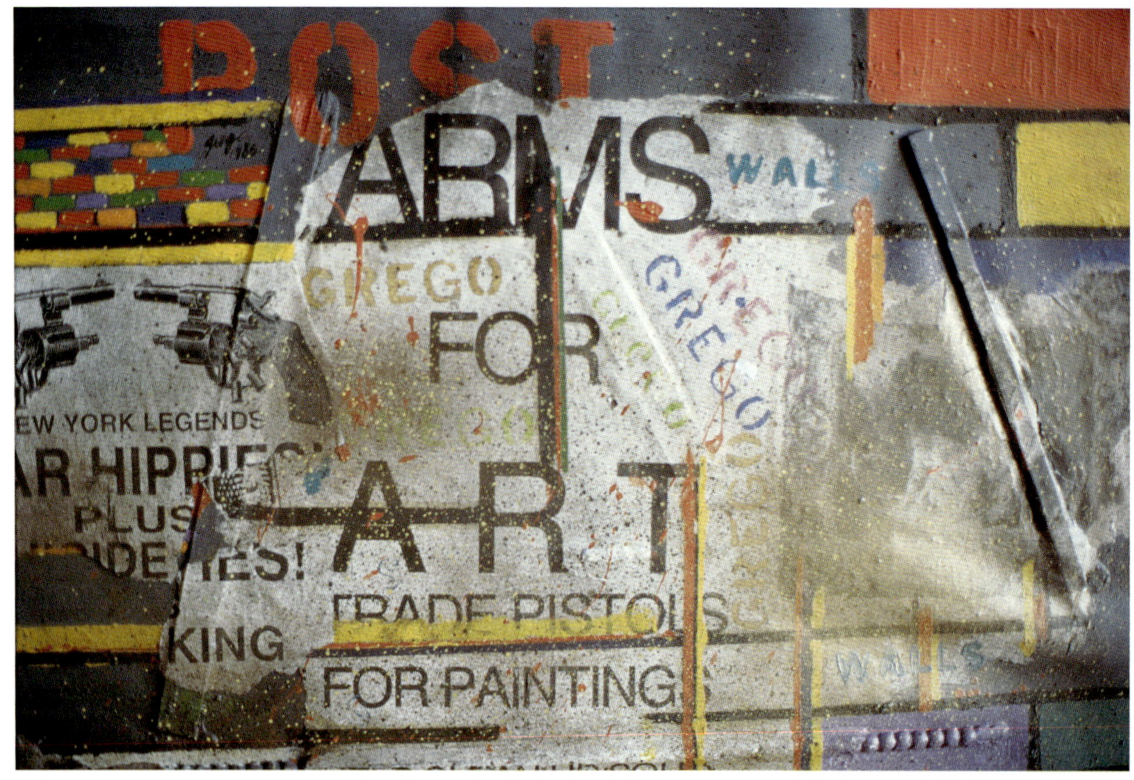

Arms for Art, 1994. Mixed media on paper, 22 × 30 in. (55.9 × 76.2 cm). Collection of the artist

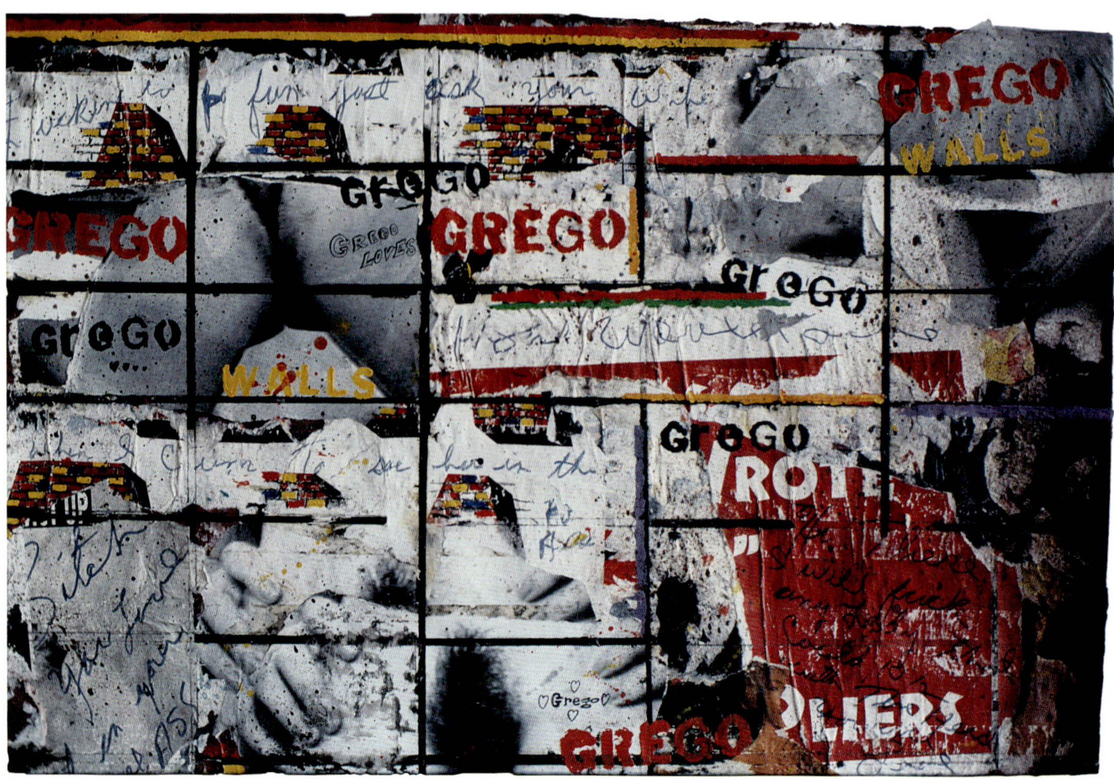

Fun, 1994. Mixed media on paper, 22 × 30 in. (55.9 × 76.2 cm). Collection of the artist

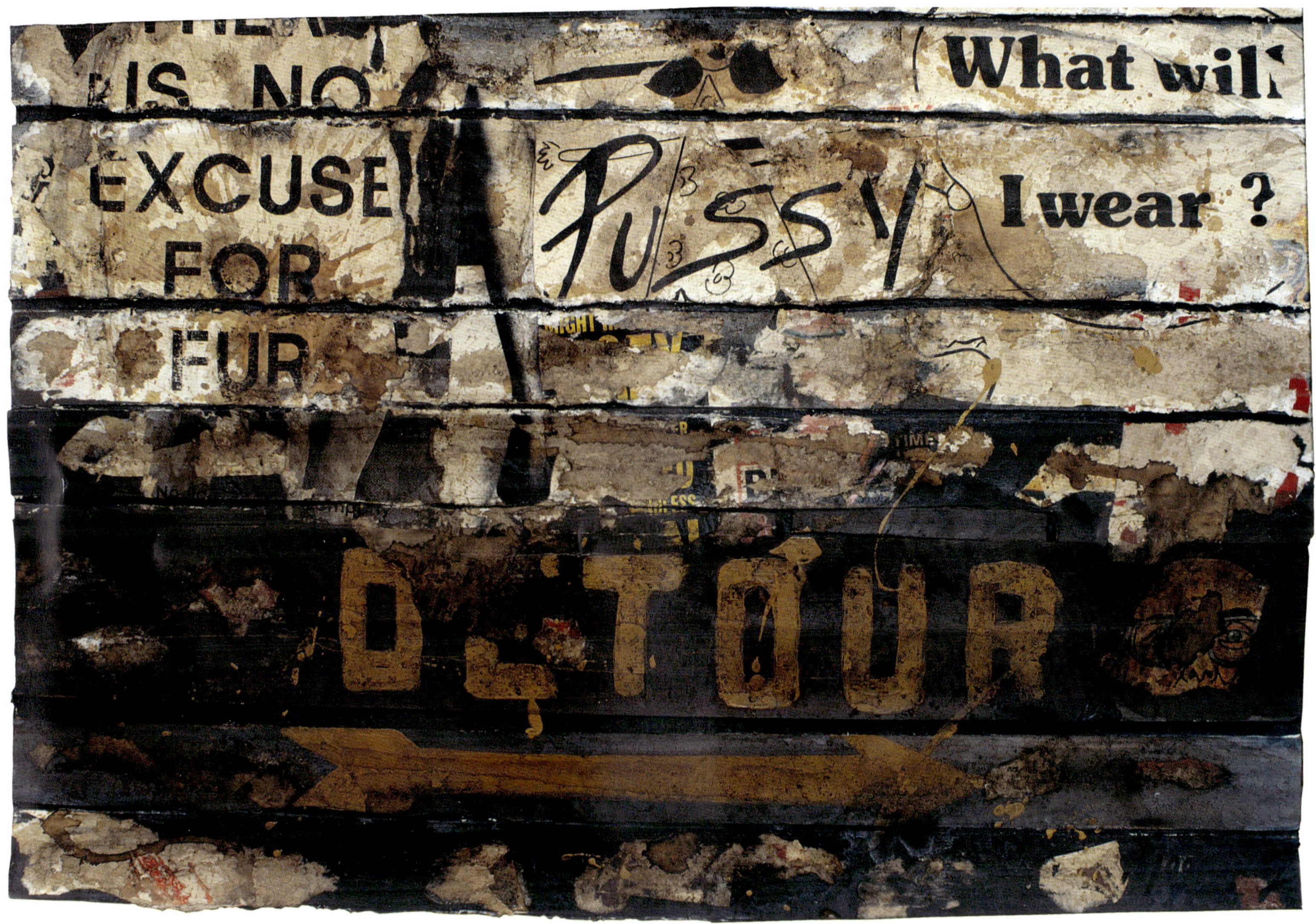

What Will I Wear?, 1995. Mixed media on paper, 22 × 30 in. (55.9 × 76.2 cm). Collection of the artist

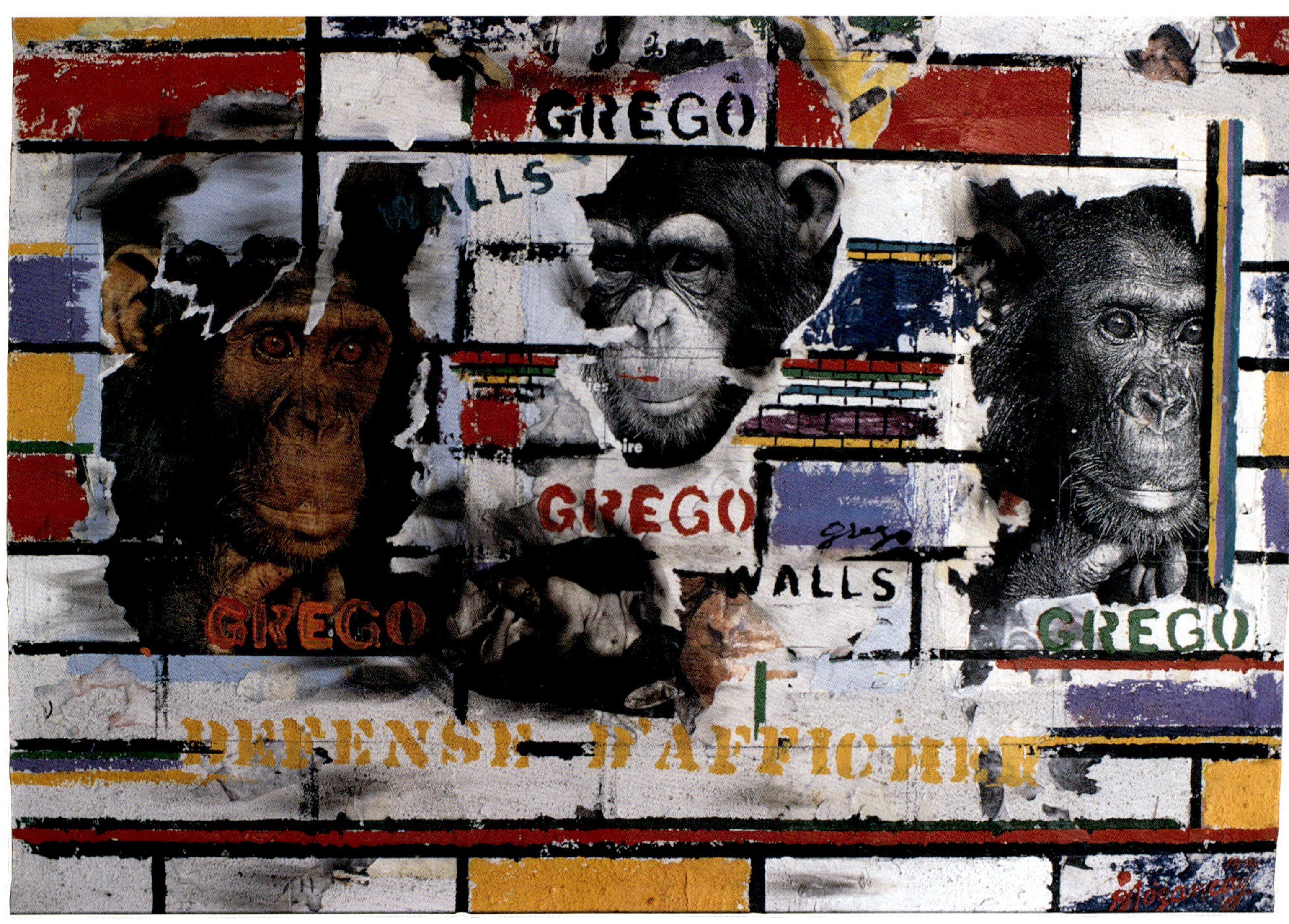

Grego's Monkeys, 1994. Mixed media on paper, 22 × 30 in. (55.9 × 76.2 cm). Collection of the artist

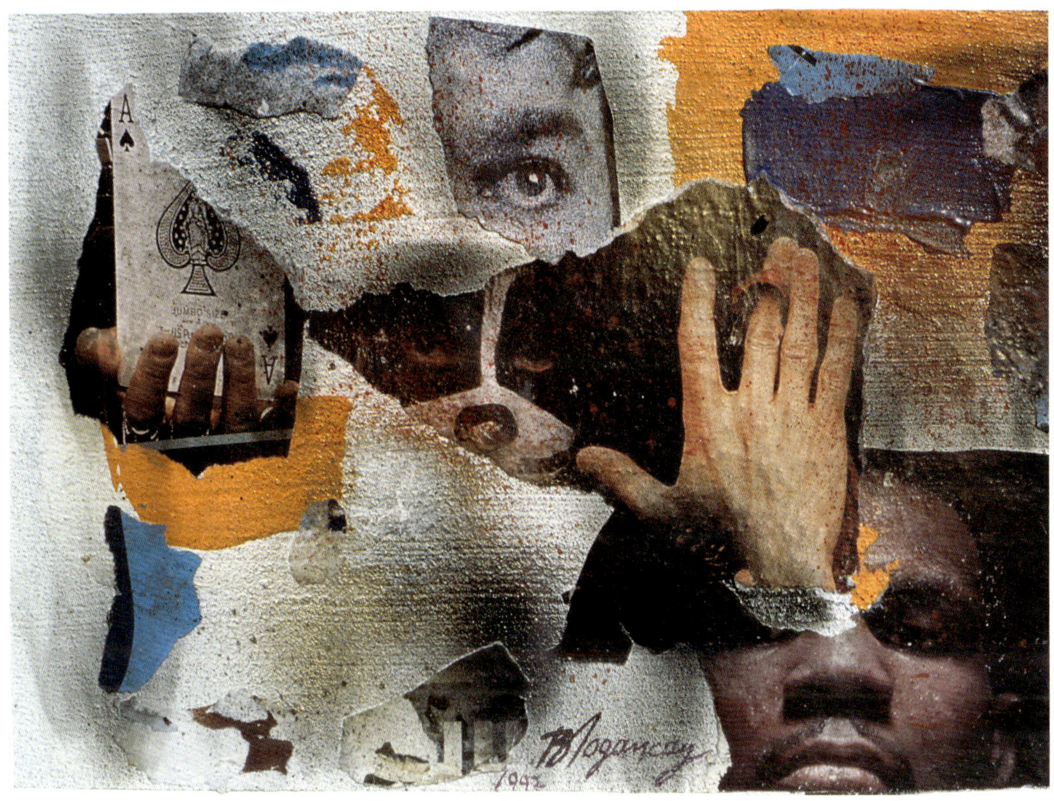

Reaching Out, 1997. Mixed media on paper, 8 × 12 in. (20.3 × 30.5 cm). Collection of the artist

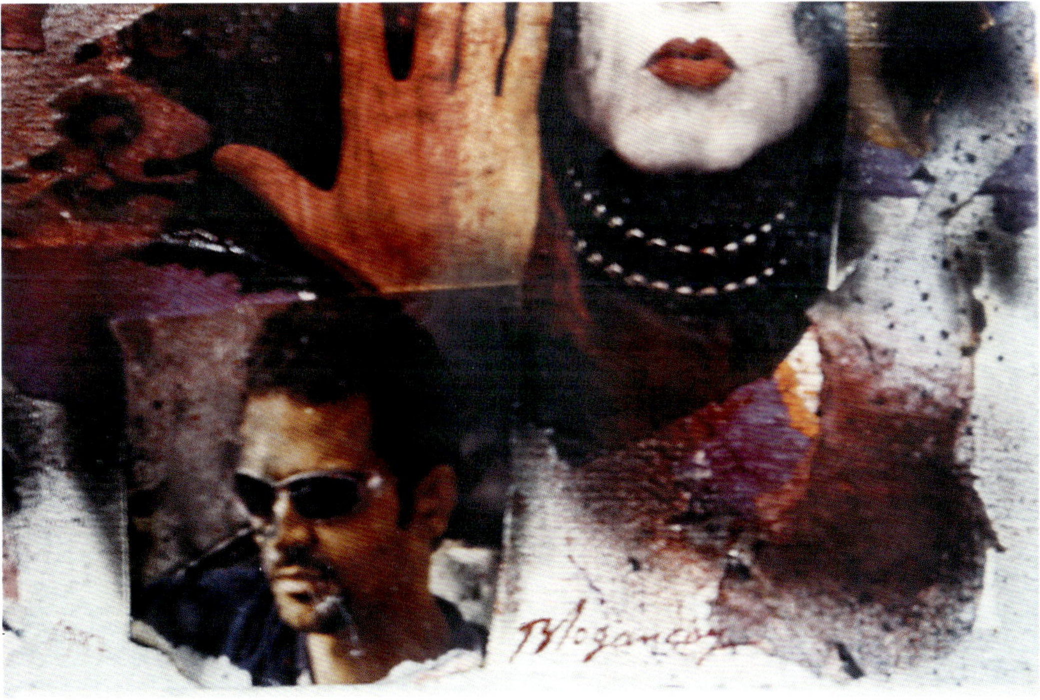

Red Lips, 1997. Mixed media on paper, 8 × 12 in. (20.3 × 30.5 cm). Collection of the artist

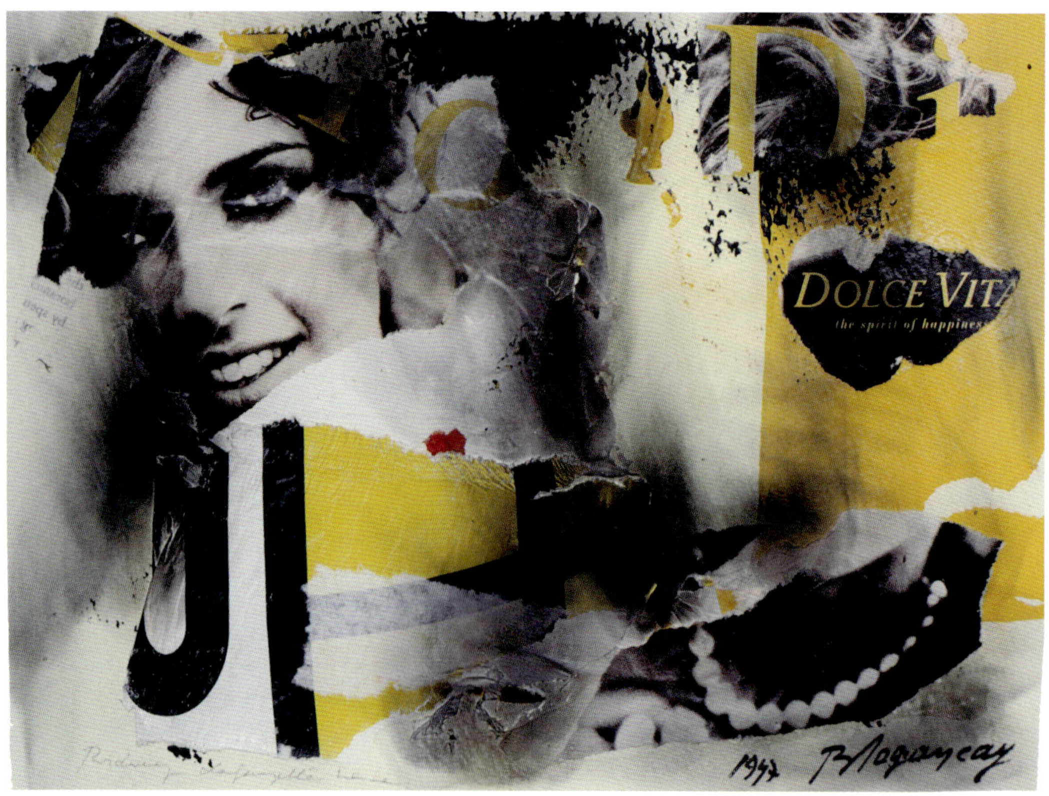

Dolce Vita, 1997. Mixed media on paper, 8 × 12 in. (20.3 × 30.5 cm). Collection of the artist

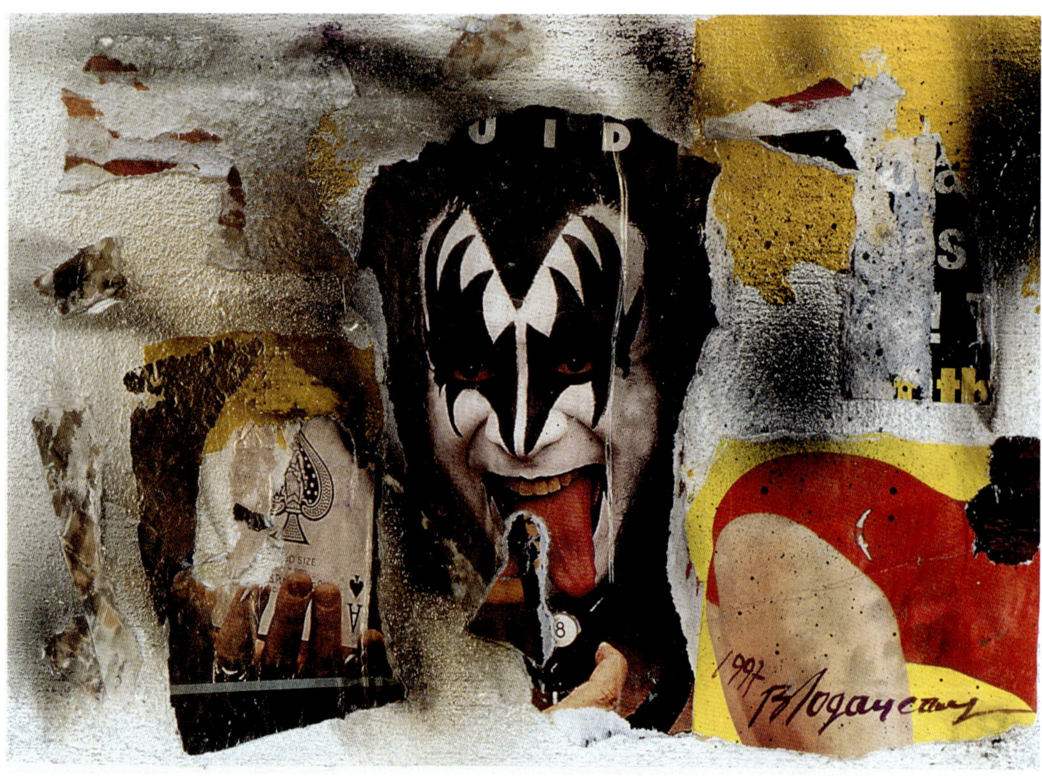

Spades, 1997. Mixed media on paper, 8 × 12 in. (20.3 × 30.5 cm). Collection of the artist

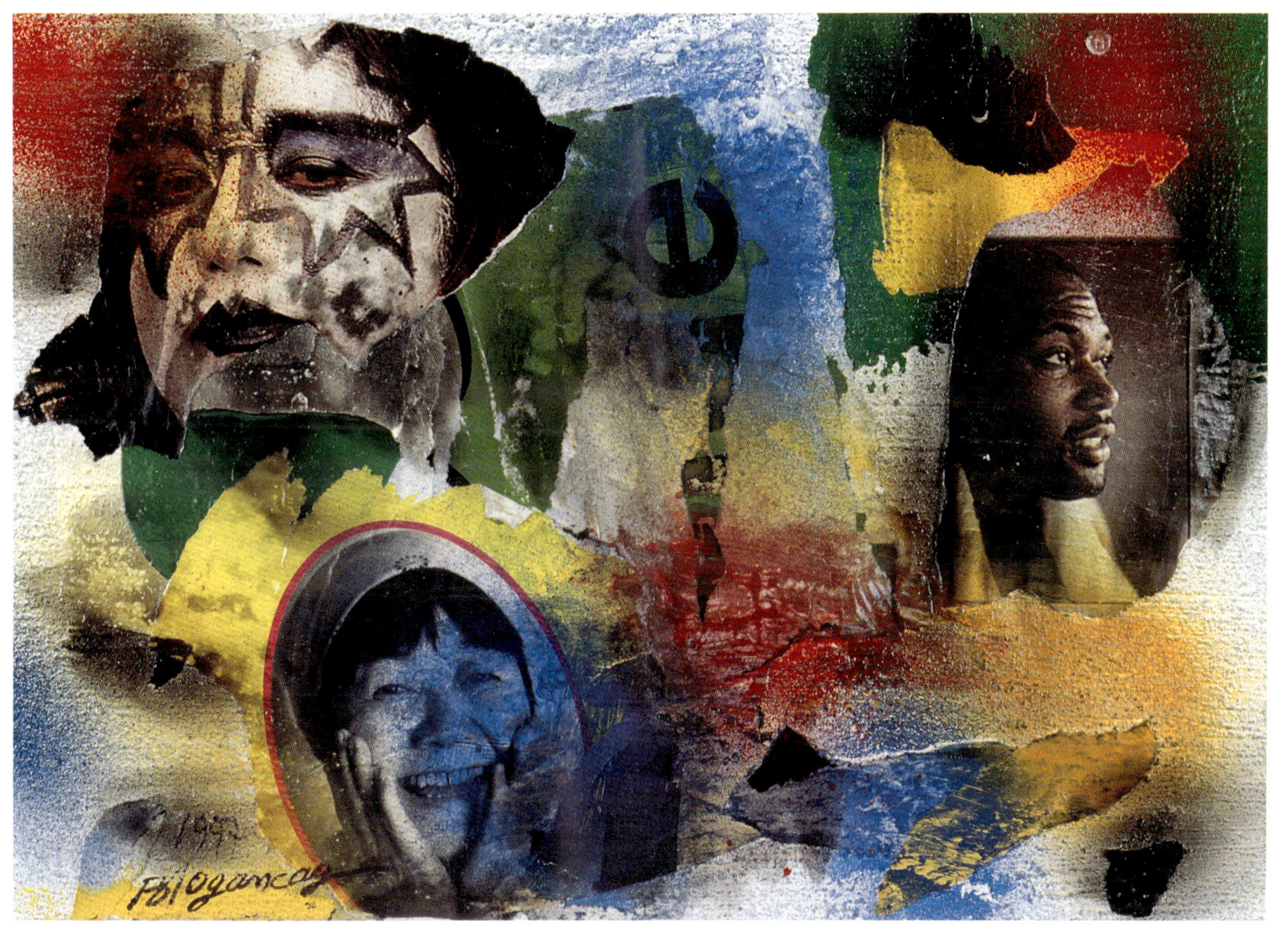

Suspended e, 1997. Mixed media on paper, 8 × 12 in. (20.3 × 30.5 cm). Collection of the artist

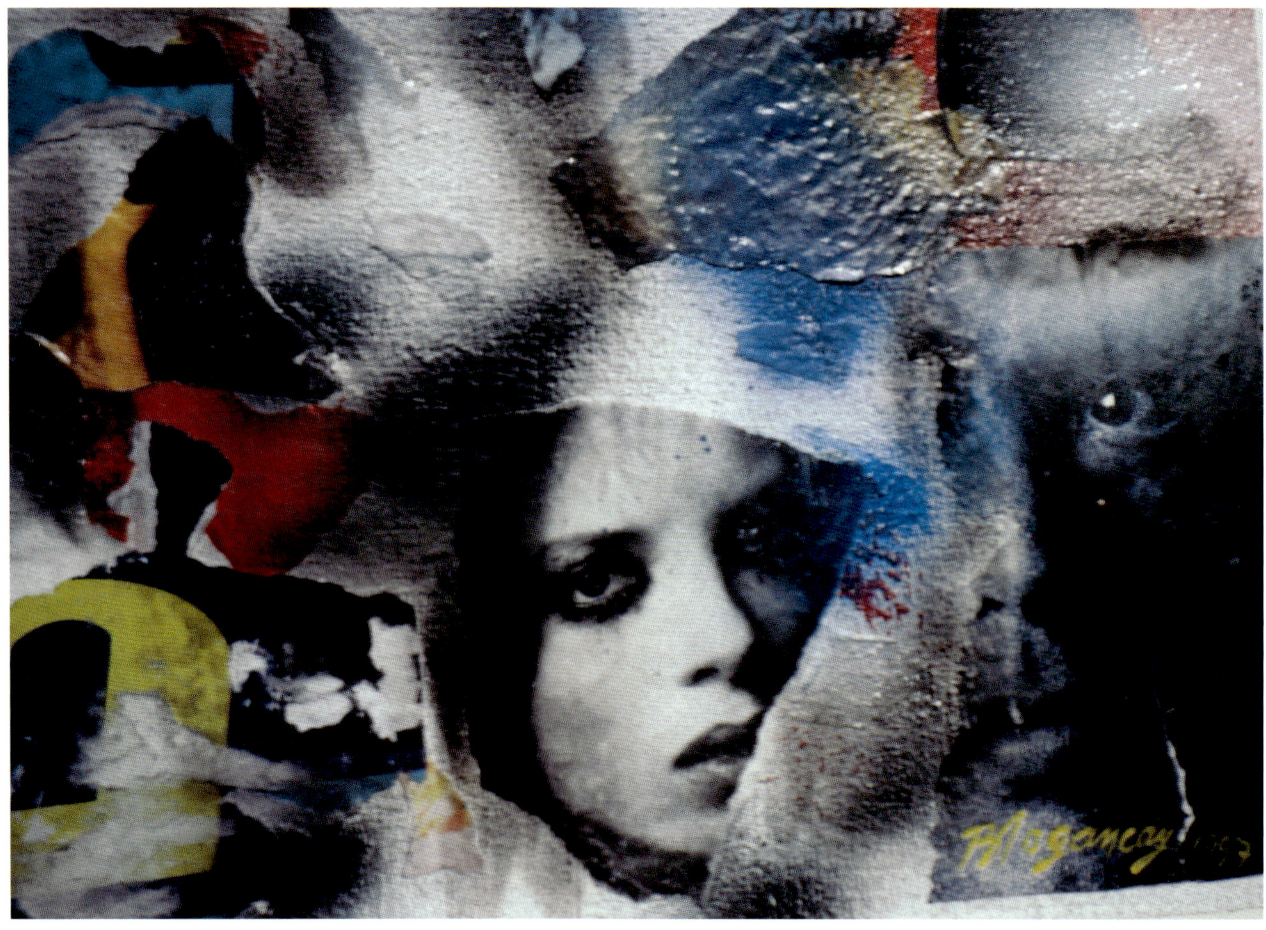

Start, 1997. Mixed media on paper, 8 × 12 in. (20.3 × 30.5 cm). Collection of the artist

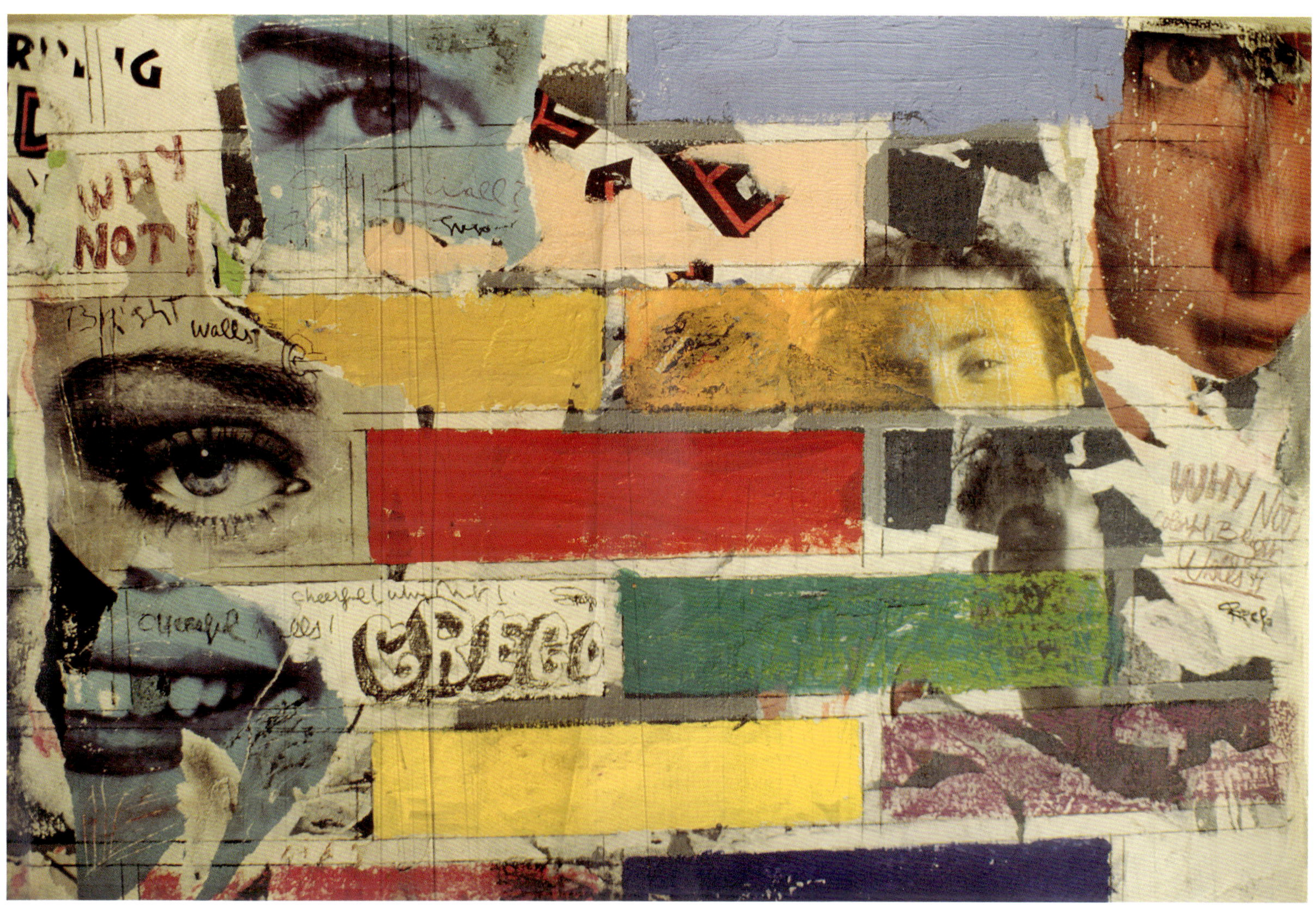

Why Not?, 1997. Mixed media on paper, 15 × 22 in. (38.1 × 55.9 cm). Collection of the artist

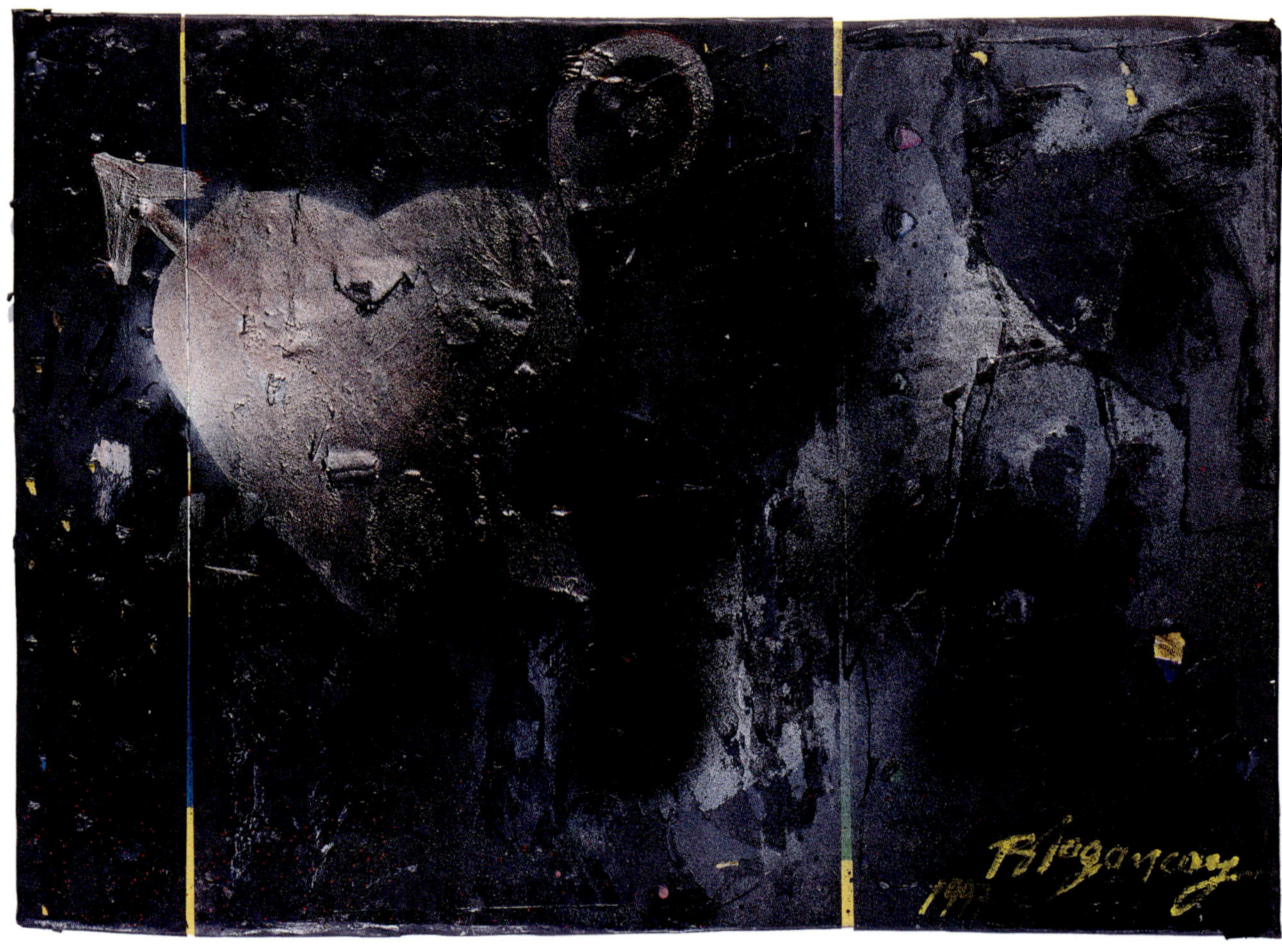

Heart in the Mist, 1997. Mixed media on cardboard, 12 × 16 in. (30.5 × 40.6 cm). Collection of the artist

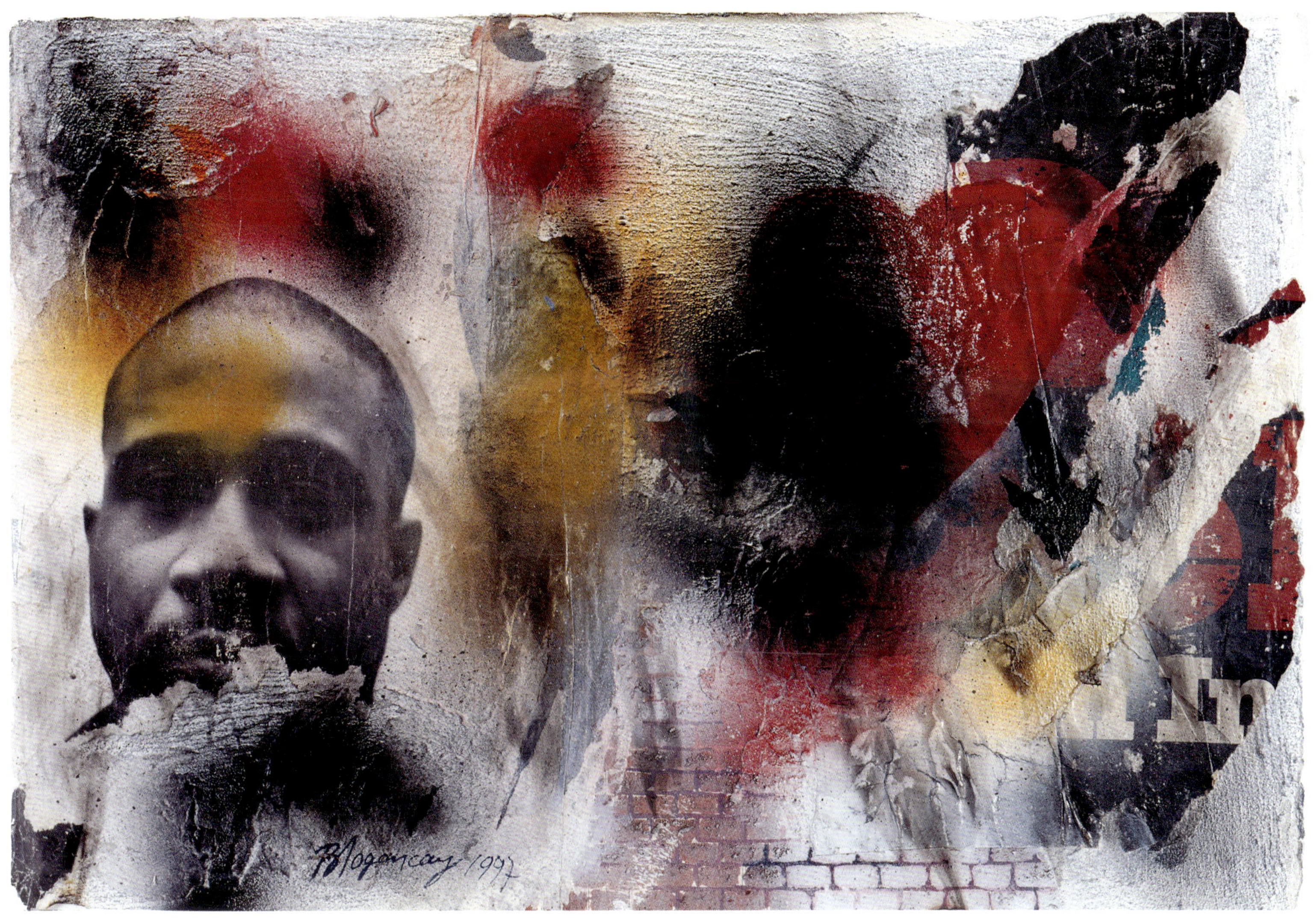

Dualistic Heart, 1997. Mixed media on paper, 15 × 22 in. (38.1 × 55.9 cm). Collection of the artist

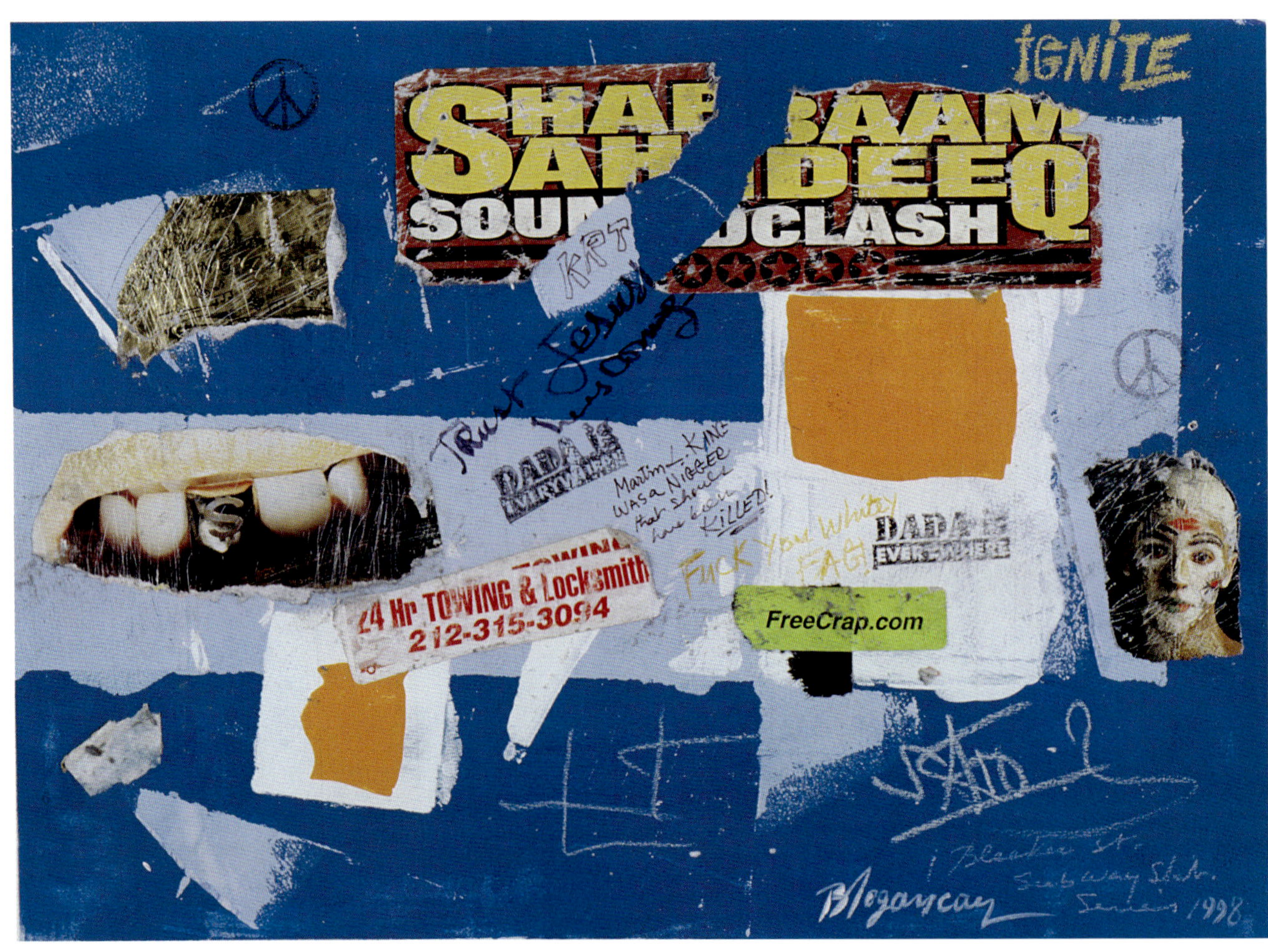

Ignite, 1998. Mixed media on paper, 12½ × 17½ in. (31.8 × 44.5 cm). Collection of the artist

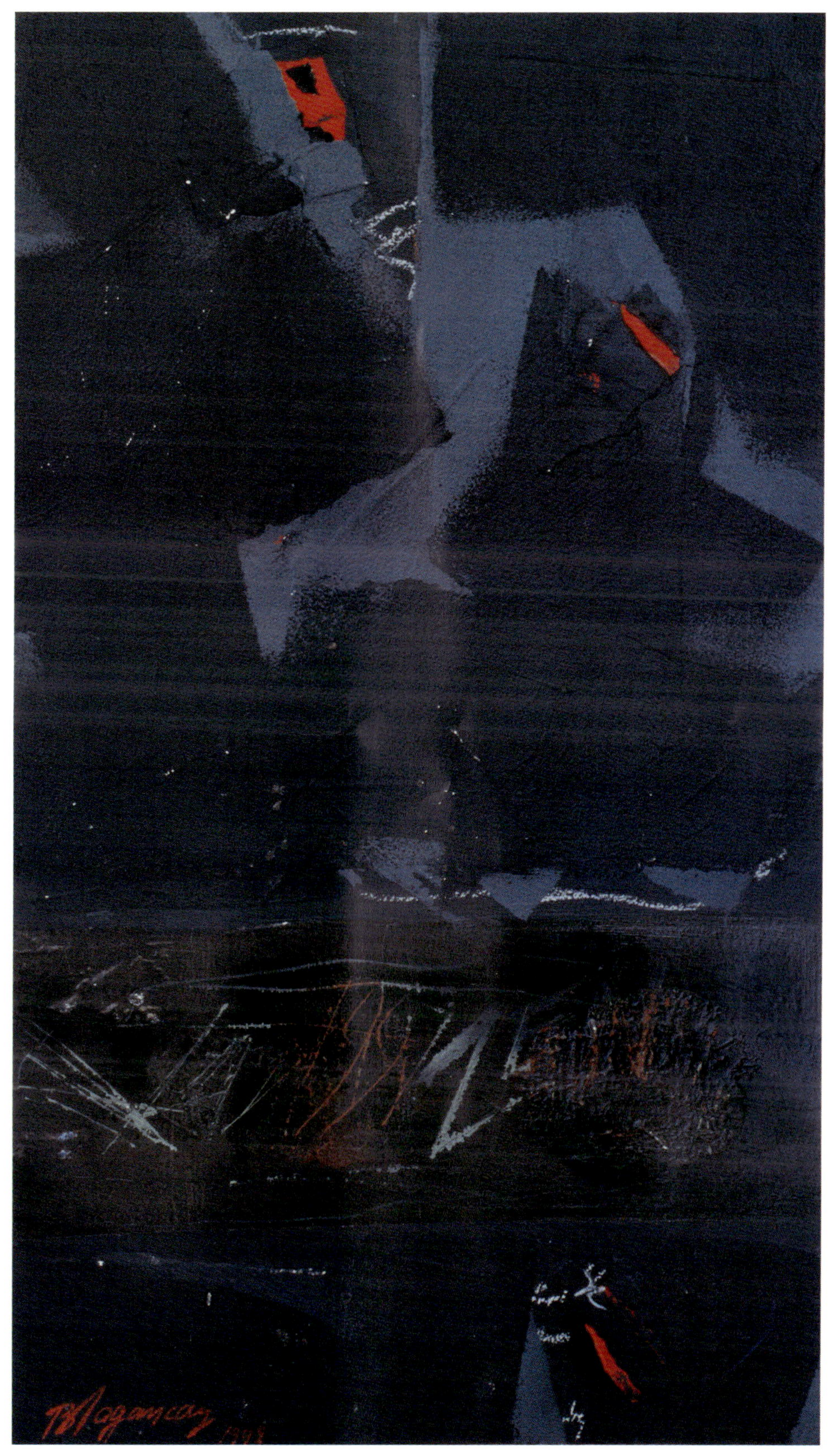

Gray Symphony, 1998. Mixed media on paper, 20 × 11⅞ in. (50.8 × 30.2 cm).
Collection of the artist

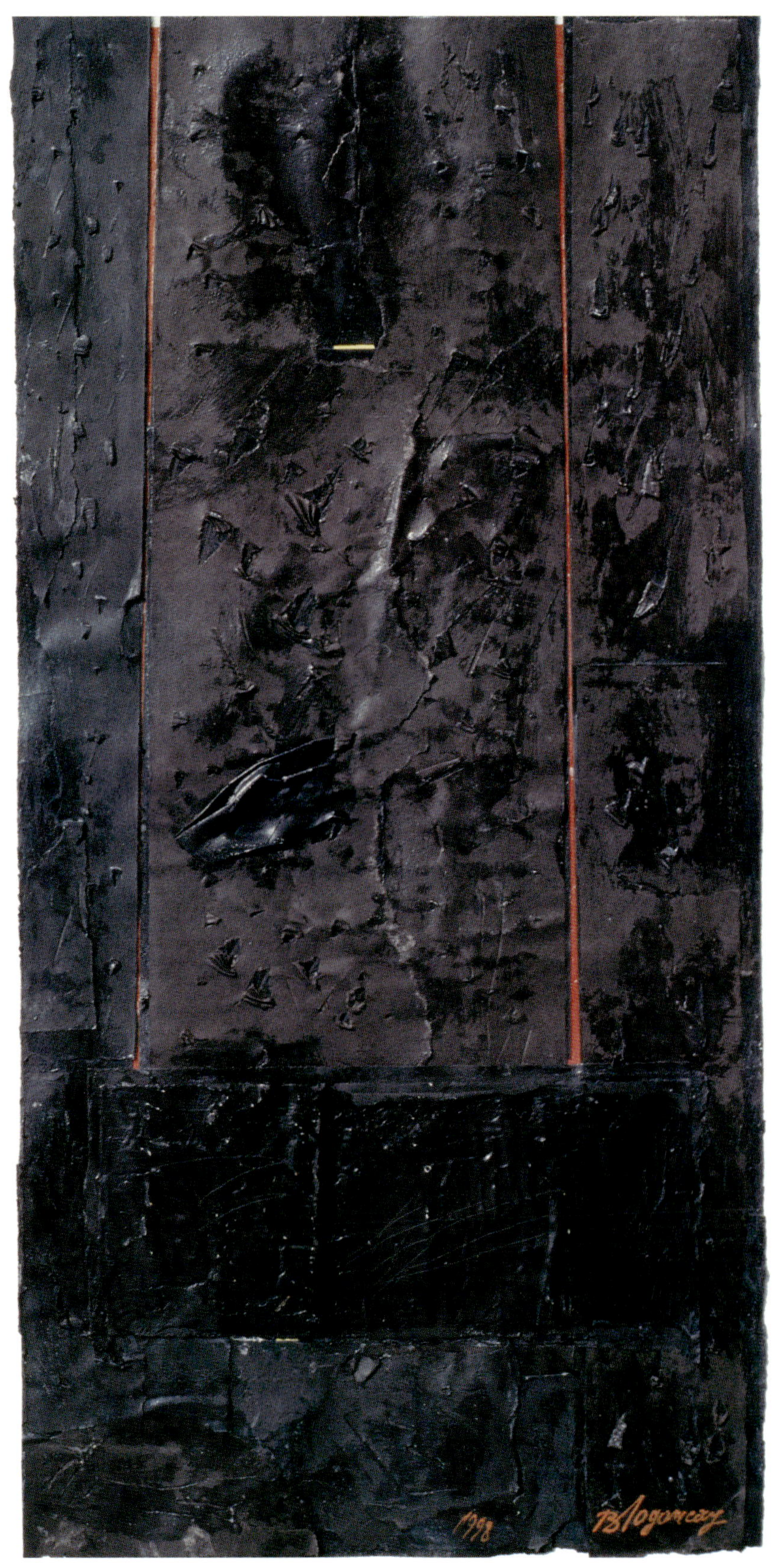

Two Fine Red Lines, 1998. Mixed media on paper, 23⅝ × 11⅞ in. (59.9 × 30 cm).
Collection of the artist

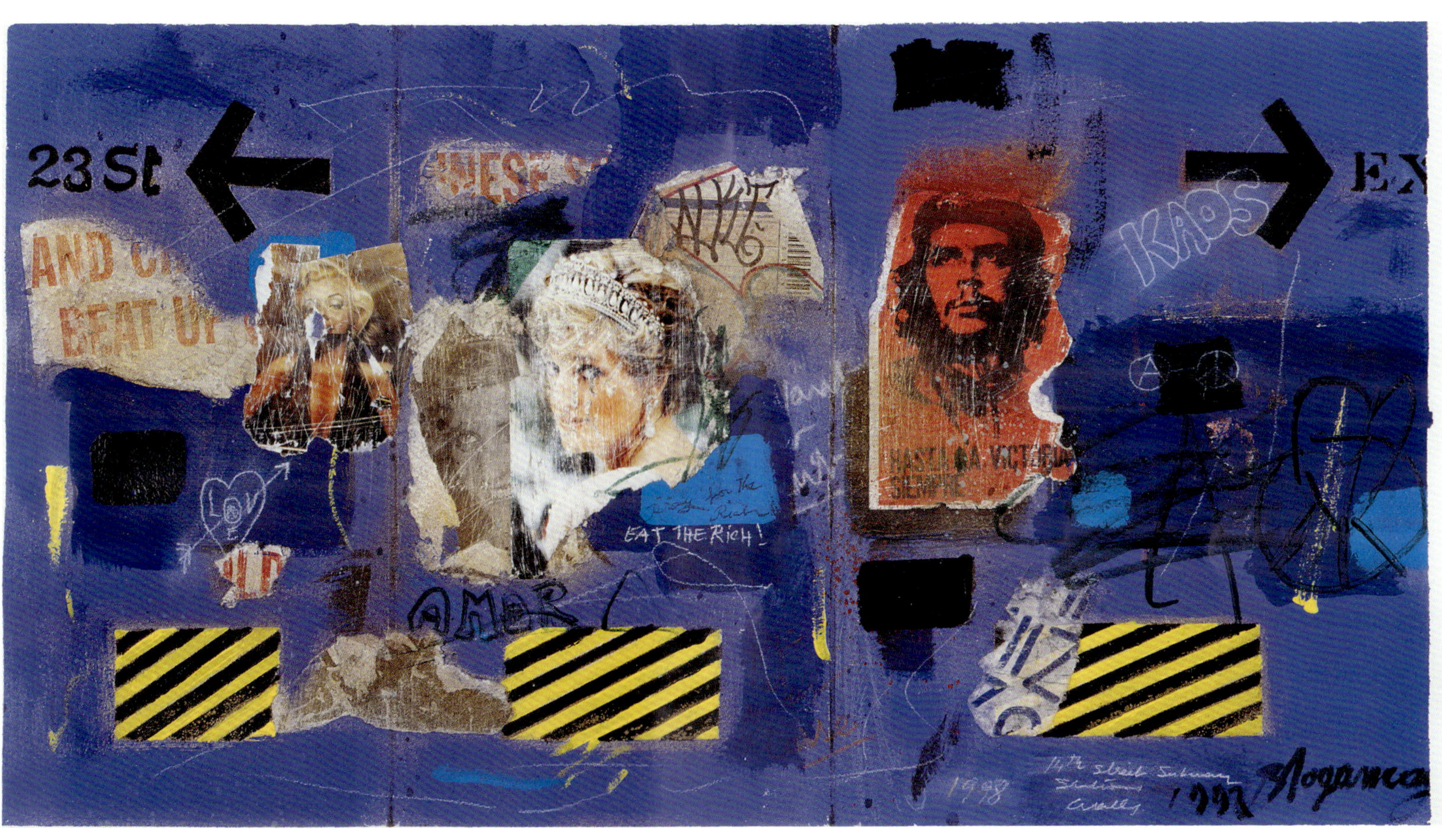

Diana & Che, 1998. Mixed media on paper, 12 × 24 in. (35 × 70 cm). Collection of the artist

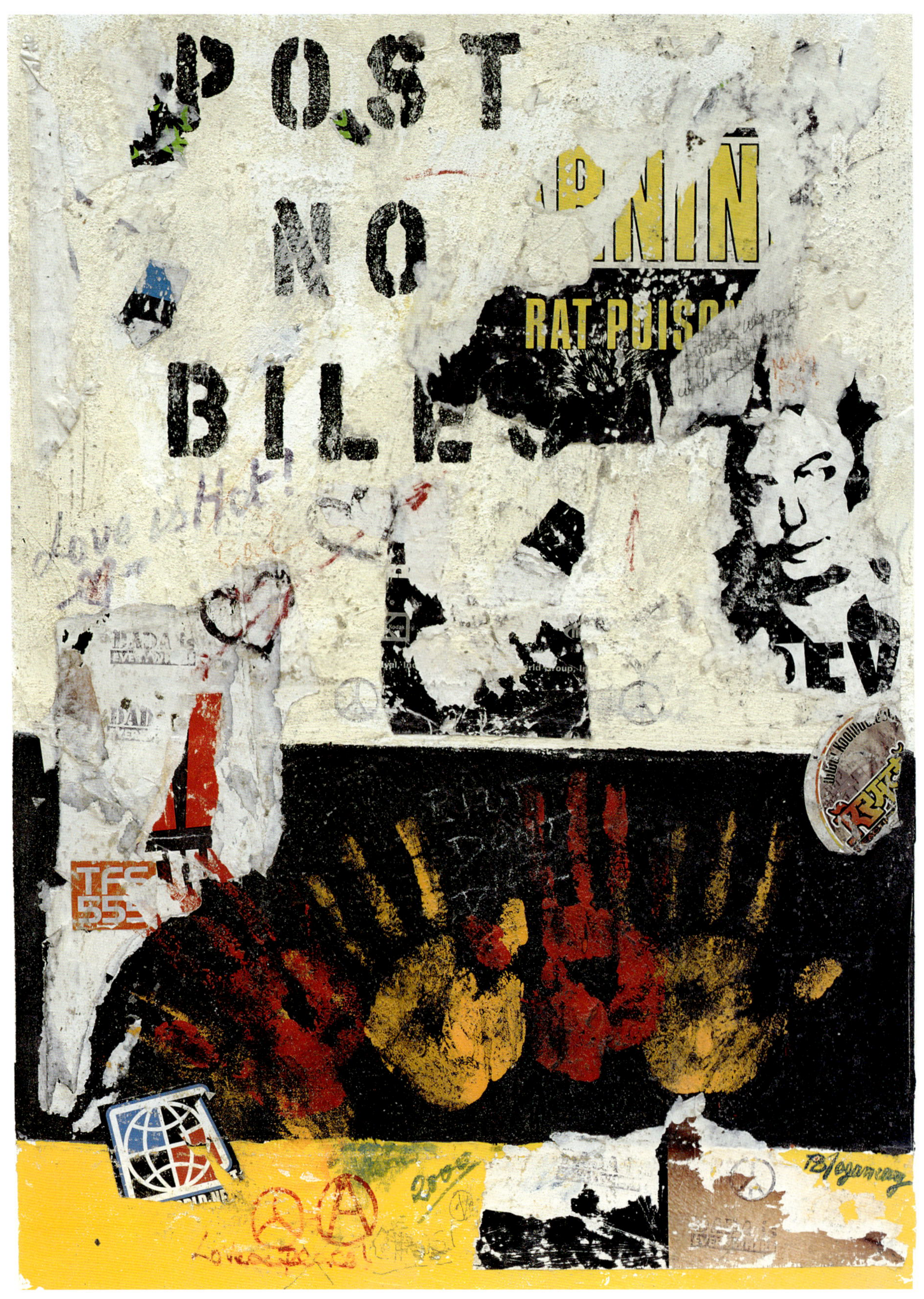

Love Is Hot, 2000. Mixed media on paper, 30 × 22 in. (76.2 × 55.9 cm). Collection of the artist

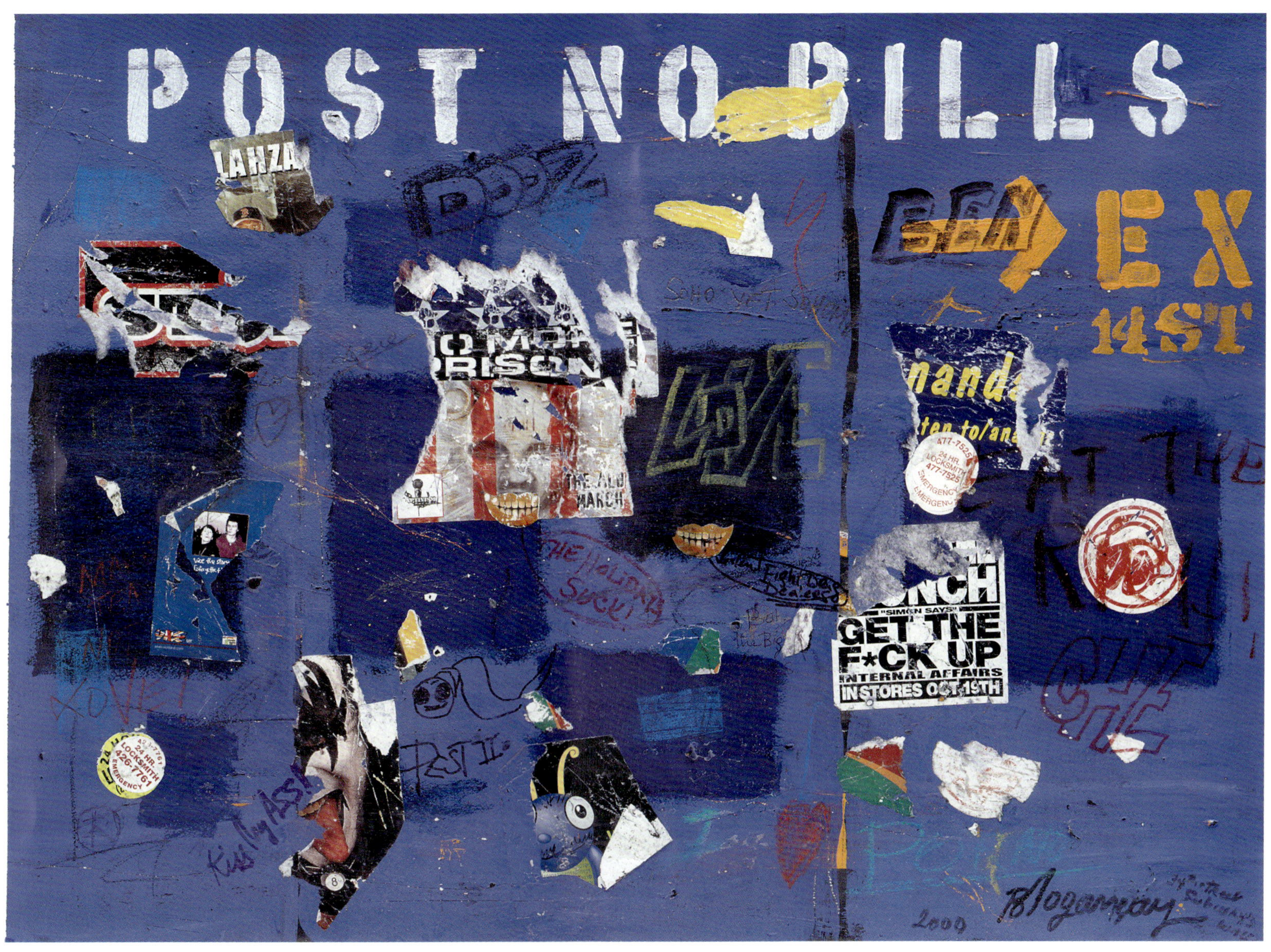

Ex 14 St., 2000. Mixed media on paper, 22 × 30 in. (55.9 × 76.2 cm). Collection of the artist

Chronology

1929

Istanbul, Turkey: Burhan Dogançay is the first of three children born to Adil Dogançay, a well-known painter and topography officer in the Turkish army, and his wife, Hediye.

1933–50

Dogançay starts drawing at the age of four.

During his high school years in Ankara, he takes courses with Arif Kaptan, a famous painter, whose emphasis, like his father's, is on drawing.

Plays soccer on the Ankara team Gençlerbirliği.

After finishing high school, he enrolls at the University of Ankara, from which he graduates with a degree in law.

1950–55

Goes to Paris to continue his studies. To learn French, he lives for several months in Honfleur, one of the impressionists' most popular places. There he plays soccer with the local team, paints, and shows his watercolors at Mme Boutiron's fish store.

Now fluent in French, he returns to Paris, where he studies economics at the University of Paris and attends art courses at La Grande Chaumière.

Travels to Denmark, where he does research for his doctoral thesis, "Le Rôle de la Coopération et les Progrès de l'Agriculture Danoise" (The Role of

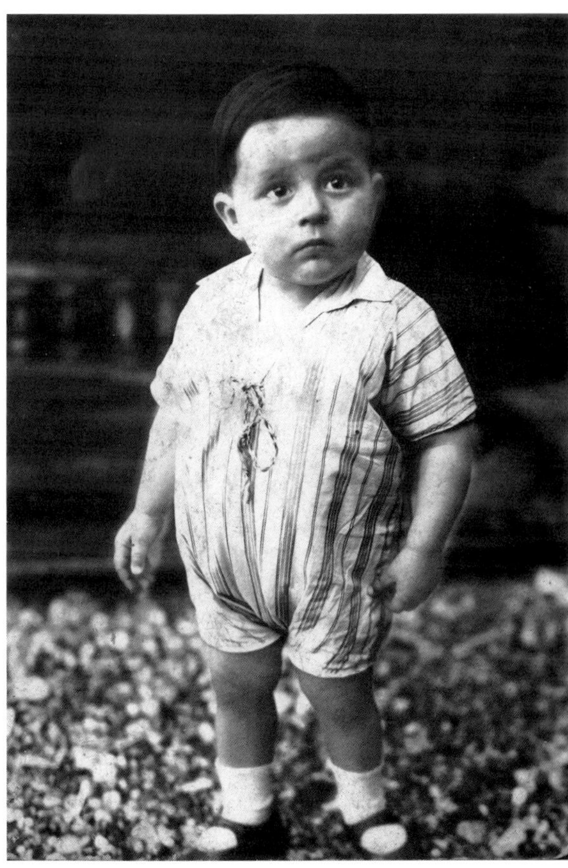

Dogançay at 1½ years.

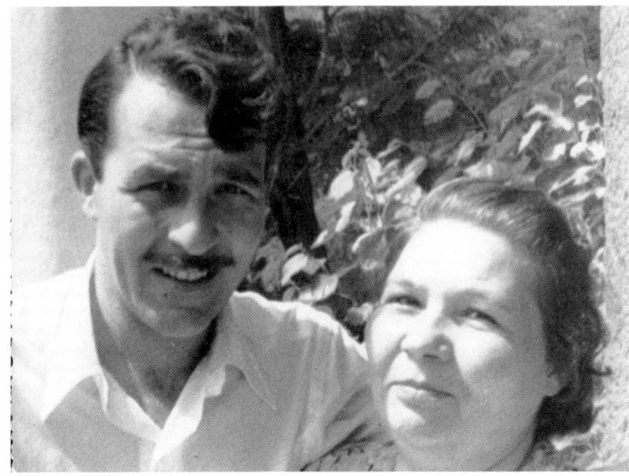

Dogançay with his mother Hediye, Ankara, 1953.

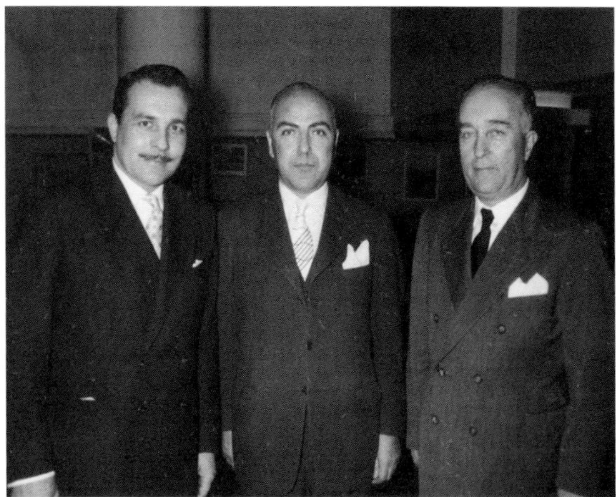

Doğançay with his father and Munis Faik Ozansoy,
Ankara, 1956.

Cooperatives and the Progress of Danish
Agriculture).
Travels to Sweden, Germany, Switzerland, and Italy.
Participates in group shows at the American House at
the Cité Universitaire, Paris.
Is a stand-in for Ronald Shiner during the filming of
the British movie *A Weekend in Paris.*

1953
Receives doctorate from the University of Paris.

1955–59
Returns to Ankara and begins to work for the
Ministry of Commerce.
Has three joint exhibitions with his father at the Art
Lovers Club in Ankara.

1958
As Director of the Turkish Pavilion at the World's
Fair in Brussels, Doğançay meets Princess Grace of
Monaco, King Baudouin of the Belgians, Prince
Bernhard of the Netherlands, Princess Beatrix of
the Netherlands, and many other distinguished
dignitaries and celebrities.

1959
Is appointed director of the Turkish Tourism
Department. Represents Turkey and the Middle
East at the XIV General Assembly of the World
Tourist Conference in Manila.
Travels around the world and visits the United States
for the first time.

1961
Five of his paintings are chosen for the *Twenty-
second State Exhibition of Painting and Sculpture*
in Ankara.

1962
Comes to New York as director of the Turkish
Information Office.

1964
Resigns from his government post to realize his child-
hood dream of being a full-time painter.
Has his first exhibition in the United States at Ward
Eggleston Galleries in New York.
Receives Certificate of Appreciation from the City of
New York in recognition of his interpretation of
New York City in a collection of eighty paintings
that depict different scenes of the city.

1965
His watercolors of New York are featured on the
cover of the *Journal American* issues of January 3
and August 8.
First inclusion of his work in a permanent museum
collection (The Solomon R. Guggenheim Museum,
New York): *Billboard.*

1966
One of his New York watercolors is again featured on
the cover of the *Journal American.*

1969
Receives Tamarind Lithography Workshop
Fellowship, Los Angeles, and produces sixteen lith-
ographs entitled *Walls V.*

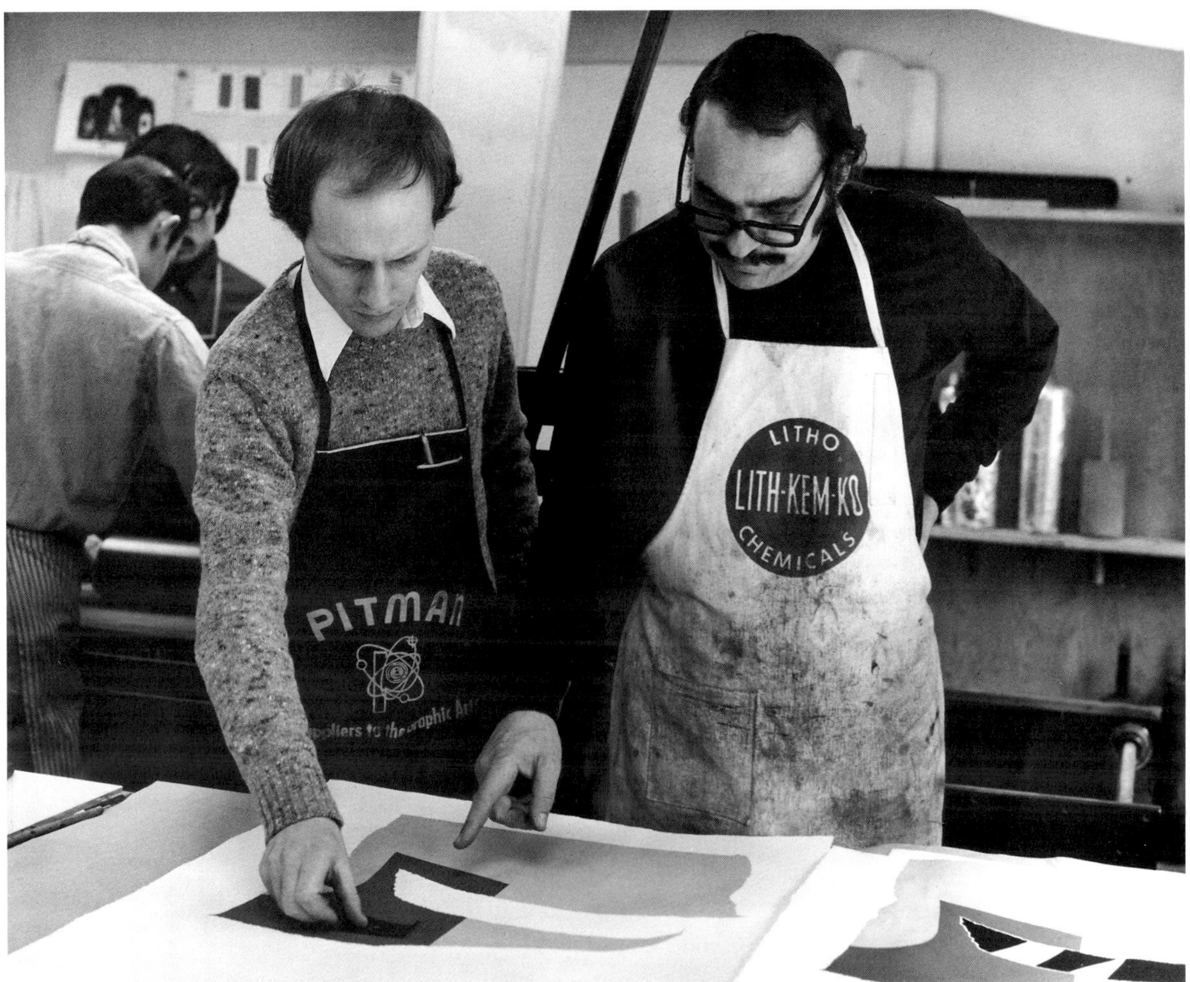

Dogançay working on *Walls 70* at Bank Street Atelier, New York, 1970.

1970
Dogançay produces sixteen lithographs, *Walls 70*, at
Bank Street Atelier, New York.

1974
UNICEF chooses one of Dogançay's pieces
(*Emergence*) as the design for a greeting card.

1975
Travels to Israel. This trip marks the beginning of his
Walls of the World photographic project.

1976–77
Lives in Switzerland and travels extensively for his
Walls of the World project.
Produces four lithographs, *Walls 75*, at Atelier
Wolfensberger, Zurich.

1978
Returns to New York City. Marries Angela Hausmann.

1979
Becomes an American citizen.

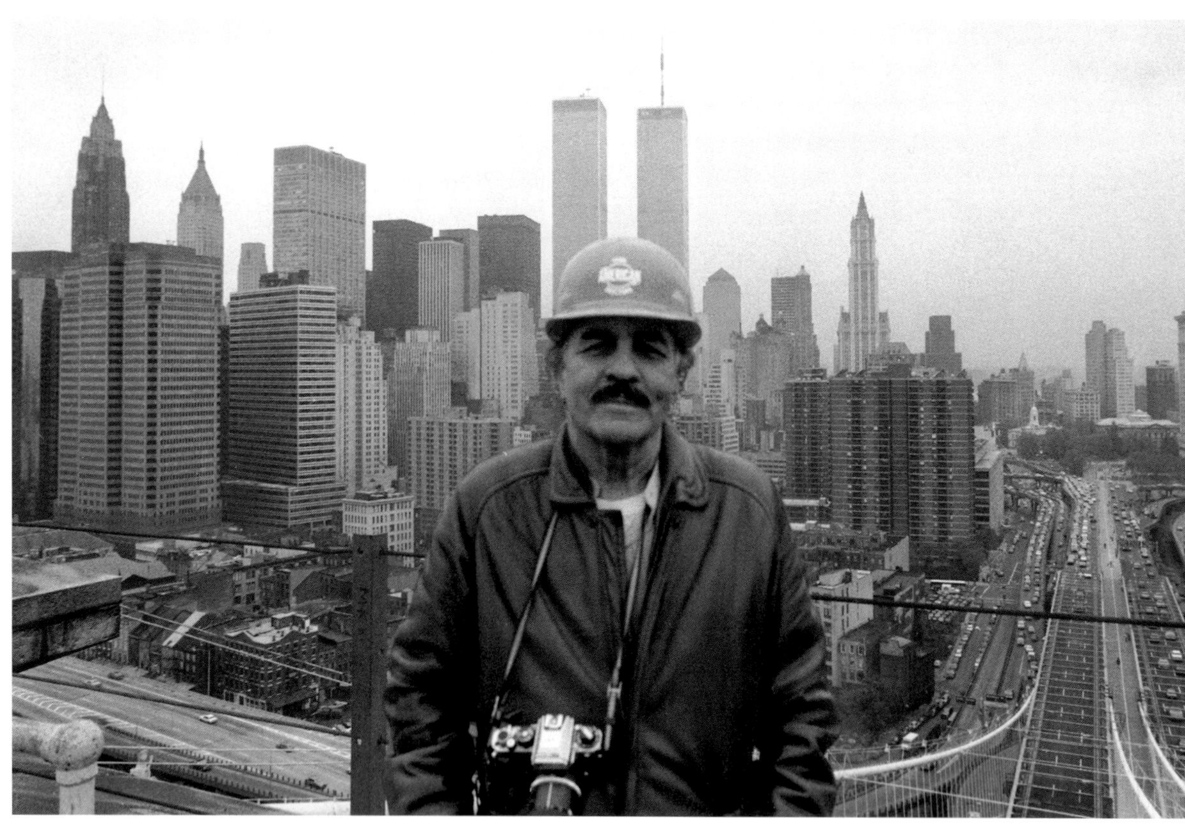

Dogançay on top of the Brooklyn Bridge, 1986.

1982
One-man show of the *Walls of the World* project,
    entitled *Les Murs Murmurent* (*Whispering Walls*)
    at the Centre Georges Pompidou, Paris.
In Walkemühle, Germany, he experiments with his
    father-in-law, engineer and inventor Gerhard
    Hausmann, to produce shadow sculptures from
    aluminum.

1983
Introduces Alucobond Shadow Sculptures, which
    are produced by the Research and Development
    Center of Swiss Aluminium Ltd., Neuhausen am
    Rheinfall, Switzerland.
Is invited to supply tapestry designs to L'Atelier
    Raymond Picaud, Aubusson, France.

Receives *Ev & Ofis*, Istanbul, Painter of the Year
    Award.

1984
Wins Enka Arts and Science Award, Istanbul.
Travels to North and West Africa for the *Walls of
    the World* project.

1984–86
Photographically documents the construction of
    skyscrapers in New York and climbs with iron
    workers to the top of several in Manhattan. This
    project leads him to the top of the Brooklyn Bridge
    during its major restoration in 1986, which gives
    him the opportunity to take exclusive photographs
    of the bridge draped in safety nets.

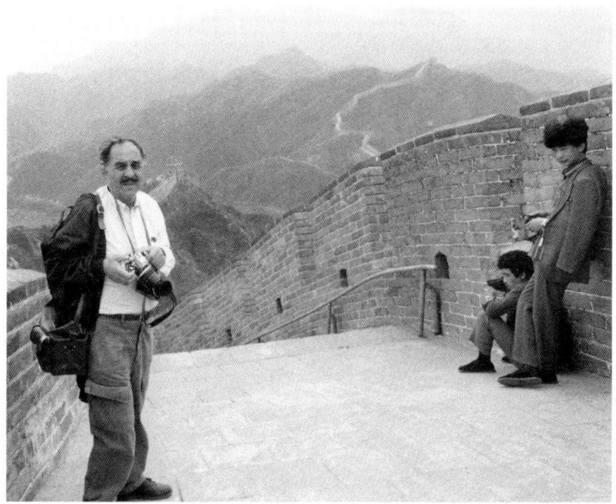

Doğançay at the Great Wall of China, 1988.

1985
The construction weekly, *Engineering News-Record*, features Doğançay photograph of Philip Johnson's Lipstick building on the covers of its September 5 and September 19 issues.

1986
Publication of his first monograph, *Doğançay* (Hudson Hills Press, New York).
Participates in the First International Asian-European Art Biennial, Ankara.

1987–88
Travels to Australia, Southeast Asia, the Far East, China, and Eastern Europe for the *Walls of the World* project.

1987
Participates in the First International Istanbul Contemporary Art Exhibition.

1989
Travels to Central and South America for the *Walls of the World* project.
Participates in the IX Bienal Internacional de Arte, Valparaiso, Chile.

1990
Travels to Central America and Cuba for the *Walls of the World* project.

1991
Travels to Togo, Benin, South Africa, Namibia, Zimbabwe, and Russia for the *Walls of the World* project.
Produces ten silkscreens, *Ribbons*, at Artess Çamlıca Workshop, Istanbul.

1992
As guest of Russia's Ministry of Culture, which honors him with its Medal of Appreciation, he is the first Western artist to have a solo exhibition (*Walls and Doors 1990–91*) at The State Russian Museum, St. Petersburg.
Publication of *Dessine-Moi l'Amour* (Editions Syros Alternatives, Paris), featuring a selection of Doğançay's *Walls of the World* photographs, with texts by Gilbert Lascault and Denys Riout.

1993
The city of Aubusson, France, acquires a tapestry designed by Doğançay and executed by Atelier Raymond Picaud.

1994
UNICEF chooses one of Dogancay's paintings as the design for a place mat.
The French publisher, Gallimard, chooses one of Doğançay's paintings for the cover of *Love, etc.* by Julian Barnes.

1995
Receives the National Medal of the Arts for Lifetime Achievement and Cultural Contribution from the President of Turkey, the highest honor that country bestows on an artist.
Travels to Vietnam, Burma, Nepal, Bangladesh, Sri Lanka, Bahrain, Qatar, Oman, United Arab Emirates, Yemen, Lebanon, and Syria for the *Walls of the World* project.

The Paris Review chooses one of Dogançay's canvases
for the cover of Issue 134.

1996
Dogançay contributes two photographs from his
Walls of the World collection for two UNICEF
greeting cards.
Moves to new studio in SoHo, New York.

1997–98
Travels to Azerbaijan, Ukraine, and Macedonia for
the *Walls of the World* project.

1998
Receives *Antik & Dekor* Painter of the Year Award,
Istanbul.

1998–2000
JFK International. Airport celebrates New York
City's Centennial with an exhibition of Dogançay's
large-scale photographs of the *Brooklyn Bridge as
Never Seen Before*.

1999
Official launch of *Bridge of Dreams* (Hudson Hills
Press), a book of Dogançay's Brooklyn Bridge
photographs, at the Brooklyn Public Library,
followed by additional book signing events at the
Brooklyn Historical Society, the Museum of the
City of New York, and Barnes & Noble bookstores.
Dogançay buys an old building in Beyoğlu, Istanbul,
and with the help of several sponsors has it
restored during the following three years. Upon
completion, this building will house a representative cross section of Dogançay's and his father's
works. The building is scheduled to open as a
private museum in 2003.

1999–2000
Inclusion of one of his Brooklyn Bridge photographs
in the Museum of the City of New York's
twentieth-century exhibition, *The New York
Century: World Capital, Home Town, 1900–2000*.

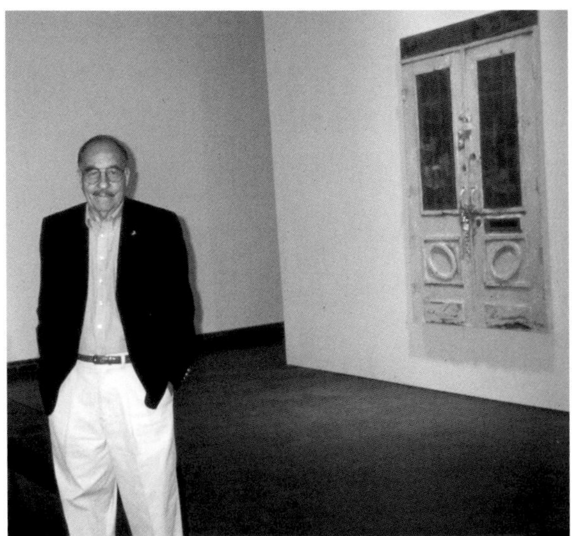

Dogançay at the Neuberger Museum of Art, Purchase,
N.Y., during the 2001 exhibition *Outside In: Selections
from the Permanent Collection*.

2000
Produces ten lithographs, *Dogançay 2000*, at Sinan
Demirtaş Workshop in collaboration with Artess
Çamlıca Workshop, Istanbul.
Travels to Kazakhstan, Kyrgyzstan, Turkmenistan,
Uzbekistan for the *Walls of the World* project,
bringing the total number of countries visited to
112.

2001
Holds his first retrospective exhibition at
Dolmabahçe Cultural Center, Istanbul.

2002
Undergoes open heart surgery.

2003
Receives *ALEM* magazine Lifetime Achievement
Award.

Solo Exhibitions

In chronological order by year, exhibitions appear in alphabetical order by city of venue

1956–59
Ankara: Art Lovers Club

1964
New York: Berlitz Gallery, *New York in the Eyes of the World*, organized by Ward Eggleston Galleries in cooperation with the Department of Public Events of the City of New York
New York: Ward Eggleston Galleries, *Watercolors*
New York: Overseas Club

1965
New York: Ward Eggleston Galleries, *The World on the Walls of New York*
Phoenix: Galaxy Gallery, *Watercolors and Gouaches*

1966
New York: American Greetings Gallery

1967
New York: Spectrum Gallery

1968
Cambridge, Mass.: Radcliffe Graduate Center

1969
New York: Spectrum Gallery, *Walls V*

1970
New York: Carus Gallery, *Walls 70*
Washington, D.C.: Lunn Gallery

1971
New York: J. Walter Thompson Company

1973
New York: Gimpel & Weitzenhoffer Gallery
Rockford, Ill.: Sneed & Hillman Gallery, *Dream Ships and Hearts*

1976
Istanbul: Gallery Baraz

1977
Istanbul: Gallery Baraz
Stockholm: Gallery Engström
Zurich: Kunstsalon Wolfsberg

1978
Gothenburg: Gallery Olab
New York: Gimpel & Weitzenhoffer Gallery
New York: The Turkish Center

1981
Sarasota, Fla.: Foster Harmon Galleries
Zurich: Kunstsalon Wolfsberg

1982–84
Paris: Centre Georges Pompidou, *Les Murs Murmurent*, an exhibition that traveled to:
Alfortville: Maison des Jeunes et de la Culture
Antwerp: International Cultural Center
Bagnères-de-Bigorre: Bibliothèque Municipale
Bordeaux: Café Librairie Vent Debout
Brussels: Palais des Beaux-Arts
Caen: Maison des Jeunes et de la Culture La Guérinière
Chamalières: A.E.D.A.P.
Chambéry: Conseil d'Architecture, d'Urbanisme et de l'Environnement

Hasselt, Belgium: Provincial Museum
Le Vaudreuil: Collectif d'Animation de la Ville
Lons-le-Saunier: Maison des Jeunes et de la Culture
Metz: Conseil d'Architecture, d'Urbanisme et de
    l'Environnement
Montréal: Musée d'Art Contemporain
Moulins: Direction Départementale de
    l'Equipement de l'Allier
Nice: Maison des Jeunes et de la Culture Magnan
Oyonnax: Secrétariat à l'Action Culturelle
Pont-à-Mousson: Centre Culturel de l'Ancienne
    Abbaye des Prémontrés
Reims: Centre Saint-Exupéry
Rennes: Maison des Jeunes et de la Culture —
    Auberge de la Jeunesse/Maisons pour Tous
Vienne: Maison des Jeunes et de la Culture —
    Auberge de la Jeunesse/Maisons pour Tous

1982
Cologne: Baukunst-Galerie

1983
Istanbul: Gallery Baraz

1984
Ankara: Vakko Art Gallery
Düsseldorf: Galerie Swidbert
Istanbul: Vakko Art Gallery
Izmir: Vakko Art Gallery

1985
Bordeaux: Centre d'Art et de Communication
Rabat: Galerie L'Atelier
Sarasota, Fla.: Foster Harmon Galleries
Vienna: Österreichische Postsparkasse

1986
Istanbul: Gallery Baraz

1987
Ankara: Gallery Nev
Istanbul: Garanti Gallery
New York: Hamideh Bayley Gallery, *Two Decades of
    Walls*

Sarasota, Fla: Foster Harmon Galleries

1988
Sarasota, Fla.: Foster Harmon Galleries

1989
Marburg: Kunstverein Marburg e. V.
Tokyo: The Seibu Museum of Art — Yurakucho Art
    Forum

1990
Odense: Gallery Torso
Paris: Galerie du Génie

1991
Sarasota, Fla.: Foster Harmon Galleries

1992
St. Petersburg: The State Russian Museum, *Walls
    and Doors 1990–91,* an exhibition that traveled to:
    Moscow: Artists' Union

1993
Istanbul: Atatürk Cultural Center, *Walls 1990–93,*
    organized and sponsored by Renault

1994
New York: Nicholas Alexander Gallery, *Doors and
    Walls*

1995
Ankara: Gallery Nev
Istanbul: Gallery Nev

1996
Houston: Hooks-Epstein Galleries, *New York —
    New Heights* (participating in *FotoFest '96*)

1997
Ankara: Artium Art Gallery
Istanbul: P & G Gallery
New York: Duggal Gallery, *The Brooklyn Bridge As
    Never Seen Before*

1998
Adana, Turkey: Görüntü Art Gallery
Istanbul: Gallery G, *Alexander's Walls and Hearts*

1999
New York: Radio House Gallery, *The Rebirth of the Brooklyn Bridge*

2000
New York: The Brooklyn Historical Society, *Bridge of Dreams*

2001
Athens, Ohio: Kennedy Museum of Art–Ohio University: *Dogançay — Wall Paintings from the Museum Collection*

Adana, Turkey: Görüntü Art Gallery, *Burhan Dogançay*
Istanbul: Dolmabahçe Cultural Center, *A Retrospective*, organized and sponsored by Dr. Nejat F. Eczacıbaşı Foundation
Istanbul: Gallery Baraz, *Recent Works*
Istanbul: Gallery Binyil, *Doors*
Istanbul: Gallery G, *Hearts*
Istanbul: Art Gallery Mine

2002
New York: Radio House Gallery, *New York Subway Walls*

2003
Siegen, Germany: Siegerlandmuseum, *Walls of the World*

Group Exhibitions

1953
Paris: American House at the Cité Universitaire,
   Exposition des Peintres Résidants de la Fondation
   des Etats-Unis

1955–57
Ankara: Art Lovers Club, *Father–Son*

1959
Ankara: Art Lovers Club, *Father–Son*
Ankara: Turkish-American Association, *Painters of*
   Ankara

1961
Ankara: Turkish-American Association, *Exhibition*
   of Modern Paintings
Ankara: University of Ankara, The Twenty-second
   State Exhibition of Painting and Sculpture

1963
New York: Washington Square Galleries, *World Show*
New York: National Arts Club, *First Sixty-fifth*
   Anniversary Exhibition

1964
New York: National Arts Club, *The Sixty-fifth*
   Anniversary Exhibition

1965
Monaco: Palais des Congrès, *Exposition*
   Intercontinentale, an exhibition organized by
   the International Art Exchange for the benefit
   of UNICEF. This exhibition also traveled to:
New York: Union Carbide Galleries

New York: Gallery of Modern Art, *About New York*
   1915–1965
New York: The Solomon R. Guggenheim Museum,
   Some Recent Gifts

1970
New York: Union Carbide Galleries, *Contemporary*
   Turkish Artists

1970–71
Binghamton, N.Y.: University Art Gallery,
   Contemporary Turkish Painting, an exhibition that
   traveled to:
   Chicago: University of Chicago
   Minneapolis: Minneapolis College of Art and
      Design
New York: Finch College Museum of Art, *Artists*
   at Work

1972
New York: Pace Gallery, *Printmakers at Pace*

1974
New York: Gallery 43, *An Exhibition of Midtown*
   Artists, sponsored by the Durst Organization in
   cooperation with the City of New York

1975
New York: The Solomon R. Guggenheim Museum,
   Recent Acquisitions

1977
Istanbul: Gallery Baraz
New York: The Solomon R. Guggenheim Museum,
   From the American Collection

New York: Union Carbide Galleries, Artists 77

1979
Chicago: Mary Bell Galleries

1980
Chicago: Mary Bell Galleries, *New Works by Gallery Artists*
Rockford, Ill.: Sneed Gallery, *Small Works by Big Artists*

1982
Cologne: Baukunst-Galerie

1982–83
National traveling exhibition *The Heritage of Islam*:
Houston: The Houston Museum of Natural Science
San Francisco: The California Academy of Sciences
Washington, D.C.: The National Museum of Natural History, Smithsonian Institution

1983
Istanbul: Alarko Art Gallery, *Fifty Rare Turkish Paintings of This Century*
Istanbul: Gallery Baraz
Zurich: Kunstsalon Wolfsberg

1984
Istanbul: Alarko Art Gallery
Rockford, Ill.: Sneed Gallery, *Who's New and What's New*
Sarasota, Fla.: Foster Harmon Galleries, *Major American Artists*

1985
La Tronche/Grenoble: Maison des Artistes-Fondation Herbert d'Uckermann, *Itinéraire d'une Galerie*
Lormont: Centre de Formation et Création Artistique, *Tapisseries d'Aubusson*
Montreux: Palais des Congrès, *Les Chefs d'oeuvre d'Aubusson*
Paris: Maison de L'Assurance, *Tapisseries Contemporaines d'Aubusson*

Talence, France: E.N.S.A.M., *Tapisseries de l'Atelier Raymond Picaud*

1986
Bordeaux: Galeries Lafayette

1987
Istanbul: Istanbul Foundation for Culture and Art
Sarasota, Fla.: Foster Harmon Galleries

1988
Paris: Foire Internationale d'Art Contemporain

1990
Sarasota, Fla.: Foster Harmon Galleries

1991
Montluçon, France: Centre Athanor, *Panorama de la Tapisserie Contemporaine*
New York: Lehman College Art Gallery, *Collage: New Applications*

1992
Aubusson: Espace Philips, *L'Hommage de Cinquante Peintres à Jean Lurçat*

1993
Münster, Germany: City Hall, *Zeitgenössische türkische Kunst*

1994
New York: Nicholas Alexander Gallery

1996
Rio de Janeiro: Arcos da Lapa, organized by Laboratoire, Grenoble

1997
Istanbul: P & G Gallery

1998
Ankara: Artium Art Gallery
Aubusson, France: Hotel Le France, *De Jean Lurçat à Nos Jours*

1999
New York: The Museum of the City of New York,
  The New York Century: World Capital, Home Town,
  1900–2000

2000
Marburg, Germany: Marburger Universitätsmuseum,
  Kunst der Gegenwart: 1975– 2000

2001
Purchase, N.Y.: Neuberger Museum of Art, *Outside In*

2002
Summit: New Jersey Center for Visual Arts, *Doors:*
  Image and Metaphor in Contemporary Art

Museum and Corporate Collections

AUSTRIA
Vienna: Graphische Sammlung Albertina
Vienna: Österreichische Postsparkasse
Vienna: Palais Liechtenstein
Wattens: Swarovski

BANGLADESH
Dacca: Bangladesh National Museum

BELGIUM
Antwerp: Royal Museum of Fine Arts
Ghent: Museum of Contemporary Art
Latem St. Martin: Musée d'Art Contemporain
Liège: Musée d'Art Moderne et d'Art Contemporain
Ostend: Museum for Modern Art

BRAZIL
Rio de Janeiro: Museu de Arte Moderna do Rio de
   Janeiro

CANADA
Toronto: University of Toronto
Victoria: Art Gallery of Greater Victoria

CHILE
Santiago: Museo Nacional de Bellas Artes

DENMARK
Aalborg: Nordjyllands Kunstmuseum
Humlebaek: Louisiana Museum of Modern Art
Odense: Museet for Fotokunst — Brandts
   Klaedefabrik

FRANCE
Grenoble: Musée de Grenoble

Paris: Banque Internationale de Commerce
Paris: Musée d'Art Moderne de la Ville de Paris
Paris: Bibliothèque Historique de la Ville de Paris
Strasbourg: Musée d'Art Contemporain

GERMANY
Marburg: Marburger Universitätsmuseum

ISRAEL
Dimona: Dimona Museum
Jerusalem: Bezalel National Museum
Jerusalem: The Israel Museum

JAPAN
Hiroshima: Hiroshima City Museum of
   Contemporary Art
Ibaraki: Ibaraki Museum of Modern Art
Tokyo: Tokyo Fuji Art Museum

JORDAN
Amman: Jordan National Gallery of Fine Arts

MACEDONIA
Skopje: Museum of Contemporary Art

RUSSIA
Moscow: The Moscow Collection
St. Petersburg: The State Russian Museum

SWITZERLAND
Geneva: DG Bank (Suisse) SA
Geneva: Farimex
Zurich: Kronenhalle
Zurich: Swiss Aluminium Ltd.

Bibliography

ARTICLES

In alphabetical order by author.

Acar, Özgen. "Kapılar ve Duvarlar." *Cumhuriyet*, Istanbul, 11 December 1994.

Akay, Ali. "Duvarın Tuval Üzerinde Yansıması." *Cumhuriyet*, Istanbul, 20 October 1998.

Allyn, Rex. "A Chance for Leisurely Study of Art Works." *Sarasota Herald Tribune*, Sarasota, Fla., 15 July 1984.

———. "Harmon Features Internationally Known Artist." *The Longboat Observer*, Sarasota, Fla., 21 February 1985.

Altuğ, Evrim. "Yedi koldan Doğançay." *Radikal*, Istanbul, 7 April 2001.

Anonymous. "Acclaimed Artist Not Your Ordinary Painter of Walls." *The Athens News*, Athens, Ohio, 17 May 2001.

———. "Açılış Tablosuz Yapıldı." *Hürriyet*, Istanbul, 6 October 1983.

———. "Altın Palet Büyük Onur Ödülü." *Sanat Çevresi*, Istanbul, no. 60, October 1983.

———. "Artist Says Walls Mirror the Surrounding World." *The Messenger*, Athens, Ohio, 14 June 2001.

———. "Boğaz Köprüsü de Doğançay'ı Bekliyor." *Cumhuriyet*, Istanbul, 8 March 1997.

———. "Brooklyn Bridge as Never Seen Before." *The Turkish Times*, Houston, 15 June 1997.

———. "Brooklyn Köprüsünü JFK Havaalanına Taşıdı." *VIP*, Istanbul, October 1998.

———. "Burhan Dogançay." *The New York Herald Tribune*, New York, 11 April 1964.

———. "Burhan Dogançay." *The New York Herald Tribune*, New York, 3 April 1965.

———. "Burhan Doğançay." *Politika*, İstanbul, 18 August 1976.

———. "Burhan Doğançay." *Die Tat*, Zurich, 2 February 1977.

———. "Burhan Doğançay." *Nieuwe Gazet*, Antwerp, 8 December 1982.

———. "Burhan Doğançay." *Ev & Ofis*, Istanbul, no. 87, November 1983.

———. "Burhan Doğançay: Duvalar ve Resimler." *Boyut*, Ankara, November 1982.

———. "Burhan Doğançay: Wände der Welt." *Litfass*, Berlin, no. 16, April 1980.

———. "Burhan Dogançay beim Kunstverein." *Ober-Hessische Presse*, Marburg, 2 March 1989.

———. "Burhan Doğançay Monografisi." *Sanat Çevresi*, Istanbul, no. 61, November 1983.

———. "Burpee Receives Dogançay Painting." *Register Star*, Rockford, Ill., 6 January 1974.

———. "Dogançay Is Attracting Great Interest." *Turkish News*, Istanbul, 25 May 2001.

———. "Foster Harmon Gallery." *The Longboat Observer*, Sarasota, Fla., 13 June 1991.

———. "Galeri G Burhan Doğançay'ın Sergisi ile Açılıyor." *Vizyon Dekorasyon*, Istanbul, October 1998.

———. "Harmon Combines Burhan Dogançay, Robert Watson and Group Exhibit." *Sarasota Herald Tribune*, Sarasota, Fla., 17 February 1985.

———. "Kunst in Zürich." *Neue Zürcher Zeitung*, Zurich, 9 October 1981.

———. "Les Murs Murmurent." *Le Républicain Lorrain*, Pont-à-Mousson, 3 February 1983.

———. "Les Murs Murmurent: Les Photos Insolites." *L'Est Républicain*, Pont-à-Mousson, 2 February 1983.

———. "Les Murs Murmurent, Ils Crient, Ils Chantent." *La Vie Nouvelle*, Chambéry, 12 November 1982.

———. "New York–New Heights." *The Turkish Times*, Houston, 15 March 1996.

———. "One-Man Exhibits to Open." *Sarasota Herald Tribune*, Sarasota, Fla., 1 February 1981.

———. "Paintings by Dogançay in Pan Am Spotlight." *Brooklyn Bay News*, New York, 17 September 1966.

———. "Peinture: Burhan Dogançay." *Le Matin du Sahara*, Rabat, Morocco, 5 March 1985.

———. "Photographie: Du Souvenir à l'Image." *Pourquoi Pas*, Brussels, 1 April 1982.

———. "Retrospectif ve 7 sergi." *Cumhuriyet*, Istanbul, 7 April 2001.

———. "Sanat ve Türkiye Üzerine." *Yeni Kona*, Konya, 19 April 2001.

———. "The Foster Harmon Galleries." *The Longboat Observer*, Sarasota, Fla., 15 July 1982.

———. "The Two Worlds of Burhan Dogançay." *The Travel Agent*, New York, 25 July 1964.

———. "Turkish Delight." *Interior Design*, New York, February 1965.

———. "Turkish Diplomat in New York is Artist of Note." *The Observer*, Nashville, 28 May 1964.

———. "Turkish Painting Presented to National Museum." *The Bangladesh Times*, Dacca, 7 November 1995.

———. "Wall Preserver." *Sunday News*, New York, 9 October 1966.

———. "Walls 70: A Powerful Pastiche." *Interiors Magazine*, New York, December 1970.

———. "Wandmalereien." *Zürichsee Zeitung*, Zurich, 14 February 1977.

———. "World Travel Aids Turkish Painter." *The Arizona Republic*, Phoenix, 17 January 1965.

———. "Yirmi Küsur Yıldan Beri Duvarları Çiziyorum." *Cumhuriyet*, Istanbul, 2 November 1984.

Antmen, Ahu. "Dokunmaya Çağıran Bir Resim." *Cumhuriyet*, Istanbul, 14 April 1998.

———. "Her 'Dünyadan' İnsan İmgesi." *Cumhuriyet*, Istanbul, 24 November 1993.

———. "Dünyanın Fısıldayan Duvarları." *Cumhuriyet*, Istanbul, 6 October 1991.

———. "Yaratıcılığı gözünün seçtiğinde." *Cumhuriyet*, Istanbul, 19 May 2001.

Aras, Funda A. "Babadan Oğula Resim Serüveni." *Skala*, Istanbul, no. 2, May 2001.

Asılyazıcı, Hayati. "Şehirlerin Duvarları'ndan Multi-Medyaya." *Aydınlık*, Istanbul, 22 November 1993.

Asselin, Hedwige. "Les Murs du Monde." *Le Devoir*, Montreal, 30 July 1983.

Atikoğlu, Ayça. "Dogançay'ın Türkiye Çıkarması." *Milliyet*, Istanbul, 2 November 1984.

Aydıntaşbaş, Aslı. "Ressamın Vizöründen." *Radikal*, Istanbul, 20 April 1998.

Badouin, Uwe. "Leidenschaftliche Kunst verbindet Orient mit Okzident." *Oberhessische Presse*, Marburg, Germany, 14 April 2001.

———. "Türkischer Künstler will Marburg auf Europas Kunstkarte verankern." *Oberhessische Presse*, Marburg, Germany, 6 September 2001.

Baharoğlu, Sarkis. "Duvarların Sanatçısı." *Yeni Asır*, Izmir, Turkey, 12 March 1997.

Bankoğlu, Hülya. "Burhan Doğançay." *Vizyon*, Istanbul, no. 100, October 1998.

———. "Burhan Doğançay: Don Kişot'luk Yapıyorum." *Posta*, Istanbul, June 1986.

Baraz, Yahşi. "Bir Dünya Sanatçisi: Burhan Doğançay" *Sanat Çevresi*, Istanbul, June 2001.

Bartlett, Maxine. "Devoted Turkish Diplomat Shows Artistic Talents." *The Arizona Republic*, Phoenix, 23 January 1965.

Bayhan, Mehmet. "Fotografın Hazırladığı Tuzaklar." *Cumhuriyet*, Istanbul, 13 April 1991.

Berkand, Necdet. "Yeni Dünya'da Bir Sanat Elçimiz." *Tercüman*, Istanbul, 10 June 1969.

Bilgin, Çetin. "Duvarların Dili." *Ankara Siyasi Halk Gazetesi*, Istanbul, 7 September 1976.

Birand, M. Ali. "SEİA mı, Süleyman ve Doğançay Sergileri mi?" *Milliyet*, Istanbul, 20 March 1983.

Bowles, Jerry, and Tony Russell. "Walls 70, Burhan Doğançay," *This Book Is a Movie*. New York: Dell Publishing Company, 1971.

Budak, Emel. "Burhan Doğançay." *Antik & Dekor*, Istanbul, no. 42, 1997.

———. "Görkemli Bir Retrospektif'in Ardinandan." *Antik & Dekor*, Istanbul, no. 65, July/August 2001.

Büber Ayman, Oya. "Gökdelenler Üzerinden Fotoğraflar." *Güneş*, Istanbul, 9 April 1991.

———. "Bir Yeraltı Sanatı Avcısı." *Tempo*, Istanbul, no. 14, 7 April 1993.

Bugay, Başak. "Dünyan'nin Duvarlari." *Aydinlik*, Istanbul, 20 May 2001.

Büyükünal, Feriha. "Burhan Doğançay." *Sanat Çevresi*, Istanbul, no. 108, October 1987.

Castle, Frederick Ted. "Burhan Doğançay at the Russian Museum." *Art in America*, New York, December 1992.

———. "Doğançay'ın Duvarları." *Türkiye'de Sanat*, Istanbul, no. 10, September/October 1993.

Cemal, Hasan. "Bir Pazar sabahi, Hayaller Köprüsü . . ." *Milliyet*, Istanbul, 10 September 2000.

C. G. "Burhan Doğançay." *Arts Magazine*, New York, December/January 1968.

Civaoğlu, Güneri. "Gemi ve kapi." *Milliyet*, Istanbul, 8 April 2001.

Corbino, Marcia. "On the Wall Paintings." *Sarasota Herald Tribune*, Sarasota, Fla., 9 February 1981.

Darcy, C. "Ière Exposition Intercontinentale à Monaco." *La Revue Moderne*, Paris, 1 August 1965.

Dean, Kevin. "Art/Foster Harmon Gallery." *The Longboat Observer*, Sarasota, Fla., 21 February 1985.

———. "A Conversation with Burhan Doğançay." *The Longboat Observer*, Sarasota, Fla., 5 February 1981.

DiLauro, Stephen. "Don't Be Quick to Condemn Graffiti; They Can Be a Blessing." *The Morning Call*, Miami, 18 August 1994.

Dormen, Haldun. "Uluslararası Bir Türk Ressamı." *Milliyet*, Istanbul, 8 May 1977.

Dunn, Helen. "Burhan Doğançay: Artist, Photographer." *People, Places and Parties*, New York, Summer 1982.

Durgun, Özgür. "İlmek İlmek Yaşam." *Radikal*, Istanbul, 17 April 1998.

Duru, Başak. "Dişarida Türklerden Ressam Çikacağina Inanan Çok Az Kisi Var." *Sanat Çevresi*, Istanbul, June 2001.

Elibal, Gültekin. "Burhan Doğançay'ın Bir Sergisi Daha." *Sanat Çevresi*, Istanbul, no. 61, November 1983.

Elkatip, Demet. "Öncesi Sonrası Duvar." *Milliyet*, Istanbul, 22 October 1998.

Erez, İrem. "Burhan Doğançay 'ın Çağdaş Resim Sanatındaki Yeri." *Sanat Olayı*, Istanbul, no. 9, September 1981.

Erfevel. "Burhan Dogançay." *La Semaine d'Anvers*, Antwerp, 17 December 1982.

Eroğlu, Özkan. "Burhan Doğançay Retrospektifi." *Yapi*, Istanbul, 1 May 2001.

Esatoğlu, Mehmet. "İnsanlığın Aynası Duvarlar." *Evrensel Kültür*, Istanbul, 18 November 1995.

Filoğlu, Lale. "Burhan Doğançay: Benim için duvarlar tutku halini aldı." *Vizyon*, Istanbul, no. 65, December 1995.

Financı, Yurdakul. "B. Doğançay'ın Resimleri İlgi ile Karşılandı." *Ulus*, Ankara, 6 January 1965.

G. B. "Dogancay." *Art Voices Magazine*, New York, volume 3, no. 4, April/May 1964.

Gillemon, Danièle. "La Photographie Existe." *Le Soir*, Brussels, 2 April 1982.

Girgin, Emin Çetin. "Türk Resmi İçin Bir Başlangıç." *Cumhuriyet*, Istanbul, 1 August 1987.

——. "Yapıtlarım Duvar Resmi Olarak Düşünülmeli." *Cumhuriyet*, Istanbul, 29 June 1986.

Göçer, Esin. "Burhan Doğançay'la Bir Gezinti." *Sanat Çevresi*, Istanbul, no. 240, October 1998.

Gören, Ahmet Kamil. "Burhan Doğançay'in Kapilari Galeri Binyild'da." *Sanat Çevresi*, Istanbul, June 2001.

Grasskamp, Walter. *Kunstforum International*, Cologne, vol. 50, April 1982.

Güncikan, Berat. "Çocuklar ressam gördü." *Cumhuriyet* Magazine, Istanbul, 6 May 2001.

Günyaz, Abdülkadir. "Burhan Doğançay Sergisi'nin Düşündürdükleri." *Sanat Çevresi*, Istanbul, no. 181, November 1993.

Gürel, Haşim Nur. "Burhan Doğançay." *Sanat Çevresi*, Istanbul, no. 155, September 1991.

Halman, Talat. "Amerika'da Modern Türk Sanatı." *Türk Evi*, New York, November 1977.

——. "Burhan Doğançay." *Ankara Sanat Dergisi*, Ankara, March 1977.

——. "Burhan Doğançay New York'ta Sergi Açtı." *Milliyet*, Istanbul, 25 November 1967.

——. "Sanatımızı Bilen, Kültürlü Kişilerden Yararlanmalıyız." *Hürriyet*, 3 November 1982.

Hekimoğlu, Müşerref. "Çöplük'ü İzleyen Gençler." *Cumhuriyet*, Istanbul, 12 November 1995.

Hizlan, Doğan. "Burhan Doğançay Güneydoğu'ya okul yaptiracak." *Hürriyet*, Istanbul, 1 March 2001.

——. "Güzel şeyler de oluyor." *Hürriyet*, Istanbul, 20 April 2001.

H. N. "Burhan Doğançay." *Die Tat*, Zurich, 28 February 1977.

Holt, Dennis. "New Photo Book on Brooklyn Bridge Reconstruction Celebrated at Library." *Brooklyn Daily Eagle*, Brooklyn, 8 November 1999.

——. "Striking Photos Distinguish Brooklyn Bridge Book." *Brooklyn Heights Press*, Brooklyn, 11 November 1999.

İşleyen, Ercüment. "Resimde Büyük Sahtekrlık." *Milliyet*, Istanbul, 6 August 1995.

Jacobs, Jay. "Personality: Back to the Walls." *The Art Gallery Magazine*, Ivoryton, Conn., vol. XIV, no. 1, October 1970.

J. D. H. "Dogançay 's Watercolors at Galaxy." *The Arizona Republic*, Phoenix, 31 January 1965.

Jensen, H. R. " Dogançay–Collagens Mester." *Morgenavisen Jyllands-Posten*, Aalborg, Denmark, 20 June 1990.

J. L. "Murmures des Murs." *La Presse*, Montreal, 30 July 1983.

Kanbay Doğantepe, Hülya. "Kalpten Kalbe, Akıldan Akıla Kapılar Açıyor." *Antik & Dekor*, Istanbul, no. 33, 1996.

Kardüz, Ali Rıza. "New York'ta İki Türk." *Sabah*, Istanbul, 7 June 1997.

——. "Ressam Babanın Ressam Oğlu." *Sabah*, Istanbul, 18 October 1997.

Kayabal, Aslı. "Acemi Sahtekr Aranıyor!" *Yeni Yüzyıl*, Istanbul, 9 August 1995.

——. "Toplumun Aynası Duvarlar." *Yeni Yüzyıl*, Istanbul, 19 November 1995.

Keskin, Hasan. "Orada kimse var mi?" *Zaman*, Istanbul, 20 April 2001.

Kınaytürk, Hamit. "Dessine-Moi l'Amour." *Sanat Çevresi*, Istanbul, no. 181, November 1993.

——. "Ressam Burhan Doğançay 'ın Sahte Resimleri Ortaya Çıktı." *Sanat Çevresi*, Istanbul, August/ September 1995.

——. "Rusya Cumhuriyet Kültür Bakanlığı Ressam Burhan Doğançay'a Takdir Madalyası Verdi." *Sanat Çevresi*, Istanbul, no. 162, April 1992.

Köksal, Ahmet. "Burhan Doğançay'la Bir Konuşma." *Sanat Çevresi*, Istanbul, no. 93, July 1986.

——. "Doğançay'ın Resimleri." *Milliyet Sanat Dergisi*, Istanbul, 17 September 1976.

Köprülü, Tuna. "Sanatımızı Doğançay ile Dünyaya Duyuruyoruz." *Hürriyet*, Istanbul, 23 June 1982.

Küçüksayraç, Elif. "Burhan Doğançay'in Istanbul Çikartmasi." *Geniş Açi*, Istanbul, 15 May 1982.

Külahlıoğlu, Can. "Doğançay Yeni Aysan Yetkin." *Yeni Gündem*, Istanbul, no. 18, July 1986.

Landau, Ian. "Bridge of Sighs." *Time Out*, New York, no. 215, November 1999.

Levick, L. E. "Burhan Dogançay." *New York Journal American*, New York, 11 April 1964.

Lieber, Joel. "Travel of Turkish Tourist Head Forms Inspiration for Painting." *Travel Weekly*, New York, 9 June 1964.

Lopate, Phillip. "Burhan Dogançay." *Bomb*, New York, no. 80, Summer 2002.

Madra, Beral. "Burhan Doğançay: Duvar tutkum peşimi bırakmaz." *Vizyon*, Istanbul, no. 14, May 1991.

——. "Burhan Doğançay 'ın Resimleri Üzerine." *Sanat Çevresi*, Istanbul, no. 93, July 1986.

Madra, Ömer. "Burhan Doğançay." *Arredamento Dekorasyon*, Istanbul, January 1994.

M. B. "Burhan Dogançay: Walls V." *Arts Magazine*, New York, March 1969.

Mesayyah, Mirey. "Duvarlar Ülkelerin Aynasıdır." *Barometre 7*, Istanbul, 22 April 1991.

Meyer, Walter. "Handwriting on the Wall Tells Artist Great Deal." *Sunday News*, New York, 18 September 1966.

Miller, Marlan. "Diplomat Offers Dashing Shows." *The Phoenix Gazette*, Phoenix, 1 February 1965.

M. M. C. "New York in the Eyes of the World." *The Villager*, New York, 1 October 1964.

Moll, Kerstin. "Auf der Suche nach Botschaften." *Oberhessische Presse*, Marburg, 17 March 1989.

Muûls, Violaine. "On Baillonne Même les Murs." *L'Evénement*, Brussels, no. 102, 25 March 1982.

Nirven, Nur. "Burhan Doğançay ile Söyleşi." *Vizyon Dekorasyon*, Istanbul, no. 10, January 1994.

——. "Burhan Doğançay ve Duvarlar." *Sanat Çevresi*, Istanbul, no. 181, November 1993.

——. "Rengarenk Bir Sergi." *Güneş*, Istanbul, 27 September 1989.

Niyazioğlu, İbrahim. "Burhan Doğançay ve Uluslararası Sanat İlişkilerimiz." *Hürriyet Gösteri*, Istanbul, September 1987.

Noël, Serge. "L'Image a des Ratés." *Pour Bruxelles*, Brussels, 25 March 1982.

Öktülmüş, Buket. "Duvarların Dili." *Radikal*, Istanbul, 15 October 1998.

Oral, Zeynep. "Duvarları Yaşayan, Duvarları Yaşatan Sanatçı." *Milliyet Sanat Dergisi*, Istanbul, no. 184, 15 January 1988.

Özgentürk, Nebil. "Duvarin kalbi." *Sabah*, Istanbul, 14 April 2001.

Pak, Orhan. "Amerika'da Bir Türk Ressamı: Burhan Doğançay." *Sanat Çevresi*, Istanbul, July 1982.

Perlman, Mişel. "Düşgücünün Sınırı Yoktur." *Cumhuriyet*, Istanbul, 20 December 1992.

P. WD. "Januaris/ Dogançay /Zeller." *Neue Zürcher Zeitung*, Zurich, 8 February 1977.

Reisner, Robert. *Graffiti*. New York: Cowles Book Company, 1971.

Rona, Zeynep. "Aubusson Duvar Halıları ve Burhan Doğançay." *Arredamento Mimarlık*, Istanbul, April 1998.

Saçar, Bekir. "Sanatseverler Doğançay'la buluştu." *Posta*, Istanbul, 7 April 2001.

Şahin, Fatih. "Doğançay'ın sergisine büyük ilgi." *Alem*, Istanbul, no. 16, 18 April 2001.

Schutz, Louis B. "Burhan Dogançay: The Man and His Art." Unpublished undergraduate thesis, Randolph-Macon Woman's College, Lynchburg, Va., June 1971.

Schwab, Christine. "Ein Türkischer Künstler in New York." *Marburger Magazin Express*, Marburg, July 1989.

Senft, Bret. "New Angle on an Old Bridge." *Photo District News*, New York, December 1999.

Şenyener, Şebnem. "Duvara Aşk Katan Ressam." *Sabah*, Istanbul, 11 August 1993.

——. "Şu Malum Köprü." *Vizyon*, Istanbul, 5 May 1997.

Shemanski, Frances. "Diplomatic Mission." *Pictorial Living—New York Journal American*, New York, 3 January 1965.

Simavi, Aliye. "Burhan Doğançay." *Vizon Gazete*, Istanbul, October 1980.

Sönmez, Ayşegül. "Beni rol model olarak alıyorlar." *Milliyet Pazar*, Istanbul, 15 April 2001.

Sönmez, Necmi. "Brooklyn Köprüsü 'Suretleri.'" *Arredamento Mimarlık*, Istanbul, December 1999.

——. "Dünya Duvarlarına Kök Salan İmgeler." *Avrupa ve Türkiye'de Yazın*, Istanbul, no. 87, September 1999.

——. "Eş Zamanlı Gerçek." *Türkiye'de Sanat*, Istanbul, no. 10, September/October 1993.

——. "Gerçekle kurgu arasindaki karşitliklar." *Hürriyet Gösteri*, Istanbul, 1 April 2001.

——. "Görüntü ile İmgenin Çatışması." *Cumhuriyet*, Istanbul, 8 November 1995.

——. "İstanbul Duvarlarının Önünde Burhan Doğançay." *Marie-Claire*, Istanbul, August 1989.

Sümercan, Aydan. "Burhan Doğançay ile Duvarlar Üzerine Çeşitlemeler." *Sanat Olayı*, Istanbul, no. 50, July 1986.

Tanaltay, Erdoğan. "Burhan Doğançay ile Bir Gün." *Sanat Çevresi*, Istanbul, no. 241, November 1998.

Tansuğ, Sezer. "Burhan Doğançay'la Söyleşiden İzlenimler." *Sanat Çevresi*, Istanbul, no. 11, September 1979.

——. "Büyük Bir Resim Ustası: Burhan Doğançay." *Sanat Çevresi*, Istanbul, no. 61, November 1983.

——. "Büyük Bir Usta: Burhan Doğançay." *Ev & Ofis*, Istanbul, no. 87, November 1983.

——. "Burhan Doğançay'ın Endüstriyel Standartlaşmayı Eleştiren Yeni Çalışmaları Üzerine." *Sanat Çevresi*, Istanbul, no. 181, November 1993.

——. Doğançay'da Formların Nesneleşme Süreci." *Sanat Çevresi*, Istanbul, no. 205, November 1995.

Turay, Anna. "Manhattan'dan Kazlıçeşme'ye." *Cumhuriyet*, Istanbul, April 1991.

Türkat, Seda. "Duvarların izinde bir ömür." *Tempo*, Istanbul, 26 April 2001.

Uluç, Doğan. "Açık Oturum." *Hürriyet*, İstanbul, 3 November 1982.

———. "Doğançay ile Bir Söyleşi." *Dünya*, Istanbul, 17 July 1979.

———. "Doğançay'a İlgi Büyük Oldu." *Hürriyet*, Istanbul, 8 November 1986.

———. "Türk Objektifinden Brooklyn Köprüsü." *Hürriyet*, Istanbul, 4 July 1998.

———. "Zirvedeki Doğançay." *Hürriyet*, Istanbul, 6 December 1999.

Uslubaş, Tolga. "Duvardan kalplere." *Türkiye*, Istanbul, 7 April 2001.

Van der Brempt, S. "La Photographie: Grand 'Art Nouveau.'" *La Semaine d'Anvers*, Antwerp, no. 336, 16 April 1982.

Wanfors, Lars. "American Graffiti." *American Trend Magazine*, Stockholm, no. 3, 1983.

Welch, Anita. "Artist Captures Tempo of Manhattan." *The Arizonian*, Phoenix, 28 January 1965.

Yilmaz, Ihsan. "Ressam Amca." *Hürriye Cumartesi*, Istanbul, 12 May 2001.

———. "Ünlü ressam sergisini TIR'la gezdirecek." *Hürriyet*, Istanbul, 5 April 2001.

Zimmerman, Dave. "Artist: Walls Mirror Society." *Register-Star*, Rockford, Ill., 6 January 1974.

BOOKS
In alphabetical order by author.

Antmen, Ahu. *Blue Walls of New York*. Istanbul: Iş Bankası, 2003.

Blanchebarbe, Ursula. *Walls of the World*. Bielefeld Kerber Verlag, 2003.

Lascault, Gilbert, and Denys Riout. *Dessine-Moi l'Amour*. Paris: Syros-Alternatives, 1992.

Lopate, Phillip. *Bridge of Dreams: The Rebirth of the Brooklyn Bridge*. New York: Hudson Hills Press, 1999.

Moyer, Roy (ed.), Jacques Rigaud, Thomas M. Messer, Stephen DiLauro, Marcel van Jole, Roy Moyer, Gilbert Lascault, and Clive Giboire. *Dogançay*. New York: Hudson Hills Press, 1986.

Rona, Zeynep (ed.), Jacques Rigaud, Thomas M. Messer, Emel Budak, Eleanor Flomenhaft, Necmi Sönmez, Jean-François Picaud, Zeynep Rona, and Phillip Lopate. *Burhan Dogançay: A Retrospective*. Istanbul: Duran Editions, 2001.

EXHIBITION BROCHURES AND CATALOGUES
In chronological order by year. Each catalogue is published by the exhibition's initiating institution.

1977
Kunstsalon Wolfsberg, Zurich. *Burhan Dogançay*. Brochure. Text by J. Jacobs and Thomas M. Messer.

1981
Kunstsalon Wolfsberg, Zurich. *Burhan Dogançay*. Brochure. Text by Thomas M. Messer.

1982
Centre Georges Pompidou, Paris. *Les Murs Murmurent, Ils Crient, Ils Chantent....* Exhibition catalogue. Essays by Jacques Mullender, Jacques Rigaud, Thomas M. Messer, Gilbert Lascault, and Burhan Dogançay.

1985
Österreichische Postsparkasse, Vienna. *Burhan Dogançay*. Brochure. Text by Roy Moyer.

1989
Seibu-Yurakucho Art Forum, Tokyo. *Burhan Dogançay*. Exhibition catalogue. Text by Tadao Ogura.

1990
Galerie du Génie, Paris. *Dogançay*. Exhibition catalogue. Text by Gilbert Lascault.

1992
State Russian Museum, St. Petersburg. *Dogançay: Walls and Doors, 1990–91*. Exhibition catalogue.

Essays by Alexander D. Borovsky, Oleg Loginov,
and William Zimmer.

1993
Atatürk Cultural Center, Istanbul. *Dogançay Walls.*
Exhibition catalogue. Essays by Frederick Ted Castle
and Necmi Sönmez.

1994
Nicholas Alexander Gallery, New York. *Dogançay:
Doors and Walls.* Exhibition catalogue (second revised
edition 1995). Essays by Eleanor Flomenhaft and
Clive Giboire.

1996
Hooks-Epstein Galleries, Houston. *New York – New
Heights.* Brochure. Text by William T. Cannaday and
Burhan Dogançay.

1998
Galeri G, Istanbul. *Alexander's Walls and Hearts.*
Exhibition catalogue. Essay by Elvan Şahinoğlu.

2001
Galeri Binyil, Istanbul. *Kapilar.* Brochure. Text by
Ahmet Kamil Gören.

Galeri G, Istanbul. *Kalpler.* Brochure. Text by Haşim
Nur Gürel.

Görüntü Sanat Galerisi. Adana, Turkey. *Burhan
Doğançay.* Brochure. Text by Mehmet Ergüven.

Mine Sanat Galerisi, Istanbul. *Dönemler.* Brochure.
Text by Esra Aliçavuşoğlu.

INTERVIEWS AND TV DOCUMENTARIES
In chronological order by year.

"Dogançay, Burhan." Interview by Cindy Adams.
Evening News. ABC TV, New York, 15 September
1966.

Dogançay, Burhan. Interview by Jack O'Brian. WOR
Radio, New York, 12 October 1966.

"Art and the Environment." Produced by Ezzedine
Harbaqui for Tunisian State TV, Tunis, 1982.

"Burhan Dogançay". Produced by Martin Kessler for
Kulturkalender, HR3, Frankfurt, 23 March 1989.

"Atölye" (Studio). Produced and directed by Güneş
Buharalı, interview by Ahu Antmen, TRT2, Istanbul,
24 January 1998.

"Kritik." Produced and presented by Nilüfer Kuyaş,
NTV, Istanbul, 26 April 1998.

"The Walls of the World." Produced by Bircan Ünver
for Cable TV Channels 34, 35, 56 and 57, New York,
1998–99.

"Gece-Gündüz" (Night-Day). Produced and presented
by Pınar Demirkapı, NTV, Istanbul, 3 December 1999.

"Bridge of Dreams." Produced by Fran Ham for
Brooklyn Community Access TV. New York, 1999.

"Bridge of Dreams." Produced by Bircan Ünver for
Cable TV Channels 34 and 35, New York, 2000.